Queer
Shakespeare

Queer
Shakespeare

Desire and Sexuality

Edited by
Goran Stanivukovic

THE ARDEN SHAKESPEARE
LONDON • NEW YORK • OXFORD • NEW DELHI • SYDNEY

THE ARDEN SHAKESPEARE
Bloomsbury Publishing Plc
50 Bedford Square, London, WC1B 3DP, UK
1385 Broadway, New York, NY 10018, USA
29 Earlsfort Terrace, Dublin 2, Ireland

BLOOMSBURY, THE ARDEN SHAKESPEARE and the Arden Shakespeare
logo are trademarks of Bloomsbury Publishing Plc

First published in Great Britain 2017
This paperback edition published 2019
Reprinted 2019 (twice), 2020, 2021, 2022 (twice)

Cover design: Irene Martinez Costa
Cover image: *The Kidnapping of Ganymede* by Rubens, Peter Paul
(1577–1640) / Furstlich Schwarzenberg'sche Verwaltung, Vienna, Austria /
Bridgeman Images

A catalogue record for this book is available from the British Library.

A catalog record for this book is available from the Library of Congress.

ISBN: HB: 978-1-4742-9524-6
PB: 978-1-350-08447-6
ePDF: 978-1-4742-9527-7
eBook: 978-1-4742-9526-0

Typeset by Fakenham Prepress Solutions, Fakenham, Norfolk NR21 8NN
Printed and bound in Great Britain

To find out more about our authors and books visit www.bloomsbury.com
and sign up for our newsletters.

CONTENTS

ACKNOWLEDGEMENTS

The core of the chapters included in this book originated in the papers discussed at the research seminar 'Queer Shakespeare', held at the annual meeting of the Shakespeare Association of America in Vancouver in 2015. I am grateful to Vin Nardizzi for responding to the proposal for the seminar with erudition, enthusiasm and skill, and and for his support while the book was in preparation. Will Stockton, Jeffrey Masten and Mario DiGangi responded to the ideas shared in the seminar with generosity, encouragement and critical sharpness. Many of their points shared in the seminar were helpful in the shaping of this book afterwards. Anthony Guy Patricia made many useful comments on a draft of the book. I am grateful to Natasha Hurley who ventured backwards in queer times with intellectual verve typical of her quick mind, and suggested how one might think differently and thought-provokingly about queerness in Shakespeare. I thank John Garrison and Stephen Guy-Bray for sharing their critical wisdom and practical advice with me. I am indebted to Mitch Redden for his help as an exemplary research assistant. It was a great pleasure for me to work with the superb editorial team at Bloomsbury. Margaret Bartley's interest in this project, her expert guidance on numerous matters and her quick e-mail replies made my work on this book a whole lot easier than I anticipated. I acknowledge the financial support from the Social Sciences and Humanities Research Council of Canada at the initial stage of this project. Most importantly, I thank all the contributors for writing intellectually inspiring, fresh and original essays.

A NOTE ABOUT THE TEXT

Throughout this book, Shakespeare's texts are cited from *The Arden Shakespeare Complete Works*, ed. Richard Proudfoot, Ann Thompson and David Scott Kastan (London: Bloomsbury, 2011). For specific purposes, Arden 3 single editions of Shakespeare's works are occasionally used in individual chapters.

NOTES ON CONTRIBUTORS

Valerie Billing is Assistant Professor of English at Central College. Her scholarship has previously been published in *Renaissance Drama* and *The Journal for Early Modern Cultural Studies*. She is currently working on a book project titled *Size Matters: The Erotics of Stature in Early Modern English Literature and Culture*.

Simone Chess is Associate Professor of English at Wayne State University. Her book, *Male-to-Female Crossdressing in Early Modern English Literature: Gender, Performance, and Queer Relations* (2016) argues that representations of male-to-female crossdressers in literature show models of queer male femininities that are relational and beneficial. She has published articles and book chapters on crossdressing and gender labour, gender and disability, bathroom activities, ballads and Shakespeare, dramatic representations of blindness and oath-making in 'murderous wife' ballads. Her next book project will bring together early modern queer and disability studies.

Holly Dugan is Associate Professor of English at The George Washington University. She is the author of *The Ephemeral History of Perfume: Scent and Sense in Early Modern England* (2011), co-editor with Lara Farina of a special issue of *postmedieval* 3 (4) (2012) on the 'Intimate Senses' and co-editor with Karl Steel of an essay cluster in *Early Modern Culture* (2016) on 'Fabulous Animals'. She is currently working on a book-length monograph that explores the prehistory of primatology through the lens of Shakespeare and performance.

John S. Garrison is Associate Professor of English at Grinnell College. He has held fellowships from the American Philosophical Association, Folger Shakespeare Library and National Endowment for the Humanities. With Kyle Pivetti, he is co-editor of *Sexuality and Memory in Early Modern England: Literature and the Erotics of Recollection* (2015). He is the author of *Friendship and Queer Theory in the Renaissance* (2014) and *Glass* (2015).

A. Eliza Greenstadt is Professor in the School of Film at Portland State University, where she teaches in media, aesthetics and literary studies. Her research focuses on gender and sexuality in early modern England, and she has published on a variety of authors from William Shakespeare to Margaret Cavendish. *Rape and the Rise of the Author: Gendering Intention in Early Modern England*, her first book, was published by Ashgate in 2009. Currently, she is researching a monograph on genital communities with the working title *Pricked Out*.

Stephen Guy-Bray is Professor of English at the University of British Columbia. He specializes in Renaissance poetry and queer theory. He is currently completing an edition of George Peele's *The Old Wive's Tale* and starting a study of Narcissus and queer inactivity.

Ian Frederick Moulton is Professor of English and Cultural History in the College of Integrative Sciences and Arts at Arizona State University. He has published widely on the representation of gender and sexuality in early modern European literature. He is the author of *Love in Print in the Sixteenth Century: The Popularization of Romance* (2014) and *Before Pornography: Erotic Writing in Early Modern England* (2000), editor and translator of Antonio Vignali's *La Cazzaria*, an erotic and political dialogue from Renaissance

Italy (2003), and co-editor of *Teaching Early Modern English Literature from the Archives* (2015).

Vin Nardizzi is Associate Professor of English at University of British Columbia. His first book, *Wooden Os: Shakespeare's Theatres and England's Trees*, was published by the University of Toronto Press in 2013. He is currently working on a second monograph project, 'Marvellous Vegetables in Renaissance Poetry'. With Robert W. Barrett, Jr., he is co-editing a forthcoming issue of the journal *postmedieval* called 'Premodern Plants', and with Tiffany Jo Stern is editing a collection of essays called *Oecologies: Engaging the World, from Here.*

David L. Orvis is Associate Professor of English at Appalachian State University. He is editor, with Linda Phyllis Austern and Karl Boyd Mcbride, of *Psalms in the Early Modern World* (2011), and, with Ryan Singh Paul, of *The Noble Flame of Katherine Philips: A Poetics of Culture, Politics, and Friendship* (2015) and author of essays on Shakespeare, Lyly, Marlowe, Herbert and Milton. His current book project focuses on the legacy of Anteros in classical, medieval and early modern literature and culture.

Kirk Quinsland is a Lecturer in the English Department at Fordham University. His current projects include a book addressing antitheatrical writing and its connection to various forms of metatheatricality on the early modern stage, and a digital project to map linguistic connections between the Blackfriars and plays performed at the Blackfriars Theatre.

Melissa E. Sanchez is Associate Professor of English and Core Faculty in the Gender, Sexuality and Women's Studies Programme at the University of Pennsylvania. She is the author of *Erotic Subjects: The Sexuality of Politics in Early Modern English Literature* (2011) and editor of three volumes: *Spenser and 'the Human'*, a special volume of *Spenser Studies* co-edited with Ayesha Ramachandran (2015); *Rethinking Femninism in Early Modern Studies: Gender, Race, and Sexuality*, co-edited with Ania Loomba (2016); and *Desiring History and Historicizing Desire*, a special volume of the *Journal of Early Modern Cultural Studies*, co- edited with Ari Friedlander and Will Stockton (2016).

Kathryn Schwarz is Professor of English at Vanderbilt University. She is the author of *Tough Love: Amazon Encounters in the English Renaissance* (2000) and *What You Will: Gender, Contract, and Shakespearian Social Space* (2011). With Holly Crocker, she co-edited 'Premodern Flesh', a special issue of *postmedieval* (2013). She is working on a book titled *Community and Mortality in the English Renaissance*.

Goran Stanivukovic is Professor of English at Saint Mary's University. His most recent publication is *Knights in Arms: Prose Romance, Masculinity, and Eastern Mediterranean Trade in Early Modern England, 1565–1655* (2016). He is currently working on a book on Shakespeare's early styles.

Christine Varnado is Assistant Professor of Gender and Sexuality Studies at Buffalo-State University of New York. She is the author of 'Invisible Sex!: What Looks Like the Act in Early Modern Drama?' and 'Getting Used, and Liking It: Erotic Instrumentality in *Philaster*'. She is at work on a book redefining queerness as a set of affective qualities inhering in the style and structure of early modern texts.

Introduction: Queer Shakespeare – desire and sexuality

Goran Stanivukovic

The production of *A Midsummer Night's Dream* directed by Emma Rice at the Globe Theatre in the summer season in 2016 staged this play as a comedy of homoerotic desire.[1] The success this production had with much of the audience who saw it at the Globe and globally in a BBC live-broadcast in September 2016 lay in 'queer goings-on'[2] as the central feature of the stage interpretation of this comedy. At the level of gender casting and directorial interventions in the play's text, this production was a Bollywood-style queer entertainment, though shorn of much of the aggression and violence that also accompanies the gender and sexuality politics of this play. The production closes the temporal gap between the articulation of desire and sexuality in Shakespeare's and our time; through Shakespeare's dramatic poetry contemporary expressions (more so than debates) spoke with seductive energy and audience approval, even occasional applause. With this production, queer Shakespeare entered the theatre centre stage. Yet it is the complexity and diversity of desire and sexuality produced by Rice's intervention in the sex-gender distinction and the gender politics of Shakespeare's text, made possible by queer resourcefulness of

Shakespeare's text, that makes this production a convenient introduction to this book. In Rice's bold production, full of desiring vitality, Helena became Helenus in love with Demetrius, Hippolyta and Titania kissed and passionate speeches about love and wooing came across as admittance of a character's acceptance of homosexuality, and as ways of coming out to themselves and the audience, when spoken by one actor to another of the same gender. And when Helenus offers himself to Demetrius,

> I am your spaniel; and, Demetrius,
> The more you beat me, I will fawn on you.
> Use me but as your spaniel, spurn me strike me,
> Neglect me, lose me; only give me leave,
> Unworthy as I am, to follow you.

> (2.1.203–7)

the female submissiveness to male power within heterosexual chase, as presented in the text begins to sound like a proposal for S/M submission within the male same-sex economy of power and desire. This may appear, as it is, an instance of Rice's radical intervention in the gendered and sexual politics at the level of text and what the text signifies. Yet in her illuminating reading of this play, which starts at the cross-over of queer and feminist theory, Melissa Sanchez has already suggested that at the conceptual, or theoretical, level these lines could be read as a kind of gender-bending appropriation at this point, with the reference to spaniel suggesting 'the masochistic element of *male* desire' in this play as much as, Sanchez reminds her readers, spaniel does in *The Two Gentlemen of Verona*. As in this early comedy, in *A Midsummer Night's Dream* these lines also reveal, Sanchez suggests, that 'abject devotion may be the flip side of aggression'.[3] If we approach Rice's staging of Helena as the abject Helenus, eagerly almost inviting to be treated roughly by Demetrius, her production should not appear as either shocking or too radical because we seem to be watching something that has already been addressed by queer theory. I am not suggesting this in order to minimize the radicalism of Rice's production, as to suggest that we can also think about this production, at this moment, not as one warping Shakespeare's text too liberally but that it visualizes the complex psychosexual dynamics at play at this moment in the text, a moment the implications of which complicate Rice's production both visually and aurally in powerful terms. This passage and the Globe performance illustrate that in Shakespeare's world of desire the choice of an object of desire and of language through which desire is verbalized are separate. This speech is not about shameful desires, not about hidden thoughts and suppressed eroticism. It is instead a moment of truth and autonomy of the sexual subject liberated in its demand for and expression of sexual gratification through submission. When the language in this passage is disembodied from the female object of desire (played by a boy actor) presented as a speaking part, which is how the scene is shown in the text and staged in the theatre; and when it is spoken by a male part, who now plays the submissive boy to Demetrius's dominant male, it is the semantics of this passage, and the structure of language, that make it still possible for sexual meanings to move freely between different objects of desire without disturbing the meaning of the power and sexual relationship. The queerness of this passage lies precisely in the capacity of the text to allow the separation of personhood from erotic desire and sexual behaviour, relationship and practice. At the end of the play, Demetrius, from whom the spell cast over him by Oberon is never lifted, says to Helenus:

> The object and the pleasure of my eye,
> Is only Helenus. To [him], my lord,
> Was I betroth'd ere I saw Hermia;
> But like a sickness did I loathe this food:
> But as in health, come to my natural taste,
> Now I do wish it, love it, long for it,
> And will for evermore be true to it.

                                                        (4.2.169–75)

The audience thus witnesses a moving moment of a public acceptance of one's own queer desire, and a kind of theatrical coming out.[4]

Rice's turning of the comedy's heteronormative plot into a production full of new stage identities reveals modalities of desire and erotic meanings that are already in the text and the plot of Shakespeare's comedy, but that have been contained by history and hidden in time. Just as Rice's production entices the audience in the Globe to view her production as homoerotic, upends our expectations of a familiar narrative and opens the text up for alternative meanings and motivations, so do the chapters in *Queer Shakespeare* encourage readers to consider Shakespeare's works as queer texts of considerable diversity and expressive power. They also demonstrate the extent to which queer theory has diversified and how that diversification has revealed meanings that were unacknowledged by previous critical practices and ways of reading desire and sexuality in Shakespeare. Although individual explorations of the representations of queer desires and sexualities in Shakespeare's works cumulatively represented one of the most radical, theoretical engagements with Shakespeare since the formulation of queer theory in the late twentieth century, critical surveys of the theoretical approaches to Shakespeare fail to acknowledge the burst of scholarship which queer theory generated in Shakespeare studies, especially in the 1990s.[5] *Queer Shakespeare* does not only address a diversity of ways in which to understand the queerness of language, time, object, style, narrative form and nature in Shakespeare, but also demonstrates that 'queer' means diversity of approaches to desire, sexuality and embodiment in Shakespeare. Rice's production knowingly plays on the queerness, not only of the play's text, but also on other texts by Shakespeare, such as Sonnet 116, 'Let me not to the marriage of true minds admit impediments', which she interweaves with her version of the play with the purpose to signal the sealing of the bond between Demetrius and Helenus.

Just as the line that separates the world of magic in the woods and the world of courtly reality is thin, so are the lines that apparently distinguish desires and sexualities within what is set out to be a heteronormative plot. The class ideology in *A Midsummer Night's Dream* has led Alan Sinfield to point out that the play's sexual politics create an 'interruption of the nuptials of Theseus and Hippolyta' and thus to an 'endemic crisis in patriarchy'.[6] Social contradictions in Shakespeare, as Daniel Juan Gil shows, often define versions of sexual subjectivities as asocial, hence queer. Such sexualities expose contradictions within the social life of early modern England, as in *Troilus and Cressida*, Juan Gil argues; one could say that *A Midsummer Night's Dream* is that kind of a play as well.[7] The manifold desires in this play have prompted Madhavi Menon to claim that passages like the one displaying Demetrius' expression of love to Helena in a scene in the woods do not 'explain desire; on the contrary, they insist on its lack of identifiable causality'.[8] Instances like these do not necessarily reaffirm heteronormative love and wooing; they cloud rather than illuminate desire that runs through such scenes. They also show that the signification and direction of Shakespearean desire cannot be pinned down easily, but that queer theory teases out different, and differing, structures and versions of that desire. Shakespeare's texts brim with similar discursive and narrative scenarios. The plurality of meaning produced by the comedy's language within a plot of coupling arises from the confusion created by the magic potion. It brings into play dramatic, syntactic, semantic and stylistic possibilities for a new erotic meaning, which can be called 'queer'. These new dramatic possibilities are queer because they originate from within the text and yield new states of being on the stage, ones that unsettle heteronormative discourse in the play. Shakespeare is queer because his language is queer.

A Midsummer Night's Dream is one of many plays in which Shakespeare's text reveals itself not only as a 'queer' but whose 'queer ability to bond affectively with the past'[9] represents a meeting point between his time and our modernity. In combination with his iconic status as a literary figure, the queer potential of Shakespeare's texts has assured that he is an unavoidable subject of queer early modern studies and a frequent object of queer experimentation and testing in theatre and popular culture. Coupled with the queer potential within his texts, this cultural visibility assures that Shakespeare has a queer future as well. Yet, despite the combined effect of these attributes, queer early modern criticism and queer theory in particular have not made as extensive a use of Shakespeare as an object of inquiry as one might expect. *Queer Shakespeare* addresses some of the lacunae in the scholarship of queer desires and sexualities within Shakespeare studies. It encourages approaches that have been left out by other explorations of queer Shakespeare that have disparately appeared in individual essays throughout journals, collections and individual chapters in monographs. Taking a broad view of what queer theory can do for Shakespeare and what Shakespeare has done for queer theory, contributors to *Queer Shakespeare* have written their chapters cognizant of the disagreement with some of the current writing on queer Shakespeare. The contributors explore multiple ways in which 'queer' manifests itself in Shakespeare's texts. *Queer Shakespeare* raises questions about what makes Shakespeare's texts queer and demonstrates utility of the term 'queer' in Shakespeare studies.

What is queer Shakespeare?

'Queer Shakespeare' is a matter of theoretical perspective as well as a subject of critical inquiry. What is queer about Shakespeare's texts as objects of critical analysis? How does queer Shakespeare affect critical practice at our current moment in Shakespeare scholarship? These questions frame this collection and underpin the individual essays. As a term of deconstruction most closely associated with post-structuralist theory of sexuality, desire and embodiment, 'queer', when it is used in early modern criticism, has denoted the four categories around which that foundational criticism has built its arguments: the sodomite and homoeroticism in representations of male same-sex eroticism; and the tribade and lesbianism in depictions of female same-sex eroticism.[10] In this historical sense in which it defined the opposition between identity and difference, 'queer' has captured the representation and the discourse of desire and sex that are historically determined in opposition to social regulation, for example, the religious doctrine of marriage and procreation. As such a term, 'queer' has also been used to contrast the cultural and political power that demands knowledge of any identity defined in transparent and fixed terms. In this sense, 'queer' represents 'a challenge to the ontological grounding of desire and politics'.[11]

Yet *Queer Shakespeare* reaches beyond the theoretical dichotomies of deconstruction and the treatment of queer as one of the theoretical versions of post-structuralism, by pushing the thinking about desire and sexuality in a direction that does not only include debates about the norm and the overturning or deviating from it, but that also takes it apart. 'Queer' in *Queer Shakespeare* captures some of the existing understanding of desire and sexuality prevalent in queer early modern criticism, but it also focuses on style, formalism, community and objects as subjects of analysis which produce new and varied kinds of desire. One of the peculiarities of queer Shakespeare as a critical and theoretical direction is that, almost paradoxically, from the start it ran against the idea that 'queer' also signals marginality. Existent scholarship on queerness in Shakespeare has located queer meanings within some of the most mainstream characters, actions and plot strands in Shakespeare. One does not have to be relegated to the social or sexual margin in Shakespeare to embody queer meaning. And *Queer Shakespeare* demonstrates that margin is not always the place that produces queer currents in Shakespeare's drama and poetry, nor is it one that 'queer' presences seek to occupy. *Queer Shakespeare* picks up on some of the new thinking about the relationship of literature, time and desire that has grown out of post-structuralist theories of desire and sexuality.

Coupled with the idea of temporality, 'queer' has recently posed challenge to the teleology of historical time; to the idea that across time and history, queer has always been a forward-oriented imagination and that 'tended to privilege the avant-garde'.[12] *Hamlet* does not come to mind immediately as a queer text on the surface of it, but there is a good reason for Elizabeth Freeman to use this play (indeed, to use Shakespeare) as a framing device for her experimental study about new social relations produced by interruptions in time and in the social order. *Hamlet* is an avant-garde play at all levels of composition. In the context of Freeman's idea of 'queer' as a marker of avant-garde art, either mainstream or popular, *Hamlet* is a queer play. It is a play that shatters orthodoxies of any kind, from theatre to semantics. Obsession with the body – body politic, Ophelia's body, Claudius's body, Polonius's body, Old Hamlet's body, Yorrick's body, Gertude's body, Rosencranz's and Guilderstern's bodies, Laertes's body – lies at heart of *Hamlet*. For Freeman, therefore, 'it's not unreasonable to read the entire play as ... a melancholic wish for the homoerotic Eden that is the play's primal scene'.[13] This claim will no doubt prompt thinking about *Hamlet*, though outside *Queer Shakespeare*, because there is no essay devoted to this tragedy in this volume. But what Freeman's thinking about *Hamlet* as a starting moment that prompts slow steps and nuanced ways of defining and illustrating queer temporality perceptively shows is that queer theory is in some of its most recent formulations indebted to Shakespeare. That Shakespeare's engenders the queer theory of temporality is a proposition that both queer theorists and Shakespeare critics might accept, at least as a starting point for further debates.

'Queer' stands for both a critical method and a theoretical system grounded in what Mario DiGangi has described as 'the strategy of examining the representation of mobile erotic relations instead of fixed erotic identities'.[14] Fixed identities, which queer overturns, are socially produced identities, which allows Carla Freccero to define 'queer' as 'naming a non-identity-based critical cultural and political practice that seeks to resist the humanist rights-bearing claims of collective identities'.[15] Freccero employs 'queer' as a theoretical term that signals an ideological departure from the idea of the erotic body defined uniformly, which DiGangi also questions. Critics of queer early modernity in England have offered arguments about different ways in which same-sex sexual acts, practices and desires manifested themselves in early modern literature and society. In these undertakings, critics have invested a significant amount of controlled speculation in drawing conclusions about what we can actually know today about the social signification of these sexual and erotic manifestations in the past that came down to us in coded allegories and literary stylizations, and a limited body of archival evidence, in the English context.

With his large canon of plays and a significant body of lyric poetry for an active playwright and actor that he was, Shakespeare has become an important case study in explaining the meeting point of queer theory and early modern literature. One of the questions that this volume also addresses is what queer theory has done for Shakespeare scholarship and how queer theory can move Shakespeare criticism in a new direction. Madhavi Menon's critical experiment, *Shakesqueer*,[16] represents a bold intervention in this regard, in that her project covers the entire Shakespeare canon of plays and poems. The contributors to this book, of whom some are not scholars of early modern studies but theory scholars writing predominantly on modern and contemporary literature and culture, found something queer in each of Shakespeare's texts. Not only does Menon's queer companion make Shakespeare a queer writer *tout court*, but more importantly, her statement that 'Shakespeare is a queer theorist ... because his work already inhabits the queer theory we occupy today'[17] raises the key question that also frames *Queer Shakespeare*: what is the relationship between queer theory and Shakespeare? The goal is to show how queer theory unfolds from within Shakespeare's texts, how to think of queer theory as formulating itself by looking backward in the past, not only forward, towards modern times and literatures, as queer theory tends to do. The overall conception and the course of the book themselves make Menon's volume a queer book. It is a very different kind of companion among many that have been steadily coming out of late. If, as Menon suggests, Shakespeare's texts and modern queer theory share common ground, then queer Shakespeare scholarship, as envisaged in *Queer Shakespeare*, shows how else one might conceive of queer Shakespeare as a queer theorist and writer, by linking queer theory with other theories and philosophical paradigms that both complement Menon's 'Shakesqueer' project and suggest new directions for the next phase of queer scholarship on Shakespeare.

Shakesqueer makes a strong claim for Shakespeare's work to contain conceptual and ideological structures of queer theory, something which queer theorists who are not early modern specialists pick up and develop in their analyses. *Queer Shakespeare* demonstrates that teasing out queer theory in analyses of Shakespeare's texts is inextricable from analyzing those texts as part of the historical, cultural and aesthetic backgrounds in which they were originally written, though not only as contexts that helped form Shakespeare's texts but also milieus against which those texts react. This critical approach is enriched by bringing together different directions and ways of using queer theory in interpreting Shakespeare. Thus, for instance, John Garrison's chapter engages new thinking in the study of object-oriented ontology and Simone Chess's chapter brings in recent thinking about trans issues in the present. In this way, these chapters remind us why scholars continue to turn to queer approaches as they seek new insights into Shakespeare: queer theory nimbly deploys multiple modes of interpretation to render visible the complexity of sexuality. *Queer Shakespeare* demonstrates that queer theory brings the present in dialogue with the past while also unsettling the teleologies that position those temporal categories as proceeding one from the other.[18]

Queer theory has allowed Shakespeare critics to unpack desires, sexualities and kinds of embodiment in ways in which previous criticism did not. It has revealed Shakespeare as a sexual radical at times, as a writer for whom the body and desire, and sex and sexuality, are as important as crowns and wars, who is in and who is out of the throne. The Shakespeare that emerges from the pages of *Queer Shakespeare* is the Shakespeare acutely curious, observant and attentive to the nuances of how sexuality and desire shape and affect his world. Queer theory has shown that Shakespeare is transgressive in order to raise questions about what might be the opposite of transgression, that we may think is the norm, but it might not be. It has suggested that the law of desire that regulates which body should desire which other body is the most malleable and unstable of the laws within his creative imagination. Queer theory has also displayed that in Shakespeare the fictional men and women, fairies and airy spirits, are driven by competing desires that cut across the lines of gender and sexual identities against contemporary expectations. In methodological terms, queer theory has deepened the link between the study of the psychic structures within interiority and the social and cultural history that shape identity. In that respect, queer theory has shown that in Shakespeare the process of a character's unchaining itself from those external constructions takes the form of a struggle that is at once political and public as well as intimate and emotional. Queer theory brought together historiography and the study of psychic processes, and inwardness and the subconscious, imagined in different terms but presented in recognizable structures in Shakespeare's text.

In Shakespeare, as in much early modern literature, queer is a coded discourse, one dependent on the rhetorical ornament or a classical allusion to convey queer meaning. A reference to Ganymede[19] or to Calisto[20] would have conjured associations with what we now call queer sexuality and desire to the early moderns just as we decode these mythical figures as queer, because we have transported the classical associations of these figures with queer sexuality to modern times. But rhetorically coded lines in Shakespeare's Sonnets, certain lexical choices and puns, for instance in *Coriolanus*[21] and *Romeo and Juliet*, and some passages in *The Merchant of Venice*[22] or *Twelfth Night*, all demonstrate that at different levels of expression and ornamentation, and to differing degrees, Shakespeare's texts produce queer moments and scenic events. As a marker of such textual moments, queer is attached to a person or behaviour that is not named by culture that regulates representation. Because that discourse is linguistically coded in ways that intersect with but are not always identical to the actual acts and forms of embodiment that early modern men and women practised and inhabited, a queer Shakespeare project depends on the critical practice of the uncovering of the linguistic, rhetorical and stylistic work of imagination that reshapes various social practices into the language of dramatic and lyric poetry. If Shakespeare the queer theorist came before queer theory, which is how the teleological argument goes, the emergence of queer theory, before it was so named, owes, as it does, much to Shakespeare as well.

Queer Shakespeare before queer theory

Queer Shakespeare collects chapters which either examine queerness as an instance of history as a cultural practice, or which treat 'queer' as an elastic and expansive notion that bears within itself the meaning of aberration from genealogical thinking of some kind. While informed by queer theory, the essays are also intent on extending the terms of queer theory in a direction in which queer theory has not gone yet. This dual purpose of the chapters in *Queer Shakespeare* is represented to different degrees in individual essays, but all of the chapters intervene in both historiography and theory. They all make it evident that the Shakespearean past is treated 'as a site that produces queer theory',[23] as Stephen Guy Bray postulates in his book *Against Reproduction.*

For Shakespeare critics who are queer theorists, *Queer Shakespeare* gives an opportunity to understand how Shakespeare anticipates queer theory, and how queer theory builds on the queer foundations of some of Shakespeare's texts. The way, for instance, in which Shakespeare represents romantic love as always contested, unsettled and frequently unromantic; in which courtship is often bound by 'homoerotic dimension';[24] and that sex and sexuality are not identical, already deconstructs heterosexual ideology, 'proleptically', by presenting 'queerness at the heart of heteronormative culture'.[25] Queer early modern criticism started by making this argument and to a large extent still continues to work within it.

If Shakespeare came before queer theory in the sense that his texts anticipate some of the ideas upon which queer theory would later be built, his texts also contributed to the queer structure of thinking about polymorphous sexuality, in a way that closes the gap between the pastness of Shakespeare and the contemporariness of queer theory. The chapter 'Swan in Love: The Example of Shakespeare's Sonnets' in Eve Kosofsky Sedgwick's influential book *Between Men: English Literature and Male Homosocial Desire* explores Shakespeare's Sonnet 20, the so called master-mistress sonnet. Sedgwick's essay gave rise to many 'startlingly crisp'[26] arguments about homosociality and gendered identities put forward in Shakespeare studies, at the same time when queer theory started to influence literary criticism. Sedgwick's chapter is at once a contribution to queer theory in the making and to Shakespeare studies in need of a nuanced awareness of the erotic energies that produce texts which give intellectual enjoyment. Her chapter also played an important role in shaping queer theory as a critical tool for unpacking dichotomies within, and the binaries of, gender and sexuality. Sedgwick, via Shakespeare, was therefore constitutive of the formative phase of queer theory and queer early modern literary criticism.

Some recent work on sex, sexuality and desire in Shakespeare, however, illustrates 'queer' work on Shakespeare outside the theoretical understanding of 'queerness', as offered in this volume. When Paul Hammond points to the fact that Shakespeare's sonnets are 'less direct'[27] than Philip Sidney's sonnets, that their distinct feature is their 'tortuous indirections' compared to the 'daring'[28] of Richard Barnfield's sonnets, without calling such aesthetic convolutions 'queer', he demonstrates that the lexicon of queer theory is a matter of selection for a literary critic. For Sedgwick and Hammond, who both wrote about Sonnet 20, 'queer' is a new method of analysis and critical reading, not an adherence to a specific theory and its technical vocabulary. For them, 'queer' lies in the tangle of linguistic subtleties with which polymorphous sexuality and androgyny become the subjects of lyric poetry and a way of reimagining the tradition of sonnet writing; of altering that tradition from within – and at the moment passed its peak as a lyrical fashion in the English Renaissance.[29] Queer, in *Queer Shakespeare*, is a repository of critical possibilities – difficult, political, probing, but also lively – which one can employ, at this moment in theory more widely, and in queer theory specifically, to interpret the incommensurate and controversial language of desire and sexuality in Shakespeare.

Queer Shakespeare in critical context

In queer early modern literary criticism and in queer criticism of twentieth- and twenty-first-century literature and culture, scholars have used the term 'queer' to analyze the changing conceptualization of sexual behaviour, the binaries of sexual identity and scenes which in some way look awry at normative representations of desire, sexuality and embodiment. The focus on desire and the querying of the sexual binaries of homo- and heterosexuality as they have been culturally and historically formulated to presume control of the definitions of sexuality in the Renaissance has also been the main objects of queer literary criticism. For instance, *Queering the Renaissance*, a volume that collects some of the grounding essays from the formative phase of queer early modern historiography, redefines the ways in which identity, gender and sexuality were conceptualized in the Renaissance and presented in literature of the period.[30] Shakespeare is explored within a critical context that covers different figures and genres of writing. Goldberg's own essay, 'Romeo and Juliet's *Open Rs*', deconstructs the energies of desire in this play that 'cross gender difference', mainly in linguistic terms.[31] In their critical overview of queer historicism, Goldberg and Menon theorized the relationship between historical and sexual difference, as an aspect of what they call the 'universalizing scope' of historicism that has a tendency to homogenize markers of sexuality as universally different in relation to normativity.[32] In his work that followed these discussions, Goldberg extended queer historiography with the aid of 'philosophical materialism',[33] while continuing to grapple with the concepts of sameness and difference that are represented as elusive and ambiguous in Renaissance art and literature – but in this project, Shakespeare is not his subject.

Yet in *Queer Shakespeare*, sameness and difference do not drive analyses in the individual essays. In differing ways, the essays in *Queer Shakespeare* show that the multifarious ways in which desire and sexuality feature in different texts demonstrate how queer theory becomes a 'perceptional opener'[34] by which object-oriented philosophy, trans theory or comparativism can yield new insights. This volume also opens up the term 'queer' to redefinition, to re-envisaging, and to a new critical awareness of its potential. It allows each contributor to understand and use the term 'queer' in an individual way; to adapt it to the texts and contexts which are the subject of queering; and even to take as much from an understanding of 'queer' as a signifier of erotic unruliness within a text and culture. Each chapter in *Queer Shakespeare* therefore brings its own perspective on 'queer', a term 'whose political efficacy is diluted through its universalization', as James Bromley and William Stockton argue in their collection, *Sex Before Sex*, but a term which continues, even at this most recent, late, stage in queer theory, to stir up controversy, even if only at the level of debate among critics of literature and stage performance.[35] *Queer Shakespeare* shows that deconstructive Shakespeare is not always the same as queer Shakespeare. It proposes that dichotomies of desire and sexuality, which are the subject of analysis in this volume, are queer, but only insofar as those dichotomies also extend to other manifestations of desire and forms of embodiment that on the surface may not strike us as queer, like glass, smell or size.

In *Queer Shakespeare*, 'queer' means not just intimacy and affection, not only sexuality and eroticism, not only acts and practices. Rather, 'queer' captures the split between representation and embodiment; the changing of texts between linguistically different cultures of the early modern period; it bridges gaps between different kinds of community, and material objects and texts. Sexual practices and types are queer; but so are rhetorical figures and styles. And 'queer' in this collection does not mark a departure from genital sex: sodomy is analysed in the context of antitheatrical homophobia and within the register of the early modern money-lending economy. When procreation, taken to be the generation or animation of material life, is shown to be a queer act, as it is in Christine Varnado's reading of *Macbeth*, then 'queer' in *Queer Shakespeare* has made an unpredictable leap by showing how the normative has become the transgressive, and a queer event of a particular, and peculiar, kind. Or, when the gigantic and the miniature are treated as queer attributes of the erotic, as in Valerie Billing's interpretation of *Love's Labour's Lost*; when clothing, jewellery, strange texts and the dilatory, baroque manner of narration turn into the signs of queerness in Stephen Guy-Bray's analysis of *Cymbeline*; and when law and the Christian articulation of virtuous and shameful sex are put in conversation with queer theory in Melissa Sanchez's exploration of *Measure for Measure* – then *Queer Shakespeare* demonstrates expansiveness of the term queer to capture the strangeness of the past to imagine desire, sexuality and the body. 'Queer' captures how the kind of writing Shakespeare employs and the ways of telling a story represent a response in his poetics to the moment of profound social, political, cultural shifts and changes in language that early modern England underwent at the end of the sixteenth and early seventeenth century. In this sense, *Queer Shakespeare* shows that queer early modern studies, and queer theory more broadly, is far from over.

On the contrary, the more queer theory evolves, the more it expands the opportunity for critical innovation; the more experimental vitality it can add to Shakespeare criticism and different cultural appropriations of Shakespeare. *Queer Shakespeare* shows that the vibrancy of Shakespearean sexualities, the vagaries and extremities of desire germane to his writing, and the resistance to epistemologically transparent articulations of sex and the body afford new critical possibilities. The Shakespearean queer is both a conceptual abstraction and an abstraction that masks the representation of desire, sexuality and embodiment of multiple significations. The most desiring of Shakespeare's fictional men and women, the ones fully consumed by *eros*, are also the ones who test rhetoric most daringly.

Queer language and queer Shakespeare

The chapters in *Queer Shakespeare* demonstrate that at any level of composition and style, stage scene and plot device, Shakespeare can be queer, even queerer than we at first think he is; and in refreshing and liberating ways, too. Queer Shakespeare displays rhetorical power that can shatter and alter meaning at any point in the text, as the following lines by Arcite, one of the two cousins from *The Two Noble Kinsmen*, illustrates:

> Let's think this prison holy sanctuary,
> To keep us from corruption of worse men.
> …
>   What worthy blessing
> Can be but our imaginations
> May make it ours? And here being thus together,
> We are an endless mine to one another;
> We are one another's wife, ever begetting
> New births of love; we are father, friends, acquaintance,
> We are in one another, families;
> I am your heir, and you are mine. This place is our
>   inheritance.

> (2.2.71–2; 76–84)

Confinement becomes a place that liberates imagination to beget new ways of belonging for two men. It is a place of fantasy. It erases the boundary between kinship and friendship, and turns both kinship and friendship into a new kind of affective bond, 'an endless mine to one another'. It is not clear what kind of exchange is imagined in this passage; whatever it is, it offers fulfillment. Imprisonment also redefines the meaning of gender and marriage, in an invitation to become (symbolically?) each other's wife. This fantasy of new affective and social coupling has rewritten what family, heritage and inheritance mean in the prison. Yet this confinement seems more like a desired bower of emotional bliss than a crushing dungeon. Prison has become a shared space of intimacy, however elusive the somatic and erotic signification of that intimacy may be. It has become a homosocial and queer space. As Arcite's language cuts through matrimonial and kinship lines, it releases desire that is at once erotic and political: his words have made

Palamon 'almost wanton' (2.2.96). Wantonness, understood
in the sense in which the *OED* defines it as 'undisciplined,
ungoverned, unmanageable, [and] rebellious', implies force
and desire to shatter the political authority that imprisoned
the cousin-friends. Arcite's use of the word reveals both
political and erotic Shakespeare and Fletcher, his collaborator
on this play. Palamon's ungoverned thoughts rebel even
against time, which may put an end to his 'friendship' with
Arcite: 'I do not think it possible for our friendship / Should
ever leave us' (2.2.124–5). The meaning of the word 'friend'
is not too far removed from that of 'cousin,' which invokes
love and intimacy. 'Friend' is also closely related to *amicitia*,
which captures the affective basis of friendship, love as a way
of bonding between friends. This dramatic moment brings
out the tension between 'the tropes of male friendship and the
cultural imperative of monogamous marriage'[36] in the plot.
To seal the bond between friends in this passionate reverie,
Arcite imagines death as the state in which shared love within
this affective friendship will never end: 'And after death our
spirits shall be led / To those that love eternally' (2.2.115). The
fantasy of eternity takes the language of emotional exchange
back to that of matrimony, and the ritualistic promise that
husband and wife are inseparate in life and death.

This passage illustrates that in its most recognizable form
the queerness of Shakespeare's text characterizes what Jeffrey
Masten has called 'the mobile quality of desire, erotics, and
affections, as distinct from identities'.[37] Arcite's language
shows the virtue of desire to be fluid; its meaning opaque. But
the text does not demonstrate that either the class or gender,
or even sexual identity of the imprisoned noblemen is affected
by these changes in the rhetoric of desire. It is desire, not
identity that is, in fact, of more interest to the two collabo-
rators at this point. For, affections that bind the friends in
Shakespeare and Fletcher's play are not imaginative constructions of a playtext only. Their cultural correlative and social
meaning lie in what Will Tosh has documented and described
as complicated 'affectional transactions'[38] between men as

friends in early modern England. Shakespeare and Fletcher's text is queer in both the historical and theoretical sense in which friendship is imagined.

Yet how transgressive is this desire? The desire imagined in this passage privileges a male-male relationship differently in relation to kinship and the Theban court, as normative units and, especially of the court, of political power as well. But that same male-male desire does not put gender and affection in tension, but in consonance. As such, desire confirms masculine agency.[39] One could say, even, that this passage confirms that Shakespeare and Fletcher think and write within the frame of his own period's idealization of friendship as one of the main social pillars, while also treating friendship as a more expansive and affective bond that registers particular, if often fluid, forms of closeness and privacy between men.[40] The state situation shows that this other, affective, side of friendship is of more interest to Shakespeare at this point in the play. The exchange between Arcite and Palamon takes place in a prison cell, in a space that emasculates men; in a place that strips men of power afforded to them by culture and society. The desire that brings Arcite and Palamon together does not come in *addition* to the power they had outside the prison walls, but *despite* having that power taken away from them. *Queer Shakespeare* shows that signs of queerness in Shakespeare are more authentic in scenes away from the tension of gender and sexuality, where the play between orthodoxy and subversion is apparent but not simplified.

The multifaceted meaning of the words in this passage conceals both the operation of the mind that thinks away from the normative gender arrangement and shows the syntactic strategy that carries this meaning. It is evidence of a historical change occurring in the English language at the turn of the centuries. It shows that the increasingly rhetorical mind of a writer writing in a deeply rhetorical culture was influenced by the changes in the English language at the point when the semantic potential of the English language significantly developed at the end of the sixteenth century.[41] The artificiality of language, which Renaissance rhetoricians advocated as an ideal to be followed over realism, even colloquialism, depended on rhetorical ornament for its effect; rhetoric also encouraged the experimentation with the invention of topics to be developed and embellished with rhetorical figures.[42] In playwrights like Shakespeare we should therefore expect rhetoric to be a malleable form in which experimenting with content means testing the meanings they can produce; and using those meanings, and the very process of their testing, to dramatic or poetic ends. In the passage from *The Two Noble Kinsmen*, these rhetorical tendencies are evident in attaching different meanings to desire as well as to the affective and corporeal bonds within such social categories as wife, cousin and friend. Shakespeare rhetorical imagination is also queer imagination.

At this moment in the history of the English language, the expansion of the meaning of words, mostly through polysemy, became an important tool for the creation of the semantic diversity of the English literary language.[43] Reflecting on the lines cited above from the angle of theory, one could say that those lines illustrate what Jeffrey Masten has recently called 'queer philology'.[44] *Queer Shakespeare* demonstrates that the origin of queer early modern theory lies precisely in the arrangement and meaning of the words as carriers of meaning, not only in meaning itself. The lines from *The Two Noble Kinsmen* on which I comment here demonstrate that the Shakespeareanism of desire,[45] that is, the specific nature and force of expression that Shakespeare attaches to the vibrancy of the language of desire, builds a bridge between the past and the present of queer theory.

The exchange between Arcite and Palamon does not make them homosexuals in modern terms; it does not reveal the homoerotic nature of their affective relationship with each other. Even friendship which they profess in idealized terms does not follow the same trajectory of same-sex relations which we find within the spaces of friendship that John Garrison, in his book on early modern friendship and queer theory, traces down to a philological and historical detail.[46] Rather, the rhetoric of new bonding between the two young noblemen captures queerness in the sense in which David Orvis treats queer as 'alternative arrangements and practices'[47] that can be established between men against dominant cultural arrangements. What exactly this arrangement, fantasized about within the prison walls and, importantly, hidden away from the family household and the scrutinizing gaze of the King of Thebes, means, is not clear. But this arrangement shows Shakespeare's queer art of the incommensurable. Queer meaning in Shakespeare is never graspable in full; it is never circled; so many meanings compete at once, and sometimes contradict one another. In that sense his linguistic art reveals itself as the queer art of words. The semantic opacity of the affective, emotional, erotic or amorous language becomes in Shakespeare's queer art of words a 'productive analytical resource'.[48] And that productive analytical resource, as a queer resource, extends Shakespeare criticism in directions in which other forms of critical inquiry do not venture. Unpacking Shakespeare's queer language enables us to not only see how Shakespeare, the writer of restless desires, pushes the limits of sexuality and desire, but also how the utility and meaning of 'queer' dilates in close analysis. In many instances in *Queer Shakespeare*, in fact, nuanced close analysis proves to be the best analytical method in finding out how Shakespeare buries queer meaning in the complexity and bravura of his language.

What is common to all the chapters that follow is that their authors search for hitherto unexplored strategies of deciphering the 'intelligibility'[49] of desires and sexualities imagined in Shakespeare's text. The authors explore Shakespeare's drama and lyric poetry in relation to other dramatic characters, against the background of the stylistic and literary contexts that helped shape Shakespeare's texts, with a view of social and cultural communities imagined in the texts as versions of collectivity separate from traditional collective units and social categories, like family, religious group and social class. Among the topics examined in this book are explorations of the forms of sexual connections formed after disease (plague), transgendered bodies at the heart of comedy, homophobia and metatheatre, glass and desire, generation as an unnatural phenomenon, the queerness of scent and writing style as queer formalism.

Queer Shakespeare between history and theory

Queer readings of Shakespeare represented in this volume are both historically and theoretically oriented. The aim of this book is to uncover as many possibilities for expanding the historiography of queer approaches to Shakespeare in the space allowed and to illustrate how different ways of theoretical thinking about what 'queer' is, or can be, influences how we read Shakesepare. A project of this scope, centred on a mainstream writer of a large and generically diverse canon such is Shakespeare, inevitably has to leave something out. This book does not feature readings of Shakespeare that are dependent on the decision-making processes and revisions undertaken by eighteenth- and nineteenth-century editors in editions, and changes in prompt books in which words were crossed out.[50] Although the way we read sexuality in Shakespeare is dependent also on those revisions, I consider this particular aspect of queer Shakespeare historiography, important though it is, a distinct area of research. This area covers related objects and fields of study and analytical practices – new bibliography, history and practices of editing, theatre history, performance and textual studies – which would make a stronger and more visible contribution to queer Shakespeare historiography in a project more focused on different instances within this field of Shakespeare scholarship. The book also does not include chapters on queer readings of stage performance and of popular film and music, despite the imprint that queer interpretations of Shakespeare have produced within popular culture and media.[51] Although I acknowledge that popular culture represents a growing area for the study of modern queer appropriations of Shakespeare, I am also mindful of the fact that different media in popular culture shift focus from text to popular culture and therefore call for a critical apparatus that is different from that of literary criticism.[52]

Queer in *Queer Shakespeare* draws on new developments in queer theory particularly attentive to transsexual theory. Comparative literary and cultural assessments reveal yet another new perspective on queer work on Shakespeare practised in this volume. In contact with texts from the European Renaissance, Shakespeare's writing reveals queerness as a difference based on suppression, occlusion and semantic difference of allied vocabulary. One of the difficulties and pleasures of unpacking queer meanings in Shakespeare, and in early modern literature more broadly, is the illegibility of the scenes which harbour such meanings. Motifs, figures, rhetorical formulations and scenarios associated with them in archival and more readily available texts can also be repetitive. A comparative perspective with queer culture in early modern Italy, where social history shows that different queer acts and practices were culturally more visible and more amply registered in the archives in explicit terms, might help us speculate differently about the nature of sins that are textualized in Shakespeare and other examples of early modern English literature.[53] It seems that there are fewer of what Traub calls 'archival impasses'[54] in Italian than in English archives of queer early modernity. What would it mean, for instance, for an analysis of queer Renaissance, the history of homosexuality in England or specifically for the queerness of *The Two Noble Kinsmen*, if an English archive yielded evidence, similar to a detailed document in an Italian archive, of a group marriage involving eight men in Rome in 1578, 'who legitimized their relationship in a rite that imitated the Counter-Reformation sacrament of marriage', as Giuseppe Marcocci describes that occasion?[55] The marriage took place in the 'ancient basilica of San Giovanni a Porta Latina', now a frequented tourist site and advertised as a popular place for weddings in Rome. The men, all from southern Europe, were found out, tried, imprisoned then hanged on the bridge over the river Tiber leading to Castel Sant'Angelo in Rome. Their bodies were burned on a stake in a southern part of Rome, an unlikely location for this act. Echoing the language from the Shakespeare–Fletcher play, these eight men became wives to one another in a group marriage ceremony, doubly troubling the idea and act of marriage because of its same-gendered nature and the multiple parties tied into a wedlock. The brief lives of these men in imprisonment became the queer space of their brief new reality of marriage. What that group marriage signified in social terms, we do not fully know. Different political cultures and social conditions in early modern Europe determined what was recorded, how much, by whom and with what purpose, especially if the record registered a draconic punishment, which in itself is an event, as this one was. Comparative queer historiography, of which we need more in queer early modern (English) studies, may shift perspectives of our knowledge and critical practice in exciting directions. Ian Moulton's comparative analysis of an unlikely pair of texts, Shakespeare's sonnets and an explicitly pornographic poem about hermaphroditic sex, embodiment and eroticism from Italian literature, uncovers a more explicit and raw form of hermaphroditism than that which is only occasionally attended to by Shakespeare.

The chapters on language, style and comparativism act as reminders that in the post-New Historicist critical environment a return to language and the study of resources as objects of inquiry represents a return to two topics which New Historicism did not address: language as material practice and source studies. When Stephen Greenblatt stated that 'the Renaissance tended to sharpen its sense of the normative by meditating upon the prodigious',[56] he gestured towards thinking about the Renaissance as a queer phenomenon. His claim sounded like a sign of theoretical possibility. And his interpretation of *Twelfth Night* in the essay from which I have quoted him here examines the play's resistance to a determined identity. *Queer Shakespeare* treats historicist research, which is in one form or another unavoidable in Renaissance studies, not as a precondition for queer criticism but as a theoretically reconfigured alternative to, and sometimes a version of, the empiricism of archival research. This volume demonstrates that Shakespeare is an unavoidable presence in the literary history of sexuality in early modern England;[57] that he is constituent of queer theory just as queer theory without Shakespeare shuts itself away from one of its most resourceful presences.

Queer Shakespeare is divided into three parts. Since all of the chapters engage with queer desire, sexuality, embodiment and practice, close analysis as a way of interpreting specific historical milieu and theoretical perspective from which each author addresses her or his topic, there are necessary conceptual overlaps between chapters as a whole. Therefore, the organization of the book in three parts should be taken as a way of stimulating further critical thinking about queer Shakespeare by identifying notions that the chapters in each part offer as a way of starting critical conversation, not clear-cut thematic categories that neatly correspond to topics explored in each of the chapters within the three parts.

Part I, 'Queer time', groups together four chapters in which queer sexuality and desire are analyzed in relation to time, history and historiography, within the English context and comparatively. The chapters in this group explore the fluid relationship between time and desire, history and sexuality and the problems of historiographical descriptions and articulations of these relationships, including a comparative, Anglo–Italian perspective as a way of accessing queer meanings that relate Shakespeare's texts to other vernacular literature in a transnational context. David L. Orvis examines how the early modern ideology of love shaped amorous and erotic discourses in *The Two Gentlemen of Verona*. Specifically, Orvis's chapter is concerned with how this early

INTRODUCTION   27

comedy consistently asks questions of the worthiness of different kinds and levels of love and desire. His chapter shows the extent to which Shakespeare's plays explore questions about the meaning and worth of queer desires and what we might call normative sexuality, and about romantic love and affectionate friendship between men. John Garrison's chapter, 'Glass: The Sonnets' desiring object', pushes the idea of queer time in Shakespeare in a different direction. He explores glass as a natural object related to the operations of time, desire, 'desirability' and aging in the sonnets. In 'The sport of asses: *A Midsummer Night's Dream*', Kirk Quinsland asks whether thinking about sixteenth- and seventeenth-century antitheatrical writing as homophobic represents a historical anachronism, in an attempt to explore the dynamics between stage representations of sexual conduct and homophobic audiences in Shakespeare's time. The 'stylistic badness' of the 'Pyramus and Thisbe' play-within-the play staged by the rude Mechanicals referred to as 'sport' is explored as an antihomophobic reaction to the homophobia of antitheatrical treatises. This part ends with Ian Frederick Moulton's chapter, 'As You Like It or What You Will: Shakespeare's Sonnets and Beccadelli's *Hermaphroditus*', which sets out to examine the relationship between texts across 'temporal and linguistic boundaries', specifically between licit and illicit desire in Becadelli's early fifteenth-century collection of Latin epigrams and a selection of Shakespeare's sonnets. Comparative analysis between temporally and generically different poetry reveals a relationship between desire and time that allows queer presences to be recognized as structurally corresponding across a longer historical arc.

Part II, 'Queer language', brings together four chapters examining language, narrative and style as carriers of meaning about desire and sexuality. These chapters focus on language as material practice, rhetoric, sound, narrative and style of Shakespeare's writing which we call 'queer'. Valerie Billing, in 'The queer language of size in *Love's Labour's Lost*', investigates size, a property neither inherently erotic nor intrinsically queer, as a linguistic and stylistic category charged with erotic potential and the source of phallic jokes, through which male-male social and physical contacts are rendered as queer desire. In 'Locating queerness in *Cymbeline*', Stephen Guy-Bray asks what makes *Cymbeline* a queer play when it 'reaffirms' natural social hierarchy and orthodoxy. Focusing his analysis on narrative rather than linguistic excess, Guy-Bray demonstrates that the heteronormative narrative of the play is conveyed in a queer manner, and in that sense his reading runs counter to criticism that has analysed identity, language and sexuality in the play as queer. Moving from macrotextual to microlinguistic forms, Holly Dugan's chapter, 'Desiring H: *Much Ado About Nothing* and the sound of women's desire', focuses on the construction of female eroticism through aural punning and sexual allusions created by it, by exploring the queer phonology and meaning of the sound produced by various pronunciations of the letter 'H' at the end of the song in which Beatrice and Margaret pun about 'the orthography of women's desire'. If Billing starts her analysis by examining the limits of the Petrarchan rhetoric to articulate desire, Goran Stanivukovic, in his chapter '"Two lips, indifferent red": Queer styles in *Twelfth Night*', examines the vocabulary and syntax of Petrarchan style as carriers of queer meaning in the passionate encounters between Viola-Cesario and Olivia.

The last part, 'Queer nature', consists of five chapters which, in differing ways, explore the relationship between desire, environmentality and nature more broadly. These chapters are concerned with the notion of nature as a broad category, from weather to embodiment but also the binary of nature and nurture; from plague to the unnaturalness of sodomy; and from vitality to antisocial procreation. In 'Queer nature, or the weather in *Macbeth*', Christine Varnado explores how the language which renders the natural world in *Macbeth* by collapsing the boundaries between natural, human and 'what is alive' disrupts 'the logic of sexual repro-duction'. Reproduction of a different kind, of money bred by way of usury, is the subject of A. Eliza Greenstadt's chapter

'Strange insertions in *The Merchant of Venice*', in which she explores sodomy as an unnatural sin against the background of early modern writing about usury. The connection between desire, gender and embodiment is the subject of Simone Chess's chapter, 'Male femininity and Male-to-female cross-dressing in Shakespeare's plays and poems', which examines male-to-female (MTF) crossdressing by 'recognizing and recentering Shakespeare's representations of male femininity'. Kathryn Schwarz, in her chapter 'Held in common: *Romeo and Juliet* and the promiscuous seductions of plague', explores how contagion, specifically plague, yokes bodies with speech acts, and explores sexuality not in relation to heterosexual marriage but in a supple vocabulary of ways in which all mortal bodies might touch. This part started with a chapter asking questions about the nature of procreation in *Macbeth* and it ends with Melissa Sanchez's chapter, 'Antisocial procreation in *Measure for Measure*,' in which she challenges the category of both the sexual and ontological female body as consigned to procreation by virtue of that body's 'nature', and examines consequence of such separateness upon social order. Vin Nardizzi's afterword extends debates about desire and sexuality as queer ecology and queer environmentalism.

PART I

Queer time

1

'Which is worthiest love' in *The Two Gentlemen of Verona*?

David L. Orvis

The question posed by this chapter's title, and the implications and stakes of which will be teased out in what follows, draws its terms from an exchange between Julia and her waiting-woman Lucetta in 1.2 of *The Two Gentlemen of Verona*. Afforded the privacy Julia's garden, the conversation broaches matters of love:

> JULIA   But say, Lucetta, now we are alone,
>   Wouldst thou then counsel me to fall in love?
> LUCETTA   Ay, madam, so you stumble not unheedfully.
> JULIA   Of all the fair resort of gentlemen
>   That every day with parle encounter me,
>   In thy opinion which is worthiest love?
>
> $(1.2.1–6)^{1}$

As the scene unfolds, it comes to light that Julia already favours Proteus, one of the play's eponymous two gentlemen, over her other suitors. Nevertheless, the sequence of questions – first, whether to love, and second, whom to choose – reveals the parameters – and hence, too, the ideological underpinnings – of the love Julia is allowed. That she paradoxically seeks 'counsel' on whether 'to fall in love', that she solicits input on which suitor 'is worthiest', suggests a forced choice masquerading as a spontaneous, uncontrollable act. Julia seems satisfied with her choice, and remains steadfast even as Proteus renounces his vows and gives away her ring in pursuit of Silvia. This constancy in the face of increasingly unnerving deeds of inconstancy may serve to redeem Proteus (in some circles, anyway), but the thoughts, feelings and beliefs underwriting Julia's devotion to a dishonest, unfaithful lover and Silvia's would-be rapist are by and large foreclosed to us, as indeed they are to Julia herself. Depriving her of the corresponding lines, the playtext quite literally denies Julia this kind of introspection, or at least prohibits her from vocalizing it. In this instance, discursive limits are demarcated by those questions left unasked, by prohibited rather than permitted speech.

If the above offers us a glimpse into the different mechanisms by which ideology circumscribes discourses of love and desire, then it likewise provides an entry point for considering ways of (not) loving that defy or exceed dominant paradigms. Julia's query about 'worthiest love' can thus be more broadly construed as an inquiry into love's conceptual field. Most immediately referring to a choice in lovers, its phrasing allows for an interrogation of love in its institutional forms. Which is worthiest: heteroerotic love or homoerotic love? Romantic love or passionate friendship? Previous scholarship has amply demonstrated that these conflicts come to the fore in *Two Gentlemen*, with ambivalent results. In his path-breaking analysis of the conflict, Jeffrey Masten has shown that 'though the play consistently places male friendship and male-female love at odds ..., it is important to recognize that this cannot be seen simply as a contest between eroticized male-female relations and platonic male friendship, for male friendship and Petrarchan love in this play speak a remarkably similar language'. By the end, Masten argues, we witness 'a massive restoration of the play's homosocial power structure, a system no longer seen to be in competition with Petrarchan love, but underwriting it'.[2] Yet, other critics have interpreted the collusion of discourses as undermining, rather than 'underwriting', social and sexual identity: for Stephen Guy-Bray, the play's representation of heterosexuality 'as a prosthesis, as part of the equipment or furniture of a man', effects a 'stress on substitution and interchangeability … to undermine the stable and individual self';[3] for Elizabeth Rivlin, 'the way in which Shakespeare maps master/servant relationships onto bonds of romantic love and friendship' exemplifies a mimetic service that 'both shows the potential of Renaissance servants to rearrange social identities and reflects on the capacity of Shakespeare's theater to generate and dismantle such identities'.[4] In different ways, then, scholarly work on the play has already begun to grapple with questions prompted by Julia's query, albeit mostly within the confines of love's institutional forms.

Far from disputing the hegemony of romantic love and friendship in *Two Gentlemen*, this chapter hopes to elucidate some ways of (not) loving that find expression despite, or rather because of, its persistence. Or to quote Masten quoting *Shakespeare in Love*, my aim is to uncover 'the very truth and nature of love in this play' by beginning to explicate attitudes and beliefs typically understood to fall outside it.[5] Excavating such ideas in what J. L. Simmons has aptly called Shakespeare's 'coming out' play indicates, moreover, the originary status of critiquing love's dominion for Shakespeare's canon.[6] The playwright's earliest and most explicit treatment of the concept, *Two Gentlemen* deploys the word 'love' (in its various permutations) more than any other Shakespeare play – a total of 210 iterations, by my count.[7] If critics argue forcefully for the primacy of textuality in shaping characters' relationships, desires and senses of self, I would add that the constitutive texts are themselves constituted by the operative lexicon of love they structure and facilitate.[8] The play's 'love-discourse' (2.4.125) takes many forms, including 'love-book[s]' (1.1.19), love 'stor[ies]' 'shallow' and 'deep' (1.1.21, 23), 'love[s] ... writ ... in rhyme' (1.2.79), 'love-song[s]' (2.1.18), 'tales of love' (2.4.125) and, of course, 'love letters' (3.1.323). This diverse array of texts animates and sustains the play's investigation of 'love- affairs': not only the many types ('foolish love' [1.2.57], 'erring love' [2.4.213], 'kind love' [2.7.2], 'true confirmed love' [4.4.102], 'love sincere' [2.7.76]: which is worthiest?), but also their source, (e.g. 'spring of love' [1.3.84]), substance ('love's hot fire' [2.7.21]), trajectory (before- and 'after-love' [3.1.95]), and strength ('instances of infinite of love' [2.7.70]). This preoccupation with 'love-discourse' conveys an anxiety befitting characters making their first forays into love. As the play's organizing principle, it invites scrutiny of love as both ideological formation and discursive practice.

Returning to Julia's question, for instance, we might ask: How is love's worth determined, and why must we choose or at least prefer one instantiation over another? Why do gender and rank, among a host of other considerations, qualify a suitor for one type of love but not others? Given the play's well-documented commingling of friendship and romantic love, why must the former conform to one profile and the latter another? Why not romantic friendship, which could accommodate either profile, or both? Why must love take the form of a pair, rather than a trio or some other more fluid network? What makes love compulsory? Why do we, or *must* we, love at all? These sorts of questions, although seemingly taken for granted by the dramatis personae, nonetheless inform the playtext's conceptualization of 'love-discourse' and 'love-affairs'. Indeed, they obtain as logical extensions of a more basic question: what are the conditions and/or constituent parts required for an expression or social relation to fall under registers of love and thus acquire the 'love-' designation? Or from a different angle: what cannot be read as 'love-affairs' or 'love-discourse'? What remains excluded from the contents of the 'love-book'? From the notes and lyrics of the 'love-song'? From the pages and enclosures of the 'love letter'? And on what grounds, exactly? Any attempt to parse these locutions, to figure out the cultural work of the qualifier, calls for further exploration of what counts as, and indeed what constitutes, 'love-' in the first place. That characters neglect to pose certain kinds of questions only underscores their value in discerning the discursive limits under examination in the play.

As the emphasis on languages of love, or rather loves, would suggest, my project benefits from the insights of recent queer-philological work, particularly Jeffrey Masten's brilliant book *Queer Philologies: Sex, Language, and Affect in Shakespeare's Time*. Especially useful is his interpretive framework for etymological analysis:

> Etymology, ... in its lingering tastes of the past and present, forces us to develop ever-expanding lexicons of erotic and affective terms and their relations. Not only backward-looking *history*, etymology as a practice looks forward to remind us that words that seem identical and familiar to modern eyes and tongues we might better see as false cognates ("false friends," as we used to say in French class) – words that only *pass* as "the same" as ours, words that, when pressed, release whole new contexts while also holding within themselves the genealogical seeds of their eventual direction.[9]

Masten finds a salient example in the word 'sweet' and accompanying rhetorics of sweetness, which feature prominently in *Two Gentlemen*. Although primarily interested in 'the syntax of affective male relations', Masten notes that sweetness 'is spoken across *kinds* of relationships in early modern England, including those we would now separate into homosexual and heterosexual'.[10] In *Two Gentlemen*, therefore, we see rhetorics of sweetness applied both to friends and lovers, both in homo- and heteroerotic contexts. In the play's opening scene, Proteus wishes 'Sweet Valentine,

adieu' (1.1.11), to which Valentine responds in kind: 'Sweet
Proteus, … let us take our leave' (1.1.56). The very next
scene reveals Julia cherishing the 'sweet honey' of Proteus's
love letter (1.2.106), in which Proteus himself pines for
'*sweet Julia*' (1.2.125; emphasis in original). Both Valentine
and Proteus address Silvia as 'sweet lady' (2.4.36; 2.4.105,
4.2.112), and on one occasion Proteus calls her 'sweet love'
(4.2.102). Yet further instances put pressure on, if not push
beyond, categories of friendship and courtship: Lance refers
to Speed casually as 'sweet youth' (2.5.2); Turio expresses
gratitude to 'sweet Proteus, my direction-giver' (3.2.89);
and, perhaps most titillating of all, the Duke enjoins his
'sweet gentlemen' (i.e. Proteus, Turio *and* Sebastian/Julia) to
follow him in pursuit of the absconded Silvia (5.2.46). This
portability of affect, erotics, and desire bears out what Masten
describes as the '*historical*[ ] queer[ness]' of sweetness *vis-à-vis*
more modern regimes of gender and sexuality.[11] It indicates,
moreover, that sweetness operates as both constitutive element
and destabilizing force for a wide range of affective and erotic
relations.

Imbrications of this rhetoric with a similarly volatile love-
discourse become clearest when Proteus arrives at court in
Mantua. There, Pantino tells Antonio, Proteus shall '[h]ear
sweet discourse, converse with noblemen, / And be in eye
of every exercise / Worthy his youth and nobleness of birth'
(1.3.31–3). The pertinent exchange is worth quoting at length:

VALENTINE	Welcome, dear Proteus. Mistress, I beseech you
	Confirm his welcome, with some special favour.
SILVIA	His worth is warrant for his welcome hither,
	If this be he you oft have wish'd to hear from.
VALENTINE	Mistress, it is; sweet lady, entertain him
	To be my fellow-servant to your ladyship.
SILVIA	Too low a mistress for so high a servant.
PROTEUS	Not so, sweet lady, but too mean a servant
	To have a look of such a worthy mistress.
VALENTINE	Leave off discourse of disability.

	Sweet lady, entertain him for your servant.
PROTEUS	My duty will I boast of, nothing else.
SILVIA	And duty never yet did want his meed.
	Servant, you are welcome to a worthless mistress.
PROTEUS	I'll die on him that says so but yourself.
SILVIA	That you are welcome?
PROTEUS	That you are worthless.

(2.4.99–115)

Interweaving languages of sweetness and courtship, this chiasmus of rhetorics establishes a discourse that accommodates a trio of lovers in Silvia, Valentine and Proteus. The interplay of key words – 'sweet lady', 'mistress', 'servant', 'duty', 'worth' – bandied about by all three characters in almost stichomythic fashion – suggests a scenario quite unlike the traffic in women performed at play's end.[12] As Julie Crawford observes, 'At the end of the play the marriages serve to recreate the triangulated economy of male emulation and identification, with and through the affections of women'.[13] In striking contrast to this economy, which as numerous critics have pointed out establishes itself in the face of Silvia's conspicuous silence (after her final line, 'O heaven!' [5.4.59]), the erotically charged invitation to service offered Proteus on his arrival at court includes Silvia as willing participant. Before exiting with Turio, Silvia says to Proteus, 'Once more, new servant, welcome' (2.4.116), to which the new servant replies, 'We'll both attend upon your ladyship' (2.4.120). Irrespective of what happens later in the play, at *this* instant, in *this* situation, Silvia 'welcome[s]' Proteus as Valentine's 'fellow-servant'.

I linger over this exchange for two reasons. First, it brings into view, if only momentarily, the disruptive potential inherent in the hegemonic discourse of courtly love. Employing conventional modes of address, the 'sweet discourse' of Antonio's court discloses one powerful way in which words exceed their normative meanings and become appropriated for resistant (re)formulations. In other words, the exchange demonstrates that courtly language contains terms of its own displacement. Second, it reminds us that not all trios enact triangulation or trafficking, and that affective and erotic moments such as this, no matter how seemingly fleeting or inconsequential, merit consideration apart from their place in the normalizing arc of narrative. Adopting James M. Bromley's anti-teleological hermeneutic, we can read Silvia's momentary interest in a courtly threesome as significant in its own right, regardless of its status elsewhere in the text, for positing an alternative to romantic love's dyadic structure.[14] Moreover, we can distinguish this fantasy of consensual polyamory sharply from the traffic in women mobilized in the play's final scene, and with Melissa E. Sanchez's radical queer feminist framework, separate out instances of sexual violence perpe-trated against female characters such as Silvia from their own pursuits of masochistic or otherwise non-normative desire.[15] To disregard such distinctions and assume, for example, that Silvia's acceptance of Proteus as Valentine's fellow-servant cannot possibly reflect her own wishes, that indeed it can only ever signify or gesture toward subjection in the service of homosocial, homonormative bonds of male friendship, is to accede dominant culture's proscriptions of women's subjective desire.[16]

My impression that the playtext does not, or rather need not, militate against a more generous, sex-positive reading of Silvia – one, however, that does not, or rather need not, overlook or diminish instances of violation and abuse – derives at least in part from the overt and extensive critique of love's normative ideologies evident from the play's beginning. As Masten points out, the first iteration of 'love', not coincidentally Valentine's and also the play's opening line, 'Cease to persuade, my loving Proteus' (1.1.1), 'signifies in both directions; Proteus is "chained" by affection for Julia but equally bound to his male friend, to whom he speaks in similarly affectionate language'.[17] This similitude simultane-ously informs and undermines the play's early attempts to distinguish one type of love from another, as when Proteus's 'honour'd love' (1.1.4) for Valentine is juxtaposed with his 'doting love' (1.1.43) for Julia. The latter expresses itself in 'groans' (1.1.29), 'heart-sore sighs' (1.1.30) and 'watchful, weary, tedious nights' (1.1.31). It overwhelms and incapacitates the lover, effecting Ovidian metamorphosis in the manner Proteus describes:

> Thou, Julia, thou hast metamorphos'd me:
> Made me neglect my studies, lose my time,
> War with good counsel, set the world at nought;
> Made wit with musing weak, heart sick with thought.

> (1.1.66–9)

This is the stuff of Petrarchanism, a discourse instantly recognizable and, as Elizabeth Williamson demonstrates, thoroughly dissected in *Two Gentlemen*. The process begins, Williamson suggests, as 'the play opens with a dialogue that encourages the audience to view courtly love as something superficial, made and unmade by words'.[18] Following Guy-Bray, we might also say that love's artifice stems from its 'mediat[ion] through textuality', since 'to some extent at least, ... relationships we might think of as especially personal and intimate are all formed out of pre-existing material, out of texts we already know'.[19] In 1.1, Valentine and Proteus emphasize the textuality of romantic love, first in their banter about the 'love-book' and well-known tragic tale of Hero and Leander (1.1.19–26), again when they allude to mythologies of Love/Cupid (1.1.38–41), and a third time when they invoke an aphorism comparing 'doting love' to 'the eating canker' 'in the sweetest bud' (1.1.43–54). This emphasis on courtly love's textuality, on its emergence from and persistent preeminence through works of narrative, not only demythologizes a dominant and particularly potent form of love, it also lays bare the process by which other, counter-normative practices and configurations may be put into discourse. Exalted male friendship, which from the play's opening scene speaks nearly the same language as Petrarchan love, points in a similar direction, submitting to a similar impulse, despite its supposed homonormative status. Critical re-evaluations of the play's representation of male friendship indicate, in fact, that the early inducement to deconstruct extends to this affective relation, as well.[20]

While critics continue to explore what Traub calls 'the unstable boundary between *philia* and *eros*', much less attention has been paid to divine or spiritual love (*agape*) in the play.[21] Yet I would argue love's most radical potential resides in its divinely inspired form. In *Two Gentlemen*, the god of godly love is Love, ostensibly of the cherubic order, reputed by various characters to have wings (2.6.42, 2.7.11), childlike mannerisms and features (3.1.124–5) and 'not an eye at all' (2.4.95; see also 2.1.66). 'Love's a mighty lord' (2.4.135), claims Valentine, who earlier in the play had informed Proteus, 'Love is your master, for he masters you' (1.1.39). Add in a keenness for penetrative violence, as adduced by the plight of '*love-wounded Proteus*' (1.2.113; italics in original), and our composite sketch of Love as the love-god Cupid is complete.[22] This 'chameleon Love' (2.1.167), to adopt Speed's phrasing, may often preside over a certain variety of heteroerotic coupling, but exceptions to the rule abound in early modern literature and culture. '[T]he multiplicity that defines Cupidean desire', writes Jane Kingsley- Smith, 'may be heteroerotic, but is also homoerotic, pederastic, maternal and incestuous'. Defying even those iterations typically and conventionally imputed to him, 'Cupid represents love's blindness, in the sense of its disregard for social hierarchy, and its transience, given that he can remove affection as easily as he imposes it. Though he plays a role in epithalamic poetry and masques, Cupid shows no necessary affinity with marriage and may just as easily inspire the kind of lust that leads to rebellion, murder and suicide'.[23] On the one hand, then, Cupidean divinity signifies Love's totality, encompassing the spectrum of erotic and affective possibilities, while

on the other, Love's tyranny at the hands of a fickle, vengeful
god who enforces and flouts his own phallically constituted
commands at will. Although he declines to appear in the play,
the close association between Cupid and Puck would suggest
the love-god is more than a mere trope or motif. He inhabits
Shakespeare's worlds – *Two Gentlemen*'s Verona and Milan
no less than *Midsummer*'s Athens.[24]

Compounding this entanglement of eros and agape is the
incarnational theology of 'God is love' and attendant tradition
of correlating Christ with Cupid.[25] Rooted in medieval
mysticism and later influenced by Neoplatonic philosophy,
renderings of Christ as divine archer, with 'Ovid and the
Song of Songs' their 'dual provenance', constitute, in the
words of Barbara Newman, 'a superb illustration of the
medieval practice of "crossover" – the intentional borrowing
and adaptation of courtly themes in devotional art and vice
versa'.[26] Absorbing Christ into Cupid and Cupid into Christ,
secular and devotional art and literature from the Middle Ages
onward depict Amor variously as supreme matchmaker and
ultimate beloved. Writing about seventeenth-century religious
literature, Richard Rambuss remarks, 'To speak … of the
allure of devotional life, of enjoying God as one's lover, of
Christ acting as Eros or Cupid, the arrow-armed male god
of love: all this is commonplace here'.[27] This conjunction
informs the identities of at least two characters, Valentine
and 'Sebastian', named for martyrs iconologically linked to
dieu d'Amors through their association with divine darts or
arrows.[28] If sacred eroticism of this texture finds particular
poignancy in the Catholic devotional practices out of which
it first emerged, then it would seem *Two Gentlemen*, which in
addition to its Catholic saints is set in Italy and teeming with
references to confession (4.3.44, 5.2.39), penance (1.2.64,
2.4.127, 5.2.36, 5.4.168) and pilgrimage (2.7.9, 2.7.30),
as well as rosary beads (1.1.18), relics (4.3.132) and other
Catholic paraphernalia, foregrounds the porous boundary
between eros and agape.[29] To speak of godly love, therefore,
is also, ineluctably, to speak of its erotic counterpart.

Thus understood as a hybrid of types and traditions, Love in *Two Gentlemen* embodies and enacts an irreducible tension that percolates the play's love-discourse. Looking back at the terms Valentine and Proteus use to describe their hetero-erotic desires, we might note that Petrarchanism and Ovidian metamorphosis echo the idiom of divine passion. Valentine, like Proteus before him, acknowledges, 'life is altered now':

> I have done penance for contemning Love,
> Whose high imperious thoughts have punish'd me
> With bitter fasts, with penitential groans,
> With nightly tears, and daily heart-sore sighs;
> …
> There is no woe to his correction,
> Nor, to his service, no such joy on earth.
> Now, no discourse, except it be of love.
> Now can I break my fast, dine, sup, and sleep
> Upon the very naked name of Love.

> (2.4.126–30; 136–41)

As Speed points out to Valentine, '[N]ow you are metamorphosed with a mistress, that when I look on you, I can hardly think you my master' (2.1.29–31). This Petrarchan notion of love as erotic violence has much in common with Augustinian *caritas*, where '[i]nsuperable love wounds the soul's affections, inseparable love binds the power of thought, singular love destroys the capacity for action, and insatiable love "leads to the brink of death and makes one despair of recovery"'.[30] Indeed, Valentine and Proteus find themselves in a position not unlike the speaker of Shakespeare's sonnets. Gary Kuchar points out 'the intersections between Pauline agape and Neoplatonic Eros in Sonnet 22', which 'bespeak a lover immoderately and insecurely in love rather than one enjoying anything like perfect mutuality'.[31] How, then, are we to distinguish erotic love from spiritual love? Thomas Hyde submits a 'poetic theology of love' as one way to reconcile the tension inherent in the Cupid/Christ coupling: 'In a Christian poem, Amor or Cupid can be a partial manifestation, a figure or image of the love that is God, but only if readers never confuse or forget the hierarchical relation between the figure and fact, between the fictive world and real one'.[32] For Hyde, this is a matter of distinguishing pagan god from passion, 'in a literary tradition in which Scripture provides an ultimate example of textual truth and therefore an ultimate model of poetic authority'.[33] In this analysis, discerning agape requires reading literary professions of love and desire within and against biblical tradition, the implication being that one can *and should* distinguish between the two, and indeed that this strategy is optimal for comprehending relations between agape and eros in sacred and secular texts.

Yet, *Two Gentlemen* resists efforts to prise apart erotic love (in all its polymorphous/'chameleon' perversity) and spiritual love, much in the same way it obfuscates clear distinctions between Protestant and Catholic forms of worship – a premise at once terrifying and potentially liberating.[34] The playtext figures the inseparability of eros and agape in Blind Cupid who, as Erwin Panofsky has shown, originated in Renaissance depictions of cherubic Love.[35] Cupid's blindness presents a representational paradox: in some figurations, blindness signifies a lesser love attributable to baser, carnal cravings, while in others, a sacred form of love grounded in Renaissance Neoplatonism and transcendent of lecherous desire.[36] In the same play, then, Cupid's blindness explains seemingly erratic, ephemeral and arbitrary erotic infatuation as well as supposedly more steadfast, substantial and spiritual love. In response to Valentine's claim to 'have loved her [i.e. Silvia] ever since [he] saw her' (2.1.64), Speed avers, 'If you love her, you cannot see her' (2.1.66). The reason: 'Because Love is blind' (2.1.68). Similarly, Silvia maintains that due to his devotion to Julia, Proteus 'should be blind' (2.4.92). In 4.4, however, Julia compares her own features to Silvia's portrait, and opines, 'What should it be that he [Proteus] respects in her / But I can make respective in myself,

/ If this fond Love were not a blinded god' (4.4.191–3)?
In the first two instances, Love's blindness blinds the lover
from all visual stimuli, including the beloved. In Julia's
case, though, Love's blindness reflects a mutability causing
Proteus to shuttle, as per his namesake, between beloveds.
If Blind Cupid presides over both types of love, then to the
extent that characters identify as, for example, a 'beadsman'
(1.1.18), a 'true-devoted pilgrim' (2.7.9) and 'Love's firm
votary' (3.2.58), both types constitute godly love. Or at least
it becomes virtually impossible to know which iteration of
love is (not) a directive of the love-god. Hence, in consecutive
scenes, Proteus and Julia implore Love's assistance, in the
form of wings, to cross-purposes: in 2.6, having committed
to violating his oath to Julia, Proteus apostrophizes, 'Love,
lend me wings to make my purpose swift, / As thou has lent
me wit to plot this drift' (42–3); in 2.7, Julia plots to follow
her beloved Proteus employing 'Love's wings to fly, / … when
the flight is made to one so dear, / Of such divine perfection
as Sir Proteus' (11–13). Appeals to Blind Cupid traverse the
godly and the erotic, frustrating any attempt to differentiate
one from the other.

Further complicating matters is the specularity of attraction
purportedly governed by a blind deity. In a song often
attributed to Proteus, we find the following lines: 'Love
doth to her eyes repair / To help him of his blindness, / And,
being help'd, inhabits there' (4.2.45–7). This paean to Silvia's
beauty ascribes to it a curative quality that could heal the
blindness of Blind Cupid himself. This is the same beauty,
of course, that impels Proteus to request Silvia's portrait:
'For since the substance of your perfect self / Is else devoted,
I am but a shadow; / And to your shadow will I make true
love' (4.2.120–2). Silvia, for her part, though 'very loath to
be your [Proteus's] idol', agrees: 'But, since your falsehood
shall become you well / To worship shadows, and adore
false shapes, / Send to me in the morning, and I'll send it'
(4.2.126–8). This language of idol worship applies, as well,
to Valentine, who answers in the affirmative when asked by

Proteus, 'Was this the idol that you worship so' (2.4.143)? During the same conversation, Valentine recounts, 'For in revenge of my contempt of Love, / Love hath chas'd sleep from my enthralled eyes, / And made them watchers of mine own heart's sorrow' (2.4.132–4). Different types of love, therefore, betray a specular quality even as they abide the commands of a blind deity.

One way to understand characters' obsession with idol worship is to argue for a shift in the play's emphasis, from superficial to substantial love and desire. According to Maurice Hunt, 'Shakespeare's dramatic art prompts the conclusion that the romantic beatification of a "sainted woman" is less attractive than a more realistic, companionate love between men and women, a love courageously represented … by Julia'.[37] Related to this shift is 'a similar displacement at the end of this comedy—from a mighty god and his romantic love to an absolute deity and the more selfless love associated with the affective phases of Christian heart's sorrow, repentance, and forgiveness'.[38] However, Proteus's reunion with Julia recalls the very terms of his apostasy. Owning his 'faults' and 'all th' sins', Proteus declares, 'Inconstancy falls off, ere it begins. / What is in Silvia's face but I may spy / More fresh in Julia's, with a constant eye' (5.4.112–14). Here, as above, contradictions bound up in the figure of Blind Cupid reveal themselves in love's specularity. Whether Proteus loves Julia or Silvia or someone else altogether, that manifestation of blind devotion – by which I mean, the full spectrum of devotion that simultaneously includes and confounds erotic love and spiritual love, situational intimacy and long(er)-term relationships – is initiated and sustained by the (in)constant eye. As if to remove any doubt about the endurance of this regime of love and desire, in the play's final moments Valentine proclaims, 'Come, Proteus, 'tis your penance but to hear the / The story of your *loves* discovered' (5.4.168–9; my emphasis). Rather than elevate the discourse from erotic love to godly love, from eros to agape, Proteus's revelations reinforce the impossibility of telling one from the other.

In collapsing distinctions between erotic and spiritual love, the playtext proffers not merely their coexistence but their interchangeability. More simply put, eros becomes, or rather *always-already is*, agape. As previously mentioned, this is both a terrifying and potentially liberating prospect. For Valentine, Love both authors and author*izes* the polyamorous arrangement implicated in the play's final lines – '[O]ur day of marriage shall be yours, / One feast, one house, one mutual happiness' (5.4.170–1) – much as it does Silvia's fantasy of a courtly threesome with her two fellow-servants and diverse other loves posited in the play: the tedious 'cate-log ... of condition[s]' (3.1.272) Lance describes to Speed in 3.1; the homosocial collective of love-outlaws Valentine encounters and briefly joins in 4.1; the 'pure chastity' (4.3.21) of Sir Eglamour that endears him to Silvia in 4.3; and yes, even the love of Lance for his dog Crab as portrayed in 4.4. This Love allows, indeed comprises, Protestant and Catholic and pagan motifs and practices, with all the sexual connotations, whether procreative or sodomitical, they may betoken.[39] In other words, Love underwrites both those erotic and affective relationships that buttress hegemonic, phallic, patriarchal culture and those that have the capacity to challenge or subvert it. So while the play may arc toward a particular kind of conventional ending, in the process it opens up myriad affective and erotic possibilities available to Shakespeare's characters as well as his past, present and future audiences. These possibilities may not predominate or pervade the play, but they nevertheless offer a powerful critique of, and thus also function as a means to undermine, prevailing permutations of Love. In this context, as in the larger play and even Shakespeare's corpus as a whole, the stakes of Julia's query, to which I now return – '[W]hich is worthiest love?' – could not be higher.

But I would like to suggest, by way of conclusion, a more emancipatory possibility, one not taken by the play's so-called gentlemen nor their respective beloveds, but available even so to characters and spectators alike. In a culture where dominant ideas about love oscillate between Cupid and

Christ, two male gods wielding divine darts igniting love and longing of the masculinist, phallic, penetrative order, where men such as Proteus dare to invoke the language of love when threatening to rape women such as Silvia (5.4.58), one might perpetrate the most radical resistance by simply refusing to answer Julia's question. If the play invites us to critique love's hegemony and the ideologies and discourses that enable it, then this critical examination extends to questions about not just how to love, but whether to love *at all*. If we find the play's ending unsatisfactory, even despite critics' attempts to justify characters' choices along religious, political and/or cultural lines, then it seems to me that the most radical option, *not to love*, is perhaps the most obvious, not to mention most palatable and most queer, of all.

2

Glass: The Sonnets' desiring object

John S. Garrison

The term 'glass' appears ten times across Shakespeare's sonnets, and it represents one of the few material objects depicted in the poems. Such prevalence corresponds with its material history, given that objects made from glass claimed a prominent place in the cultural imagination of the early modern period. Crystal mirrors had recently emerged as a new technology, replacing old versions made of metal, offering another way to see oneself. Innovations related to the glass lens fuelled the scientific revolution – including improvements upon the microscope, telescope and prism – and thus opened the promise that one could view the world from new angles and with new perspicuity. In turn, early modern writers seized upon terms related to glass to describe the poetic process. Herbert Grabes has traced 398 English books published between 1500 and 1700 whose titles refer to mirrors, and Margaret Ezell notes a startling increase in texts about mirrors and glass in the seventeenth century.[1] As Rayna Kalas has shown, Renaissance poets frequently deployed glass-related vocabulary – ranging from 'framing' to 'perspective' to 'reflection' – in order to talk about the making of a poem.[2] With their frequent references to glass, Shakespeare's sonnets invite us to explore how the material object shapes discussions of identity and *poesis*.

Shakespeare seems particularly keen to tap into the properties of glass for a meditation on the operations of desire and of desirability.[3] And this meditation seizes upon glass' inherent queerness, both in the material's refusal to be singularly categorized and in its ability to skew the way a subject sees a desired object (as well as how a subject sees her- or himself when desiring). The sonnets seem to associate the material with same-sex desire, as glass appears in only those typically understood to be addressed to the young man.[4] As this essay will argue, glass offers a particularly apt vessel for contemplations about the operations of erotic desire, both clarifying how and why one *wants* while simultaneously emphasizing the complexity and stubborn opacity of what drives our experience of *wanting*. Such contemplations inevitably link to *identity* and to *making,* as desire continually renders and undoes us as subjects and objects. Thinking about the ties between glass and sexuality, one might immediately think of narcissism or the Lacanian mirror-stage. However, reflection is only one of the possible functions of glass that has purchase on the nature of sexuality. In a world of objects, glass constitutes a particularly queer object. As a material substance, it provocatively disturbs fundamental distinctions often used to define objects. Scientists continue to debate whether glass is a liquid or a solid, as it stubbornly refuses to fall squarely into either category. Glass is marked by a profound instability, and not simply because the threat of it cracking or shattering seems always imminent. It can be either (and sometimes simultaneously) reflective, opaque or transparent. It can be used to gain clarity or to obfuscate, as well as to demarcate a surface while giving the illusion of depth. Certainly, physical operations often associated with glass – gazing, mirroring, transparency – have been translated into more abstract concepts by those thinking about how we perceive the world and ourselves. Yet even these common understandings of glass are perverted and queered by Shakespeare in ways that still feel startlingly new. Taking glass as an object of study in the sonnets calls our attention to how the very thing that should be transparent mitigates relations between people, as well as between people and their desired objects and experiences. Glass reveals mediation to always be present (even when transparent or invisible) and desire to be fluid (even when solidified into a seemingly static state).[5]

Object formulation

The complex etymology of the word 'glass' renders visible its vexed properties as an object, as well as its vexing effect on other objects. The word comes to us from Old English, and the *OED* suggests that the ultimate root may be the Germanic *glă-, glæ̂* – ablaut-variant of *glô-* 'to shine'. By transitioning from an action to a thing, the object's effects came to be grounded in the essence of the object itself. 'To shine' enables something to stand out, to look new or promising. Beginning in the sixteenth century, the word 'glass' also functioned as an adjective that indicated the colour grey, and this use may derive from the Welsh term *glas*. This strand of the genealogy suggests another operation of glass, which paradoxically is at the heart of the material's operations as well. Grey seems innocuous and perhaps acts as a marker of the undesirable if we understand the colour to be associated with decay and lack. While it can be used to showcase something, glass is also used for its transparent qualities; glass exists to make us notice; glass exists to be ignored.

We can see the conflation of these effects – making something shine while making something grey – in Sonnet 22, which opens:

My glass shall not persuade me I am old,
So long as youth and thou are of one date.

(1–2)[6]

The poet may gaze at himself in the mirror, but he thinks of the young man. Indeed, the poem itself is offered as a mirror into which the addressee is invited to gaze upon his reflection lovingly rendered by the poet. Thus both speaker and addressee look into the glass and encounter a face other than his own. This mirror functions as an object that takes them away from themselves. Like all mirrors perhaps, this one urges the gazer to look at the surface in an effort to understand better the interiority of the individual reflected there. However, as André Greene nicely puts it, surface representation is 'an unreliable ally, vulnerable to every trap, the scene of every trick with mirrors'; his metaphor of the mirror is an apt choice to emphasize that glass uniquely toys with us to suggest that it could hold 'knowledge which might lay claim to some solidity, even if it is unable to be an object of certainty.'[7]

In Sonnet 62, the poet's encounter with his own reflection in the mirror leads him to admonish himself and alter his sense of identity:

> But when my glass shows me myself indeed,
> Beated and chopped with tanned antiquity,
> Mine own self-love quite contrary I read.

> (9–11)

He cannot understand why he would love himself and chastises himself in the next line, 'Self, so self-loving were iniquity' (12). The encounter with oneself in the mirror awakens one to how narcissism generates a shine in the mind that often serves to counterbalance awareness of the limits of one's attractiveness. Here, glass serves to remind us of how unlovable we are and how brief states of eros can be. But perhaps Blondie captured this best in 1978:

> Once I had a love and it was a gas
> Soon turned out had a heart of glass
> Seemed like the real thing, only to find
> Mucho mistrust, love's gone behind.[8]

At the end of the affair, glass brings clarity alongside fragility. In the song, glass points to the lover's changing state from airy and light to solid and breakable. Glass' dynamic qualities – at times molten, finding its origin in sand and fire, becoming smooth, brittle and cold – resemble the changeability of love.

We find a useful instance of glass' queer tendencies in John Donne's poem, 'The Broken Heart', which contains a vivid depiction of glass' ability to articulate the fragility of the self, especially in the throes of a bad romance. The speaker laments, 'what did become / Of my heart, when I first saw thee? / I brought a heart into the room, / But from the room I carried none with me' (17–20).[9] One of Cupid's arrows 'at one first blow did shiver it as glass' (24). The heart takes on the qualities of glass only once exposed to love, not simply at the scene of the break-up. Donne's poem ends:

> Yet nothing can to nothing fall,
>   Nor any place be empty quite;
> Therefore I think my breast hath all
>   Those pieces still, though they be not unite;
> And now, as broken glasses show
> A hundred lesser faces, so
>   My rags of heart can like, wish, and adore,
>   But after one such love, can love no more.
>
>   (25–32)

'The Broken Heart' shows us rejection's capacity to make us feel, to borrow the title of Ian Bogost's 2012 monograph on object studies, 'what it's like to be a thing'. Unrequited attraction can undermine the dominant position of the desiring subject because the subject is transformed into an object under the catastrophic duress of another subject's rejecting gaze. To drive his point home, Donne structures his poem to resemble shattered glass. The easy flow of stanzas while the speaker pursues his beloved transitions into a final stanza made jagged and stilted with caesurae to coincide with the breaking of his heart. Rayna Kalas's argument that glass offered a powerful heuristic device that was seized upon by early modern poets has purchase here. I believe we can see an instantiation of Kalas' argument in Donne's poem, as well as an example of what Samuel Daniel describes in his 1603 *Defence of Ryme*: that 'All verse is but a frame of wordes confined within certain measure', a claim which Kalas interprets to indicate that 'the musical and lexical harmony of the world's frame manifests itself in verse.'[10] This poem and Shakespeare's sonnets underscore the ways that glass can disturb that harmony.

Glass is an object made complex by what humans project onto it. In the same way, people who are objects of our affection become screens upon which we project our desires. Shakespeare's sonnets, Blondie's song and Donne's poem underscore both how we become objects when under the scrutiny of another's desire and how we feel like we've lost our subjectivity when we are rejected. As Tristan Garcia observes, humans need the world of objects to reinforce ontological claims of superiority. He remarks, 'Humanity identifies with machines to self-differentiate from other animals. Humanity identifies with other animals to self-differentiate from machines'.[11] Glass offers a fascinating case study for Garcia's claims, as it is the material machine that enables us to see ourselves and to see others.

Beginning in the medieval period, the term 'glass' was used as a noun to denote a mirror and, beginning in the Renaissance, indicated an hourglass.[12] Thus the object was very much a tool for gaining perspective on space and time. Today, we think of glass primarily as a material or a substance, something from which other, recognizable objects are constructed. We can see an intriguing instance of glass's multiple connotations and its power to drive fantasy in Sonnet 126, which opens with these lines:

> O Thou my lovely Boy, who in thy power,
> Dost hold time's fickle glass, his sickle hour,
> Who hast by waning grown, and therein show'st
> Thy lovers withering, as thy sweet self grow'st.

(1–4)

Lines 3–4 parallel the structure of the *hemiepes* in ancient Greek and Latin elegiac poetry, where a line is clearly divided into two half-lines. The line form itself resembles the queer form of mirroring that takes place in the sonnet. That is, the two sides of the caesura are not equivalent. They are each other's obverse. One side is grey, the other shines. The two halves of the line seem dialectical, as well. While mirroring renders visible desire based in difference within the sonnets, the mirroring and gazing operations here do not track to the complementary, reproductive logics of heterosexual difference. The mirror suggests subtler forms of difference tied to queerer forms of desire. Garcia reminds us that 'signification is a circulation of things in networks, in meta-relations.'[13] Glass complicates these logics because its significations are fluid as they shift according to who gazes into or through it. Aranye Fradenburg describes the sonnets as 'go-betweens – public relations, perhaps, for growing boys. They are transitional (and transitioning) objects'.[14] The material glass enables the addressee and speaker to project themselves into each others' positions, while the reader is invited to imagine her- or himself in either role.

Glass enables multiplicity, then, in ways that grant access to queer erotic arrangements. Melissa Sanchez has recently traced possibilities for female promiscuity in the sonnets, and the poems' mirroring capacities open opportunities for male promiscuity as well. Sanchez argues that 'Shakespeare's poetic language makes legible the cultural work of the stigma attached to women who desire non-monogamous sex—women who, as it were, desire like men', and I would extend her argument to claim that glass enables readers to *desire someone else* and to *desire like someone else*.[15] The trope of multiplication within the sonnets also links to rhetorical strategies favoured by early modern writers. George Puttenham explains that repetition enhances a word's 'beautie', and Henry Peacham lauds repetition for it adds 'much comelynesse' to a word.[16] In *The Garden of Eloquence* (1577, rev. 1593), Peacham attributes the terms 'pleasure' and 'pleasantnesse' to repeated words.[17] He goes on to stress that repetition enables 'affinitie' and 'affections' between words, as well as between words and feelings.[18] Peacham emphasizes that likeness is generated by repetition, an idea later echoed by Jacques Derrida.[19] It also adds 'swéetnesse' in the sound of the words, a term which Jeffrey Masten has shown to resonate with homoerotic valences.[20] Like other poems that use popular early modern rhetorical devices such as *epanalepsis* (repetition) and *epanadiplosis* (doubling) for effect, Shakespeare's sonnets embrace mirroring and reflection – at the level of language and at the level of conceptual relations made possible by glass objects – to emphasize the evocative complexities in the relations between poet and reader.

Sonnet 126 uses glass to describe the power that the addressee has over the speaker. Like in many of the sonnets, the speaker suggests ways that he functions as a double of the young man and presents his poem as a double as well. Both strategies use forms of multiplicity tied to pleasure and to reproduction. The addressee holds 'time's fickle glass', yet the exact nature of that glass object is ambiguous. Does the young man hold a mirror, which might show Shakespeare aging, show the young man aging or emphasize Shakespeare's age compared to the reflection of the young man? Or is the glass held by the young man an hourglass? If so, we see that young people serve to remind us that youthful beauty will fade and that we ourselves are not as young as we once were. If we imagine the object to be an hourglass, then youth is aligned with the movement of sand to mark time. Given that glass itself is generated from sand, we see an example of how glass comes to be associated with time in general, as well as how the passing of time can change how we see glass. The hourglass began as sand in its raw material, and later was crafted into the object that now captures sand. In the same way, the aging speaker was once young and now captures the young man in his depiction.

In either of these cases – whether the glass contains the reflection of an aging lover or the glass controls the flow of sand to mark the aging of the lover – we see glass linked to time and to desire. The connection is underscored in Sonnet 77, where 'Thy glass will show thee how thy beauties wear, / Thy dial how thy precious minutes waste' (1–2). The speaker's concern with aging runs through the sonnets because it 'leads to death, destroys beauty.'[21] That is, the speaker depicts the young man as desirable by throwing into relief the speaker's own lack of desirability as an older man. In this sonnet, the 'lovely boy' seems simultaneously to be the speaker's beloved and the boy-god Cupid, who inspires the miserable madness of love and who is depicted in the final two sonnets of Shakespeare's overall sequence. A reading of the boy as Cupid makes it difficult to ignore the presence of 'sick' in Sonnet 126's 'sickle', as the events in the final two sonnets (153 and 154) can be understood to depict baths for the treatment of gonorrhea or syphilis.

The erotics of containment

Sonnet 126 ultimately uses its glass object to remind us that desire and time are inextricably connected, as the young man is described as 'minion of [Nature's] pleasure' all-the-while he is cautioned that Nature 'may detain but, not still keep, her treasure!' (11–12).

The speaker imagines that glass would allow him to do what Nature cannot. Sonnets 5 and 6 imagine ways in which the young man's beauty might be distilled and preserved before he ages. Though these poems rest at the heart of the 'procreation sonnets', they use glass in order to urge forms of stasis.[22] In Sonnet 5, the poet likens the urgency to have children to the onset of winter. We seemingly assuage ourselves about the coming of colder weather and of old age with 'summer's distillation' as 'a liquid prisoner pent in walls of glass' (9–10). The scent of flowers transforms into perfume trapped in a glass bottle and can recall for us the sensorium we associate with a summer's day in the same way a child recalls the youth of the parent. As Stephen Guy-Bray puts it, 'the other person is a mechanism like a sonnet: something that enables one to remember things about oneself.'[23] 'The point that Shakespeare's sonnets make about erotic memory', he continues, 'is that erotic memory is essentially the memory of oneself, of one's own thoughts, feelings, and experiences.'[24] We need the perfume or the sonnet to remember what has been forgotten. Glass enables this powerful 'remembrance' because

> flowers distilled, though they with winter meet,
> Leese but their show; their substance still lives sweet.

(13–14)

We encounter a *hemiepes*-like structure again here in the first line of this couplet. That is, the line seems broken about evenly between two states of being. And those two states of being are queerly juxtaposed as related unequals: the arrival of winter and the dissipation into liquid. In her study of perfume in the Renaissance, Holly Dugan notes that 'olfaction, like other sensory ways of knowing, emphasizes the fungible relationship between material objects, the body, and embodiment.'[25] This holds particularly true in Sonnet 5, where the young man's desirable body becomes liquid encased in a glass object.

In Sonnet 6, Shakespeare leaves it evocatively ambiguous whether the young man will be encased in glass or whether he will become glass:

> Then let not winter's wragged hand deface,
> In thee thy summer, ere thou be distilled:
> Make sweet some vial.

(1–3)

Metaphorically, the young man can be kept beautiful by preserving some part of him in his prime in the form of a child.

In the fantasy, though, either he becomes perfume that makes the vial sweet or he is made into the vial itself. Shakespeare invites us to read line 3 as 'make thee some sweet vial'. Further, the young man has transformative powers, as we can interpret the line to read 'make sweet something vile', if he can synaesthetically transform an object such as glass (which has no real flavour) into a flavour. Shakespeare chooses the material object of the vial because glass can be beautiful in its own right. We choose glass, rather than wood or metal, to contain perfume because it allows us to see the liquid and because the container itself can suggest the beauty one will acquire when donning the scent. Shakespeare's sonnet and Dugan's claim help us see that glass is not solely linked with sight as a sensory operation. In the case of perfume, glass allows a scent to be powerfully and beautifully contained, and it allows for a sudden release of a scent that sparks the pleasure centres, corresponds with memory and entices for potential contact to come. As Garrett Sullivan puts it, 'literary texts don't invalidate normative conceptions of memory, sexuality, and selfhood'; instead 'they expose the wishful thinking residing at the core.'[26] Sonnets 5 and 6 crystallize (so to speak) the wish at the heart of the speaker's and addressee's shared desire to defy age within the space of poetry, while simultaneously exposing the fantasmatic underpinnings of that wish.

In Shakespeare's time, 'glass' could be used as a verb meaning to enclose in glass or to place an object in front of a mirror. We can see in Sonnets 5 and 6 a combination, perhaps, of the two meanings. To enclose something in glass is at once to preserve it at its best and to showcase it for viewing. Glass calls our attention to other objects, but it calls our attention in a specific way: it 'persuades' us, as Shakespeare describes in Sonnet 22. And while glass seems to take on a subjectivity of its own, it transforms subjects into objects. In the sonnets, glass shows us how both desirability and rejection possess the capacity to make us sense how 'human being and thinghood overlap'.[27] The role of glass in the sonnets illuminates how queer studies and object oriented ontology share common ground. We are all *things* as a result of desire and as a result of being desired. Shakespeare's queer glass reveals what Leo Bersani pointedly describes as 'the very essence of the sexual [that consists] in a shattering of ego boundaries produced by any number of "unaccountable", unclassifiable objects'.[28] What seems particularly at stake in the sonnets is a model of desire that admits that we lose subjecthood by gaining access to more complex experiences of love. The sonnets immortalize the young man, but they also seize upon glass objects in order to render the young man as a liquid prisoner. The speaker's poetry creates this textual mirror or glass container, yet both speaker and addressee are rendered objects in the process. Unrequited attraction can undermine the dominant position of the desiring subject because the subject is transformed into an object under the ego-dissipating effects of rejection by another subject.[29]

It is worth noting here that glass mirrors in the Renaissance differed from our own contemporary mirrors and from mirrors in previous periods. Pre-Renaissance mirrors were largely polished metal. The introduction of the crystal mirror in the Renaissance introduced an object more similar to our own in look and feel, yet the glass was curved and thus did not truly give an accurate reflection of the physical self. Subjects saw themselves in miniature – rendered more precisely than with previous surfaces but also made less knowable, significantly smaller. Assessing one's desirability in a Renaissance mirror was a strange science, where either one accepted the reflection as an inaccurate depiction of how one looked to others or admitted that all looking is refracted through the warped lens of subjectivity. As Deborah Shuger has shown, mirrors in early modern art or literature are rarely depicted as used for examining one's own physical characteristics.[30] Instead, mirrors are depicted where individuals view an aspirational figure, such as Christ or the Virgin Mary, looking back upon them, or individuals might see the future state of their face in the form of a skull gazing back. These were speculative selves, one might say.[31] That is, one aspired to be like one of these individuals in the future – if one sought the virtue of Mary, for example – or one faced the inevitability of becoming like the image in the mirror, in the case of *memento mori*. At the same time, mirrors were imagined to translate nature (the human body) into art (a painting, a literary figure).

Object orientations, sexual orientations

Objects are central to the process of orientation, including the process of navigating sexual orientation. Sara Ahmed remarks, 'to be orientated is also to be turned towards certain objects, those that help us find our way'.[32] And, indeed, as we begin to ask which objects have particular power in the sonnets and in our world, we inevitably run into questions about erotics. Ahmed invites us to consider:

> What does it mean for sexuality to be lived as orientated? What difference does it make 'what' or 'who' we are orientated toward in the very direction of our desire?[33]

The sonnets' speaker and addressee orientate towards each other and repeatedly orientate themselves towards glass. If ones orientates towards an object as a mediator for desire, and if that object is one that both reflects back the gazer and multiplies the person being gazed upon, might that object enable new forms of erotic engagement? Objects, orientation and desire collide in the sonnets.

Ahmed's reflections on object orientation help us see why patron relations offer an incomplete explanatory model for what we see when we take as glass our focus when reading the sonnets. Indeed, Jonathan Culler remarks that 'our attention should be directed towards experiencing the poem as an event, not to discovering what the author might have experienced.'[34] To set aside biography and to explore 'queer Shakespeare' is to explore Shakespeare's (and, by result, our own) queer ways of knowing and being. Such an approach opens up new readings of not only the sonnets, but also a volume such as George Gascoigne's *The Steele Glas* (1576). Its epilogue on one level pleads with the patron for support. When we focus on the role of glass in sparking new ways to desire and be desired, though, we can trace more imaginative possibilities. Gascoigne writes, 'my lord, let shut the glass apace, / High time it were for my poor muse to wink', and moves into the mode of flirtation:

> But if my glass do like my lovely lord,
> We will espy, some sunny summer's day,
> To look again, and see some seemly sights.[35]

If the patron likes what he sees, the author might show a bit more. Yet, one cannot help but wonder if the first line is not necessarily inverted syntax. Perhaps glass does the desiring here. If the book, which contains a reflection of the speaker and the addressee, likes the patron, more pleasure might yet be yielded. In these few lines, we see how glass emphasizes surface and tantalizes us with the promise of depth. To reach out and touch the mirror is to discover that the three-dimensional world beyond it cannot be reached. Yet Gascoigne's text itself constitutes the very glass that the reader is invited to desire. Within it lies a mirror world that can be explored.

As a final line of inquiry into how queer theory, object studies and desire intertwine in the sonnets, consider how Sonnet 3 closes:

> Thou art thy mother's glass and she in thee
> Calls back the lovely April of her prime:
> So thou through windows of thine age shalt see,
> Despite of wrinkles this thy golden time.
> But if thou live remembered not to be,
>   Die single, and thine image dies with thee.

> (9–14)

Shakespeare urges the young man to see his mother in his face and to see his aging self within the face of his aging mother. The realization rejuvenates both the aging woman's face and the addressee's own sense of youth still dwelling inside of him. His youthful countenance recalls her youth or 'April', offering an opportunity to interpret his own appearance as 'windows' into her youth and into his own 'golden time.' The addressee of Shakespeare's poem is reminded that to 'die single' is to foreclose the replication of his appearance in future generations. Sonnet 3 opens, 'Look in thy glass and tell the face thou viewest / Now is the time that face should form another' (1–2). By insisting for the formation of 'another' (printed 'an other' in the original), the speaker insists that the addressee generate *another him* and *an Other*. This depiction of an encounter with versions of oneself in glass reminds us that the material collapses time in ways that generate diverse responses: at times celebratory, optimistic and brimming with expectation, while at other times melancholy, maudlin and meditating upon what it means to be finite.

John Dee nicely calls our attention to how glass simultaneously estranges us from ourselves and encourages a flirtation with ourselves imagined to an Other:

> if you, being (alone) nere a certaine glasse, and proffer, with dagger or sword, to foyne at the glasse, you shall suddenly be moved to give backe (in maner) by reason of an Image, appearing in the ayre, betwene you & the glasse, with like hand, sword or dagger, & with like quicknes, foyning at your very eye, likewise as you do at the Glasse.[36]

When we see ourselves constructed from a physical object, it becomes easy to render our self as a stranger. And when we encounter that Other, our impulse is to engage in play. 'Our fantasies', as Adam Phillips notes, 'may reveal that we are not excessively sexual, but excessively frightened of other people.'[37] Indeed, this opens the possibility that 'what we call love is our hatred of the future; and it is because other people represent our future as objects of desire, what might happen next to us, we fear them.'[38] This helps us see the erotic appeal of glass, which alloerotically and autoerotically presents us with an attractive and extremely safe sexual partner.[39] In the quotation above, Dee is engaged in a dance that simultaneously entices the other individual and fights him off.

Foucault's description of the mirror as a heterotopia offers a fitting description of the dynamic in Dee's depiction and in Shakespeare's sonnets:

> From the standpoint of the mirror I discover my absence from the place where I am since I see myself over there. Starting from this gaze that is, as it were, directed toward me, from the ground of this virtual space that is on the other side of the glass, I come back toward myself; I begin again to direct my eyes toward myself and to reconstitute myself there where I am.[40]

The sonnets show us how encountering a reflection of ourselves does not necessarily wake us to self-knowledge. The experience is *ecstatic,* in the sense that it only drives our desire to be outside of ourselves and underlines that such a desire has sexual implications. José Esteban Muñoz observes that the self-shattering potential of *jouissance* connects to ecstasy's ability to take one out of oneself, especially given the etymology of 'ecstasy' from the Greek *ex-* meaning 'out' and *-stasis* meaning 'to stand.'[41] Muñoz argues that ecstasy cannot be disaggregated from a yearning for a time-defying experience that 'contains the potential to help us encounter a queer temporality'.[42] Indeed, most of us can relate to the notion that looking in a mirror has, at times, made us wish we were someone other than ourselves, somewhere other than where we were or someone we used to be. Rather than offering clarity and self-knowledge, the glass mirror estranges the gazer from her or his subjecthood. We can wish we were elsewhere, but we can also inhabit other worlds or other personas (just as the poet can). The gazer is no longer a single, discrete entity. The subject also understands itself as an object – as the object of another's gaze and as an entity made of glass. The tantalizing appeal of glass in the sonnets – for the speaker, the addressee, reader and for the queer scholar – involves the promise that we might see our objects of study and objects of desire just as they see us.

3

The sport of asses:
A Midsummer Night's Dream

Kirk Quinsland

Like Judith Butler's Gender Trouble, *[...] also
widely considered a founding text in queer theory,
Epistemology doesn't use the word queer.
So what is queer about it?*[1]

To what extent is it correct, appropriate or fair to call English antitheatrical writing of the sixteenth and seventeenth centuries homophobic? I ask this question not in the spirit of further widening the gulf between the pre-modern sodomite and the modern homosexual, or to further engage the well-worn and 'by-now ritualized statements that "of course, there was no homosexuality back then" and "it is wrong to speak of sexual identity back then."'[2] Instead, I am interested in the extent to which this body of writing insists on conflating gender presentation with sexual conduct, and how this conflation creates the context in which the Mechanicals in *A Midsummer Night's Dream* present their version of *Pyramus and Thisbe* to a homophobic audience. The ventriloquized antitheatrical homophobia expressed by Theseus and the court turns on the play's linguistic insistence that the inset play is a 'sport,' a piece of bad theatre available for mockery. Whether or not *Pyramus and Thisbe* really is a bad play is, in this essay, something of an open question; I am suggesting that the entertainment's stylistic badness is a metatheatrically antihomophobic strategy for exposing antitheatrical homophobia. The mockery itself fuses together antitheatrical concerns about homosocial groups of theatermakers, who cannot be comfortably integrated into the community because of their perceived otherness, with *Midsummer's* larger concerns about marriage and reproduction, ultimately positioning theatre as a site of deferred heterosexuality.

In pursuing these claims, however, I am largely avoiding the word 'queer'. The word 'queer' in much scholarship on the queer renaissance, and in recent queer readings of *Midsummer*, primarily refers to one of two things – the homoerotic (non-normative or otherwise non-heterosexual sexual activity)[3] or the homosexual (a psychologized sexual identity)[4] – and both present challenges to the kind of reading that I will be doing in this essay, and to the question of what it means to perform a queer reading of an early modern text.[5] As David Orvis phrases it, the term 'queer', when used in the context of early modern studies, is a 'deliberate anachronism whose strategic application to premodernity always runs the risk of obfuscating rather than elucidating precisely those discursive formations that most interest lesbian and gay and queer critics'.[6] Among other possible obfuscations that the term produces is that there is a largely uncrossable chasm between homoeroticism and homosexuality, despite both conceptions of queerness being fundamentally rooted in bodily experience.[7]

I share Elizabeth Freeman's concern about the word's potential to become divorced from embodied eroticism. Freeman writes, 'To me, "queer" cannot signal a purely deconstructive move or position of pure negativity. In enjoining queers to operate as agents of dis- or de-figuration, critics

[...] risk evacuating the messiest thing about being queer: the actual meeting of bodies with other bodies and with objects'.[8] If queerness is dissociated from either sexual practices or identitarian sexualities, it can be expanded to include virtually anything that seems non-normative, regardless of the term's original connection with embodied sexuality. And some critics take the tack of radically expanding the categories that queer theory can be made to analyze. Carla Freccero explicitly identifies her work as having been 'mostly about advocating for queer's verbally and adjectivally unsettling force against claims for its definitional stability, so theoretically anything can queer something, and anything, given a certain odd twist, can become queer', but still insists that the term should be applied in connection with sexuality, ultimately defining it as 'the name of a certain unsettling in relation to hetero-normativity.'[9] Madhavi Menon goes further in expanding the category to include language, ahistorical identities and temporality. Despite her insistence that queerness cannot 'mean anything at any time and in any place', the reason is that 'queerness cannot "mean" in any final sense of that word. If queerness can be defined, then it is no longer queer – it strays away from its anti-normative stance to become the institutionalized norm. Queerness is not a category but the confusion engendered by and despite categorization'.[10] To which I would ask: if 'queer' simply refers to confusion and cannot be defined, why use the term at all? One might simply adopt 'non-normative' or 'confusing' as theoretical terms, since they do not have specific connections to a category of inquiry like sexuality and are therefore likely to produce less uncertainty or instability concerning the subject of what a critic using queer theory is inquiring into. With this glomming on of subjects possibly unrelated to sexuality, 'queer' appears to become so expansive a category that it ends up a self-negating term: queerness is predicated on difference in that to be or to act queer is to be different from, or outside of, normativity. If queerness exists everywhere, or if all things can be read as queer or can be queered, then queerness becomes a de facto normative position and thereby ceases to function as a position of difference.

As a means of navigating these fraught splits, in this essay I am largely not engaging with the terms of the seemingly polar opposite positions of the homoerotic and the homosexual, or even with the term 'queer' itself. What I am interested here isn't sexual activity or identity, but rather the perception of its possibility. It is this potential – rising nearly to the level of gay panic – about the prospect that male theatregoers will become sodomites that fuels the notion that antitheatrical writing is homophobic.[11] I am arguing that Shakespeare positions the Mechanicals as outsiders but not as sexual others, in the sense that they neither display queer erotic behaviour nor possess solidified sexual identities. I am also distinguishing between how Shakespeare positions the Mechanicals and how Theseus's court and antitheatrical writing positions them: Shakespeare's deployment of the strategically antihomophobic inset play points out the extent to which Theseus and the antitheatricals fundamentally misunderstand the Mechanicals and their play.

While the term 'queer' often means homoerotic or homosexual, it is not limited to these meanings exclusively, as a different thread within queer theory reminds us. As articulated by Lee Edelman, '[Q]ueerness could never constitute an authentic or substantive identity, but only a structural position determined by the imperative of figuration.'[12] Edelman's larger point is that the queer-affirmative investment in queerness as an identity is not all that different from the logic that animates homophobia; the only option is for queerness 'to oppose itself to the logic of opposition' and refuse to participate in 'every substantialization of identity, which is always oppositionally defined.'[13] As a structural position rather than an identity, the queer thus stands not in opposition to the heteronormative, but outside of it, refusing to be integrated while also pointing out the extent to which the construction of the heteronormative relies on the homophobic rejection of the queer subject.

And it is in this space that I am locating the Mechanicals' *Pyramus and Thisbe* (and indeed *Midsummer* itself). But rather than identifying it as a queer play, I am instead, following Sedgwick, discussing it as being antihomophobic. To name the Mechanicals as hetero or homo, queer or not queer, is to invest in a binary – can a person or a thing be partly queer?[14] – that Sedgwick's notion of antihomophobic theory can undo through its emphasis on the indeterminacy of the thing in question: one need not be a homo to be on the receiving end of homophobia. This reading does not, in the manner of antitheatrical writing, insist that the Mechanicals are either homoerotic or homosexual figures. Instead, I am focused on the reaction to the play, the court's homophobic perception of the possibility of queer sexuality within it and the rejection of the performance on the basis of this perception of possibility. Whether or not that embodied sexuality or activity is actually there is entirely beside the point; all that matters is that the court believes that it could be. Sedgwick describes this antihomophobic theory, and its relationship with indeterminacy, as being

> deconstructive, in a fairly specific sense. The analytic move it makes is to demonstrate that the categories presented in a culture as symmetrical binary oppositions—hetero-sexual/homosexual, in this case—actually subsist in a more unsettled and dynamic tacit relation according to which, first, term B is not symmetrical with but subordinated to term A; but, second, the ontologically valorized term A actually depends for its meaning on the simultaneous subsumption and exclusion of term B; hence, third, the question of priority between the supposed central and the supposed marginal category of each dyad is irresolvably unstable, an instability caused by the fact that term B is constituted as at once internal and external to term A.[15]

Antihomophobic theory thus functions as an attempt to understand, respond to and potentially reconfigure the asymmetrical relationship between hetero and homo, not by elevating the homo to the position of term A in the dyad, but instead by drawing attention to the way in which the hetero, legibly or not, relies on the rejection of the homo in order to construct itself. Shakespeare follows this deconstructive mode through the metacritical presence of the Mechanicals' *Pyramus and Thisbe* within *Midsummer*: *Pyramus* being constituted as being both inside and outside of *Midsummer*, and the meaning that it contributes to *Midsummer* – calling into question *Midsummer*'s resolution on marriage and reproduction – requires *Pyramus* to be repudiated by its on-stage audience.[16] Theseus and the court, in other words, think that rejecting *Pyramus* affirms their heterosexual pursuits, but Shakespeare uses the rejection of *Pyramus* to show the homophobic logic that drives it and animates antitheatrical sentiment.

Antitheatrical writing consistently befogs the distinction between gender presentation and sexual practices in a way that may indicate that this body of work thinks about sexuality as identity as opposed to being merely a set of practices. The primary ground on which antitheatrical writers attacked the theatre was that plays presented morally dissolute actions that would so infect and inflame spectators that individuals would be unable to resist imitating them. Some of this anxiety gets attached to the prospect of sodomy.[17] In *A Refutation of the Apology for Actors* (1615), for example, I. G.[18] argues that theatergoers see 'such wanton gestures, such dishonest speeches, such laughing and fleering, such lipping and kissing, such clipping and culling, such lustful passions [...] as is wonderful and exceeding shamefull to behold'. These actions being observed, then, cause theatregoers 'to repeat the lasciuious acts and speeches they haue heard, and thereby infect their mindes with wicked passions, so that in their secret conclaues they play the Sodomite, or worse'.[19] Seeing the signs of sodomy on stage – if perhaps not the thing itself – are in Greene's mind enough to provoke men to commit acts of sodomy, and whatever Greene's rather breathless 'or worse' might entail. Or perhaps Greene's meaning is that watching theatre inspires spectators to go and be theatrical in their own lives, privately playing sodomites in imitation of the sodomites on stage, and in some cases taking their Method training a little too seriously and actually becoming sodomites.

Even more striking than Greene's fever dreams about what men might do in private is the extent to which antitheatrical literature conflates sodomy with cross-dressing,[20] and the way in which this conflation sets up sodomy as more than a bodily practice. William Prynne's *Histrio-mastix* (1633) is particularly vociferous on this point:

> And is this a laudable, as many; a trivial, venial, harmless thing, as most repute it? Is this a light, a despicable effeminacy, for men, for Christians, thus to adulterate, emasculate, metamorphose, and debase their noble sex? Thus purposely, yea, affectedly, to *unman, unchristian, uncreate* themselves, if I may so speak, and to make themselves, as it were, neither men nor women, but monsters (a sin as bad, nay worse than any adultery, offering a kind of violence to God's own work) and all to no other end but this: to exhilarate a confluence of *unchaste, effeminate, vain companions*, or to become competent actors on a stage, the greatest infamy that could befall an ancient pagan Roman, or a Christian?[21]

Prynne sets up a nexus of gender stability, chastity, religion and ontology itself: to be an effeminate man is to be a sodomite is to be unChristian is to no longer be at all. Short-circuiting the causal logic leads to the somewhat hysterical claim that cross-dressing will destroy the world, yet Prynne's larger point is that all of these sinful actions are interconnected and inextricable. Collectively they contravene God's laws, and for doing so, theatre poses a legitimate existential threat. While Prynne follows a logical chain of events to this conclusion, John Rainolds' earlier *The Overthrow of Stage-Plays* (1599) supplies an epistemological (if less logical) route to the same end. Rainolds writes, 'How much greater outrage of wickedness and iniquity are the actors and plays themselves likely to fall into? Seeing that diseases of the mind are gotten far sooner by counterfeiting than diseases of the body, and bodily diseases may be gotten so, as appeareth by him, who, feigning for a purpose that he was sign of the gout, became (through care of counterfeiting it) gouty in deed'.[22] If Rainolds is to be believed, it is possible to contract a medical condition simply by feigning that one has said condition. And if even this is possible, Rainolds goes on to argue, the 'disease' of sodomy is even easier to catch: 'And do you grant that you and your youth have unclean affections, to the intent you may blame my speech? [...] Besides, can you accuse yourself, or any other, of any wanton thought stirred up in you by looking on a beautiful woman? If you can, then ought you be aware of beautiful boys transformed into women by putting on their raiment, their features, looks and fashions'.[23] Boys dressed as women provoke men to feel the same lust toward boys as they have toward women, Rainolds argues, positioning sodomy as an externally provoked cancer rather than as an inherent vice. And yet, as Rainolds' etiological logic would have it, one becomes what one does: the boys who wear women's clothing are '*transformed into* women', and one who engages in sodomy, or even who thinks about practicing it – the mere fantasy of one of Greene's secret conclaves – becomes a sodomite. For Rainolds, it seems, there is little distinction between the homoerotic and the homosexual, and the distinction matters very little. What matters for Rainolds is that sodomy exists, and that its mere presence on stage can infect others and pull them into the sodomitical fold.

The homophobic logic of the rejection of the performance of *Pyramus and Thisbe* turns on this notion that one is what one does. The court's rejection begins with the insistence on positioning the Mechanicals as outsiders. Philostrate frames the play as one in which 'There is not one word apt, one player fitted' (5.1.65).[24] Responding to Theseus' evident enthusiasm to see a play introduced as 'A tedious brief scene of young Pyramus / And his love Thisbe, very tragical mirth'

(5.1.56–7), Philostrate objects that the play was written by 'Hard-headed men that work in Athens here, / Which never labored in their minds till now' (5.1.72–3) and can provide no measure of entertainment 'unless you can find sport in their intents' (5.1.79). Theseus responds with some measure of magnanimity: 'I will hear that play; / For never anything can be amiss / When simpleness and duty tender it' (5.1.81–3). When Hippolyta objects that the play cannot possibly be good and the players liable to embarrass themselves, Theseus responds, 'The kinder we, to give them thanks for nothing. / Our sport shall be to take what they mistake: / And what poor duty cannot do, noble respect / Takes it in might, not merit' (5.1.89–92). Theseus sets up the conditions under which the on-stage audience should receive and understand the play: even as the product of simpler minds than their own, *Pyramus and Thisbe* should be regarded as a sincere attempt at an intellectual craft, and is all the more admirable for the bettering effect that it will have on the 'hard-headed men' who created it. As Theseus sees it, the Mechanicals will become better through imitating their betters. More implicitly, they will become better through presenting heterosexual discourse in a culturally approved way: the play, on its face, might fail at completing heterosexuality – Pyramus and Thisbe die, after all, but at least they get to be in straight love for a while first – but Theseus seems to regard the play as something which will allow the outsiders to enter the cultural world and practices of the court. But of course they are not actually allowed access to this space, except as theatrical interlopers.[25] The perpetual outsiderness of the Mechanicals highlights the logic behind their rejection, and it is this perpetual outsiderness that allows the play to occupy the structural role of negation and anti-normatvity. As a result, *Midsummer* rejects the very logic on which people like Theseus construct otherness and the idea of the structural role of the 'queer': it reveals that Theseus and the others, like the antitheatricals, insist on the co-incidence of being and seeming, while Shakespeare makes it clear that the two do not coincide. Instead, the Mechanical's play functions to lay bare the homophobic logic that excludes based on perceptions of difference.

This exchange between Theseus and Philostrate repeats the word 'sport' in referring to the entertainment. 'Sport' occurs eleven times in the play, typically to connote trickery, cruelty or mean-spirited mockery.[26] Helena uses the word frequently, in all three instances referring to herself as the victim of the 'sport' of the other three lovers. To Lysander she declares, 'None of noble sort / Would so offend a virgin, and extort / A poor soul's patience, all to make you sport' (3.2.159–61), and upon Hermia joining the fray, she complains, 'Now I perceive they have conjoin'd all three / To fashion this false sport in spite of me' (3.1.193–4). Refusing to believe Lysander's and Demetrius's declarations of love, she assumes that they 'counterfeit sad looks, / Make mouths upon me when I turn my back, / Wink at each other; hold the sweet jest up; / This sport, well carried, shall be chronicled' (3.2.237–40). Puck picks up the word and uses it to explain his lack of regret at having made a mistake in carrying out Oberon's instructions: 'And so far am I glad I do did sort, / As this their jangling I esteem a sport' (3.2.352–3). This concentrated use of the word, four times in under a hundred lines, and its connotations of taking delight in the suffering of others, sets up its use in the context of *Pyramus*, especially after Snug uses it in calling the play 'our sport' (4.2.17). For Philostrate, the only value in the piece is the sport that it will provide the on-stage audience in mocking it; even for Theseus, the 'sport' is to rescue the play from itself through his own superior powers of cognition, finding in it the good qualities that the actor-creators were unable to make themselves.

Shakespeare grants his on-stage audience control over interpreting the proceedings: it is they who can determine the value of the dramatic entertainment presented to them, which in turn allows them to reject the Mechanicals as outsiders. Yet Shakespeare, signalling his awareness of and engagement with antitheatrical writing, also makes it clear that the staged audience goes too far in turning *Pyramus* into grounds for sport. As soon as Quince concludes the prologue, the mockery begins: Lysander declares, 'He hath rid his prologue like a rough colt; he knows not the stop'; Hippolyta likens the prologue to 'a child on a recorder; a sound but not in government'; and Theseus draws an analogy to 'a tangled chain; nothing impaired, but all disordered' (5.1.119–25). Yet none of them seem to have actually listened to Quince's words:

> If we offend, it is with our good will.
> That you should think, we come not to offend,
> But with good will. To show our simple skill,
> That is the true beginning of our end.
> Consider then, we come but in despite.
> We do not come, as minding to content you,
> Our true intent is. All for your delight,
> We are not here. That you should here repent you,
> The actors are at hand; and by their show,
> You shall know all, that you are like to know.
>
> (5.1.108–17)

Theseus' initial response, that 'This fellow doth not stand upon points', indicates his belief that Quince has mispunctuated his speech.[27] Presumably the speech should have run as follows, and this seems to be the meaning that Theseus and the rest of the on-stage audience takes from the prologue:

> We do not come as minding to, content you;
> Our true intent is all for your delight.
> We are not here that you should repent you.
> The actors are at hand, and by their show,
> You shall know all that you are like to know.

Repunctuated, the speech indicates that the play *is* available as an object of sport: the actors do not come to instruct, but only to delight – and if that delight happens to include the derision and interruption to which the play is subjected, then the play has served its purpose. Yet it is in the 'incorrect' punctuation that we can see Shakespeare's engagement with antitheatrical theory: the actors are explicitly *not* putting on the play exclusively for the delight of its audience. Instead, their purpose is 'that you should here repent' – the motivation is explicitly corrective. The audience should, the prologue argues with Quince's punctuation, look to the play for moral correction delivered by the actors. Bottom reveals the outcome of the events presented in *Pyramus*, namely that 'the wall is down that parted their fathers' (5.1.337–8), indicating that putting up artificial barriers to love will inevitably end badly. Shakespeare has Theseus determinedly miss the point: in responding to Bottom's inquiry as to whether or not the players should present their epilogue, he says, 'No epilogue, I pray you; for your play needs no excuse. Never excuse; for when the players are all dead, there need none to be blamed. Marry, if he that writ it had played Pyramus, and hanged himself in Thisbe's garters, it would have been a fine tragedy— and so it is, truly, and very notably discharged' (5.1.341–7). Theseus cannot resist sneaking in a final dig at the quality of the play, wishing that it would have been a good play had its author killed himself, before catching himself and once again offering a condescending compliment to the players.

The staged audience uses a broad linguistic arsenal to insult and override the play. Taking aim at the players themselves, when Theseus wonders if even the lion will speak, Demetrius responds, 'No wonder, my lord; one lion may when many asses do' (5.1.153). Theseus returns to the ass insult in an exchange following Pyramus' death:

DEMETRIUS   No die, but an ace for him; for he is but one.
LYSANDER   Less than an ace, man; for he is dead, he is nothing.
THESEUS   With the help of a surgeon he might yet recover, and prove an ass.

(5.1.296–9)

The play provides the characters with the opportunity to display their own wit and wordplay, beginning with a quibble on 'die' as 'dice' and ending with Theseus intentionally puncturing the theatrical illusion with the obvious and wholly unnecessary note that Pyramus isn't really dead. The longest sustained rhetorical display occurs around Moonshine, who is not allowed to finish his speech owing to the number of jokes about cuckolding and puns concerning the Man in the Moon, the moon's light and its phases. Finally Moonshine simply gives up trying to deliver *Pyramus's* poetry and says, 'All that I have to say is, to tell you that the lantern is the moon; I the Man i'th'Moon; this thorn-bush my thorn-bush; and this dog my dog' (5.1.247–9). Most of the jokes in this scene focus on the unfitness of the players, positioning them as outsiders, asses and cuckolds, and culminate in Moonshine's refusal to continue playing along. Moonshine's plainspoken rebellion against the rejection highlights just how different the everyday speech of the Mechanicals is from the stylized mien of the court's 'sport'.

So what makes this rejection homophobic? As Theseus and the court see them, the 'hard- headed men' putting on *Pyramus and Thisbe* belong to a homosocial community of their own, and their community cannot be comfortably integrated into the play's motivating questions concerning marriage and procreation. The absence of any mention of the men in the company being married stands in stark contrast to the rampant coupling of the other characters, fairy and human alike. They are also not all full-grown men: Flute's request that Quince 'let not me play a woman: I have a beard coming' (1.2.43–4) indicates his position as not-yet a man, one who has yet to achieve masculinity, and his effeminacy sets him up, within Prynne's logic, as a potential sodomite. A critical reader could, upon this point, take me to task for reproducing, maybe even endorsing, this homophobic logic: after all, *Pyramus* does present homoerotic language and behaviour. As Thisbe (Flute) describes 'her' relationship with Pyramus (Bottom), 'My cherry lips have often kiss'd thy stones, / Thy stones with lime and hair knit up in thee' (5.1.188–9),[28] and soon thereafter Pyramus invites Thisbe to kiss him through a hole in Wall (Snout), and Thisbe complains, 'I kiss the wall's hole, not your lips at all' (5.1.199). The homoerotic implications of kissing stones and holes are unmistakable, and it is tempting to take these references as indicating the lack of control the Mechanicals have over their material and their linguistic expression. And following this line of reasoning would indeed endorse the homophobically antitheatrical rejection of the play: it allows us to recognize the Mechanicals as homoerotic and/or homosexual figures, and then mock them for not knowing what they do. But within my argument in this essay, in which *Pyramus* functions as a rejection of antitheatrical homophobia, the lines take on a different valence. They have to be available for homophobic interpretation and mockery in order to function as critique. In other words, *Midsummer* can itself perform homophobia in order to reject homophobia. This provides no simple yes or no answer to the question of whether I am signing on to Prynne's logic, but only a hearty 'it's complicated.'

As a group of presumptive bachelors, possible sodomites and linguistic outsiders, the Mechanicals exist in opposition to the play's marriage complications and its teleological orientation toward marriage and procreation.[29] The entire reason that the court watches *Pyramus and Thisbe* is that Theseus needs to fill a few hours between the end of dinner and the point where all of the newly married couples can retire to their bedrooms for some procreative sporting. As Theseus phrases it, 'Come now; what masques, what dances shall we have, / To wear away this long age of three hours / Between our after-supper and bed-time', going on to ask Philostrate, 'Is there no play / To ease the anguish of a torturing hour?' (5.1.32–7). Once the play is concluded, Theseus rather insists upon heterosexual intercourse taking place: 'Sweet friends, to bed. / A fortnight hold we this solemnity / In nightly revels and new jollity' (5.1.354–6). If this exhortation were not enough, Oberon and Titania appear to offer blessings for the fruit of the unions ostensibly taking place immediately off-stage:

OBERON   Now, until the break of day,
          Through this house each fairy stray.
          To the best bride-bed will we,
          Which by us blessed shall be;
          And the issue there create
          Ever shall be fortunate.
          So shall all the couples three
          Ever true in loving be.

                                              (5.1.387–94)

Oberon's blessing, of course, elides the fact that Demetrius is still under the spell at the end of the play, which means that his marriage to Helena is rather not one that could be fairly described as 'ever true in loving'. His blessing then goes on to emphasize that the fairies have the power to ensure that the children being conceived as he speaks will not be deformed – 'Never mole, hare-lip, nor scar, / Nor mark prodigious, such as are / Despised in nativity, / Shall upon their children be' (5.1.397–400) – which in turn emphasizes the ways in which procreation can go wrong. Nature cannot be left to her own devices; she requires a magical shove in order to produce stable relationships and non-deformed babies. By ending *Midsummer* with such an emphasis on the improbability of heterosexuality, and ostentatiously delaying heterosexual intercourse in favour of drama, Shakespeare ends up establishing theatre as a site of deferred heterosexuality. No one from Theseus's court is in reality, at least presumably, fucking off stage; those sitting or standing in the theatre watching *Midsummer* are ostensibly not fucking either. Theatre is non-generative, in a fairly specific sense: as Shakespeare points out, it alone does not bring about reproduction, or marriage or heterosexuality. Instead, it interrupts while reminding its audiences that social constructions of heterosexuality rely on a repudiation of what heterosexuality constructs as its other.

In short, the court relies on rejecting the Mechanicals and their play as a means of constructing its own heterosexuality and its own aesthetic superiority. In an essay on *Midsummer's* engagement with aesthetics, Hugh Grady argues that the inset play lets us see 'all the artifice of the theater, its rehearsals, its props and costumes, its calculations of audience reaction, on display before us' to the end of using the 'travesty that is the rude mechanicals' play [to] present us with the final truth of his own masterpiece—its madeness, its materiality, its resistance to the artist's shaping fantasies'.[30] The inset play is, in other words, a foil that through its awfulness highlights the brilliance of the play that contains it.[31] The trouble with this conclusion is that it assumes that *Pyramus* has no aesthetic value or purpose of its own, and Grady's focus on the aesthetics of the piece denies it any practical value beyond highlighting *Midsummer's* beauty and brilliance.

And indeed it does seem to serve a practical purpose: Shakespeare deploys *Pyramus* as a metatheatrical antihomophobic tool for exposing the lapses and gaps in the notions of heterosexuality and aesthetics that *Midsummer* presents,[32] and therefore it works as a means of critiquing the audience's homophobic rejection of the entertainment. Such a reading requires reading the court's reaction to *Pyramus* as something more than humorous.[33] The court's reaction to the play is one of distancing: they insistently shove it aside as if to say that nothing so terrible could have anything to do with them. Yet it is only because the play is bad – showily, attention-grabbingly bad – that it can function as an object of ridicule that the court needs in order to construct and demonstrate its heterocentric superiority. Precisely because it functions as the butt of the joke, *Pyramus* becomes more than galumphing poetry when we read it to see Shakespeare as siding with the Mechanicals against the homophobic court. In this event, the inset play asks for a complicated kind of double-consciousness from *Midsummer's* audience. We may laugh at *Pyramus* (and at *Midsummer*), but cannot reject it as thoroughly as Theseus and the others do, for to do so means rejecting *Midsummer*, and all other plays, as well. This complicated interplay sets up a 'bad' play not merely as a foil to the 'good' play that contains it; it insists that the bad play is an integral part of the good play at least to the extent that it emphasizes *Midsummer's* anxiety about marriage and reproduction. What Shakespeare reveals through *Pyramus* is theatre's capacity to disrupt and defer heterosexuality, quite literally, but more importantly in the sense that *Pyramus's* badness exposes heterosexuality's dependence on homophobia in order to reassert and reassure itself of its own dominance.

4

As You Like It or What You Will: Shakespeare's Sonnets and Beccadelli's *Hermaphroditus*

Ian Frederick Moulton

Is queer history a continuum, or is it best understood as a discontinuous series of moments, of interventions, of gestures? When searching for evidence of queer practices, passions and affections in the pre-modern period, should one attempt to construct a genealogy, finding evidence of continuity and tradition, or is it better to focus on individual moments, texts and pieces of evidence?[1] There is no genealogical connection whatsoever between Antonio Beccadelli's collection of Latin epigrams, *Hermaphroditus* (c. 1425) and Shakespeare's *Sonnets* (published 1609). And yet, juxtaposing the two allows one to interrogate notions of queer historiography and to query what useful relationships can be established between texts across temporal and linguistic boundaries within the

larger culture of late medieval and early modern Europe.
Beccadelli's collection draws on models of classical epigrams to
express a range of licit and illicit desire in a socially prestigious
mode of discourse: elegant Latin poetry. Shakespeare's sonnets
do the same work in the later elite genre of the English sonnet
sequence. What is to be gained by bringing these two collections into dialogue with each other? While Beccadelli's and
Shakespeare's collections of poems both centre on questions
of queer desire, sonnet sequences as a genre have little to do
with collections of epigrams and there is no reason to believe
that Shakespeare had any knowledge of Beccadelli's work.
Yet both collections can serve as crucial markers for the possibilities of articulating queer desire in early modern Europe.

The title of Beccadelli's collection, *Hermaphroditus*,
touches on the issue of gender ambiguity – an idea that was
central to Shakespeare's poetry.[2] Shakespeare's Sonnet 20
famously plays with gender categories in its description of a
'master-mistress' who is a 'man in hue' with a woman's face
and heart; who has been 'pricked out' for woman's pleasure
by the belated endowment of a 'thing' which is also 'nothing.'[3]
('Prick' and 'nothing' were early modern slang for male and
female genitalia.) In his extant writings, Shakespeare never
uses the word 'hermaphrodite,' but his sonnets are – among
many other things – an extended meditation on the blurring of
gender boundaries. Sonnet 20 is just the most explicit manifestation of a theme that runs throughout the sonnets, and is a
major focus of much of Shakespeare's drama as well.

The term 'hermaphrodite' originates as the name of a
mythological figure in Ovid's *Metamorphoses*,[4] and it appears
in English as early as 1400 to describe beings that combined
male and female features and characteristics.[5] The term was
commonly used in Shakespeare's lifetime, often with negative
or ambivalent connotations.[6] In Ovid, Hermaphroditus is a
male youth beloved of the nymph Salmacis. He rejects her
advances (as Shakespeare's Adonis rejects Venus), but bathes in
her pool. Salmacis leaps in and seizes Hermaphroditus, asking
the gods to let them be together forever. The two of them are

then transformed into one united being, 'you could not call it a
woman or a boy; it seemed neither, and both.'[7] Then, in response
to Hermaphroditus' prayer, his parents Hermes and Aphrodite
curse Salmacis' pool, so that any man who enters it will lose his
virility, 'quickly softened by the touch of the water'.[8]

In this mythic version, the hermaphrodite is an image
of heterosexual union, but also of the loss of masculinity.
A moralized English translation of the Ovidian tale by
Thomas Peend, published in London in 1565,[9] identifies
Hermaphroditus as representing 'such youths as yet be greene'
(sig. B1[r]) and Salmacis as 'eche vyce that moveth one to ill'
(sig. B1[v]). Peend provides the following moral to the story:

We change our nature cleane,
    being made effemynat.
When we do yeeld to serve our lust,
    we lose our former state.

(sig. B2[v])

The implication is that, for men, sexual contact with females
is effeminizing, and leads to unmanly softness. Heterosexual
union is thus not a source of strength or fertility, but of
sterility and weakness.[10]

A similar dynamic occurs in the conclusion of the 1590 first
edition of Spenser's *Faerie Queene* with the hermaphrodite
embrace of Amoret and Scudamore. Recalling the Biblical
injunction that man and wife shall 'become one flesh',[11] as the
two long-separated lovers are reunited, they are described as if
they have become a single being with two genders:

Lightly he clipt her twixt his armes twaine,
    And streightly did embrace her body bright,
    Her body, late the prison of sad paine,
    Now the sweet lodge of love and deare delight:
    But the faire Lady overcommen quight
    Of huge affection, did in pleasure melt,
    And in sweete ravishment pourd out her spright:

No word they spake, nor earthly thing they felt,
But like two senceless stocks in long embracement dwelt.

Had ye them seene, ye would have surely thought,
    That they had beene that faire Hermaphrodite,
    Which that rich Romane of white marble wrought,
    And in his costly Bath causd to be site:
    So seemd those two, as growne together quite,
    That Britomart, halfe envying their blesse,
    Was much empassiond in her gentle sprite,
    And to her selfe oft wisht like happinesse,
In vaine she wisht, that fate n'ould let her yet possesse.

Thus doe those lovers with sweet contervayle
    Each other of loves bitter fruit despoile.[12]

As in Ovid, the hermaphrodite here represents the union of a heterosexual couple. This hermaphroditic body then inspires heterosexual desire in Britomart, the female knight of chastity who longs for her destined husband Artegall.

But the figuring of the couple as hermaphrodite is ambivalent; it at once idealizes their union and suggests there is something unnatural about it. And as Lauren Silberman has pointed out,[13] Spenser is careful to compare the lovers not to an actual hermaphrodite, but to a marble statue of a hermaphrodite from an ancient Roman bath.[14] The comparison of a living couple to a statue suggests both stasis and sterility, and the context of a pagan Roman bath lends overtones of exotic eroticism and voyeuristic excess.

One might say that this is a queer way to imagine the customary heterosexual embrace that concludes traditional romance narratives. In any case, it proved to be a lame and impotent conclusion; the entire passage describing the hermaphroditic embrace was famously excised in the second edition of The Faerie Queene, ostensibly to defer the couple's union for narrative purposes. Whatever the motivation, Spenser's removal of the hermaphrodite erased its provocative representation of heterosexual union as lascivious, unnatural and oddly sterile – not a living being but a cold stone statue.

Thus, rather than providing an idealized image of heterosexual union, in both Ovid and Spenser the hermaphrodite embodies an unnatural and sterile confusion. These negative connotations of the term are clear in Thomas Nashe's use of the word 'hermaphrodite' in his 1593 pamphlet *Strange Newes* to mock Spenser's friend Gabriel Harvey for using overly learned terms like 'addoulce' and 'entelechy':

> Doe you knowe your owne misbegotten bodgery: *Entelechy* and *addoulce*. With these two Hermaphrodite phrases, being halfe Latin and halfe English hast thou puld out the very guts of the inkhorne.[15]

Nashe does not specify which language – Latin or English – is masculine or feminine. Perhaps Latin, the language of masculine erudition is male, and English, the mother tongue, female. Or perhaps it is the other way around – English is the manly language of the streets, and Latin the effeminate language of the cloister and university. The indeterminacy is part of the point. Harvey's misbegotten bodgery makes nonsense of the very concept of category. The guts are out of the inkhorn and everything is a sticky mess.

While Shakespeare was quite familiar with the concept of the hermaphrodite, it is extremely unlikely that he (or Nashe, or Spenser) had ever heard of Antonio Beccadelli's *Hermaphroditus*, a collection of obscene Latin epigrams written in Italy in 1425. Beccadelli's text, divided into two books containing over eighty poems, is a deliberately irreverent, crude and offensive work. Its title is explained in a poem near the end of the first book that comments on the volume's structure:

> I have divided my book into two parts, Cosimo,
> For the Hermaphrodite has the same number of parts.
> This was the first part, so what follows is the second.
> This stands for the cock, the next will be cunt.[16]

The organizational principle articulated here seems clear, but it does not work in practice. Although both cocks and cunts appear frequently throughout the text, they are in no way separated into one book or the other. Both books are filled with both.

Holt Parker, the text's most recent editor, suggests that in calling his volume *The Hermaphroditus*, Beccadelli may be thinking of Boccaccio's description of Hermaphroditus in his *Genealogy of the Pagan Gods* (*Genealogia deorum gentilium*, started in 1360):

> Hermaphroditus ... born from Mercury and Venus, [may] symbolize speech that is unnecessarily lascivious, which when it ought to be manly, seems effeminate because of the excessive softness of the words.[17]

This explanation too, does not quite fit. Many readers have judged Beccadelli's volume 'unnecessarily lascivious' but his tone, diction and prosody are anything but soft.

Modelled on the second century Latin epigrams of Martial as well as the works of more recent Italian *poeti giocosi* such as Cecco Angiolieri,[18] Beccadelli's collection deals with a wide range of sexual activity from various points of view. Women are generally seen as objects of sexual desire, often in a negative and misogynist context. There are several poems mocking a woman named Ursa, a grotesque embodiment of aggressive feminine desire, who has an enlarged clitoris (1.8),[19] prefers to be on top and insists on anal sex (1.5). She has insatiable appetites and sexually exhausts the speaker (1.21); he is afraid her vagina will swallow him (2.7); and he is disgusted by her smell (2.8, 2.10). And yet there is also a breathtakingly hypocritical poem where he comforts her hurt feelings and swears his devotion to her (2.9). Other poems, written to an 'ideal' mistress named Alda, are more complimentary:[20] 'Alda is the equal of any goddess in beauty and morals' (2.5). But even the poems to Alda are at times ironic and derogatory: 'She doesn't piss, but if she did piss, she pisses

balsam. / She doesn't shit, but if Alda did shit, she shits violets'
(1.18). Other poems deal with brothels and whores: there are
two epitaphs for a whore named Nichina (2.30, 2.32) and a
lengthy poem that imagines Beccadelli's book being accepted
as a customer into a Florentine brothel (2.37).

While many of Beccadelli's epigrams are bawdy or sexualized,
others are not. There is a poem mocking cuckolded husbands
(1.6), but there are also several epitaphs for children dead of
the plague (1.24, 1.25, 1.32, 2.32), a scatological poem about
a defecating peasant (1.40), poems dedicated to friends (1.21,
1.27, 1.38, 1.41, 2.22, etc.), poems attacking enemies (1.10,
1.11, 1.16, 1.17, 1.20, etc.), poems on drunkards and misers
(2.12, 2.36), one on an old horse dying of hunger (2.36)
and another praying that a mistress's childbirth be easy and
safe (2.25). The enormous variety of tone and subject matter
echoes the classical precedent of Martial, but Beccadelli's
collection also fits Thomas Hobbes' later characterization of
'hermaphrodite' writing as 'partly right and comely, partly
brutall and wilde,'[21] though on the whole, the brutal and wild
get more emphasis than the right and comely.

Almost one fifth of the poems in *Hermaphroditus* deal
with sexual relations between males. Several poems praise
male homoeroticism – either explicitly or implicitly. Poem
1.9 compares a Frenchman who fucks boys to an Italian who
fucks girls, implying that there is little to choose between them
– both are voracious, but the speaker himself is even more so.
Poems 1.14 and 1.15 both argue for the superiority of sex with
boys over other forms of sexual activity. In poem 1.28 the
speaker (identified with the author of the volume) says he is
held captive by his love for a boy named Carlo, from Perugia.
And poem 1.34 invites the poem's recipient, Amilus the
Pederast, to 'butt fuck' the messenger who brings him the text.

There are several poems that are critical of men who desire
males, but they are either condemnations of men who are
attracted by ugly partners (1.26, 1.36, 2.6) or men who enjoy
being penetrated themselves rather than taking pleasure from
penetrating others (1.12, 1.13, 1.33). Epigram 1.19 combines

both themes, attacking a man named Coridon for loving an ugly and foul-smelling boy named Quintius ('If you smell his mouth, you'll think you've smelled his ass / but even his ass is cleaner than his mouth'), and then attacking the boy Quintius for taking pleasure in being anally penetrated:

> Who can count the number of members your gaping
>   asshole has swallowed?
> As many ships that Scylla devoured by the Sicilian shore.
> He openly takes the woman's passive role for any man
>   (the shame of it!)

There are also seduction poems from men to adolescent boys (2.17, 2.18, 2.28, 2.34) – though these are always coyly presented as being written for Beccadelli's friends rather than for the author himself. These poems written to lovely boys are no less romantic and effusive than traditional poems written to lovely girls:

> You are more beautiful than silver, but you will be
>   handsomer than gold, if you return kind words,
>   generous boy.
> Your family is good: brothers, sisters, parents;
>   you should be just as gentle, since your whole family is
>   good.
> Your appearance is handsome; let your mind be beautiful
>   too

> (2.17)

In a much cruder register, Epigram 1.7, an 'Epitaph for Pegasus, the Lame Pederast' openly praises anal sex with boys. Written in the traditional style of an ancient Roman tomb inscription, the passage pleads with passing travellers to stop for a moment and pay their respects:

> When you're about to butt fuck your submissive youth,
>   please do it on this tomb, traveler,

> And so honor my soul with fucking, not with incense.
>   Grant this rest to my spirits, I pray.

The poem goes on to approvingly cite Achilles and Hercules for buggering their partners and suggests that anal sex is part of an ancient and sacred tradition:

> This type of solace counts the most among the shades,
>   as established by the fathers of old.
> Thus Achilles satisfied the ashes of Chiron,
>   and your ass felt it too, blond Patroclus,
> Hylas knew it, spitted by Hercules on his father's burial
>   mound.
> Perform for me the rites our ancestors taught us.

At no point in any of the poems, no matter how ironic, sarcastic or vituperative they may be, is it suggested that sex with boys is any more to be condemned than sex with women. In Beccadelli's text, a pederast may be attacked for being a slave to his passions, but in this he is no better or worse than a man who is obsessed by sex with women. One poem, in fact, argues that once a man has had anal or oral sex with boys he will never go back to vaginal sex:

> *Lepidinus Asks the Author Why Once Someone*
> *Begins to Butt Fuck He Never Stops*

> O author of trifles, why is a man never able to give it up
>   once he's fucked someone in the ass or mouth?
> In fact, even a blockhead Breton, when he's barely had a taste,
>   willingly competes with Siena itself in this sort of love.
> Naples yields to the French, Florence to the Germans,
>   once they get a chance to touch a boy.

(1.14)

As long as men take the active role, for Beccadelli their object choice – boy or woman – is not particularly important.

Men who take pleasure in being anally penetrated, on the
other hand, are mocked for being effeminate. Epigram 1.13,
'Against Lentulus, the Effeminate, the High and Mighty, and
a Man of the lowest Vice' concludes:

> You keep everything to yourself, except for one thing.
> That one thing is your asshole, Lentulus, which you
>   do not keep to yourself, but share with everyone,
>   effeminate Lentulus.

On the whole, *Hermaphroditus* comes across as a scholarly
humanist effort to revive a classical view of sex which
sees adult male sexual desire as natural, somewhat foolish,
pleasurable and vulgar, but not by any means sinful in
itself.[22] In this view, men naturally seek pleasure in the sexual
penetration of the bodies of others. This may make them
ridiculous if they overindulge, or if they become obsessed
with a particular partner, or choose an inappropriate one (old,
hairy, foul-smelling or ugly), but the desire itself is accepted
and can be celebrated. The key to appropriate behaviour, in
sexual pleasures as in other desires, is moderation: enough
sex, but not too much, all penetrative, and ideally with
an appropriate partner, male or female, under appropriate
circumstances. As one poem puts it:

> Even if my cock often desperately wants cunt,
>   or sometimes my dirty dick goes after boy's thighs,
> nevertheless my lust is not so crazy or swollen,
>   that I would ask for a bang openly or in company.
> I wouldn't want to bugger Hyacinthus in public,
>   I wouldn't fuck Helen herself with a lot of people
>   around.

> (2.24)

The poem that jokingly contrasts the sexual tastes of a
Frenchman and a Tuscan, says that the Frenchmen fucks all

the boys in the city, whereas the Tuscan fucks any female, including new mothers, widows and members of his own family: 'In short,' Beccadelli concludes, 'you want for your own everything in the whole city that pisses. / He wants everything in the whole city that shits' (1.9).[23] Neither is better or worse.

Although the subjects and language of Beccadelli's poems may frequently be crude, from a poetic point of view, such low topics and language are perfectly decorous for the genre of the epigram. The Roman poet Martial's twelve books of epigrams are often rude and sexually explicit, but they are also by turns humorous, solemn, self-deprecating and satirical. They combine poems in praise of the Emperor with poems on oral and anal sex as well as serious and solemn epitaphs for dead children.[24] The range of Beccadelli's tone and subject matter mirrors Martial's in many ways. Technically speaking, Beccadelli's poems are not particularly impressive, but they tend to be metrically and generically correct according to rules of Latin poetics deduced from classical models. Thus, Beccadelli, a sophisticated courtier and scholar could think not only that a volume dealing with cocks, cunts, assholes, catamites, whores, peasants, farts and shit was decorous, but he could also dedicate it to the most powerful man in Florence, Cosimo de' Medici. As indeed he did. In a poem advising de' Medici how to read the volume, Beccadelli suggests that it is an ideal after-dinner diversion, 'something for you to read to a guest after lunch, Cosimo … reading material for those in their cups after dinner is done.'

Hermaphroditus was widely and fiercely criticized, but Beccadelli had a very successful life and career all the same. Antonio Beccadelli (1394–1471), also known as Panormita,[25] was a humanist scholar who spent his long life in the service of various Italian princes. He was court poet to the Visconti in Milan, was crowned poet laureate by the Holy Roman Emperor, and spent his later life in Naples at the court of King Alfonso V, where he was instrumental in the founding of Academia Neapolitana, the first of the great Renaissance Italian academies.

The *Hermaphroditus*, composed when Beccadelli was in his late twenties, was clearly written to draw attention to its author, demonstrating his mastery of a wide range of subject matter as well as his daring choice of material. The project proved more controversial than Beccadelli probably intended. A host of humanist writers and church authorities spoke out against the volume, and the popular preacher Bernardino da Siena staged public burnings of the book. Beccadelli was burnt in effigy in both Bologna and Milan. Beccadelli and his allies defended the book, but in the general manner of humanist quarrels this only provoked greater outrage and accusations. Beccadelli was accused not only of sodomy, but of having murdered his wife and of pimping out boys.[26] Some claimed the Pope himself threatened readers of *Hermaphroditus* with excommunication. Eventually, to silence the criticism and end the controversy, Beccadelli issued a retraction and recanted his dedication to Cosimo de' Medici.[27]

Contrary to what some critics had claimed, de' Medici had not burned his own copy – the presentation copy of *Hermaphroditus* is still safe and sound in the Medici library.[28] But neither did de' Medici give Beccadelli any patronage or protection. Like Thomas Nashe's later attempt to become the English Aretine by writing erotically explicit verse,[29] Beccadelli's gambit had failed. The remainder of his literary and scholarly output kept both cunts and cocks to a minimum. His most successful and influential work ended up being *De dictis et factis Alphonsi regis* (1455), a volume in praise of Alfonso V of Naples that represents the King as an ideal humanist prince, who reads Virgil and Livy and spends his spare time debating philosophy with the many scholars at his court.

Over time, *Hermaphroditus* was largely forgotten. Manuscripts of the collection gathered dust in libraries and *Hermaphroditus* did not appear in print until the French Revolution. It was first published in 1790 in a rare edition attested in collections in Berlin and Vicenza. A larger edition attributed to Abbé Mercier was published in Paris in 1791.

Another edition, with extensive scholarly annotations, appeared in Germany in 1824. Beccadelli's collection was not translated into English until 2001. Most surviving manuscripts of the text date to the fifteenth century and are found in Italian collections.

So what does *Hermaphroditus* have to do with Shakespeare's sonnets? Sonnet sequences as a genre have little to do with collections of epigrams. Beccadelli was a courtly humanist writing in Latin. Shakespeare was a popular dramatist writing in the vernacular. Shakespeare's sonnets are revered as being among the greatest lyric poetry in English. Beccadelli's Latin verse is not nearly so distinguished, and for centuries the critical consensus on the *Hermaphroditus* was well represented by Ludwig Pastor's statement that it embodies 'the spirit of the false [heathen] Renaissance ... in all its Hideousness'.[30]

Yet Beccadelli's and Shakespeare's collections of poems both centre on questions of queer desire, and both can serve as crucial markers for the possibilities of articulating queer desire in early modern Europe. In both collections, models of sexual and affective relationships are put forward that challenge and contradict prevailing modes of accepted relations, as well as subverting fixed categories of gender and desire. Shakespeare turns Petrarchism on its head by having a male poet pine for an unattainable (and not particularly virtuous) young man instead of a distant virtuous lady. Then in the so-called 'dark lady' sonnets he explores the frustrations and pleasures of a consummated relationship with a flesh-and-blood woman rather than Petrarchan longing for a chaste ideal. Beccadelli's poems equate boys and women as objects of desire, and posit a world where sexual object choice (for elite men) is irrelevant rather than a matter of life and death.

By juxtaposing Shakespeare's erotic poetry with Beccadelli's one is made aware of the potential of elite verse forms to communicate queer relations and desires. The cultural capital of the Latin epigram or the English sonnet can be subverted to suggest ideas and explore relationships that would be unspeakable in other, less refined, contexts. These expressions were not uncontested, but they endure nonetheless. Whether or not de' Medici read *Hermaphroditus* to approving friends after dinner, he kept his copy carefully, and did not burn it, whatever Bernardino di Siena might have thought.

Both Shakespeare's Sonnets and *Hermaphroditus* were circulated originally in manuscript, and it can be argued that this more restricted form of dissemination allowed their authors more latitude to explore risky subject matter. Besides Frances Meres' 1598 praise of Shakespeare's 'sugred Sonnets among his private friends'[31] we know few details of the dissemination and reception of Shakespeare's sonnets before their publication in 1609.[32] Thanks to the controversy over *Hermaphroditus*, the early circulation and reception of Beccadelli's text is easier to trace. Early readers such as Guarino da Verona and Francesco Filelfo were enthusiastic, and praised the volume in letters, but as the text spread more broadly, it was widely condemned[33] and its early defenders abandoned it.[34] In the case both of *Hermaphroditus* and of Shakespeare's sonnets, the dissemination of the texts quickly spread beyond coteries of sympathetic friends. Beccadelli's text came into the hands of moralist preachers and was publicly condemned and burned. Shakespeare's sonnets were printed in an edition that he presumably neither condoned nor directed. They were left out of the Folio publication of Shakespeare's plays, and were not reprinted until 1640.

While Beccadelli's poems were unknown in early modern England, Latin epigrams functioned nonetheless as a conduit for sexual knowledge and discourse. While many editions of Martial published in Catholic Europe in the sixteenth century were expurgated to remove lewd poems,[35] a complete edition of Martial's epigrams was published in England in 1615, edited and annotated by Thomas Farnaby, and printed by William Welby.[36] The volume was dedicated to Sir Robert Killigrew, a member of Parliament, friend of John Donne and Francis Bacon, and close to James I's favourite, Robert Carr, Earl of Somerset.[37] A second edition was published in 1633.[38] Included in the collection are unexpurgated poems on male masturbation, anal sex, oral sex and much else besides. Though Shakespeare may not have read Martial unexpurgated, other early modern English readers certainly did, not least Ben Jonson, whose own English epigrams – though polite by comparison – are clearly modelled on Martial's example.[39]

Jonson owned at least three different complete editions of Martial,[40] and his annotations show that he was well aware of the poem's bawdy connotations. For example, Martial's epigram 2.28 lists all the sorts of penetrative sexual activity a man named Sextillus abstains from, and then ends by saying 'two possibilities remain'. In the margin of his copy, Jonson wrote 'Fellator cunniling'.[41] It was obvious to Jonson that Martial was suggesting that Sextillus takes pleasure from sucking men and women's genitals. This annotation is particularly significant since early modern erotic writing in English seldom mentions oral sex in any context.[42] Latin poetry was clearly functioning as a conduit for sexual discourse in a way that vernacular poetry did not.

Indeed, English readers like Jonson could only read the unexpurgated Martial in Latin. English translations of Martial were published in 1629 and 1656, though both are partial and omit the most scurrilous materials.[43] Perhaps more significantly, the complete and unexpurgated Latin editions of Martial were supplanted, beginning in 1655, with a selected edition intended for use in Westminster School.[44] This text was frequently reprinted during the remainder of the seventeenth century.[45] No complete edition of Martial was published in England between 1633 and 1700. Even today, complete and unexpurgated English editions of Martial are relatively rare. Loeb Classics provides the complete epigrams in Latin with facing page English translations, but the Penguin and Oxford Modern Classics editions offer relatively decorous selections, even though both volumes are entitled simply *Epigrams*, as if to imply that all the epigrams were included.[46] Even W. C. A. Kerr's original Loeb edition from 1925 translated some of the more salacious texts into Italian instead of English. (These were eventually replaced by English translations in reprint editions).

Not surprisingly, Martial himself predicted that some readers would want to censor his text: In epigram 1.35 he warns the reader not to castrate his poems. 'Like husbands,' he says, 'they can't please without a cock' (lines 4–5). By the laws of poetry, epigrams must be provocative.[47] In *Hermaphroditus*, Beccadelli used Martial's epigram as a model for one of his own:

> *To Mino, That He Should Not Castrate This Book*[48]

> Mino, you advise me to take the cock out of my book.
>   That way you think my songs will please everyone.
> Mino, please don't castrate my book.
>   Phoebus has a cock. Calliope has a pussy.

> (1.23)

For Beccadelli, both the god and the muse of poetry are sexual beings. Whatever the gender of eloquence – male, female, hermaphrodite – it must be sexualized to be potent, and, like Shakespeare's master-mistress, to appeal to all.

Shakespeare's sonnets have been read in a wide variety of registers and their radical relation to Petrarchan traditions is abundantly clear. Reading Shakespeare's sonnets through the lens of Beccadelli's epigrams allows one to see their eroticism in a different light. Shakespeare's treatment of queer desire rejects many of the traditional attitudes of the classical epigram. He avoids the epigram's explicit language, as well as classical norms of male desire which see penetration as the essence of masculine sexuality. Shakespeare's sonnets incorporate romantic and affectionate feeling in ways that are absolutely alien to the discourse of Martial and Beccadelli. The result is a body of poetic work that is arguably more destabilizing than Beccadelli's scandalous collection. In their articulation of the male speaker's passionate and frustrated attraction to an elegant male social superior, Shakespeare's sonnets reimagine the possibilities of masculine desire.

Beccadelli's epigrams, on the other hand simply reassert a classical model that is deeply traditional in its definition of masculinity as the physical penetration of social inferiors: women, boys and slaves. Though *Hermaphroditus* was clearly transgressive in the context of early modern Christian sexual morality, Beccadelli's collection looks defiantly to the past and to strong hierarchies of sexual power and desire rather than imagining a queer present or future.

PART II

Queer language

5

The queer language of size in *Love's Labour's Lost*

Valerie Billing

Madhavi Menon calls Shakespeare's *Love's Labour's Lost* (c. 1594–5) 'a comedy in drag' because it seems to possess all the traits of a comedy, yet the ending fails to resolve the many potential pairings in marriage.[1] The play is supposedly about four aristocratic men – the King of Navarre and his lords Berowne, Longaville and Dumaine – courting four women – the Princess of France and her ladies Rosaline, Maria and Katherine – while, in the sub-plot, the rustic clown Costard and the Spanish knight Don Armado compete for the affections of the dairymaid Jaquenetta. These courtships, however, experience continued delays and are ultimately thwarted when news arrives of the Princess's father's death. Instead of successfully wooing the women, most of the men spend their time writing Petrarchan love lyrics that are as much for each other as for their female beloveds and engaging in eroticized verbal and physical struggles with other male figures. The play's language of love and desire, especially as articulated by the male characters, relies on terms and phrasing that suggest size, and it is size, I will argue, that underwrites both the delay that forestalls the comic resolution and the male-male struggles that comprise much of the plot. Size, though rooted in the physically measurable, becomes a fluid category whose vocabulary at once connotes physical and social stature and carries with it erotic potential through its ability to construct hierarchies based on often-sexualized dynamics of dominance and submission.

The vocabulary of size in *Love's Labour's Lost* often seems deceptively conventional: characters use it both literally and metaphorically to express physical dimensions, social stature and the pleasure and pain of love in Petrarchan love poetry. Applying queer analysis to this language of size, however, reveals this language's capacity to turn expressions of hetero-erotic desire into homoeroticism, cross and unsettle categories of the physical and the social and trouble the circulation of sexual knowledge in the play. As a category with queer potential, size offers a new way of thinking about embodiment and asks us to consider physical dimension as a trait that operates alongside gender to inspire and drive desire. The desires articulated throughout *Love's Labour's Lost*, and in Shakespeare's canon more broadly, cannot always adequately be understood and described by the gender-focused terms we use today that divide homoeroticism from heteroeroticism. These erotic categories overlap in *Love's Labour's Lost*, with the desire for largeness or smallness often causing the hetero-erotic to shade into the homoerotic. In this chapter, I first trace the lexicon of size's queer engagements with Petrarchan tropes, then analyze the erotics of physical and social largeness and smallness through the characters Moth, Armado and Costard. Finally, I consider the role of size in the dissemi-nation of sexual knowledge throughout the play.

Size, as a category and a language, is inherently neither erotic nor queer, yet it provides new points of entry into the queer erotics of *Love's Labour's Lost* by inviting us to reimagine the metaphorical struggles often articulated in Petrarchan love poetry. The play's lampooning of Petrarchism has been well documented, but I would suggest that the play is also testing the limits of what kinds of desires Petrarchan tropes can articulate.[2] Mark Breitenberg argues that violence is endemic to masculine desire in the Petrarchan tradition and, drawing on the work of Nancy Vickers, formulates Petrarchism as a response to the pain of frustrated heterosexual desire: Petrarchism is 'an enabling discourse of masculine heterosexual desire and ... a socioliterary convention that provides a compensatory form of masculine empowerment in response to the perception of psychic and emotional vulnerability'.[3] At the same time, however, Petrarchism 'rests on a "necessary" contradiction: the frustration of desire impels desire itself'.[4] Though Breitenberg goes on to argue that the play does not empower the female characters because their rejections of the men only fuel, rather than neutralize, male desire, I want to put more pressure on the vulnerability Breitenberg describes. Though violent language permeates the play's Petrarchan love language, that violence is often directed back at the masculine self and serves to articulate an embrace of the erotics of vulnerability through language that connotes size.

The seemingly conventional speech in Act 3 in which Berowne first declares his love for Rosaline takes up the Petrarchan trope of love as a physical struggle while pointing toward a queer erotics produced by fusing the languages of love and size. Berowne admits his love not by actually talking about Rosaline, but by casting himself as a slave to a simultaneously miniature and gigantic Cupid. He calls Cupid 'This Signor Junior, giant dwarf, Dan Cupid', formulating Cupid as a series of size contradictions (3.1.179).[5] He calls Cupid a 'wayward boy', but he also bemoans his own 'little heart' (3.1.178, 185). Despite the absence of a physical body portraying Cupid on the stage, Berowne's vivid language of size conjures Cupid as a third participant in his relationship with Rosaline and turns his confession of love into a polyamorous fantasy. When Berowne finally describes his lady love, he devotes only two lines to her appearance, which he depicts unflatteringly: she is 'A whitely wanton with a velvet brow, / With two pitch-balls stuck in her face for eyes'

(3.1.195–6). Berowne may be confessing his love for Rosaline, but he does so with language that eroticizes his relationship not with her, but with Cupid, who grows in stature while Berowne shrinks. Berowne remembers his former dominance over Cupid when he was 'a domineering pedant o'er the boy', but Cupid has become an 'anointed sovereign', 'dread prince' and 'great general', among other appellations (3.1.176, 180, 183, 184). Here, Berowne engages in a struggle with Cupid that produces both pleasure and humiliation as he switches from the dominant to the submissive role – from a pedant to a slave – in conventional Petrarchan rhetoric of submitting to the bonds of love. This seemingly conventional imagery, however, expresses ostensibly heterosexual love in homoerotic terms. Following Jeffrey Masten's efforts to think beyond conventionality in men's affectionate addresses to each other in early modern letters and plays, I argue that in Berowne's soliloquy, the vocabularies of size, dominance and submission create a male-centered homoerotics deserving of attention as an expression of desire that resonates beyond convention.[6]

This analysis of size in Berowne's confession of love lets us rethink Breitenberg's strictly heterosexual formulation of Petrarchism and consider the queer potential of Petrarchan tropes. The dynamic of dominance and submission in Berowne's soliloquy does not occur across a strict gender binary, but rather is mediated through Cupid's diminutive yet conquering form. As a boy, Cupid occupies a gendered position separate from both femaleness and adult maleness, and submission to Cupid offers Berowne an alternative to erotic submission to a woman. Berowne couches his final admission of surrender in the language of size: he gives in to Cupid's 'almighty dreadful little might' (3.1.202). Cupid is 'little', and yet the repetition of *might* in the first and last words of this quotation suggests that his triumph over Berowne was inevitable. As both an irresistible conqueror and an object of desire, Cupid embodies the erotic potential of the category of the diminutive, which was associated in Renaissance England with children, sonnets, miniature portraits and other objects thought to be both highly desirable and collectible.[7] Susan Stewart argues that the toy, as a category of the small, 'is a device for fantasy, a point of beginning for narrative', a definition that resonates with Berowne's imaginary Cupid.[8] Cupid functions as an object of fantasy for Berowne, who transfers his erotic feelings for Rosaline to Cupid's small male body, and it is through this small body that Berowne begins to construct a narrative that will enable him to woo Rosaline. Though Berowne nominally resists Cupid, he also desires this toy-like enemy who inspires him to express his love for Rosaline as a homoerotic fantasy of submission to a diminutive male. Through this sort of fantasy, the play's language of size causes Berowne's articulations of desire to slip between the hetero and the homo and between monogamy and polyamory.

While Berowne's Cupid remains pure fantasy – he never appears on the stage – a host of other characters who are sexualized by their size offer their bodies to the gazes of both the other characters and the play's spectators alike. The diminutive Moth and the enormous Don Armado and Costard embody size as an erotic category that shifts easily between the physical and the social, and, as in Berowne's homoeroticized expression of love for Rosaline, size for these three characters of excessively small or large stature creates homoerotic potential out of heteroeroticism. Through language that conflates physical and social stature, these characters also eroticize social categories by linking them with the vocabulary of size used to describe highly desirable bodies. The Spanish braggart Armado and his young page Moth's first scene together supposedly deals with Armado's confession of his passion for Jaquenetta, yet it dramatizes the erotic friction between Moth and Armado through talk of physical size and social stature. Armado, who in the opening lines of their first exchange addresses Moth as 'boy', 'dear imp' and 'tender juvenal', expresses intimate fondness for Moth as, specifically, a small dependent boy (1.2.1, 5, 8). These terms of endearment primarily refer to age, but they also connote smallness, as suggested a few lines later when Armado affectionately calls Moth 'pretty', because 'little' (1.2.22). The cause-and-effect implied by this phrasing suggests that Moth's attractive wit and physical desirability originate with his small size. Ruth Stevenson even connects Moth to a boyish Cupid and notes the similarity of Moth's name to the French *mot*, meaning *word*, arguing that Moth 'represents male-child sexual drive that is inherently related to language'.[9] With a name that evokes words, a small unit of language, Moth embodies size as a lexicon as well as size as a physical trait. At the same time, Moth is not simply an erotic object: throughout this scene he engages in a battle of wits with Armado that anticipates Cupid's domination of Berowne and takes part in constructing the scene's erotics by describing Armado in terms of largeness. In response to the affectionate diminutives Armado uses to address Moth, Moth calls Armado 'my tough señor' and later compares him to the biblical Samson, 'a man of good carriage, great carriage, for he carried the town gates on his back' (1.2.9–10, 68–9). Moth and Armado's flirtatious exchange quickly morphs into more explicit sexual banter, with Moth teasing Armado with the phallic insinuation that he 'will praise an eel with that same praise'; Armado responds, 'thou heatest my blood', indicating anger, sexual arousal, or both (1.2.26, 29–30). Here, as in Berowne's fantasy, male confessions of love for a woman become entangled in an eroti-cized struggle with another male that is made both rhetorical and physical through its reliance on the language of size. Moth and Armado bicker and tease while Berowne expresses his internal struggle in terms of a common poetic trope, but the physical terms of size in both scenes also ask the audience to imagine the characters' embodied, eroticized struggles for dominance.

Armado and Moth's banter not only adds a physical edge to their rhetorical interaction, but also illustrates the fluidity of size as a language that both crosses categories such as age, status and physical dimension and troubles these categorical distinctions altogether. When Armado says to Moth, 'comfort me, boy. What great men have been in love?' (1.2.63), he names the 'boy' as a particular figure who can offer comfort, underscores Moth's small stature and contrasts Moth's smallness with the 'greatness' of men whom he fancies are like himself. Moth's first answer to this question is Hercules, a hero famous for loving both boys and women (1.2.64). In response, Armado exclaims, 'most sweet Hercules!', and then immediately addresses Moth again as 'sweet my child' (1.2.65–6). This exchange revolves around 'boy' and 'sweet', words Masten has analysed in terms of an instability connected to their erotic potential. He argues that the early modern 'boy' is characterized by a 'categorical fluidity' or 'categorical unfixity' that contributes to his status as a 'universal object of desire'.[10] Elsewhere, Masten demonstrates that '*sweetness* is a part of the syntax of affective male relations'.[11] In Moth and Armado's banter, the word 'sweet' connects Armado, Moth and the imagined Hercules, and in the exchange between Moth and Armado as well as in Berowne's Cupid fantasy, the language of size specifically underwrites expressions of male-male intimacy. In Moth and Armado's conversation, sweetness, boyhood and size intersect in an affectionate exchange that unsettles Armado's articulation of his ostensibly heterosexual passion for Jaquenetta.

Armado's use of 'sweet' to address both Moth and the imagined Hercules implicitly connects these two figures despite Moth's diminutive and Hercules' 'great' stature, and Moth's depiction of Hercules in the performance of the Nine Worthies at the play's end illustrates both the erotic physicality of size and its fluidity. The schoolmaster Holofernes suggests that Moth play this role in their performance for the King, the Princess and their retinues, but to Armado, the difference in stature between Moth and Hercules should be obvious and important. He objects to this casting based on size: 'Pardon, sir, error! He is not quantity enough for that Worthy's thumb. He is not so big as the end of his club' (5.1.122–4). Using figurative language to make a joke about the size of Moth's body – and also a phallic joke about the size of his penis – Armado insists on Moth's unsuitability for portraying Hercules by suggesting that size is fixed and measurable rather than performable. Holofernes, however, has a solution that draws on the fluidity of size to suggest age as well as dimension: 'he shall present Hercules in minority. His enter and exit shall be strangling a snake' (5.1.125–7). Holofernes conflates smallness and youth here, and, similar to Armado who compares Moth to Hercules's thumb, reduces Moth to the status of a cute little boy. This diminutive cuteness remains sexualized, however: Holofernes assigns Moth the action of 'strangling a snake', or playing with an animal that recalls the phallic eel from Moth's earlier conversation with Armado. Moth, with his little body, reduces the great Hercules to diminutive, sexualized entertainment for Holofernes and for the royal spectators. And like the boys who acted in the London children's playing companies during the early years of Shakespeare's career, Moth as a diminutive Hercules might appeal erotically to both the King and the Princess, to both male and female spectators on the stage and seated throughout the theatre.[12]

The fat, clownish Costard, another character sexualized for his size, participates in the performance of the Nine Worthies alongside Moth and both adds a new dimension to the performance's potential eroticism and further obscures the line between the physical and social aspects of size. Costard, whose name refers to a type of large apple and whose obsession with eating and extreme aversion to fasting in Act 1 further suggest that he is apple-shaped, dwarfs Moth, and in his depiction of Pompey he offers both comedy and an enormous, sexualized male body. Holofernes assigns Costard his part specifically because of his largeness: 'this swain, because of his great limb or joint, shall pass Pompey the Great' (5.1.119–20). The two uses of 'great' in this statement conflate greatness as a physical property with greatness as a social designation, a conflation Costard himself perpetuates when he enters during the performance and declares himself '*Pompey surnamed the Big*' (5.2.546). Berowne takes up this category-crossing blunder for a joke of his own, proclaiming Costard 'Greater than "Great." Great, great, great Pompey! Pompey the huge!' (5.2.681–2).

These references to Costard's largeness, particularly in the context of the 'limb' and 'joint' in Holofernes' description of him and his own admission that he will 'stand for' Pompey, not only make a joke out of Costard but also sexualize him as the possessor of a large sex organ (5.2.505). It is worth noting that this sexualization occurs through words that connote size as uttered by other men: Holofernes makes the first remark about his 'great limb or joint', and it is Berowne, not one of the ladies, who responds enthusiastically to Costard as 'Pompey the huge'. Even here, in what should be the final stages of his wooing of Rosaline, Berowne is focused on a male body that, as in his fantasy of Cupid, grows in stature through Berowne's own inflated language; Pompey goes from simply 'big' to 'Greater than "Great." Great, great, great' and then to 'huge'. Berowne's exclamation fuses comedy with erotic delight in the oversized male body, and the exhibition of male bodies of excessive size in this performance delays the cross-sex courtships to the point that they are ultimately thwarted, suggesting that the language and performance of size work against heterosexual marital resolution in this play.

Costard, with his immense body, moves easily between the main plot and the sub-plot and male and female spaces, bringing with him the erotic potential of largeness and his tendency to conflate physical dimension with social stature. When he delivers a letter to the Princess in Act 4, he has an odd exchange with her that focuses on the size not of his body, but of hers:

COSTARD Which is the greatest lady, the highest?
PRINCESS The thickest and the tallest.
COSTARD The thickest and the tallest. It is so, truth is truth.
         An your waist, mistress, were as slender as my
             wit,
         One o' these maids' girdles for your waist
             should be fit.
         Are not you the chief woman? You are the
             thickest here.

                                                (4.1.47–53)

To modern European and Anglo-American audiences, this exchange seems shocking: Costard calls the Princess fat, and she encourages him to do so. At stake here, though, is the inseparability of the physical from the social dimension of size and the Princess's ability to control the representational terms of her own body – and its erotic potential. The Princess's social stature as the 'greatest lady' apparently corresponds to a largeness of waist that seems at once to confirm and produce her high social station, but the interaction between princess and clown also functions as an example of what Patricia Parker has termed the play's myriad 'preposterous reversals' that invert social order and deflate the highbrow to the status of the lowbrow.[13] By punning on 'greatest' and 'highest' to call attention to the physical properties of her own body, the Princess makes herself as corporal as the similarly corpulent Costard and establishes a surprising intimacy between her royal female body and a male clown's body through their shared largeness, which he then takes up and elaborates on in his reply.

In flaunting her physical largeness and her body's connection to Costard's, the Princess associates herself with Costard's form of enormous male sexuality and rewrites the terms of the Petrarchan language the male characters use throughout the play to describe the ladies. The King clearly admires the Princess for her largeness: his descriptions of her rely on Petrarchan clichés that obscure her physical body, replacing it with metaphors of largeness. His love letter to her opens by figuring her as both the sun and the moon, enormous celestial bodies associated, appropriately, with royalty:

> So sweet a kiss the golden sun gives not
>   To those fresh morning drops upon the rose,
> As thy eye-beams when their fresh rays have smote
>   The night of dew that on my cheeks down flows.
> Nor shines the silver moon one half so bright
>   Through the transparent bosom of the deep
> As doth thy face, through tears of mine, give light.

(4.3.25–31)

In this passage from the King's letter, the Princess as the beloved becomes bodiless and genderless, defined only by celestial largeness, while the King as the lover is miniaturized and feminized through his association with roses and tears. The Petrarchan metaphors dwarf the King and enlarge the Princess while blurring gender and obscuring bodies, suggesting that the King perhaps desires largeness more than femaleness. Indeed, Armado's description of an intimate moment he shared with the King suggests that the king's desires are not oriented exclusively toward women. Armado describes the King as 'my familiar' and 'very good friend', recalling that 'it will please his grace, by the world, sometime to lean upon my shoulder and with his royal finger thus dally with my excrement, with my mustachio' (5.1.88–9, 94–7). 'Mustachio' is often read as a gloss for 'excrement', which, when the play was first performed, could have meant 'an outgrowth, esp. of hair, nails, feathers', but the word also carried the meaning familiar to us today: faeces.[14] Whether the King only caresses Armado's face or engages in a sexual encounter involving his finger in both Armado's anus and mouth, Armado's description casts the King as intimately involved with Armado's large, blustering body in a way he is not with the Princess's, which remains distant and unobtainable in the King's celestial metaphor. The Princess, however, embraces the physicality of her thick waist in her dialogue with Costard, using puns on size to reject metaphors that take away her corporality and leave her unable to compete with Armado for the King's anally and orally-oriented erotic affections.

The question of what Armado means – what acts or relations he refers to – with his mention of excrement raises larger questions about sexual knowledge throughout the play. *Love's Labour's Lost* both opens and closes with questions about sexual knowledge that attach specifically to a trio of characters associated with largeness: Costard, Armado and Jaquenetta. In sharp contrast to Berowne, Armado and the King, who only half-heartedly woo women, Costard engages in a sexual relationship with Jaquenetta at the beginning of the play, though descriptions of that relationship are left curiously ambiguous. Almost immediately after the three lords reaffirm their oath to the king in the play's opening scene, the constable enters with Costard, seeking disciplinary action by the king. When asked what has happened, Costard responds with vagueness, euphemism and legal wordplay: 'The matter is to me, sir, as concerning Jaquenetta. The manner of it is, I was taken in the manner' (1.1.198–200). When Berowne asks him to elaborate, he responds with unhelpful details: 'I was seen with her in the manor-house, sitting with her upon the form, and taken following her into the park' (1.1.203–5). This explanation provides some information about location, but it leaves obscure what, exactly, about this episode deserves the term 'villainy', as the constable calls it (1.1.186). Armado's letter describing what he saw is similarly opaque: while walking in the park, he writes, '*I did encounter that obscene and most preposterous event that draweth from my snow-white pen that ebon-coloured ink*' (1.1.234–6). Armado provides extensive sensory detail about the pen and ink he uses to write about the 'event', but no clear details about the event itself; when he elaborates, he says only that he found Costard '*sorted and consorted*' with Jaquenetta (1.1.248). Costard at first owns up to this charge – 'I confess the wench' (1.1.269) – but then, when told that the penalty for such an act is a year in prison, he revises Jaquenetta's status first to a 'damsel', then to a 'virgin' and finally to a 'maid' (1.1.276, 278, 281). The status of Jaquenetta's virginity shifts rapidly during this dialogue, leaving it unclear whether what she and Costard were caught doing might jeopardize her status as a 'virgin' or a 'maid'.

Few scholars have questioned whether what transpired between Costard and Jaquenetta might be anything other than penile-vaginal intercourse that results in Jaquenetta's pregnancy, revealed in Act 5. However, the vague Act 1 descriptions, whether Costard's or Armado's, fail to indicate that what Costard did with Jaquenetta could result in a baby. Costard's Act 5 assertion that Jaquenetta 'is two months on her way' gives a time frame to the moment of conception, but it is not clear how much time has passed since Costard's arrest for the 'preposterous event' at the beginning of Act 1. Indeed, Costard's vehement assertion that the baby is Armado's (5.2.673) should further make us question our assumptions about what it means to 'confess the wench', be 'taken in the manner', have 'sorted and consorted', witness an 'obscene and most preposterous event', and be a wench, a damsel, a virgin or a maid. Christine Varnado cautions scholars against assuming that we know what happens in any given depiction of offstage sex, pointing out that modern readers tend to fill in gaps in evidence with the assumption of vaginal penetration. Analyzing the 'morning-after' scene in Act 3 of *Romeo and Juliet*, in which the title characters bemoan the coming of the dawn, Varnado argues that the offstage night of passion that preceded this scene might have involved any number of sex acts and that 'there is no textual reason to assume that this offstage act of "sex" (whatever it is) follows the strict phallocentric plot telos that furnishes the patriarchal definition of sex', by which she means sex 'of the legally significant, penis-in-vagina variety'.[15] As we have seen, the text of *Love's Labour's Lost* provides no explicit details that suggest 'penis-in-vagina' sex and, instead, includes a great deal of language that encourages a queer reading of what Armado saw. Armado's description of the act as 'preposterous', a word that means putting in front what should come behind, raises the specter of sodomy, a term early moderns used to refer not only to same-sex sex acts but also to extra-marital or non-procreative sex between a man and a woman.[16] Though Jaquenetta is apparently pregnant at the play's end and thus seems to have engaged in procreative sex with a man at some point, the arsy-versy connotations of the word 'preposterous' raise the possibility that Armado witnessed anal sex or another non-procreative sex act. The confusion surrounding the child's paternity might also suggest that Jaquenetta has engaged in multiple instances of offstage sex with at least two partners, and, as I have claimed, there is no reason to assume that the 'preposterous event' Armado describes is the same act that made the baby.

Throughout the play, the language of size is part of what lends verbal struggles their homoerotic potency, but this language drops out of descriptions of Costard and Jaquenetta's sexual encounter, creating a knowledge vacuum surrounding their sex act or acts. Valerie Traub embraces just such gaps in knowledge, arguing for enhanced attention to 'the opacity of sexual knowledge' and proposing that we not only challenge our own presumptive knowledge about sex, but approach sex as a knowledge relation that should make us interrogate 'not only what we know, but also how we know it'.[17] Traub analyses a moment in Richard Brome's 1638 play *The Antipodes* in which a female character named Martha expresses 'a yearning simultaneously for knowledge and sex', arguing that Martha can function 'as an heuristic for accessing strategies of knowledge production'.[18] We might approach Costard and Jaquenetta's encounter as well as Armado's narrative of the event through a similar attention to the function and dissemination of sexual knowledge. The play devotes nearly 100 lines in its first scene to Costard's confession and Armado's letter, and yet, as we have seen, these two narratives say next to nothing about what actually happened; sexual knowledge and its transmission remain opaque. Armado's verbosity and strange word choice as he describes the 'obscene and most preposterous event' are typical of his character and might indicate his jealousy, rage or embarrassment at what he has witnessed, but they might also suggest in this instance that he has just learned something new about sex that he is struggling to articulate. Perhaps his wording is not euphemism but rather an attempt to know and express an unfamiliar form of sex.

The gap in knowledge about the 'obscene and most preposterous event' stretches to the play's final scene, in which Jaquenetta's pregnancy is revealed and the paternity of her child contested. As knowledge about sex in the play's first scene remains opaque, so too does knowledge about pregnancy and the reproductive consequences of any particular sexual act in its final scene as Costard and Armado dispute Armado's paternity. Costard interrupts the performance of the Nine

Worthies to deliver the news that Jaquenetta is pregnant and accuse Armado, and Armado reacts defensively, denying the accusation and threatening Costard (5.2.673–5). The exchange quickly takes a violent turn, with Costard and Armado preparing to duel. Here, the duel stands in for the characters' lack of knowledge regarding which particular sex act resulted in the pregnancy. Like the main plot, however, which forestalls marital resolution, this sub-plot reproductive triangle fails to resolve. The news of the Princess's father's death – the same news that halts marriage in the main plot – stops the duel, and the question of the child's paternity is left open. Dorothea Kehler argues that the possibility that Costard is the father, and that he either tricks Armado or Armado willingly accepts care of another man's child, endues the play with a 'radical subtext' in which 'not only are male/female and menial/non-menial binarisms reversed but also the stigmas attaching to cuckoldry and female promiscuity disappear.'[19] Kehler is certainly right in arguing for the radical potential of Costard's paternity, but I would expand her claims to consider the radical queer potential of unresolved or dual paternity that endures beyond the end of the play. This seemingly hetero sub-plot, characterized by male-female sex and procreation, ends with a struggle between two male characters both associated with largeness, suggesting that this struggle might be more evenly-matched than the one Berowne imagines having with an alternately small and large Cupid. Costard and Armado's potential interchangeability as large men hints that their struggle might continue without mastery and also speaks to Jaquenetta's potential delight in maintaining two large male suitors as she, too, grows larger in pregnancy. Alternatively, perhaps the two men will not struggle at all but will create a polyamorous family with Jaquenetta and her baby. The queer potential of this family is nearly as expansive as the bodies of those who comprise it.

Love's Labour's Lost concludes with four thwarted aristocratic couplings on the one hand, and an indefinably queer family that materializes out of the chaos of the sub-plot on the other hand. This chapter's analysis of the verbal, physical and social implications of size and its lexicon seeks to make sense of the many erotic alternatives the play offers to monogamous cross-sex bonds and heterosexual teleologies. Attention to size complicates the play's erotic economy, letting us unmoor size and desire from their exclusive connection to gender in order to see new ways of organizing and articulating erotic experience. In this play, size works with gender to provoke desire and produce articulations of desire in which the homoerotic becomes inextricable from the heteroerotic. Whereas size in this analysis most clearly gives us access to male-oriented queer desires, it also allows us to glimpse the Princess's and Jaquenetta's erotic desires and histories and opens new questions about women's desires and sexual knowledge in the play. In these ways, *Love's Labour's Lost* provides a case study for what we stand to gain by considering size in queer analyses of Shakespeare. Attention to size and its lexicon gives us new methods for interrogating embodiment, sex and desire in Shakespeare, in the process broadening the objects of and possibilities for queer analysis in his works.

6

Locating queerness in *Cymbeline*

Stephen Guy-Bray

In some ways, *Cymbeline* might seem like an obvious choice for a queer analysis: its status as relatively obscure and lesser – or even bad – Shakespeare (even in relation to the other romances, now, with the exception of this play, increasingly popular – even *Pericles*!), its focus on disguise, on fractured families, on disobedience at various levels, its frequently tortuous language and its almost crazily elaborate narrative might all seem to make the play inescapably queer. In one of the best essays on this play, Amanda Berry – referring to Dr Johnson's notorious critique of the play – comments that '*Cymbeline* is a staggeringly excessive play'.[1] This excess can be understood as queer (as can the dramatic adverb 'staggeringly'). My interest in this paper is in narrative excess rather than in the play's linguistic excess, although this is remarkable too. As Ros King points out in her book on the play, *Cymbeline* 'has a plot of such complexity that there are some thirty denouements in the final scene, except that they are not revelations to the audience, who know all but one of them already.'[2] Thus – and crucially – it is not merely the case that

the narrative is very complex, but that Shakespeare emphasizes it and in the play's final scene gives us a complexity
that is no longer necessary so that it can only appear like
complexity for its own sake. Both this narrative excess itself
and the remarkable and drawn-out emphasis on this excess in
the entirely excessive final scene are things that we have learnt
to recognize as queer.

On the other hand, the play contains no homoeroticism
and remarkably little homosociality, at least by the standards
of Renaissance drama. The most promising potential site of
homosociality is the relationship between Posthumus and
Iachimo. Still, even in this case the implications of their
relationship remain latent and they get very little time together
on stage. The frequent comparison between Iachimo and Iago
is instructive here: Iago is present throughout the play and
has deep homosocial bonds with Othello and with others,
while Iachimo's role, although crucial to the narrative, is
brief: he has very little more time on stage than is needed
for his narrative function. Perhaps a more promising source
of homoeroticism is suggested by King: 'Belarius and the
boys, aided by the disguised Posthumus, win victory over the
invading Romans in a "narrow lane" by effectively threatening the rape and effeminization of their fellow Britons.'[3]
In this persuasive reading, the spectre of male-male sexuality
plays an important part in the British triumph and produces
an all too familiar image of British masculinity and continental effeminacy. Nevertheless, this spectre is no sooner
invoked than put aside: the image is not taken up in the rest of
the play, nor is it echoed by the other events of the narrative,
and I think it is altogether forgotten in the play's final presentation of the conflict between Britain and Rome.

What is more, I would argue that *Cymbeline* ultimately
reaffirms marriage, the family and the naturalness of the social
hierarchy; or, at least, I would argue that the idea that the play
is socially orthodox is a reading of the play's conclusion that is
easy to defend. The marriage between Imogen and Posthumus
becomes a regular union after having a somewhat uncertain

status throughout the play, primogeniture is re-established and the inherent nobility of the two princes who have been brought up as mountaineers demonstrates that social rank is natural (a point also made in *The Winter's Tale* and *Pericles*, of course). From this point of view, then, it could be argued that the play ranks as one of Shakespeare's more conventional plays. My purpose here is not to settle the questions I have raised in this and the preceding paragraphs: that is, I do not intend to pronounce that *Cymbeline* either is or is not queer Shakespeare (or, at least, queerer than any other of his plays). Instead, I want to use the play to think about the ways in which we define queerness: subject matter, which, as I have shown, does not really apply here, is the most obvious of these, but we should also include the use of language and narrative and the relationship among these and other factors. I want to consider the extent to which what we think of as queerness and what we think of as normativity can coexist.

I'll begin with the issue of identity. In Lee Edelman's influential formulation, queerness is not to be seen as an identity, but rather as something that troubles identities of all sorts.[4] And indeed, identity is arguably the most important issue in *Cymbeline* and is usually troubled. Nancy Simpson-Younger has pointed out that '*Cymbeline* is a play about the construction of identity, but it never seems to have a stable identity itself.'[5] Identities of all sorts are troubled in the play, including the generic identity of the play itself (although this will not be my concern here), so I want now to look at some of the ways in which the play puts identity in question. We could say that the primary source of identity – especially in a patrilineal society and especially at the royal level – is the family, but families in *Cymbeline* are noticeably odd and incomplete. Cymbeline himself, for instance, has only a daughter to inherit his kingdom; his wife is dead and his sons are missing and presumed dead. On the other hand, his wife has a son from her previous marriage. Cloten's existence complicates the royal family and the question of succession; it also puts him and Imogen in a very queer relationship indeed:

he and Imogen are siblings, more or less, but this bond apparently does not rule out the possibility of their marriage: the
only objections to their marriage raised in the play are that
Imogen is already married and that Cloten is unworthy of her.
The fact that they are step-siblings does not seem to bother
anyone in the play.

The character of Posthumus troubles identity even further.
For one thing, his family is even more incomplete than the
British royal family: not only does he, like Imogen, have
two dead brothers (of course, it turns out that his brothers
really are dead), but both his parents are dead as well. In
fact, his father died before he was born and his mother
died at the moment of his birth. In other words, Posthumus
has as little family as it is possible for a person to have.
While Imogen seems to illustrate the ways in which royal
succession can become complicated (certainly a common
enough theme throughout Shakespeare's career), Posthumus
seems to be situated at the very limits of biological possibility.
Furthermore, although marriage is presumed to create a
socially legible and meaningful relationship, his own marriage
to Imogen fails to do this. While the marriage of Imogen and
Posthumus will ultimately be celebrated and reaffirmed by the
play's conclusion, its status throughout the play – especially
since it has not been consummated – makes it difficult to know
exactly what and how it means. Even the possible political
importance of the marriage between a British princess and a
Roman patrician never emerges as an important issue in the
play despite the war between these powers. Finally, for most
of the play what we learn about his character is not encour-
aging, so his emergence as a suitable husband is arguably
problematic.

For most of the play, then, marriage seems to be rather a
queer thing instead of the epitome and guarantee of normalcy.
Berry's persuasive analysis focuses on precisely this fact, and
specifically on the oddness of what she calls 'marriage time' in
the play. Pointing out that Posthumus remains in Britain for
some time after his banishment by Cymbeline and that Imogen

is not punished for this, Berry argues that 'the gap between the past act of banishment and the present not-consequences of it characterize the work of marriage time throughout *Cymbeline*, a temporality produced between performative utterance and the state of being that utterance presumably confers'.[6] This is emphasized in the gap between the representation of the couple on stage and the summary we are given in the opening exposition. As Heather Love suggests in her essay on *Macbeth* (published, like Berry's, in *Shakesqueer*), 'Given the fact that the time of the family and the time of the couple define time itself, we might understand deviations from normative time – rather than any specifically sexual form of transgression – as queer'.[7] The queerness of the marriage of Imogen and Posthumus, who are, after all, the play's central couple, queers the whole world of the play. The shifting meaning of their marriage bond, the difficulty involved in figuring out its weight in the world of the play, makes the play's meaning as a whole difficult to determine. The marriage of a princess, especially of one who is the heir to the kingdom as Imogen is at the beginning of the play, should be firmly a part of dynastic time, but this appears to be impossible in *Cymbeline*.

Identity does not only inhere in the descent and pedigree enabled by marriage, however. In a society like Shakespeare's, with its sumptuary laws, clothing also marks – and may even establish – the rank that is a basic part of Renaissance identity.[8] *Cymbeline* has an unusual focus on clothes and accessories, particularly in relation to Cloten and Imogen. In Imogen's case, the primary accessories are the bracelet Posthumus gives her as a token of his love and the ring he wagers on her chastity – both, in their perfect circularity, attesting to the untouched vagina that Imogen, the wife who is still a virgin, must simultaneously embody and represent in order to keep Posthumus' favour. This dual function is, I think, precisely the problem in *Cymbeline*. The point is that embodiment is not enough in the world of the play (and perhaps not in any world): as the play demonstrates numerous

times, that which is true in the body must also be represented
so that it is apparent to sight. To some extent, it is in the turn
to representation made so frequently throughout the play that
Cymbeline is queerest. The action of the play serves (however
temporarily) to separate embodiment and representation and
to substitute (again, temporarily) a queer world of ever-
shifting relationships, statuses and genders for the patrilineal
descent on which the world of the play depends.

The representation is seen in clothes as well as in jewellery,
of course. The most obvious example is Imogen's disguise as
a boy, but more interesting to me in the context of this paper
is her insult to Cloten and its consequences. Fairly early on,
Imogen, at the end of her patience after Cloten's attempts at
courtship, compares him unfavourably to her husband:

> His mean'st garment,
> That ever hath but clipp'd his body, is dearer
> In my respect, than all the hairs above thee,

$$(2.3.134-6)[9]$$

The insult rankles, as we see when Cloten repeats it after she
leaves. Later on, when he goes in pursuit of her he actually
wears Posthumus' garments; and when he faces Guiderius,
whom he takes to be a peasant, he attempts to overawe him
with these borrowed clothes:

> Thou villain base,
> Know'st me not by my clothes?
> GUIDERIUS   No, nor thy tailor, rascal,
> Who is thy grandfather: he made those
>   clothes,
> Which (as it seems) makes thee.

$$(4.2.80-3)$$

Both men are right: Cloten's borrowed clothes do accurately
show his noble rank, but as Guiderius points out, Cloten's

nobility inheres only in the clothes. For Imogen, while Cloten is of high status, he is not Posthumus and can never replace him. For Guiderius, Cloten's high status is both inauthentic and beside the point.

Of course, Guiderius does not know Posthumus at this point, but he accurately estimates – or diagnoses – the difference between what Cloten represents and what he embodies. In one of the oddest moments in this very odd play, Imogen shows less discernment, however. When she wakes out of the trance into which the drugs have put her, she sees Cloten's headless body and makes a mistake that is very nearly fatal:

> A headless man? The garments of Posthumus?
> I know the shape of's leg: this is his hand:
> His foot Mercurial: his Martial thigh:
> The brawns of Hercules.
>
> (4.2.308–11)

Imogen slips from representation, in accurately recognizing her husband's clothes, to embodiment, insofar as she infers that it is her husband's headless body that she sees.[10] It is a queer error, and one that threatens to undermine the union of representation and embodiment that Shakespeare must bring about if the play is to end happily. Cloten is in many ways the crucial character from this point of view, as the contrast between his high status and his extraordinarily low-grade nature would appear to indicate a serious problem with *Cymbeline*'s social hierarchy. This problem is solved both by the fact that he is only the king's stepson and by his death. That it is Guiderius who kills him is itself significant, as the split between representation and embodiment is enacted in this scene by the difference between Cloten, who enjoys the rank of prince without deserving it, and Guiderius, who is inherently princely but enjoys none of the benefits of that rank.

Representation is a problem elsewhere in *Cymbeline*, as well. The best example of these problems (or, at least, the example that sets the greater part of the play's plot in motion) undoubtedly arises in Iachimo's visit to the chamber of the sleeping Imogen, or rather in his representation of this visit to Posthumus. First he describes her jewels, which he employs as testimony to Posthumus that he really was in her chamber. As Katherine Gillen has pointed out, however, Iachimo's sense of what representation means is mistaken: 'Iachimo has misrepresented the proper relationship between Innogen's chastity and her jewels. He reconfigures what should be a relationship of signification, with the jewelry representing but not replacing Innogen's value, as a commercial relationship of exchange, with Innogen's chastity presented as a fungible commodity'.[11] Like Imogen in the scene in which she discovers the headless corpse, Iachimo is mistaken not in what he sees but in the conclusion he draws from what he sees. His theory of representation is that it forms part of a general and economic system of exchange, which leads him to regard women's sexuality as only an element in this system. In contrast, Imogen jumps to the wrong conclusion based on evidence that should not be regarded as conclusive. These two errors can be seen as paradigmatic for the way in which Shakespeare presents representation in *Cymbeline*. The process of looking at something and making a judgement based on it, something that is obviously essential for theatre audiences, is queered in the play.

The most important example of embodiment for Iachimo and for Posthumus (and, indeed, for the play as a whole) is Imogen's birthmark, which Iachimo sees when he has himself entered her bedchamber while she sleeps:

> On her left breast
> A mole cinque-spotted: like the crimson drops
> I' th' bottom of a cowslip. Here's a voucher,
> Stronger than ever law could make.

> (2.2.37–40)

Throughout this scene we see Iachimo carefully making mental note of everything he sees in the chamber, but it is

the birthmark that he sees as decisive. And it turns out that
he is right. When Iachimo returns to Italy and describes
the chamber and Imogen's jewellery in considerable detail,
Posthumus continues to doubt his word, but the mention of
the birthmark changes everything:

> You do remember
> This stain upon her?
>
> POSTHUMUS   Ay, and it doth confirm
> Another stain, as big as hell can hold,
> Were there no more but it.

(2.4.138–41)

For Posthumus, the body is a kind of evidence that cannot lie.

Posthumus is wrong, as are Iachimo and Imogen, but it
is easy to be wrong in *Cymbeline*, a play that queers our
sense of what dramatic representation means. I have already
mentioned Berry's point about the discrepancy between what
we learn from the (unusually long) exposition at the beginning
of the play and what we actually see on stage; other examples
can be found throughout the play. Nor are these discrepancies
restricted to the audience. For instance, Bruce Smith notes
that at one point 'The onstage spectators *see* Posthumus strike
to the ground a man he takes to be a traitor; the onstage
audience *hears* a different story from Posthumus's servant
Pisanio'.[12] This split between what we see and what we hear
– the two modes of dramatic representation – is crucial to the
play. In fact, Smith suggests that 'the real issue in the final
scene of *Cymbeline*' is 'seeing versus speaking'.[13] Given that
there is no real suspense left in the plot (at least for us; the
characters are still in the dark), he has a point. For me, the
implications of this point are highly significant. In so often
and so decisively divorcing what we see and what we hear,
Shakespeare prevents us from seeing dramatic representation
as something that is relatively unproblematic for the audience
and forces us to consider representation separated from what
it represents.

In making the two modes of dramatic representation non-self-identical, Shakespeare queers representation in *Cymbeline* and makes it the focus in much of the play. Jeremy Lopez has argued that this focus on representation is to some extent typical of Renaissance drama: he writes that 'language, character, action become, rather than the subject of representation, sites for admiring the act of representation itself'.[14] But while it is certainly the case that representation in Renaissance plays often appears to be doing much more than simply conveying facts or emotions, representation emerges as the subject of *Cymbeline* to an extent that is unusual and, I think, unprecedented.[15] In this play, we are certainly invited to admire the act of representation, but we are also reminded again and again that we cannot be sure either of exactly what is represented or of whether the visual or the verbal mode of representation is to be regarded as more trustworthy. A useful comparison is with the Dover cliff scene in *King Lear*. There is an obvious difference between what Edgar describes and what we see, but we are never in doubt that what we see can be trusted. In contrast, *Cymbeline* returns obsessively, over and over, to doubt. The queerness of representation is not something that the play can ever overcome.

Furthermore, although we all know that Posthumus is wrong in his reaction to Iachimo's speech, the play does endorse the idea of the body as a voucher – or, to put the point in the terms I have been using in this essay, it endorses the idea that embodiment trumps representation. A particularly good example is provided by the identification of the two lost sons of Cymbeline in the last scene. Belarius, whenever possible, has tirelessly pointed out that these young men act like princes and not like the mountaineers they appear to be: that is, they embody their royal status instead of, or to a greater extent than, their humble upbringing. Confirmation of their status is also found in the immediate emotional connection (highly stressed in the play) between the princes and the boy who will turn out to be not only a woman but also their sister. But in order to be accepted as princes, their embodiment must be represented to Cymbeline himself. Belarius begins with the younger son:

> he, sir, was lapped
> In a must curious mantle, wrought by th' hand
> Of his queen mother, which for more probation
> I can with ease produce.

(5.5.361–4)

The proof that the supposed Cadwal is actually Arviragus, second in line to the throne, can be established by a piece of representation, a garment like those that deceived Imogen. The turn from false to true representation is a hopeful sign in *Cymbeline*.

For Guiderius, who will after all be the next king, the burden of proof is higher, however. Immediately after the lines I quoted above, and without responding to them, Cymbeline refers to this proof:

CYMBELINE Guiderius had
Upon his neck a mole,
a sanguine star;
It was a mark of wonder.
BELARIUS   This is he,
Who hath upon him still that natural stamp:
It was wise Nature's end in the donation
To be his evidence now.

(5.5.365–9)

When Imogen mistook Cloten's headless corpse for her husband, she let embodiment depend on representation. Now, in this final scene, at the political climax of the play (if not the emotional one) we pass from representation to embodiment once again, but this time not logically – if this corpse wears my husband's clothes, it is my husband – but sequentially – first, the less important son can have his status proved by representation and then the more important son can have his proved by embodiment. What's true of this passage is true of the play's conclusion as a whole: an embodiment that is ultimately heteronormative is paramount, but the queer power of representation is not completely excised.

The importance of this queer representation to *Cymbeline* (despite its triumphant re-establishment of patrilineal descent) can be seen in two aspects of the conclusion. The first of these is the story of Posthumus. It is important to remember that one of Shakespeare's tasks in the conclusion of the play is to make Posthumus a more estimable character after what has been a very shaky start. Part of this task is done through his success at fighting and part through his resignation in the face of death. But what is most important in this connection, I think, is the masque in the penultimate scene. This masque features Posthumus' entire family (i.e. people he has never known and to whom the audience has no connection) and the god Jupiter himself, who puts what he calls a 'tablet' (5.4.109) on Posthumus' chest, after which they all vanish. When Posthumus awakes, he remembers the masque as a dream; the only tangible sign of it is the tablet, which he calls a 'book' (5.4.133). Significantly, he hopes that the tablet or book will not be 'as is our fangled world, a garment / Nobler than that it covers' (5.4.134–5). Everything leads us to see the text as something that embodies the truth, but the shifting terms used for it – as well as the fact that Posthumus is unable to understand it – should be enough to let us know that this text – potentially, as his language suggests, a garment that anyone could wear – is yet another example of queer representation.

The text, now called a 'label' (5.5.431) – or, in other words, either a small part of a garment or an addition to a text (both meanings would have been available to Shakespeare) – is interpreted in the next and final scene by Philarmonus, the court soothsayer, so the meaning is ultimately fixed even if the name is not.[16] The lack of fixity here is significant. As the audience would of course be able to see the text, the use of multiple synonyms, not all of whose connotations can easily be reconciled, would have the effect of keeping the gap between embodiment and representation (literally) front and centre. The main importance of this text is that it ties Posthumus and his marriage to Imogen directly to the restoration of the princes and the prosperity of the realm. On the other hand, that's not saying much. As everyone has recognized, the final scene of *Cymbeline* is crowded with revelations – indeed, far too many and done in far too much detail. The interpretation of the text would not have been missed and really contributes nothing to the play's ending. Sarah Wall-Randell has argued 'The last scene of the play underscores the sense that Posthumus's book represented a false or empty interpretive crux'.[17] Indeed, I would argue that its unimportance is stressed by the fact that it is the final revelation in this crowded scene, coming just before Cymbeline's final speeches. This position might seem like the place of honour, but I think instead that it is anticlimactic and is experienced primarily as yet another delay before the conclusion that has seemed both inevitable and imminent for some time.

The role of Jupiter's text in this concluding scene is part of the second way in which the queerness of representation remains important to *Cymbeline* despite the re-establishment of a patriarchal order that had often seemed to be in jeopardy through the play. Here, I refer to what I see as Shakespeare's foregrounding of telling (rather than showing). This foregrounding begins at the beginning of *Cymbeline*, which features a lengthy scene of exposition. At this late stage in his career, Shakespeare was obviously capable of conveying the information necessary for the spectator more briefly and efficiently, so I think we must see the long and clumsy exposition as a deliberate choice. At the end of the play, telling has gotten entirely out of hand. First, there is the elaborate masque I mentioned above. While masques were undeniably very popular at this point and the inclusion of a masque could arguably be seen as a crowd-pleasing strategy, a comparison with *The Tempest*, written quite soon after *Cymbeline*, is instructive. The masque in that play is part of the marriage ceremony and thus functions as a way to heighten the importance of the scene: it makes perfect dramatic sense. In this case, however, as I have already pointed out, the information is not especially important and the masque feels more like an interruption towards the end of what is already (by Shakespeare's standards) quite a long play.

As should be clear to everyone, the final scene carries the idea of telling to an extreme that could be considered ridiculous.[18] It is generally the case that a play's final scene solves narrative complications, but in the last scene of *Cymbeline* more narrative complications are solved than is strictly necessary and they are solved in much greater detail. At this point, we could speak of a split between the narrative and the way in which it is conveyed. If we paraphrased *Cymbeline*'s narrative, we would have a story about how a family – and not just any family, but the central family of the world of the play – is re-established and both social and political order are safeguarded; if we described the way in which the story is presented, explicated and resolved, we would be obliged to speak of baroque complexity, delay, and what Renaissance people would have called 'ambages'. From my point of view here, I would characterize the narrative as heteronormative and the method of conveying it as queer. Returning to the choice I mentioned in the first paragraph, I would say that the play is thus at once queer and not queer. But perhaps the important choice is not whether we see the *Cymbeline* as queer or not, but rather whether we see the play as an example of how heteronormativity can use queerness for its own purposes, or as an example of how queerness always underpins (and possibly subverts) its other.

7

Desiring H: *Much Ado About Nothing* and the sound of women's desire

Holly Dugan

Late in Shakespeare's *Much Ado About Nothing,* Beatrice and Margaret pun about the orthography of women's desire. This, perhaps, is not all that surprising in a play that mocks the language of love, especially its ornate conventions. Out of tune with her friends, and confessing that she is feeling ill, Beatrice interrupts Margaret and Hero in order to remind her cousin that it is time to leave for her wedding to Claudio: ''Tis almost five o'clock, cousin; 'tis time you were ready. By my troth, I am exceedingly ill. Hey-ho!' (3.4.47–8) Her cryptic exclamation 'hey-ho!' confounds contextual meaning, which Margaret quickly realizes. Recalling the festivities earlier that week, especially Beatrice's quoting of 'Hey-ho for a Husband', a ballad about single women's longing, Margaret queries: hey-ho '[f]or a hawk, a horse, or a husband' (3.4.49)? Expanding on both the song's syntax of desire and Margaret's clever rejoinder, Beatrice replies that hers is a desire '[f]or the letter that begins them all, H' (3.4.50).

Beatrice and Margaret's staccato exchange moves quickly through a host of allusions that draw on diverse sources and seem to require critical explication. Their puns about songs such as 'light of love' and 'Hey-ho for a husband' lead to puns about dancing and being 'light' in the heels, which leads to jokes about dancing and kicking, then animals and breeding, then sexual desire, its aches and itches, and finally circles back to puns about women's honour, all while Hero dresses for her wedding to Claudio. The dramatic irony is overwhelming, the breathy sound of the women's excessive Hs in this scene emphasizing what's about to be lost in the next: honour.

H, the eighth letter of the Roman alphabet, seventh in the Greek, signals a host of meanings, a point that Beatrice cleverly uses to trump Margaret's excessive puns.[1] A majuscule that embodies perfect symmetry, its graphic form mirroring itself, Beatrice's desire for the letter H is curious, marking while also obfuscating any precise meaning. When read silently on the page, her pun, like the letter, doubles back on itself, producing a need for critical explication.

Glossed as an aural pun, editors explain Beatrice's desire for H as a trick of early modern pronunciation.[2] When said aloud, H rhymed either with bodily 'aches' or 'itches' and was thus a homonym of pleasure and pain. As a pun, it focuses not on the object of desire but on its bodily effects, a clever point in this scene that discusses both. But it is one that appears often in early modern literature, fourteen other times in Shakespeare's works, with comic (*The Tempest*, *The Comedy of Errors*) as well as somber effects (*Hamlet*, *The Rape of Lucrece*). Consider, for example, Scarus's pun late in *Antony and Cleopatra*: wounded on his arm, 'bleeding apace', he quips that his wound was 'like a T, / But now 'tis made an H'. The line (both the actor's and the one on his body to which it alludes) draws attention to the physicality of the letter itself, the character's wounds and the actor's body. To make a T an H involves turning it on its side and adding an additional stroke, which may be what happens as Scarus moves and his wound bleeds. But Scarus also puns on the sound of 'H', noting that only now does the 'I' start to 'ache'. Scarus's pun, like Beatrice's, offers H as a cryptic sign of embodied histories, ones both hidden and marked.

In this play, where love is described as a 'turn' to 'orthography', Beatrice's curious desire for H reorients the lexical crux at the heart of the play, pointing towards arcane allusions and marginal characters. Beatrice is, as Ursula quips earlier in the play, capable of 'spelling men backwards', a description that suggests not only witchcraft but also Hebrew and Arabic textual traditions. In love, Beatrice 'turns Turk', converting to a new spatial and social realm, but one in which the co-ordinates of desire are much more complicated. Her H goes both ways.

In this way, Beatrice's desire for H matches my own, signalling a commitment to both the rigour of material history in the past as well as the pleasure in refusing to spell out certain meanings. That Beatrice dwells on this sound matters, I think, particularly if we think of it as part of a much longer history of women's desire, one whose textual trace is less legible in the historical record that has come to define queer historiography.[3] That we cannot know for certain what Beatrice's H sounded like, whether it denoted pleasure or pain, marks it as the kind of literary citation I've come to love, a textual cipher, an ephemeral trace, a juncture of fiction and material history, one that cannot possibly bear the weight of meaning placed upon it, but still beckons for it.

Following both Joel Fineman and Bruce Smith's influential work on the sound of 'O' in early modern drama, Miriam Jacobson's novel work on the links between zero, ciphers and 'o' in early modern poetry, and Jeffrey Masten's paradigm-shifting work on the letter 'Q' in early modern literature, I explore Beatrice's desire for H as both a sound and a letter in this essay. In doing so, I connect it to the textual and theatrical mystery of Margaret's role in the play. Margaret, I argue, explicates, aspirates and frustrates Beatrice's desire for H, providing a complicated model for me on thinking through what can and cannot be spelled out in our histories of sexuality.[4] My goal is thus in line with Masten's call for a queer philology, one that attends to the nuances and arcane particularities of an early modern lexicon of desire. As Masten argues, '[t]here can be no nuanced cultural history of early modern sex and gender without spelling out its terms—for what alternatives do we have?'[5]

Masten's meticulous and inspiring argument demonstrates how a literary love of letters might animate aspects of the history of sexuality that remain barely legible in the textual record. Yet some aspects of this history remain occluded. The problem is summarized succinctly by Valerie Traub: if, as Masten argues, 'the study of sex and gender in historically distant cultures is necessarily a *philological* investigation', then, as Traub asks, 'what might happen when terms refuse to be spelled out?'[6]

The arcane 'historical particularities' of early modern orthography offer a useful way to start; indeed Masten begins his book by reading early modern orthological anxiety about the majuscule letter Q, whose tail (at least in print) exceeds the square space allotted to it. Q, according to early modern orthographers, is exceptional, exceeding its lines and signalling an inability to function (in English and French) without its attendant v.[7]

H is not queer in this way. Indeed, for many early modern orthographers, H is not considered a letter. In George Tory's *Champ Fleury* (1529), for instance, H is only 'l'aspiration', an exhalation or an accent; if it functions as a letter, then it is only through poetic license, a point that French classical scholar Michel Maittaire corroborates 200 years later in his *English Grammar* (1712) along with Samuel Johnson's *Dictionary*.[8] Sidestepping this controversy, Ben Jonson in his *English Grammar* (1640) emphasizes that whatever it is – 'be it a letter or a spirit' – and whatever work it does, it is feminine. He writes:

> H, whether it be a letter or no, hath been examined by the ancients and by some of the Greek party too much

condemned, and thrown out of the alphabet as an aspirate merely … But be it a letter or spirit, we have great use of it in our tongue, both before and after vowels. And though I dare not say she is (as I have her one call her) the "Queen mother of Consonants", "yet she is the life and quickening of c, g, p, s, t, w, or also r when derived from the aspirate Greek rh."[9]

Though Jonson's point is lexical, his claims about H fascinate me, particularly its ability to quicken, aspirate and alter the meaning of other sounds. What work, then, does this queen mother of consonants do in this play and how might we begin to approach its varied textual and sonic meanings?

For me, Beatrice's H animates a problem latent in *Much Ado About Nothing,* namely the textual inconsistencies that centre on the complicated character of Margaret.[10] Margaret is an enigma in the play – both an intimate member of Leonato's household yet also clearly a servant within it, Margaret too easily frustrates claims about the bonds between women in this play. What is her role in the Hero plot? How culpable is she in her betrayal? The play is not clear and at times offers contradictory evidence. But her role is an important one. Articulated in an odd exchange between minor characters, H in *Much Ado* hints at the complex ways in which women related to one another in the past, especially when aspirated on stage.

Merely pronouncing it moves us towards complicated histories, ones rooted in the body. For instance, as one of John Heywood's *An Hundred Epigrams* claims, 'H is worst among letters in the crosse-rowe', for if it is found in 'elbow', 'arm', 'leg' or into 'what place soever', H may 'pike him', concluding: 'Wherever though find ache though shalt not like him.'[11] Piking, or losing oneself, is here imagined as finding 'ache', a pun that works in two ways (at least in early modern pronunciation).[12] It is a pun that Benedict makes as well, warning Margaret that wanton wit is dangerous 'for maids', for it leads to putting pikes in a vice, a sexualized image that is also martial and violent (5.1.20–1).

John Taylor, the water poet, also links the letter H with bodily aches in the 1635 edition of his prose pamphlet *The World Runs on Wheels*: 'Every cart-horse doth know the letter very understandingly; and H hath he in his bones'.[13] Another epigram about 'dolo intimus' does the same, explaining that 'Nor Hauk, nor Hound, nor Hors, those letters hhh, But ach it self, 'tis *Brutus* bones attaches'.[14] H 'it self" attaches not to the aspirated sounds of 'hawk', 'hound' or 'horse', but the embodied pain of aging. Margaret's pun and Beatrice's reply draw on these meanings: H is a sign both of pleasure and of pain.

Yet hearing H is not so easy. As the epigram 'dolo intimus' makes clear (and as any student of phonics quickly learns), H 'itself' functions differently than other letters. Unlike 'A for apple', or 'B for bat', the letter H is *not* pronounced similarly to the sound it signifies (heard in the word 'hat'). Confusingly, one must drop an aspirate sound in order to pronounce the letter correctly: 'aitch'. This trick of the aspirated and un-aspirated H is a historical irony, one steeped in the variances of language transmission across cultures and time.[15] Unlike, say, the dictionary definition of the letter F, n. ('the letter, and the sound it represents'), the definition of H, n., involves alphabetical orientation and complicated etymologies.[16]

It is perhaps too much to claim that the lost aspirate can be found through historicism, even one that models itself on a queer philology. Yet original pronunciation, like original staging practices, aspires to rediscover just that. How did an early modern actor say Beatrice's line? How do we? Original pronunciation holds out the tantalizing prospect of aspirating the dropped Hs of history, especially those that might breathe new life into old lines, a point that most critics (and most teachers like myself) emphasize when teaching *Much Ado About Nothing*. To hear the pun in the title, for example, is to engage with both early modern philology and pronunciation. 'Nothing', editors gloss, was a homonym of 'noting'.[17] And what kind of queer philology does she reveal when Beatrice turns orthographer?

Pronounced in early modern English, the play becomes *Much Ado About Noting,* the dropped h allowing us to weave the play's complex allusions into a compellingly resonant theme, one that makes a certain amount of sense even to those reading or watching the play for the first time. The play's emphasis on notes, both written love letters as well as the musical notes that animate its many songs, connects with the broader cultural emphasis on noting that the play stages; who notes what about whom matters in Messina, whether it's a beloved's beauty (in Act 1) or her constancy (in Act 4). Editors emphasize that this noting is gendered and misogynistic: 'nothing' is visually linked to 'no thing', unlocking yet another pun in the title, one that drew upon the slang term for women's vaginas. One only needs to cross-reference similar puns made by Hamlet and Iago to see how early modern misogyny is embedded in this 'nothing'.

Yet this historical insistence on airy nothing becomes hazier when we dwell on its silent h, an absence that widens the gap between the misogyny of the play, imaginatively located in the past, and its resonance with misogyny in the present. We can't know for sure how H sounded. Early modern H and its aspirated and unaspirated sounds at times seems to function much in the same way as modern H does – a dropped H usually marks class and education (such as when Bottom pronounces 'Hercules' as 'Ercules' in *Midsummer Night's Dream*) but so too does insistence on its pronunciation establish educational credentials (such as Holofernes, in *Loves Labours Lost,* who insists on adding an h to *abominable*). Likewise, H rhymes with both 'ake' and 'aitch', a point that the critical explication of Caliban's line in the *Tempest* – 'I'll rack the with old cramps, fill all thy bones with Aches ...' (1.2.433) – brings home. The meter is better if Caliban's 'aches' rhymes with aitches; and Boswell, in making a case for this pronunciation, uses Beatrice's joke in *Much Ado* as evidence for this.

Other times, its arcane pronunciation seems only to emphasize how much time has passed. Original pronunciation has the potential to aspirate some lost meanings; whether we can hear them is more complicated. For instance, one of the hardest aspects for modern audiences engaging with original pronunciation performances are the linguistic contextual cues. In his work on staging a performance of *Romeo and Juliet* with an emphasis on original pronunciation, David Crystal noted that H was particularly tricky: knowing when and where to drop the h signalled in multiple ways, locating a character within complex social co-ordinates, including provenance, education, class status and class mobility. It simply wasn't clear which characters would drop their Hs and why.[18]

Likewise, we may hear H differently. It is possible, for instance, that H is a modern phenomenon, a claim that Helge Kökeritz makes in *Shakespeare's Pronunciation*. Noting that West-Midland dialects included a notable amount of dropped h's, Kökeritz hypothesizes that Shakespeare would have dropped his hs more than not. London-based actors, Kökertiz argues, would have done so as well. Pointing towards Shakespearean puns like 'art-heart, eat-hate, heir apparent-here apparent, here-year, and perhaps Hiren-Irene-hiring', Kökertiz argues that the evidence suggests a weak articulation of initial hs, though he notes that it's near impossible to know for sure how these puns were articulated in the past or whether this was a localized phenomenon.[19]

Margaret, for instance, hears in Beatrice's cry of 'Hey ho' a number of potential cultural references. Her quick response suggests possible ways to finish the sentence, all of which emphasize the aspirated sound: '*h*awk, *h*orse, *h*usband'. H patterns as an opening consonant in all three words, blurring distinctions between their different vowel sounds. To pronounce Margaret's list of aitches is to pun on disappearing differences.

It is also to engage with complex cultural tropes that shape the articulation itself. Is Beatrice mimicking the sound of a falconer, whose cry of 'hey-ho' is a key part of taming the falcon to serve its master? Is she positioning herself as the tamer and not the tamed? Does her cry of 'hey-ho' for a horse mimic the salacious and diabolical calls of witches, marking her desire for diabolical mastery? Or is she echoing the popular ballad 'hey-ho for a husband', a cry linked to the longing of a sad, single woman? Margaret's quick reply (with its own breathy articulation) offers a number of complicated ways to finish the sentence.

As an aural pun, Beatrice's pronunciation of desire for 'H' shifts the sounds of the scene, away from Margaret's excessive assonance in her emphasis of *h*awk, *h*orse and especially *h*usband. Just prior to Beatrice's entrance, Margaret mocks Hero's 'heavy heart' by connecting it to desire to feel a 'heavy' husband (3.4.22–5). While Hero finds her joke about the weight of love obscene – 'Fie upon the! Art not ashamed?' – Margaret refuses such shame, suggesting that it is only 'bad thinking' that 'wrests true speaking' (32). She asks Hero, and the audience, breathily: 'is there *h*arm in the *h*eavier for a *h*usband'?

Margaret seems to know that the answer is yes. In this minor scene, she puns about not just the objects and effects of desire, but also its articulation. Margaret is quick-witted; too often, she is ignored. Beatrice's playful foreclosing of textual expli-cation, shortening both the sentence and the word that names her desire, produces a different kind of pleasure, one rooted in speaking and hearing words. Malapropisms, homonyms and word play abound in *Much Ado About Nothing,* as does slander; the pleasure of noting may also be a revelry in nothingness, the airy breath of language that provides the tenuous connection between Beatrice and Benedict, just as it undoes the bond between Claudio and Hero. Margaret seems to know this, spelling out what some refuse to hear.

Beatrice's brilliant and short rebuke refuses such wordplay. Not to be bested, Margaret interprets Beatrice's desire for H as a sound as well as a sign that she has 'turned Turk', converting from a spinster into a lover of Benedict. No longer imagined as a witch with the power to 'spell him backward' (3.1.61), Beatrice is now a renagado, converting for love.[20] The metaphorical implication of this particular phrase suggests not only a profound shift in orientation,

marked by religious conversion, but also, potentially, a performance style. In early modern travel writing, the aspirated H
sound was a sonic marker of ethnic difference, especially of
religious others too easily categorized as 'barbarous'.[21] Pietro
Anghiera, for instance, emphasizes that the inhabitants of
Hispaniola 'breath out these aspirations *ha, he, hi, ho* as the
Hebrewes and Arabians are to pronounce theirs', that is, 'with
open mouths and shaking breasts'.[22] Rerouting Beatrice's
desire for H back into the gulling plot of the play, Margaret
connects Beatrice to a histrionic performance style, one linked
with barbarous others.[23] Confused, Beatrice questions her
meaning. Margaret replies, continuing the alphabet/homonym
play from airy Hs to empty Is and Ayes: 'Nothing I, but God
sends everyone their heart's desire' (3.4.54).

That it is Margaret, and not Beatrice, who aspirates the
most in this scene is ironic: if Beatrice's desire for H marks a
textual crux, Margaret's airy nothing here threatens to upend
the play itself, marking not only important textual incon-
gruities, but also plot holes. What does she desire and why is
she invested in Beatrice's sigh? What kind of character is she?

We might, for instance, read her as a female analogue to
Don John, a character who is outside of the romantic plot, yet
can interpret its narrative clearly and more easily than others
within it. Margaret knows there is no sound of H in honour,
a point that soon damns Hero. And so does Don John; merely
pronouncing her name – 'Leonato's *Hero*, your *Hero*, every
man's *Hero*' – is enough to alter Claudio's perception of
her honour.[24] Likewise, the assonance of Don Pedro in the
accusation scene is striking:

> see *h*er, *h*ear *h*er, at *th*e hour last night
> Talk with a ruffian at *h*er chamber-window,
> Who *h*ath, indeed, like a most liberal villain,
> Confess'd the vile encounters they *h*ave *h*ad
> A *th*ousand times in secret.
>
> (3.5.10; emphasis mine)

This is part of the proof that damns Hero. Don Pedro's aspirated, angry exhalations animate the missing scene but also link it to a chain of others.

Margaret's Hs rather than Beatrice's have come back to haunt Hero. But Margaret is no plain-dealing villain like Don John, nor is she a 'liberal' one like Borachio. Rather, she is a bit of a textual cipher, so much so that some critics argue that her character's inconsistences – her sudden appearance during the masque ball (when additional women characters are needed) and her notable absence at Hero's wedding – reveal more about Shakespeare's writing process then any theme of the play.[25] Like other 'ghost characters' in the play, Margaret suggests that Shakespeare may have shifted the plot as he was developing it. For example, Hero's mother, Innogen, is mentioned in stage directions for Acts 1 and 2 in both the Quarto (1600) and Folio (1623) editions of *Much Ado,* but she seems to have been wholly forgotten by Act 3, and it's hard to imagine what her reaction would be to Hero's humiliation in Act 4. It's hard to imagine how a director might stage her.[26]

Most editions (from Lewes Theobald's onwards) erase her, 'tidying up' the text.[27] The same is true for Leonato's nameless 'kinsman', whose presence is equally confusing. Some editors interpret Balthasar as this kinsman, but as Stanley Wells quips, such interpretations only reveal how far we are willing to go to assume 'that the play is not itself confused'.[28]

Margaret functions in this way: she and Ursula suddenly appear during the masque sequence of 2.1, though no mention is made of their entrance.[29] Likewise, her role in the plot is equally confusing: a minor character, one that is essential to the Hero plot, she seems both intimately at home in Leonato's household and not fully welcome in it. Her absence at the wedding scene for which she helps her mistress dress seems all the more striking, as does her silence afterwards. In his essay on Shakespeare's use of his source materials, literary critic Allan Gilbert begins with a simple question, one that I have often pondered with my students and one that critics link to the play's defect in the plot: 'In *Much Ado About Nothing,* when Claudio rejects Hero, why does not Margaret tell the truth'?[30]

Though she is absent in the immediate accusation, one imagines that it would not be hard, narratively speaking, to summon Margaret and clarify what happened. The public humiliation that Claudio and Don Pedro stage at Hero's wedding along with Leonato's subsequent private attack on his daughter certainly would warrant a response. But Margaret remains silent, offering no easy solution: rather, the constables of the watch and their bumbling leader Dogberry track down Margaret's lover, Borachio, who in a fit of conscience confesses (both the plot and his love for Margaret). In the absence of plot, we get dramatic comedy.

In a play that stages the ways that Hero both is and is not 'the sign and semblance of honor', what is Margaret? Michelle Dowd, for instance, describes her as 'a substitute and, ultimately a scapegoat for her mistress'.[31] Although Hero is ultimately exonerated from the textual shame of slander, Margaret is not. Leonato's final words on the matter pronounce her culpable: 'Margaret was in some fault for this, / Although against her will, as it appears / In the true course of all the question' (5.4.4–6).

Like Innogen, Margaret's evolution from Shakespeare's source materials seems to suggest clues about the development of the play. Matteo Bandello's *La Prima Parte de le Novelle* (1554), which may have provided Shakespeare with the Hero-plot as well as the setting of Messina, does not involve a disguised female servant. Rather, the Hero character (Finicia) is undone by an elaborate ruse devised by the Don John character (Girondo), involving a perfumed servant (Borrachio) making bold claims that are overheard by the Claudio character (Sir Timbreo). Shakespeare's elaboration of Bandello's plot included adding Margaret, though her culpability in the play is less clear than in the source materials he drew upon. Critics compare Margaret, for instance, with her literary antecedents – Delinda in Ariosto's *Orlando Furioso*, Pyrene in Spenser's *Faerie Queene* – in order to emphasize what is uniquely Shakespearean about the play (most notably, the Beatrice and Benedict sub-plot), but also Margaret's hazy guilt.

In Shakespeare's source material, this episode is presented more 'directly and forcibly', and there is no question about her character's culpability.[32] In the fifth canto of Ariosto's *Orlando Furioso,* for instance, Dalinda, a servant who is much poorer than her mistress, Generva, understands that her lover Polynesso desires her mistress for her beauty and for her social status; at his request, she dresses in Generva's clothes, and welcomes him into her mistress's bedchamber purportedly to help him over his love for Generva through sexual role-playing. Dalinda is unaware that her lover has duped her; when given the chance, she confesses her role in deceiving Generva's betrothed.[33] Likewise Spenser's plot elaborates on the role of the maid. Whereas Dalinda wears her mistress's clothes to please her mate, Spenser's Pyrene does so to please herself. As Alwin Thaler summarized: 'Spenser's Pyrene is less obtuse than Ariosto's Dalinda, less blameworthy for her part in the deceit, and less disproportionately obtrusive in the action. In all this she anticipates Shakespeare's Margaret'.[34]

For the plot to work, we must believe that, like Dalinda, Margaret is willing to engage in such sexual role-playing with Borachio. But how much or what exactly this involves is unclear. Shakespeare's play references too many, yet also not enough details. One's left hunting for clues in the text itself. Borachio's seduction of Margaret is mentioned no less than five times: Borachio's initial boast to Don John (2.2.44), Don John's baiting of Claudio (3.2.101–2), Borachio's boast of what happened to Conrade (3.3.138–45), Don Pedro's accusation of Hero (4.1.88–94) and finally Borachio's confession to Claudio (5.1.221–34). Read together, they suggest strikingly different narratives of what happened. Does Borachio woo Margaret in Hero's clothes from the ground like in Ariosto's tale? Does he merely enter the room, pretending that he is welcomed by a lover as in Bandello's novella? Shakespeare's play is unclear.

The critical reception of Margaret has varied over time. For some, Margaret's willingness to wear her mistress's clothes is plausible, especially since, in the words of David Bevington, Shakespeare 'mitigates' the 'kink-iness' latent in Dalinda's plot.[35] Likewise, Alwin Thaler concludes that for all of her 'spicy talk', there is 'no harm in her'.[36] For others, Margaret is culpable and her sex with Borachio was a 'piece of shabby knavery, done in the dark for money'.[37] Some find her plot tangential: Stephen Booth connects Margaret (and her unexpected word play) with the history of performance. Her spontaneous quick-wittedness on the morning of Hero's wedding, for Booth, is part of a pattern in Shakespeare's plays, one in which young women characters routinely and unrelatedly erupt in bursts of quick, mean-spirited exchanges with one another. This, he surmises, may have had more to do with providing young male actors practice in playing the female part before taking on more substantial roles.[38]

Other critics find her essential: Diana Henderson, for example, argues that Margaret's role is key to depicting how women speak to one another in private, an important juxta-position to the male realm of Messina, allowing women to talk amongst themselves.[39] In performance, this may allow the audience to hear a very different Hero, a point that Henderson brings to bear on Branagh's 1993 film, which in Henderson's opinion foreshortens such possibilities by cutting this scene entirely and visually depicting what Borrachio only describes in the playtext.[40] Branagh drops Beatrice's desire for H in order to solve a much bigger textual mystery: how Borachio could pull off this elaborate and ornate ruse. Shot from the perspective of the peeping Claudio, the film stages Borachio's consummation of sex with Margaret. Such visual evidence smooths over textual inconsistencies, a choice that was seen as key to the film's critical success.[41]

Part of the pleasure of *Much Ado About Nothing*, though, is its textuality, especially its wordplay. Dropping Beatrice's H may simplify the plot, and resolve some of the textual incon-sistencies about Margaret, but it does so at a cost, namely erasing any trace of the uneasy and fraught alliances between women, especially when talking about sex. And it's harder to excise H completely: while Claudio penitently mourns at Hero's grave, a song of woe is played, whose refrain asks for help 'to sigh, and groan, / *Heavily, Heavily*', ... 'till death be uttered, / *Heavily, Heavily*' (5.3.17–20).

Much has been said about the queer and not-so-queer aspects of this romantic comedy, especially the ways in which it enacts a seemingly inevitable reproductive futurism even as it renders women replaceable: 'Another *Hero!*' (5.4.62). If, as Benedict argues, the 'world must be peopled', then the play stages the stakes of that social pact. As Ann Pellegrini summarizes, 'the will to be single cannot hold against the call to be married, or be no one at all'.[42] Beatrice and Benedict are gulled into happy coupledom: '*H*ere are our own *h*ands against our *h*earts' (5.4.91). Pellegrini's queer critique focuses on Don John, reading his 'will to be single' as one way to imagine the 'other scenes' and 'other pleasures' seemingly impossible within the social world of the play. Toggling between Sondheim's *Company* and Shakespeare's play, Pellegrini argues for a different way of imagining both queer communities and queer company. H, and other textual ciphers hidden in the play text, including Margaret, may do the same.

Mentioned in the stage directions of 5.4, Margaret is onstage throughout the final scene, including when Leonato pronounces that she was 'in some fault', yet she is silent throughout. This wedding day is markedly different then before. The play offers no clues of Hero's reaction to her presence, or of Beatrice's: all four women are silent, brought onstage by Leonato only to be dismissed again.

When the women return, they are masked; called forth by their paramours, Hero and Beatrice reveal themselves. Unhailed by what Pellegrini terms the 'call to marriage', Margaret and Ursula remain silent throughout the final scene. Indeed, Margaret is silent for most of Act 5, except for some quick-witted, obscene punning with Benedict in 5.2 about sonnets and sex, punning on her social position in Leonato's household and the implicit social effects of marriage on one's station in life ('why shall I always keep below the stairs') a point that resonates rather ominously since she has, indeed, ascended them in order to play the part of Hero.

Leonato's questioning of her, especially her culpability in impersonating Hero, is left for another day. The play ends without clarifying whether she was aware of Borachio's plan or not (or whether either of these couples will last). Instead, it offers us a theatrical spectacle. Calling for the music that will end the play on a comic note, Benedict asks for a dance before 'we are married, that we may lighten our own hearts and our wives' heels' (5.4.115–17). That he echoes Margaret's previous pun about heavy hearts and heavy husbands is perhaps a coincidence, but I prefer to interpret it as a sign that, somehow, he has heard the women of the play, and how they speak to one another. Beatrice's desire for H and Margaret's ability to aspirate it does not clearly animate an alternative orthography of love. But if we listen closely, we may hear in Benedict's 'halting sonnet' more than just a 'hard' rhyme attuned to normative desire and misogyny. Its pronouncement might contain a queer exhalation that's hard to explain, but equally hard to dismiss.

8

'Two lips, indifferent red': Queer styles in *Twelfth Night*

Goran Stanivukovic

Queer style is colloquially understood to be about excess, breaking a code and 'camp'. It instantiates a performance which associates desire with spectrality and it facilitates re-examining history from a queer lens, while also being a source of visual and aural pleasure. In literature, style is a material and formal property of a text. In art, it is 'material-istic incarnation' and an instance of history.[1] Ernst Gombrich's idea of style as a feature of art and of art analysis is of use to a philological exploration of style in drama, which is the subject of this essay, because style viewed as a formal feature opens up the possibility to think about the materiality of language as an incarnation which the theatre of the body and desire expresses. The Elizabethans paid attention to the material weight of language as an oral-aural phenomenon both in theory and in literary and dramatic practice. Shakespeare responded to this affiliation in his drama: 'Shakespeare's witty

exploitation of the sound and weight of words suggests that
... the reification of language is a virtue, that stressing the
materiality of the word is one of his principal goals, and that
consciousness of its sensory properties unites the audience in a
common experience'.[2] In *Twelfth Night*, in which 'words are
very rascals', words can be turned inside and out, can make
things wholesome or wanton at a whim, and can make things
understandable at the same time that they strip things of all
meaning (3.1.11–24). It is no accident then that Feste sees his
role not as fool but as a 'corrupter of words' (3.1.24–35), for
words can be played with, toyed with, twisted and turned to
make something material before the audience's very eyes.

The materiality of language is inextricable from the materiality of the body that speaks it, and from the means by which
that body is represented. Style and body have a long history
of association.

Early modern writers and theorists were closely bound by
the notion of style as linguistic materiality. Constituent of
early modern theories of poetry, for early modernists, style
represented a choice and arrangement of words and phrases
in the first instance. Political, philosophical and ideological
meanings of style in poetry came second in early descriptions
of style. For instance, the late sixteenth-century theorist of
poetry, William Scott, advises the poets among his contemporaries to 'consider that to the coupling and framing of style
goes the words as the matter and the connection or composition of these words in sentences and clauses as the form, in
both which need diligent choice in the poet'.[3] In keeping with
Cicero's advice about style in *De Oratore* (3.31.125),[4] fullness
of style (*copia verborum*) was equally important as fullness of
matter (*copia rerum*). The materiality of the parts of language
that make up style is also the central idea in Puttenham's
definition of style – itself stylistically sonorous definition –
'a constant and continual phrase or tenor of speaking and
writing', being 'of words, speeches, and sentences together a
certain contrived form and quality'.[5] The idea that style was
made up of small and large linguistic units was ingrained, not

only in the early theory of poetic development, but in poetic practice as well. This sense of style that was not only a part of rhetoric in the practice of teaching young boys to write and speak effectively and persuasively, but that was also understood to be a vehicle which communicates meaning, alerts a critic of queer style to the fact that sexual meaning is both embodied in, and produced at, the level of language itself.[6] Shakespeare's dramatic and non-dramatic poetry shows that the rhetoric of persuasion is also the rhetoric of passion, and thus gives new force to the material weight and presence of words and the styles used to frame them. Scott highlights that 'coupling' is essential to the practice of style, already presaging that intermingling is both the venue for and the goal of stylistic performance.

I propose that queer style emulates as well as embodies queer meaning in *Twelfth Night* in a way that preserves a memory of time when desire was not determined by sexual dichotomies. I share Carla Freccero's notion of 'queerness understood as a certain effect 'in and of language'.[7] The effect that a style produces is a difficult and slippery notion to locate with surety, especially when those would be receivers of the language addressed to them are either historical subjects that left no records of such an impact of language upon them, or because effect as such can be considered too subjective to lead to universal conclusions. But a formal approach to the queerness of language uncovers directions in which language operates in order to produce desires, just as – and this is a feature of *Twelfth Night* that stands out – linguistic parsing can show that desires also produce language.

As a formal and materialist mode of expression, language forms queer style, a subject to which queer literary theory has recently directed some of its critical acuity. Kevin Ohi's idea of the 'queerness of style'[8] that emerges from his nuanced close readings of the language of Henry James and Jeffrey Masten's approach to the history and historiography of queer sexuality as a 'detailed study of the terms and related rhetorics that early modern English culture used to inscribe bodies, pleasures, affects, sexual acts and, to the extent we can speak of these, identities', investigation, that is, which he calls 'queer philology'.[9] Queer early modern critics have practiced the semiotics of sexuality, because modern critics' textual encounters with early modern sexualities has inevitably been through language and through the unpacking and decoding of the erotic meaning hidden from us by the archives. But 'queer philology' sharpens our sense of the depth and extent of those meaning, by revealing historical instantiations of small, isolated and diverse linguistic and verbal instances in print and in rhetoric. Thinking about queer style in Shakespeare's romantic comedy entails, in fact, a philological process of uncovering layers of erotic signification in this play.

In his assessment of sexual meaning expressed in terms of sensual experience in *Twelfth Night*, Bruce Smith points out that 'Queer theory … is concerned with what comes *after* words, with the arbitrariness of language, the failure of words to match the realities they purport to name, even as the speakers of a given language use those words to construct personal identities and outlaw certain forms of sexual behavior'.[10] Feste's aforementioned discourse on words with Viola in 3.1 serves as a reminder of such arbitrariness and of such failures. This essay on *Twelfth Night*, however, is engages with lexical and semantic properties as carriers of erotic meaning and conduits of desire. If words come *before* queer theory, as Smith defines queer theory as a field of theoretical inquiry, then queer style manifests openly how those words produce meaning in the first place that makes it possible to grasp them as material instances that queer theory claims for its own arguments. This essay explores the role desire plays in the philological composition of certain passages and, crucially, how desire shapes the literary.

Queer style and erotic desire

One of the most remarkable plays in which cross-gendered casting creates illusions of desire and attraction in Shakespearean drama, *Twelfth Night* has elicited much analysis of the body as a signifier for the sexuality and desire released by the transvestite theatre.[11] The emphasis on the cross-dressed body of a boy actor playing a female part at the heart of the romance plot characterized by miraculous turns of events has led Stephen Greenblatt to observe – in an intriguing and perhaps unintentional play on words – that 'The play's delicious complications follow from the emotional turbulence that Viola's transformation [to Cesario] engenders'.[12]

Explorations of such 'delicious' moments have been taken up by critics in formulating arguments about the engendering of love and erotic desire. As Valerie Traub has pointed out, the transvestite theatre of *Twelfth Night* has offered 'literary critics an initial point of access to the textualization of homoerotic desire'.[13] Writing along the lines of Traub's argument, David Orvis has captured the critical polemics about the operation of desire produced by cross-dressing in *Twelfth Night*, stating that 'For feminist and queer critics, the important debate is not whether transvestism instantiates homoerotic desire, but rather how this homoerotic desire operates in a play that attempts, or at least gestures towards, heterosocial marital closure'.[14] Such debates are further complicated by the play's actual ending, which calls for marriage without dramatizing it, which opens up the possibility of Malvolio refusing to bring the captain holding Viola's 'maid's garments' out of 'durance' (5.1.269–70), and which leaves one genuinely wondering whether the 'solemn combination[s]' called for by Orsino will ever actually take place (5.1.373); in fact, what closure is provided may be hinted at by Orsino closing the play still calling Viola by the name of Cesario. Yet neither homoerotic desire so presented or the heterosexual marital closure as suggested in this comedy could be discerned without considering how both are further by the verbal style that blurs boundaries between sameness and difference, that shatters the illusion of heterosexual bonding leading to marriage, and that determines identities, not via, but with the linguistic terms themselves. In other words, the queer style of *Twelfth Night* is both an audible and linguistic property of the play. As such, it marks an entry into the body. It is not the body itself that produces the style of its representation, but the verbal style that makes an entry into the body.

What do we make of the wooing in 1.5? This first encounter between Viola-Cesario and Olivia illustrates more expressly and more complexly than other stage encounters in the play the range of emotional and erotic meanings created by language in *Twelfth Night*. Is Viola-Cesario's speech only 'something rehearsed and insincere'? Is this scene about '[m]utual feminine curiosity to see [Olivia's] competition with Orsino, or for ... more subjectively erotic reasons'?[15] What kind of erotic reasons might be implied? The scene raises more questions than critics have raised thus far. A boy actor playing a young woman (Viola) playing a male youth (Cesario) already creates confusion by virtue of this double act of transvestism and at the moment in the scene at which a delayed entry of Viola-Cesario is accompanied by the verbal excesses and peculiarities that accompany this entry. 'Most radiant, exquisite and unmatchable beauty' (1.5.165), says Viola-Cesario, as she enters the stage. She continues: 'I would be loath to cast away my speech, for, besides that it is excellently well penned, I have taken great pains to con it. Good beauties, let me sustain no scorn: I am very comptible, even to the least sinister usage' (1.5.167–71). If Feste is the play's 'corrupter of language', Viola serves as its controller, and it is her words, as much as her 'outside', that have charmed both Olivia and audiences (2.1.18). The persuasive effectiveness of Viola-Cesario's speech engendered in language – the speech is linguistically self-referential – is aimed at winning Olivia's interest in Viola as a prospective servant, not as a desirable cross-dressed body. But the desire that fuels this intention exceeds its purpose; its doubles as an affect produced by the cross-dressed and cross-gendered body, even if its full signification and direction is not revealed, or clear. Putting language before the body at the point of this main entry is a reminder of the 'overwhelmingly linguistic'[16] school training that gave the language of literary invention and ornamentation multiple signifying possibilities; it is also a reminder of the play's original audience, for the young law students and barristers who saw the play in 1602 at the Middle Temple would have been well versed in classical rhetoric and the powers of invention and ornamentation.[17] Yet Shakespeare uses this linguistic resource to craft desire that exceeds social signification of service. The semantic function of a single word, 'comptible', within a speech whose subject matter is language and whose use is persuasion, is much more complex than it might seem on the surface of the word's invented, obscure form.

Yet the word 'comptible' complicates the affective basis of Viola-Cesario's intention to be considered by Olivia as only a prospective servant. According to the *OED*, the word appears to be Shakespeare's coinage, used only once, in this instance and in this play only. Its meaning is 'liable to answer to, sensitive to' (1c). David and Ben Crystal define the word as 'sensitive, thin-skinned, impressionable'.[18] Adopting some variations in spelling, modern editors gloss the word in a similar way, following the *OED*.[19] But earlier editors, more liberally, considered other meanings of 'comptible', which opened up the erotic politics of the speech. Henry Howard Furness's gloss in the *New Variorum Shakespeare* edition of *Twelfe Night* registers those early editors' solutions for 'contemptible'. Furness suggests replacing 'comptible' with the French 'domptable', meaning 'apt to be subdued or tamed' (John Monck Mason) to glossing it as 'being treated with scorn, because she is very submissive' (George Stevens).[20] It is not just the immediate semantic environment in which 'comptible' teasingly pushes the idea of sensitivity into the realm of sexual submissiveness, suggested by 'sinister usage', which Viola proposes to Olivia. The dramatic situation that invites editors to speculate on the semantic possibilities of this phrase further complicates the erotic plot caused by cross-dressing. The affect that conflates the economic need for service and the pleasure of offering oneself to submission and usage gains power from a double meaning in this linguistic introduction. The meanings of submission and of being tamed intersect with erotic meaning in a way that makes servitude and sexuality (and power relations therein) conjoined, rather than separated. Viola is accountable to Orsino both as his servant and as her love, while she has 'taken great pains to con' both her words and her performance as a young man (1.5.165–7). Words and body have come together in this performance. The meanings with which editors in the past toyed when glossing and speculating about this dramatic moment but that modern editorial decisions passed over, nevertheless represent inextricable parts of the history of editorial glossing the erotic meaning of the play. Such past editorial comments reveal signification of the queer style of the play that has been occluded by the history of critical annotation. Given that the textual history of *Twelfth Night* is relatively straightforward, in that the earliest printed text of the play is that in the Folio of 1623, and given that the play's text in the Folio is 'generally clean' and that none of the 'obvious errors'[21] which appear in the text show up in 1.5, we can conclude that 'camptible' carries within itself layers of these competing, erotic, meanings, and that Shakespeare's incommensurate language itself works just in the direction of the creative multifariousness offered by this chosen word.

Through an analysis of lexical, rhetorical and textual arrangements in this scene, a new emotional reality unfolds. It comes out of the manipulation of the Petrarchan convention of amorous address whose register, vocabulary, tone and syntax in turn manipulate the audiences' perception of the bodies and identities that are the subject of rhetorical addresses. Petrarchism in *Twelfth Night* is not an ornament that corresponds to the kind of love and courtship performed within its poetics, but a stylistic form used to energize new erotic possibilities, emotional fantasies and vicissitudes of love that run counter to that familiar convention and style; before we take the cross-dressing dimension into consideration even having one's servant woo on one's behalf is already to break with convention. Such breaks are further suggested dramatically by Viola's confusion upon entering the stage, as she tries to make sure that she has the right Olivia and that her speech is not wasted. This note of confusion is soon shared by the audience, as Shakespeare upends conventional Petrarchism in order to explore its new possibilities in performing desire and sexuality. This dramatic tactic on Shakespeare's part shows how 'the queerness of style'[22] alters the expectations this love encounter offers, because the emotional and erotic purpose of the speech is not easily definable. This upended Petrarchism gives new emphasis and force to Viola's image of the knot that is too hard for her to unite (2.2.40–1). Not only does this use of Petrarchism suggest complications that time itself may not be able to untie, but it also suggests both erotic intertweaving and entanglement. Such use of Petrarchism also show the ways in which such entanglements dissolve definition and difference, with no one person or no one gender distinguishable or separable from the rest. Not even time can untie such knots. Dramatized on the stage, Petrarchism itself acquires a new purpose in serving to facilitate ideas about the kind of desire and sexuality for which there was no clear-cut name within the context of transvestite theatre.

Offered as a way into the world of erotic desire and sexuality in *Twelfth Night*, queer style is explained through the strategies of reading that bring detail into focus within a larger discussion[23] of both how Shakespeare's text produces queerness, and how it anticipates queer theory, not just how the play text releases new meanings when captured by queer theory. Shakespeare's use of Petrarchism to express female-female desire in 1.5 shows Shakespeare's engagement with the Petrarchan style as a philological and speech act underpinned by the action involving the women. This specific philological exercise, which is at the same time an exercise in imaging other erotic options, gives critics an opportunity to move away from a more general consideration of homoeroticism in the play to a consideration of specifically female homoeroticism as an erotic fantasy of linguistic and stage performances.

The language of the play and the details of its verbal style do not capture the body and identity at the point of their cultural formation as they are represented on the stage; rather, the main subject of the play is not the body but the linguistic form by which the body is presented. In that sense, Lorna Hutson has cautioned that 'even the disembodied nature of the language in which it articulates the desires of its protagonists, [*Twelfth Night*] has nevertheless become the touchstone of [the] "body" criticism within Shakespeare studies'.[24] Hutson's 'counter-argument' to post-structuralist criticism about the body in *Twelfth Night* rests on the point that the plot structure of this romantic comedy depends, 'not on the emergence of identity', but on the strategies of rhetorical invention and structures aimed at enabling 'men's discursive ability to improvise social credit, or credibility',[25] strategies offered as compositional models in Terence's and Plautus's plays, with their clever slaves such as Pseudolus constantly and comically always having to think on their feet, which served as the sources for this and other romantic comedies. Along similar lines of argument, Arthur F. Marotti has suggested that in Shakespeare's romantic comedies 'marriage for love was a metaphor for advancement by merit rather than by birth or influence'.[26] Both imaginatively and emotionally, the subject/object relation and the love-match in *Twelfth Night* play simultaneously along and against this dramatic pattern in comedy. The style in which this intersection of economic and erotic concerns itself is meant to bring lovers together as partners in marriage, that presenting desire between women as a more embodied poetic exchange before heterosexual love is expressed. The 'interdependence' of the verbal and the social, which Russ McDonald characterized as a feature of Shakespeare's romantic comedies[27] and which Hutson explores in her interpretation of rhetoric as a formative strategy of representing a particular kind of the social body, represent ways of reading the body in *Twelfth Night* that are alternative to the history of the somatic body. As a medium through which desire speaks and bursts out on the stage, style is the textual, verbal and audible, as well as cultural and historical, form through which ambiguous and conflicting discourses about the body contained within the cross-dressed body articulate themselves rhetorically. In other words, and to slightly alter the meaning of Buffon's adage that '*Le style c'est l'homme même*', 'the style is the body'.

In his introduction to the Arden 3 edition of *Twelfth Night*, Keir Elam emphasizes the dependence of emotion and sexuality on the figurative rhetoric of the play. He uses rhetorical tropes as illustration for his point and states that '[h]yperbole, usually in the form of exaggerated metaphor or simile, is at times used as earnest, as in exchanges of intensely polite and possibly homoerotic compliments',[28] showing style to be in the service of the expressions of love, though mostly of parody. To put it more plainly, Elam's reading of figurative rhetoric oscillates between acknowledging the possible erotic underpinnings of language and speculating about the trope's effect (always a difficult feature to establish because of the lack of records of audience's reception and reaction to specific rhetorical forms). The relationship between hyperbole and youth is noted by Aristotle, who says in *Rhetoric* that 'There is something youthful about hyperboles; for they show vehemence. Wherefore those who are in a passion most frequently make use of them'.[29] Aristotle's definition of the trope draws attention to the relationship between rhetorical ornament, or decorous style, and nature, in a way that is pertinent for a discussion of the queerness of hyperbole in Shakespeare's text. The association of hyperbole with high emotions establishes a more obvious Aristotelian relationship between hyperbole and various scenarios in which young lovers speak in terms of incredibility and excess, as they do, for instance, in *Love's Labour's Lost*, *A Midsummer Night's Dream* and *Romeo and Juliet*. In the latter, Juliet even chides

Romeo for knowing so well the love language of incredibility and excess – the staple of the Petrarchan aesthetics of love – that he may not truly love; she, on the other hand, needs only 'three words' to impart her message of love, namely that he will marry her before their affair can go any further (2.1.185). Apart from the fact that hyperbole is one of the key tropes of the Petrarchan poetry of courtship and in the blazons of lady's beauty within the Petrarchan poetics of love (*Canzoniere* abounds in it), this trope shapes literary meaning in ways that exceed its primary definition as a figure of exaggeration. At a deeper level of meaning at which hyperbole operates in an utterance, this trope implies that nature reveals its full meaning in, paradoxically, the language that exceeds its properties, that goes beyond what can be believed about that natural subject of persuasion. Thus love and desire in the wooing scene are couched in the language of excess and exaggeration to create another kind of truth from the one that the ornament, hyperbole, has exceeded.

Henry Peacham defines hyperbole as 'when a saying doth surmounte and reach aboue the truth'.[30] This possibility of hyperbole reaching for a higher truth while also possibly containing a greater falsehood, informs Puttenham's description of hyperbole as both 'the over-reacher' and the 'loud liar'.[31] Hyperbole that offers a lie as truth allows Shakespeare to stylize expressions such as 'If you will not murder me for my love, let me be your servant' (2.1.323) or 'Most radiant, exquisite and unmatchable beauty' (1.5.165) both as flattery that is not true and as passion different from the one claimed in the utterance. These possibilities intersect in John Hoskins's description of the ways hyperbole can be used: 'Sometimes it [hyperbole] expresseth a thing in the highest degree of possibility, beyond the truth, that it descending thence may find the truth; sometimes in flat impossibility, that rather you may conceive the unspeakableness than the untruth of the relation'.[32] Hoskins leaves it to the speaker or the hearer to make the truth out of the possibilities yielded by the utterance. Shakespeare leaves it to his audience to grasp the truth about the wooing in *Twelfth Night*, truth enabled by hyperbole and by the context of the transvestite theatre that the trope serves. Shakespeare's hyperboles are an important feature of Shakespeare's queer style in *Twelfth Night* because, by giving attention to going beyond truth and by presenting the improbable as probable, they guide the audience to think about the improbability of 'lesbian' desire as the probability enacted before their eyes, now. If we merely register the presence of hyperbole in a text without delving into the semiotics this trope draws on from the context in which it is used, we lose sight of how its nuanced history offered early modern writers 'directions', to echo Hoskins, for using the trope in order to craft nuanced and surprising meanings. If Olivia hid her growing love by losing her tongue and by speaking in 'starts, distractedly' (2.2.20–1), the audience could see in such silences and broken language the beginning of desire. Elam speculates that the Balkan setting of the play offers a further context to imagine homoeroticism underpinning the wooing in Shakespeare's Illyria, which is a claim that deserves a more developed and documented justification from cultural and social history but that nevertheless indicates the role this setting plays in this discussion,[33] especially given how Shakespeare's English contemporaries perceived the historical Illyria of their times. Yet, the play reveals its queer meanings elsewhere in more stylized and bold ways.

Petrarchan aesthetics and the queerness of style

In 1.5, Shakespeare's text is richly endowed with stylistic characteristics that give form to sexual ambiguities and uncertainty about identity, as Viola proclaims: 'I am not that I play' (178). Discussing the politics of sexuality and erotic identity in *Twelfth Night*, Valerie Traub has argued that:

In the course of the play's action, Shakespeare teases his
audience with a culturally available, if implicit, association
between crossdressers, hermaphrodites, and tribades; then,
through the force of the marriage plot, the audience's
attention ultimately is directed away from the specter of
such erotic possibilities.[34]

This audience teasing resulting from valences of queerness
that may be adopted in a staging of the play, is also enabled
by Petrarchism, which defines one of the most dramatically
striking moments in the play – the first long wooing scene
involving Olivia and Viola. And Shakespeare 'teases his
audience' first by troubling the gender boundaries of the
conventional Petrarchan aetiology of love that 'constitutes
itself in relation to a feminine object',[35] as Carla Freccero
puts it, by an adoring and speaking male subject. Then he
consequently changes the gendered and erotic perspectives
from within which the lexicon, syntax and style of such
emotional expressions are directed from Viola-Cesario to
Olivia. Again, the note of confusion and unsettlement that
opens their meeting is meant to confuse and unsettle more than
simply Olivia and Viola. In moments like this, Shakespeare's
text invites the audience to consider that service, the motive
that brought Viola to the door of Olivia's household, matters
as much as all the lexical choices articulating desire which
muddles the socio-economic need that Viola has and that
Olivia is ready to respond to, despite her initial surprise and
confusion. Olivia says:

> O sir, I will not be so hard-hearted. I will give out divers
> schedules of my beauty. It shall be inventoried, and every
> particle and utensils labelled to my will, as, item, two lips,
> indifferent red; item, two grey eyes, with lids to them; item,
> one neck, one chin and so forth. Were you sent hither to
> praise me?

> (1.5.236–41)

The catalogue of female beauty is all too familiar as it stands out by the obviousness of items included in the inventory of female beauty: lips, eyes, neck, chin. The list goes 'so forth', and Shakespeare knows that his audience knows it too, that there is a limit to which playing with a convention can be an exciting game. So the catalogue of virtue breaks off with a cue, in the form of a question, to Viola to pick up on the theme of praise ('Were you sent hither to praise me?'). What is, however, more curious about this inventory of beauty parts is that, being recognizable clichés, those parts are subordinate to the meanings that combine legal, textual and print forms in which trust, loyalty and virtue are confirmed and materialized. The now obsolete meaning of the word 'schedules' refers, the *OED* informs us, to 'a separate paper or slip of parchment accompanying or appended to a document, and containing explanatory or supplementary matter' that was in '16-17th c. sometimes used for a codicil to a will'. For example, the scroll that mocks Arragon's choice of the silver casket in *The Merchant of Venice*, a choice grounded in the marriage contract, is described as a 'schedule' (2.6.54), while the oaths and commitments made by the young men in *Love's Labour's Lost* are also contained in a statue, or 'schedule' (1.1.18). The mixing of the vocabulary belonging, on the one hand, to the aesthetic of Petrarchan praise of lady's beauty with the lexicon of legal bonding that is an addition to a will, on the other hand, makes this curious relationship a kind of 'codicil' to the marriage theme pursued in the play at this point. In contemporary stylistics, Olivia's Petrarchan vocabulary renders her the submissive object to Viola's desire, confirming the bond between two women in terms that render female homoeroticism that complements other forms of desire in the play.

Viola's response to Olivia, 'if you are the devil you are fair. / My lord and master loves you. O, such love / Could be but recompensed, though you were crowned / The nonpareil of beauty' (263–6), not only develops the blazoning praise into the master–mistress relationship familiar from sonnet 20, but also it teasingly transposes those terms in such a way that Viola becomes the conduit through which both a

woman's praise of another woman is conveyed and the absent
male lover's desire for a distant lady is transmitted. Viola's
body is thus doubly transvestized, through dress and through
poetry. The speaking subject of the line 'I am not that I play'
(179) and of 'If I did love you [Olivia] in my master's flame
/ With such a suffering, such a deadly life, / In your denial
I would find no sense' (256–8) undergoes, what Catherine
Bates has called in her discussion of cross-dressing in Philip
Sidney's prose romance, *New Arcadia*, 'a radical dislocation'
of identity, and of 'a fragmentation into multiple parts'[36]
– as Viola can be read as either a young man or a young
woman; either looking for service or falling in love, or both;
playing a part or performing identity; appearing to know
and to 'not understand' (258) what love flame is. While the
dramatic poetry gives room to interpret the relation between
Olivia as the object of Viola's courtship, and Viola playing a
messenger of Orsino's love to the mourning Olivia and the
subject initiating one's own desire for Olivia, in heterosexual
terms, that poetry also delineates other scenarios of desire
and identification: a woman wooing and blazoning a woman,
a young man blazoning a woman (a boy actor dressed as a
woman); a castrated youth, Cesario, wooing a woman.[37] The
subject/object relation initiated by Viola's appropriation of
the Petrarchan love aesthetics to woo a lady on behalf of a
master points to a parody of the tradition of love poetry, so
that difference of erotic desire from that tradition has been
replaced by sameness as well.

The circular, and circulating, desire in *Twelfth Night*,[38]
desire that involves Viola-Cesario, Olivia and Orsino, makes
Petrarchan style the main language exchanged between
lovers. This scenario, as Bruce Smith has already suggested,
raises 'the prospect of female homoerotic flirtation'.[39] But the
passage further expands the play's erotic scenarios. Petrarchan
style depersonalizes both the subject and the object in this
passage because the play's lexicon shifts identities beyond the
proposed historical accuracy of the one-sex model[40] used to
explain its stylized presentations in the transvestite comedies.

Viola's appropriation of the Petrarchan style in a courtship situation in which the subject/object referent is shifting shows that Shakespeare uses Petrarchism not to 'underwrite [...] the economy of masculine desire'[41] but to expose the arbitrariness of any attempt to attach desire to a gendered body, by promoting desire as a force that brings different kind of staged bodies together and outside the heterosexual matrix.

The roles of the subject and the object of praise and adoration are exchanged between Viola and Olivia, whose blazoning of Viola ('Thy tongue, thy face, thy limbs, actions and spirit / Do give thee fivefold blazon' [1.5.284–5]), turns the Petrarchan style into a verbal medium of shared desire between two speaking parts, two bodies present on stage, two speakers using clichés of flattery as the form for a shared desire that is neither charged with overtones of monstrosity, as early modern lesbianism sometimes was, nor presented as transgressive. This complete lack of disapproval, and of any form of reprobation, suggests that this is not a play that has been injected with modern readings and interpretations that Shakespeare would have been unable to foresee; instead, it suggests that the freedom and liberating queerness of the play and its complete upending of heteronormativity was there from the beginning. Bruce Smith has argued that at the end of the play, when Cesario is called a man ('Cesario, come; / For so you shall be while you are a man' [5.1.378–9]), 'the sexual sameness of lover and beloved', which 'has not been emphasized earlier in the play' is 'certainly flirted with in the end'.[42] But as we have seen, these linguistic markers have been confused very early in the play. They are confused at the beginning and throughout, and they will remain, wholly and unapologetically, confused at the end.

The dialogue that follows expands the idea of female same-sex desire coded in terms of Petrarchan stylistics.

VIOLA Make me a willow cabin at your gate
And call upon my soul within the house;
And sing them loud even in the dead of night;

> Hallow your name to the reverberate hills
> And make the babbling gossip of the air
> Cry out 'Olivia!', you should not rest
> Between the elements of air and earth
> But you should pity me.

(1.5.260–8)

The speed with which Viola runs through these lines owes much to the passage consisting of mostly monosyllabic words, which both formally and semantically are caught by the ear easily. Rhyme, or 'concord', as Puttenham calls it because it produces the effect of harmony that pleases the ear or the listener, is missing in this passage that lacks rhyme, but it is compensated for, 'cunningly',[43] as Puttenham might say, by the feminine endings (gate, house, night, hills, air, rest, earth, me). These produce a different kind of 'concord', pair or harmony: between women at the heart of the Petrarchan dialectic of love. Thus the queerness of style extends from vocabulary to prosody. The use of feminine rhyme adds an additional acoustic dimension to the presentation of lesbian desire. On the one hand, feminine rhyme provides an acoustic dimension to the queer textual moment. On the other, feminine rhyme shows that prosody is a producer of erotic meaning as much as ideas crafted by poetry are.[44] The difference between the acts of viewing the play and that of reading it inevitably plays part in the perception of the queer style generated through prosody. What the reader would 'hear' on the page might not be the same that an audience member might hear coming from the stage.[45] However, printed text enables the idea that the female-female desire and wooing are supported by feminine rhyme. Desire is here positioned in relation to language and the forms with which desire is associated.[46] The queerness of Shakespeare's style is realized through an awareness of versification, and it is recognizable because Shakespeare invented a style that offers formal grounds for thinking about that style as queer. The context of queer style expands beyond the frame of prosody, and sharpens our sense of the textual milieu that shapes the life of *Twelfth Night* in the history of queer early modern drama.

Bruce Smith has offered a compelling comparative reading of this passage alongside a passage from Ovid's *Heroides*, 'in the verse epistle [in which] Ovid imagines the Greek poet Sappho writing to the male lover Phaon, who has just abandoned her for another woman'. As the complaint, which was translated by George Turberville and printed in 1567, continues, Sappho recollects delights she had with other 'Lesbian lasses',[47] now forgotten. Phaon, Smith reminds us, won Sappho because of his androgynous look, being a youth without facial hair and of tender age. As a thematic resource for *Twelfth Night*, Ovid's text reveals desire charged with lesbianism, even where that desire might be obfuscated behind the stylistic ornament of Petrarchism. Regarded from this comparative perspective, this parallel reading shows that Shakespeare's verbal practice of emulating the classical past in a new creation shows *Twelfth Night*, even if only in this particular case, cannot be treated as an isolated textual whole, if a full range of possibilities for reading desire in it is to be made apparent. Queer style reveals itself fully in a comparative reading of related texts from different time periods. Such a style dilates queer meaning of Shakespeare's drama. So understood, queer style covers the study of sources as influences that cannot be determined by establishing a direct and linear contact between texts but that constitute a resource, one that spurns new creation.[48]

At a time when the understanding of a stable, coherent idea of the subject did not exist, both in actuality and in drama – Shakespeare's favourite poet, after all, was Ovid, who depicted and praised instability and mutability of body and desire – the notion and practice of style as a medium that would convey the idea of the coherence of identity did not exist either.[49] Shakespeare's use of the Petrarchan style shows that he imagines desire without gender boundaries. In that sense the notion of desire stylized without gendered limits dispenses with the chronological boundaries of desire and puts

Shakespeare's text in close proximity to modern queer theory. In its search for disciplinary, conceptual and ideological space in contemporary critical dialogue between the past and the present, queer theory has made the past a domain of queer historiography and the present of theory. Sharon Holland has argued that *Twelfth Night* is 'as much a play bout how to play at love as it is about the fact that whom we love is of little consequence'.[50] Yet the interplay of language and desire in this play sharpens, rather than blurs, our perception about the erotic charge that creates relationships between desiring objects in *Twelfth Night*.

In *Twelfth Night* Shakespeare's handling of the Petrarchan poetics exceeds parody, with which this well-worn aesthetic ideal in poetic composition has often been met in his works. The handling differs from the straightforward parody of Petrarchan poetics in *Romeo and Juliet*, for instance, where Mercutio, talking to Benvolio about Romeo, says: 'Now is he for the numbers that Petrarch flow'd in, Laura to his lady was a kitchen wench' (2.4.39). This parody fits the consistently heteroerotic orientation of this tragedy; it is an overt parody of heterosexuality. In *Twelfth Night*, however, Shakespeare treats Petrarchism as a resource with which he transforms expectations of erotic desire. He enlivens a convention deeply moored in artifice in ways that he also does when he uses it to imagine male same-sex desire in the *Sonnets*. For Shakespeare, Petrarchism is more than a cliché and more than a love convention: it is a source of new sexual meaning by which he turns a romantic comedy into a series of stage performances of queer desire. A style of writing is more than a set of clichés and ornaments. It is a series of formal linguistic signs coded in such a way that they transmit new meanings transformed by the action on the stage. The queer style of Petrarchan desire also shows that in *Twelfth Night* Shakespeare emerges as a poet of new sexual range and morality. The lesbianism of this passage is neither crushed by action, nor is it rendered monstrous, rather, the lesbianism in *Twelfth Night* is imagined as a powerful source of sexual teasing and rhetorical invention as combined processes. In that sense, queer style is not a repressive but a progressive aesthetics of desire and sexuality in *Twelfth Night*. Queer style animates, moves and energizes the speakers to discover erotic meanings that are produced by the Petrarchan poetics.

PART III

Queer nature

9

Queer nature, or the weather in *Macbeth*

Christine Varnado

From the play's opening moments, when thunder, lightning and rain are uncannily invoked upon (or perhaps used to conjure) the portentious heath, there is something queer about nature in *Macbeth*. Something about the way the natural world is made and animated in the language of the play thwarts the logic of sexual (let alone heterosexual) reproduction, blurring the distinctions between what is natural, what is human, what is alive – and what is not. Nature has frequently been posited, in modern and Western contexts, as the antithesis of queerness, or that which queerness disrupts. This idea of nature is premised on a complementarism of opposites mingling in generation; a fixity of order in which kinds of life (plant, animal, human) are distinguishable from each other and from that which is not alive; and a unidirectional model of growth as development and propagation. This is not how the natural world works in *Macbeth*; in our own time, scientists and philosophers of science are demonstrating that this is not how the natural world actually works; and, as other scholars have shown, this is not how nature was constructed in the early modern period.[1] Shakespeare and other early modern writers have left us a rich archive of alternative models in which nature is queer, or works in queer ways; texts we can use to rethink both queerness and nature, in order to understand how they function in literature as mutually inter-implicated, rather than exclusive, terms.

In what follows, I use *Macbeth* to probe the queer potential of nature through the problem of what constitutes 'life'. The problem of life is everywhere in *Macbeth*, called forth by the play's recurrent language of uncanny birth and bloody death. In this essay, though, I want to extend the question of generation in the play beyond the boundaries of human bodies or sexual reproduction, shifting focus to the forces and particles that make and un-make the material universe. I am asking how something resembling life is generated in *Macbeth* through other kinds of animate, inanimate or quasi-animate material phenomena: thunder, lightning, wind, rain, waves, witch-life, plant-life and the hybrid lives of the various apparitions that beckon from the text. Life enters the world, and can be seen, not only in the myriad mechanisms of plant and animal generation, but in the qualities of animacy and generativity ascribed to elements in the natural (and unnatural) world, and to forces of affect. Attending to the play's figurations of non-anthropomorphic life, I argue, reveals a queer model of generation, and a queer model of nature, at work in the play.

This chapter is informed by two rich theoretical conversations taking place in our field: the first, embodied in this volume, is the project of refining the utility of 'queer' as an analytic for early modern literature. One direction in which I would like to move that conversation is toward thinking about queerness as a structuring condition which operates at the level of systems. The material mechanisms of generation figured in a dramatic universe, for example, can be described as 'queer'. Queerness, in this structural sense, opposes and circumvents developmental *teloi*, flouts normative calibrations of sameness and difference, generates weirdness and excess, embraces the degraded, reveals the ostensibly-natural as artifice and/or sits uneasily between categories. Though this usage expands 'queer' beyond its usual referents of persons, genital sex acts and social identities, it has *not* lost its constitutive, originary connection to the history of dissident sexualities that gave us the term. To start, each of the qualities I have just listed as hallmarks of structural queerness is rooted in that history: each has been used to characterize same-sex desire and same-sex desiring people, or has been a fruitful, communally-cultivated value of queer cultures and cultural productions, or both. The other conversation in which this essay participates is the one interrogating the category of 'life'; specifically, the recent turn in philosophy and science studies known variously as new vitalism or new materialism (the works of Karen Barad, Jane Bennett and Mel Y. Chen provide a foundation for the thought I am engaging with here).[2] This line of inquiry has been invited into pre-modern English literary studies through the related interventions of Jeffrey Jerome Cohen, Eileen Joy, Julian Yates, Vin Nardizzi and others pursuing the stakes of object-oriented ontologies and the agencies of the post-, extra- and other-than-human.[3] One idea this work can offer to queer scholarship, in my view, is its move to de-centre early modern studies' long fascination with the human subject as the central locus of ideological and dramatic exploration in the period. In turning a queer eye on the materials of the natural world, this essay turns towards those areas of existence which might appear resistant to queering (the weather, how life and matter are constituted) but which, I find, are actually central to a queer analysis of *Macbeth*.[4]

My particular approach in this piece – of attending to ecological forces in order to complicate the cosmological underpinnings of a text – comes from Eve Kosofsky Sedgwick's practice, in her posthumously published essay 'The Weather in Proust', of close-reading the weather as an entrée into a non-dualistic, thoroughly vital literary universe. I also make substantial use of Mel Y. Chen's concept of 'animacy': a quality of agency, awareness, mobility or activity which Chen uses to de-essentialize the categories of 'life' and 'death'. Chen explores how forms of matter considered 'insensate' are instead uncannily animate in their operations and effects.[5] This concept allows for readings which interrogate 'the fragile division between animate and inanimate – that is, beyond human and animal' and the work done by that distinction; for example, thinking of animacy as a quality that can be enacted or possessed by metals, fluids, airborne particles or plant life.[6] Reading *Macbeth* in terms of 'animacy' makes visible the surface effects – the affects, motions and senses – that go into the ideological production of human-ness and alive-ness, allowing us to consider how these properties operate across human, non-human animal, organic and inorganic kinds of matter.[7]

The first question raised by the forces of the weather in *Macbeth* is one of the most often-asked: the question of the witches' ontological status. In fact, as this chapter will go on to show, the weather and the witches are connected, not only by the language of generativity, but by the kinds of attention they have – and haven't – received in criticism. One new line of questioning might begin thus: what can a shift in attention to the weather, the air and the heath tell us about the relationship between the first and second scenes of the play – the witches' invocation, and the chaotic battle scene that follows? The witches, ushered onstage by a technical effect of theatrical 'thunder and lightning', situate themselves in the weather ('in thunder, lightning, or in rain'), in time (projecting themselves into the future, 'ere the set of sun' that same day), in geographical space ('Upon the heath') and then, finally, 'through the fog and filthy air' (1.1.2–10). More than a mere, unconnected prologue, this brief scene establishes the witches' presence in the immediate future place and time of the action. The second scene opens with a hearsay narrative of carnage, told by a nameless, bleeding 'Captain', which segues at the moment Macbeth 'unseams' his enemy into an image of the sun running backwards and the weather's violent eruption: 'As whence the sun 'gins his reflection, / Shipwrecking storms and direful thunders break, / So from that spring, whence comfort seem'd to come, / Discomfort swells' (1.2.25–8). This weather refuses a clear connection to the action; it breaks into unexpected menace, delivering comfort and danger from the same 'spring', just as victory and defeat are mixed up and uncertain in the Captain's account. Do these scenes, then, take place on alternate planes, which intersect only at liminal moments when witches appear to men? Or do the continuous figures of thunder and lightning indicate instead that the witch-scenes and the human scenes take place in the same material world? Are the witches apart from or against 'nature', in other words, or are they part of it?

One of the ways in which an investigation of the weather in *Macbeth* is a queer project has to do with the degraded, juvenile, superseded quality of much of the extant critical knowledge produced about it. Explicit discussions of 'thunder and lightning' and other weather phenomena in the text are found almost exclusively in the realm of elementary, pedagogical literature – guides and summaries which treat it as a 'motif' or 'theme', in terms of 'symbolism' or 'foreshadowing'. It also gets substantial play in outright reading-substitutes: the weather, along with 'nature' and 'animal symbolism', are heavily and reductively covered in Cliffs Notes, Spark Notes and Yahoo Answers ('How is the weather used as a symbol in Shakespeare's *Macbeth*?').[8] There is virtually no literary criticism taking the weather as a central object of analysis. When the weather appears in scholarship, it is usually taken as a given that it reflects the crisis in the human action of the play, and that the non-human world puts forth legible signs of an unnatural threat disturbing its natural order.[9] Critics are mostly still working within the framework set out in the 1940s by E. M. W. Tillyard, who in *The Elizabethan World Picture* articulates the idea of great governing 'correspondences' between the cosmic, human and natural 'planes' of the universe.[10] In Tillyard's elegant model, 'storms and perturbations in the heavens' signal a crisis in the 'body politic', reflecting and duplicating the 'commotions and disasters in the state'.[11] In my view, however, these phenomena, which have been read as 'correspondences' in virtually all of modern criticism, instead occasion open questions and unsolved problems about how matter and agency work, questions which the text raises, plays with and refuses to put neatly to rest. It is a queer methodology to suspect that there must be much more to say about something only discussed in dated and de-legitimated terms. What queer potentials, as Jack Halberstam asks in *The Queer Art of Failure*, are opened up by experimenting with knowledge frameworks regarded as 'over', or 'backward', or by questioning the devaluation of childish ways of being (in this case, talk about the weather)?[12] Here, I want to take the weather and other natural phenomena in the play seriously, not as symbols, but as the material elements bodying forth a complex universe, through what Eve Sedgwick calls 'the changeable medium' of the text's 'cosmologies and weathers'.[13] None of the ideologies of the relation between 'man' and 'nature' informing most existing criticism successfully accounts for the full queerness of how nature works in the play; and I argue that this queerness can specifically be seen in the link between the weather and the problem of generation, or the question of what is alive and how it came to be that way.

Wind- and storm-raising are powers usually attributed *to* witches *over* nature. For example, the witches' activities as they gather on the heath include both 'killing swine' (1.3.2) and harassing a sailor's 'rump-fed' wife (1.3.6), and the uncanny promise to sail in a sieve on witch-raised winds to tempest-toss and torment her husband. I have previously read this scene as staging a collision between two different historical cosmologies of witchcraft: the quotidian forms of destruction associated with English witch beliefs, and the necromancy associated with Continental influences. But here I want to shift the frame, to look at how the witches instead are figured as integral to nature – and what that says about nature. What if the weather, the winds, the shipwrecks, the losses and illnesses figured in the witches' chants are of the

same substance as a dead swine: all attributable to one indifferent cause, an undifferentiated, roiling force which churns
materials to uncertain consequence; all part of the chaotic,
brutal course of natural events?

At the first witch-human encounter, Banquo juxtaposes the
witches' 'withered', 'wild' natures and the nature in which
they are situated:

> What are these,
> So wither'd and so wild in their attire,
> That look not like th'inhabitants o' th' earth,
> And yet are on 't? Live you? or are you aught
> That man may question?

(1.3.39–43)

The 'or' in this interrogative can be read as counterposing
'living' things against things 'that man may question' as two
distinct, exclusive possibilities. *Or*, the second question can
be read as drawing a wider ontological boundary around
the first (e.g. 'Are you sleeping? Or are you even alive?'). In
this reading, the living and the non-living alike fall under
things 'that man may question'. The question of the witches'
alive-ness is subordinated to their materialization on the
earth, and their questionability as parts of an organic whole.
Banquo continues to question the witches' place in the
temporal world, asking them 'If you can look into the seeds
of time, / And say which grain will grow, and which will not'
(1.3.58–9). The first striking thing about this image is that the
'seeds of time' are, from Banquo's perspective, in the future. In
this model of space-time, generation does not just run forward
from past (seed) to future (flowering). Time contains multiple,
quantum possibilities, in which some seeds of possible futures
will grow, and others will not. Moreover, time has materiality;
it is made of particles which constitute the germ of what has
happened and what will happen. If time comes into being
through matter, it looks very much like quantum physics'

concept of 'spacetimemattering'. This is Karen Barad's word for expressing how 'temporality and spatiality are produced and iteratively reconfigured' by what she calls material 'intra-actions', which do not take place *within* time and space, but co-create it.[14] Barad emphasizes that matter's coming-into-being is implicated in the production of time and of space; in other words, 'space, time, and matter are mutually constituted through the dynamics of iterative intra-activity'.[15] In this model, which I see evoked in Banquo's 'seeds of time', 'changes do not follow in continuous fashion from a given prior state or origin, nor do they follow some teleological trajectory – there are no trajectories'.[16]

In this iterative process, the world is constantly being made and unmade. Moreover, everything is an intra-active material part of everything else. The heath scene looks different when read in this light – less like a human epistemological or theological problem and more like a confrontation with the bubbling stew of spacetimemattering, or what is. The witches' disappearance reinforces this reading:

> BANQUO   The earth hath bubbles, as the water has,
> And these are of them. –Whither are they vanish'd?
> MACBETH Into the air; and what seem'd corporal,
> Melted as breath into the wind.
>
> (1.3.79–82)

The witches transmogrify into the very substance 'of' the earth's bubbles, creating a state-change effect that makes the earth act like water turning into air. They seem to cause all forms of matter to merge into each other – or to reveal these seemingly distinct materials' underlying fungibility or non-difference – in transforming 'corporal' solid into air. Thus the earth and air of the heath do in the play's third scene what the thunder and lightning do in the first and second scenes: they materialize the witches' strangeness as immanent to, not apart from, the pervasive queer materiality of nature itself. Banquo's next line also alludes to the interpenetration of different forms of matter, and extends it to the interface between plants, bodies and consciousness: 'Were such things here, as we do speak about? / Or have we eaten on the insane root, / That takes the reason prisoner?' (1.3.84–6). The possibility is raised that the witches 'here'-ness (just embodied onstage) could emerge out of, and be part of, the men's bodies – actually, their digestive incorporation of a plant body, an 'insane root', which also has a subjectivity, a mental theatre and an agency ascribed to it. In this image, witch bodies, human bodies, root bodies, human minds and root minds are all knitted together in an assemblage (which is literally rhizomatic – the 'insane root' makes the men into part of itself, as it becomes part of them – and schizophrenic, as well as inter-dependent and multiple, and thus triply evocative of Deleuze and Guattari).[17]

In 'The Weather in Proust', Sedgwick brings non-dualistic thought (Neoplatonism and Buddhism) together with psycho-analytic theory and close reading to describe the universe being posited in Proust's language. Here I want to look to her extended meditation on a fountain described in Volume 4 of *A la recherche du temps perdu* for what it can offer a reading of *Macbeth*.

> Simultaneously a spring and a fall, and with the narrator's repeated emphasis on the state-changes of condensation and cloud formation, it offers a stylized, artificial epitome of the unending processes by which water is propelled through its life-giving round of physical metamorphoses. (3)

In the uncanny state-changes effected by the witches at the end of Act 1, Scene 3, I see Shakespeare doing with the motions of earth and air something like what Sedgwick sees Proust doing with water. Proust's fountain, she says, figures

> an endlessly mutable but ultimately closed system where what goes around comes around, where linear narrative is propelled through a perpetual recycling of elements,

lives, positions, structures, and desires that honors the
conservation of matter and energy, that operates according
to law. In the framework of reincarnation, such a system
might be called strictly karmic; in a more familiar Western
mythology, Oedipal. But compelling as this vision may be,
it is no sooner finely articulated than it goes wastefully,
farcically off course. The full- scale weather system comes
athwart the fountain's condensed and elegant version [...]
Sometimes things that come around don't go around, and
vice versa. (3)

What happens if we take this cosmological vision as a key to
reading the weather in *Macbeth*, and, by extension, the weather
as a key to reading the ontological universe of *Macbeth* as a
whole? Though *A la recherche* and *Macbeth* traffic in very
different moods of what Sedgwick calls 'mysticism' – Proust's
'quotidian, un-special, reality-grounded' (4) and *Macbeth*'s
occult, portentious, spectral and bloody – *Macbeth* also
takes up the problem of 'how open systems relate to closed
ones, or perhaps better put, of how systems themselves move
between functioning as open and closed' (3), a concern which
is accessible through its figurations of chaos and complexity
in the non-human world. 'The weather has a privileged
place in discussions of complexity', Sedgwick observes (3);
it forces us to encounter 'the absolutely rule- bound cyclical
economy of these processes, on the one hand, and on the
other hand the irreducibly unpredictable contingency of the
actual weather' (4). 'Yet this kind of juncture', she continues,
'is the matrix, the growing point, of narrative and reflection
in Proust' (4). Thus, for my argument, the juncture presented
by the figurations of weather and other natural phenomena in
Macbeth – between a rule-bound, non-dualistic system, and
the violently unpredictable contingencies its very rules bring
into being – serves as the matrix, the growing-point, for a
queer theory of generation and 'life' in the play.

Nature's queer animacy can be traced through *Macbeth*
in the myriad animals, winds, voices and apparitions that

populate its universe. I see it at work in the uncanny inter-mingling of material and sensory phenomena around Duncan's murder. Macbeth addresses questions about the sensibility of matter to a hovering dagger; but then the capacity to sense – and to act on that sensing – is distributed over human, inhuman and nonliving things alike. Dreams in their 'wicked' agency 'abuse' sleep. Witchcraft celebrations secretly enchant ordinary time (2.1.49–50). '[W]ither'd Murther' takes on an animate personification, with the wolf as his animal familiar whose howl sets him in motion 'like a ghost' (2.1.51, 56). All of this takes place on an earth that is itself a sensing being, which can hear the steps that fall upon it, and can also speak: the 'very stones prate of my where-about' (2.1.58). The 'owl scream, and the crickets cry' (2.2.17) are heard at the moment of the murder, and the Macbeths startle to a succession of vague and un-placed voices whose origin neither can trace. What nature is bringing forth in this assemblage is the bloody deed of murder, and not of birth, though Duncan's murder has been figured as a perverse act of queer, non-biological political self-generation.[18] But in my view, the non-dualistic interplay of 'natural' and 'unnatural' animacies in this scene – indeed, the obliteration of any clean distinction between those two categories – opens up the possibility that murders (and births) are part of a rule-bound, chaotic, animate universe, neither less nor more natural than any other activity of 'life'.

Others, within and without the house, can see the strange weather 'hatched' by the murder:

> The night has been unruly: where we lay,
> Our chimneys were blown down; and, as they say,
> Lamentings heard i'th'air; strange screams of death,
> And, prophesying with accents terrible
> Of dire combustion, and confus'd events,
> New hatch'd to th' woeful time, the obscure bird
> Clamour'd the livelong night: some say, the earth
> Was feverous, and did shake.

> (2.3.54–61)

This recurring image, of the wind buffeting and knocking down man-made towers (chimneys, churches, castles), challenges a human-centred idea of agency. The wind acts with animacy, with voice; the air laments, screams and prophesies. Although these images are narrated in the passive voice (in contrast to their recurrence in Act 4), the lines emphasize that these actions have recipients; these utterances have animate hearers, who then repeat what happened ('they say'). The wind has not only action but language, even rhetoric – 'lamenting', 'prophesying' – with palpable affective and cosmological content. The earth not only shakes, it can be felt to have a fever, like a person. Likewise, the untimely darkness described in the following scene is an animate actor: 'By th'clock 'tis day, / And yet dark night strangles the travelling lamp' (2.4.6–7). This weather, and the strange animal behaviour that follows it (an owl killing a falcon, Duncan's horses going wild and eating each other), are called 'unnatural / Even like the deed that's done' (2.4.10–11) by the Old Man, who is gossiping about Duncan's murder. This comment is usually taken at face value as an exposition of the ontological status of these phenomena in the play, allowing all such disturbances to be read as inversions of the natural order which reflect Macbeth's disruption of the moral universe. However, a few lines later, Ross and the Old Man agree with Macduff that the guards Macbeth killed must have done the deed, and Malcolm and Donalbain must have suborned it, because they have fled. The next thing called ''Gainst nature still' (2.4.27) is Malcolm and Donalbain's killing their father. I'd like to argue that a reading of this scene should not grant Ross and the Old Man's ontological opinions more credence than their political ones: that the easy designation of these events as 'unnatural' is, like their attributions of guilt for the murder, an error, because the distinction between natural and unnatural is undone by the uncanny animacies of the material world.

The queer generativity of nature in *Macbeth* comes to a head at the beginning of Act 4, when Macbeth returns to the heath, crazed with anxiety and desire. As Act 3 ends, Macbeth remarks on the state which, 'like a summer's cloud', comes upon him unbidden and makes him strange (3.4.109). The natural world is animate, he fears – even articulate. 'Stones have been known to move, and trees to speak' he worries, to reveal the act of murder (3.4.121). If the subjects and verbs are reversed, this figure both refers back to the earlier Biblical allusion to stones crying out, and prefigures the animate, moving woods which portend Macbeth's vanquishment. Birds, too, speak: 'Augures, and understood relations, have / By magot-pies, and choughs, and rooks, brought forth / The secret'st man of blood' (3.4.122–4). These non-human agents possess a potential for signification that is dangerously performative and generative: they can 'bring forth' secret knowledge about secret, bloody men. This is also what Macbeth aims to do as he seeks out the witches one last time.

Some of the most striking language of nature's queer generativity in *Macbeth* is probably not by Shakespeare. The Folio version of the text that survives contains material from subsequent revisions of the play which post-date, and draw from, Thomas Middleton's *The Witch* (1611), though the web of intertextual influences connecting the texts is far from clearly known. The witches' scenes at the end of Act 3 and the beginning of Act 4, including the role of Hecate, are suspected of being at least partially Middleton's work (the song titles are directly lifted from his play). What these scenes have in common with similar scenes in *The Witch* are copious lists of witchcraft ingredients: profusions of animal parts, organic materials and physical phenomena which populate the witches' speeches and songs. Like the language of the weather in *Macbeth*, its witchy set-pieces have been under-analyzed in criticism, relegated to the status of spectacles. Diane Purkiss's reading of these scenes has stood as canonical: that the witches of *Macbeth* figure the problem of unreadability; and that the play refuses any single discourse of witchcraft, through a mish-mash of contemporary images and ideologies to be understood for the thrill of their stage effects rather than their substantive content.[19] However, close analysis of the interplay of animate and inanimate materials, natural and unnatural forces in Act 4, Scene 1 reveals an alternative, chaotic, queer theatrical model of how life enters the world. Though the interpolated witch-spectacles may not relate to the main action of the play in any philosophically coherent way, we can still attend to their content. Attracted by the critically degraded status of these scenes, perhaps due to their dubious authorship – Purkiss calls them 'a low-budget, frankly exploitative collage of randomly chosen bits of witch-lore'[20] – I want to look for what such dismissals might be obscuring, to ask how the idea of queer generativity can allow us to discern a thematic through-line within the sensational stage spectacle, and to think about what it adds to the play.

What is staged in Act 4, Scene 1 is a chaotic assemblage of the stuff that makes up the world: partial, fragmented materials which carry in themselves histories of violence, and are the products of violence. The scene flouts any hierarchy of the natural, bringing all different, dismembered parts of animals, plants, unnatural creatures and human bodies together in one violently generative jumble. The ingredients described are not passive or inert; they are active, dynamic, in motion. The witches are dependent on the activities of animals – the thrice-mewing of the 'brinded cat' and the whining of the hedge-pig – to bring about the space-time of the spell. Some materials have been cured or treated to spark their animating properties, like the toad that has spent thirty-one days under a cold stone, sweating venom (4.1.6–8), or the 'mummy', preserved and powdered human remains (23). Both these processes of curing problematize the line between dead and alive, pointing to the ongoing chemical activity of bodies that seem to be in deathly or dormant states. Other ingredients acquire their animating powers from how they enter the world, like the 'Finger of birth-strangled babe / Ditch-delivered by a drab' (30–1). This tiny finger's powers are particularly contingent on a series of liminal conditions: separated from the rest of its members, it was a part of something that was, in some sense, alive, though not quite human, which became not-alive at the moment of its becoming human – by birth-strangling, a cause which could, it is important to note, as likely be an accidental, *natural* outcome as a deliberate act of killing, especially in a ditch-birth – at a marginal, abjected place on the earth, in and through a marginalized, abjected woman's body. And yet this seemingly random object is produced in the speech alongside the specific dismembered body parts of people who were marked as Jews, Turks and Tartars (26, 29). These artifacts of human violence and human tragedy, born out of social oppression, are indifferently mingled in with the other substances, neither more nor less natural than anything else that happens in the spell, or in the world.

This 'thick and slab' gruel (32) is animated by violent state-changes: burning, bubbling, boiling and baking. Energy and matter both are animate, doing their mutual ongoing work of co-becoming in the language of the refrain: 'Fire, burn; and, cauldron, bubble' (4.1.11). The boiling and bubbling of the stew, which is aurally emphasized by the repetitions of 'double, double' and 'trouble', hearkens back to the 'bubbles' of the earth that Banquo remarks on at the witches' first appearance ('The earth hath bubbles, as the water has' [1.3.79]), and their ability to effect uncanny state-transformations. I would argue that the language of the spell offers *bubbling* as a pervasive, ongoing mechanism for material generation and animation which informs the entire play: a seething, frothing collectivity of life and all its bloody, undifferentiated parts, bubbling up beyond the control of any single agency, human or otherwise.[21]

That this scene was probably added in from a later stage production makes it of greater, not lesser, interest in this light, because it reflects a desire – *someone's* desire, at some un-traceable moment in the life of the play – to augment and point up the uncanniness of material life in the play using these specific, spectacular images.[22] And the understanding of the play that that decision reflects is now, in turn, part of the text. Art and artifice are intrinsic to generation in the witch scenes (which makes sense considering their theatrical provenance), as evidenced by the witches whipping the stew into an animating 'charm' by performance and ritual (singing and dancing). This, too, is part of what the spells and songs add to the play's theory of how matter becomes animate life: not without intensive acts of imaginative art, which cannot be separated out from what looks like nature. In sum, I see the witches, like the weather, in *Macbeth* as doing much more than 'representing the unnaturalness of the Macbeths' tyranny' or symbolizing the threat of disorder to an otherwise-orderly nature.[23] Instead, the witches' spells blur any easy distinction between natural and unnatural forms of generation; they signal that this fragmented, dismembered, bubbling chaos *is how nature works*, by demonstrating the thorough inter-dependence of destruction and generation, and of nature and artifice.

These are also the questions raised in the rest of Act 4, Scene 1, beginning with the powers Macbeth attributes to the witches in his quest for knowledge:

> Though you untie the winds, and let them fight
> Against the Churches; though the yesty waves
> Confound and swallow navigation up;
> Though bladed corn be lodg'd, and trees blown down;
> Though castles topple on their warders' heads,
> Though palaces, and pyramids, do slope
> Their heads to their foundations; though the treasure
> Of Nature's germens tumble all together
> Even till destruction sicken, answer me.

(4.1.52–60)

These images of weather-magic and destruction are connected to contemporary witch beliefs; I am more interested, however, in reading them as physical phenomena, holding open the question of causality. And in fact, the agencies posited in this speech are more multiple, the cosmology much queerer, than a simple narrative of disruptive witchcraft. Grammatically, the witches' agency drops out of this speech after the first clause

– the waves, plants and buildings go in their chaotic ways of their own accord, related to the witches only proximally. The witches only 'untie' the winds, and 'let' them fight, releasing a violent force inherent in the winds, which can only imperfectly be contained. The passage plays with the linguistic concept of animacy, which informs Mel Chen's analysis: an 'animacy hierarchy' embedded in language informs speakers' expectations for which words will perform the actions of verbs and which will be the objects. These culture-bound intuitions reveal 'a conceptual order of things, an animate hierarchy of possible acts', which is dependent on the assumptions of a specific cosmology.[24] The 'yeasty waves' that confound the ships here also confound a conventional animacy hierarchy of the English language – or, they posit an alternative hierarchy, in which winds and waves *do* these actions. The adjective 'yeasty', characterizing the waves as foaming and fermenting with yeast, adds another dimension to this new animacy hierarchy: the waves seem to be inhabited by the animacy of a living fungal organism which creates motions of air and foam (in the form of teeming bubbles) through its digestive cycle. The crops and trees blown down are the objects of the diffuse force that is unleashed, but the grammatical emphasis again is on the action that the plants physically do. Even the non-living materials – the castles, palaces and pyramids – are the animate subjects of their actions. Overpowering their human auxiliaries, they embody much larger-scale, super-anthropomorphic forms: giant macro-bodies sloping their heads to their foundations. Natural and unnatural materials act in this passage alongside, simultaneously with, but in an unfixed relation to, the witches' agency, as different kinds of equally, queerly animate matter.

I see the causal relations among witches, winds, waves and stones here as akin to what Deleuze and Guattari describe as the rhizomatic inter-dependence between the orchid and the wasp, in which agents are neither primary causes nor mere effects, and causality is constantly being lost and re-gained in different form: 'something else entirely is going on: not imitation at all but a capture of code, surplus value of code, an increase in valence, a veritable becoming'. The non-individual entities formed in these multiple becomings 'interlink and form relays in a circulation of intensities', but it is an '*aparallel*' process, in which there is 'neither imitation nor resemblance'.[25] Describing the actions of weather, witches and natural materials in these terms allows these seemingly disparate dramatic elements to be considered as a single 'circulation of intensities,' as 'Nature's germen' or germ-seeds which 'tumble all together'. This final image in the speech can easily be read as an image of destruction or anti-generativity (in line with a reading of Macbeth's queer, un-lineal rise to the throne and his traffic with the witches' anticipatory/inter-fering prophecies), in which the natural order of germination is thwarted or undone. However, in the new reading of the play which I am advancing, 'Nature's germen' are not a repro-ductive mechanism which gets disrupted by queerness – they are the queer seeds of space, time and matter, the tumbled-together raw materials of a queerly generative universe.[26] I read the tumble of 'Nature's germen' as the seminal image (pun very much intended) in the play's figuration of what Sedgwick has inspired me to recognize as 'an endlessly mutable but ultimately closed system where what goes around comes around'; until it *doesn't* – until it goes violently, 'waste-fully' off course (3) – but where such irreducible eruptions are also part of an 'absolutely rule-bound cyclical economy' (4) of queer generation.

Though there is undoubtedly much more to say about these matters, I must conclude with an image that directly gives the lie to clear distinctions of life or animacy: the third apparition to appear to Macbeth in the phantasmagorical tableau of partial men and spectral children in Act 4, Scene 1 is a 'child crowned, with a tree in his hand'. Macbeth cannot pin down the nature of 'this' – this thing that is like a baby or an heir, but neither: 'What is this, / That rises like the issue of a king / And wears upon his baby-brow the round / And top of sovereignty?' (4.1.85–8). This apparition, which embodies both human reproduction and plant life, predicts another kind of uncanny animation: 'Macbeth shall never vanquished be, until' (it says), 'Great Birnam Wood to high Dunsinane Hill/ Shall come against him' (4.1.91–3). Hearing this, Macbeth insists on the fixity of trees, and of the one-way binary distinction between lively and dead matter:

> That will never:
> Who can impress the forest; bid the tree
> Unfix his earth-bound root? Sweet bodements! good!
> Rebellious dead, rise never, till the wood
> Of Birnam rise; and our high-plac'd Macbeth
> Shall live the lease of Nature, pay his breath
> To time, and mortal custom.
>
> (4.1.93–9)

The irony of this speech set in the reading I have offered is that, though he doesn't know it, Macbeth is already living outside of these rules. Not only because he has departed from all supposedly natural logics of filiation in his untimely birthing of himself as king – but because the universe does not hold to the 'animacy hierarchy' he insists on here, and never has. And indeed the woods do not stay fixed: 'a moving grove' (5.5.38) of woods-becoming-men – or men-becoming-woods – creeps toward Dunsinane, signalling Macbeth's doom. Thus the movement of woods reveals 'life' to be something quite other than an individuated, natural or linear progression, and 'agency' to extend far beyond the human subject, to seen and unseen forms of animacy whose consequences cannot be predicted in advance. Looking outside the human, to the materials and forces of nature, makes visible the construction of *Macbeth*'s queer universe: tending toward non-dualistic similitude rather than Oedipal difference; powered by uncanny fragmentation, proliferation and bubbling as modes of generation; and moving toward 'unlineal' collapse.

10

Strange insertions in *The Merchant of Venice*

A. Eliza Greenstadt

When in *The Merchant of Venice* Antonio negotiates a loan to stake Bassanio's courtship of Portia, he makes a point of distinguishing his bond with his friend from the one he seeks with the usurer, commanding Shylock, 'If thou wilt lend this money, lend it not / As to thy friends, for when did friendship take / A breed for barren metal of his friend?' (1.3.127–8). Antonio's vivid image was typical of the period's anti-usury discourse, which described this practice as the unnatural breeding of money. Some polemicists underscored the point by comparing usury to another unnatural sin: sodomy. Invoking this fact, critics have interpreted Antonio's condemnation of 'barren' usury in light of his homoerotic feelings for Bassanio.[1] In the 2011 anthology *Shakesqueer*, Arthur L. Little, Jr. contends that when Antonio disdains the breeding of interest he is rejecting 'the ability of usury, of sodomy, to speak for queer friendship and desire.'[2] And Lauren Garrett argues in a 2014 article that 'Antonio's perverse movement toward self-destruction, his solitary position outside of the marriage bond at the play's conclusion, and the homoerotic nature of his love for Bassanio all link him ... homologically to conceptions of usury as unnatural generation', and hence to sodomy.[3]

These interpretations rely on influential scholarly investigations from the 1990s, which claim that the link between sodomy and usury was based on the early modern belief that both sins involved unnatural procreation (sodomy is sex without breeding; usury is breeding without sex). In what follows, I return to the sources to show that this conclusion turns out to be incorrect. While their lack of reproductive purpose was often the common ingredient uniting the sins that appeared on sodomy's rotating menu, this was not the version of this transgression anti-usury writers loathed. Instead, they compared usury to sodomy because both violated communal values associated with friendship. Thus we should understand the usury/sodomy analogy via Alan Bray's indispensable insight that in the Elizabethan era male friendships were vulnerable to imputations of sodomy when they appeared exploitative or to serve mercenary ends.[4] The double vision that made amity difficult to distinguish from sodomy could also confuse a friendly gesture with usurious manipulation. Recognizing this version of sodomy is important because scholars have a tendency to pit homoeroticism and sodomy on the one hand against heterosexuality and procreation on the other, in a dyad that speaks more to contemporary struggles with the religious right than the complex formulations we find in Renaissance texts. By attending to its opposition to friendship – a form of intimacy whose dream of perfect equality was normatively restricted to a homogeneous male elite – we can better perceive the ways sodomy included gender difference. We know that this sin could involve male effeminacy – not just the desire to be penetrated but any craving thought to overrun masculine restraint.[5] In addition, sodomy could encompass versions of heterosexuality and reproduction in which the female exceeded her prescribed role as a means for reaffirming the masculine same. Bringing this perspective to *The Merchant of Venice* should cause us to question interpretations that view Antonio as isolated and barren by virtue of his homoerotic urges. Instead, I will consider the merchant a strange character whose interactions with Portia, another interloper to the male friendship tradition, have queerly generative potential.

My interpretation has affinities with that of Lara Bovilsky, who has critiqued the recent tendency to argue that 'Antonio exemplifies the friend [and hence] the competition between homosociality and heteronormativity'. Rather, Bovilsky contends that 'Shylock's loan increases Bassanio's affective and financial debts to Antonio' so that the 'resultant asymmetries in intensity and suffering within the Bassanio-Antonio relationship make it an outlier friendship for the period, even as it continues to be classed as friendship and love by Antonio and other characters in the play'.[6] Here I go further: more than an outlier, Antonio violates the code of friendship by attempting to manipulate Bassanio into a permanent state of emotional debt. Although Bovilsky does justice to the extremity of Antonio's behaviour, like other critics she emphasizes his self-destructive tendencies, which can be assimilated into the selflessness expected of the friend.[7] However, Antonio's actions are also *other*-destructive; when this aspect comes into focus, they appear legibly usurious and sodomitical. Antonio admits as much when, at the climax of *Merchant*'s courtroom scene, he says that he is 'tainted' (4.1.113). I agree with critics who interpret this statement as redolent with sodomy, but I disagree that it signals Antonio's status as scapegoated by his homosexual desires. Instead, to bind Bassanio all the more tightly to him the merchant theatrically displays his taint in an abject inversion of amity's rhetoric.

Since in doing so Antonio paradoxically pursues a bond of masculine privilege by displaying a stain associated with both sodomy and femininity, his strategy complicates the common argument that Portia's victory in their rivalry over Bassanio signals the triumph of heterosexual marriage over masculine friendship.[8] Little, for example, claims that Antonio stands for 'queer mourning' while Portia represents a 'generic fantasy world' of 'heterosexual marriage (and reproduction) … as the ritualistic rejection of mourning.'[9] One problem with such readings is that they must downplay the extent to which Portia is not only an unusual wife in the marital equality she achieves but also a queer character through both her cross-dressing and assumption of patriarchal authority. Like Little I view Antonio and Portia as competing avatars of mourning and procreation; but in a play that, unusually for Shakespeare's comedies, barely mentions human sexual reproduction, the lovers' rivalry instead centers on textual reproduction. Before they ever meet in person, Antonio and Portia confront each other in the form of epistles. These letters depict alternative modes of literary influence, with Antonio representing the work of memorialization and Portia the humanist practice of *imitatio*, or the imaginative reinvention of sources. When, in the play's final scene, Portia hands Antonio a letter, this does not represent a reconciliation of these modes but rather opens the question of how texts collide. Here, as elsewhere, *Merchant* calls attention to the conditions of its own making: the first of Shakespeare's comedies drawn from an Italian novella – Ser Giovanni Fiorentino's 1558 *Il Pecorone* – the play intercuts its main source with subplots, variations and myriad mythological, biblical and topical allusions. The interactions of these sources mirror those of the foreigners who meet on Venice's famously cosmopolitan shores. Like these alien characters, the intertextual fragments that are often awkwardly inserted into the drama carry the sodomitical threat of difference in their potential to divert the plot from the path it takes onstage. These other, imaginary, narrative possibilities become the terrain on which, I want to hazard, early modern sodomy can open onto a queer present in which unruly, perhaps monstrous, offspring might breed.

* * *

Recent scholarship has formulated two, related, explanations for why anti-usury writers linked this sin to sodomy. First, critics claim, both usury and sodomy were thought to couple like with like: in usury, money breeds with itself; in sodomy, one sex copulates with itself. Second, both sins unnaturally combined breeding with barrenness: as David Hawkes elegantly puts it, 'sodomy is sinful because it makes what is properly generative sterile, while usury is sinful because it makes what is properly sterile generative'.[10] Both claims, on closer examination, prove inaccurate. Instead, anti-usury polemics compared this sin to sodomy because they perceived both to be forms of exploitation distorting a natural state of communalism among men.

According to Peter C. Herman, 'the anti-usury tradition … recoiled at the idea of like breeding with *like*, money with money, which creates a further homology between usury and homoeroticism, a practice medieval and early modern discourse also figured as fundamentally "unnatural"'.[11] Yet it is anachronistic to equate 'sodomy' with 'homoeroticism'. The paradigm that arose in nineteenth-century sexology opposing an aberrant 'homo' to a normative 'hetero' sexual orientation was largely absent from and often antithetical to the Christian sin of sodomy, which was instead a wide and shifting category of behaviour including acts between different sexes or even species.[12] Under the influence of a modern formation that so strongly associates sexual transgression with same-sex eroticism, otherwise sensitive interpreters have detected references to the coupling of like with like where they do not exist, including in Aristotle's influential statement on usury from the *Politics*:

> Usurie deserveth to bee hated, for that by it menne gaine and profite by money, not for that intent and purpose for which it was ordained, namely, for the exchaunging of commodities; but for the augmenting of it selfe: which hath procured it the name of τόκος, to witte, issue or engendring: because things engendred, are like the engendrers; and Usurie is naught else but money begotten of money: in so much, that amongst all the meanes of getting, this is most contrarie to Nature.[13]

Aristotle plays on the double meaning of the Greek *tokos* as both 'interest' and 'birth' to depict usury as unnatural monetary reproduction. According to Jody Greene, 'in the most literal reading of Aristotle's notion of usury as the breeding of like with like, usury was linked with the fantasy of procreative homosexual sex, of getting "something" from male-male sodomy'. Aristotle, however, does not discuss the breeding of like *with* like. In specifying that 'things engendred, are like the engendrers', his sole focus is the similarity between parent and offspring, the breeding of like *from* like. Elsewhere in her discussion Greene contends, 'The issue for Aristotle is that breeding like from like, "money from money," is "unnatural"'.[14] Although here Greene correctly notes that Aristotle described the breeding of like *from* like, he did not consider this process unnatural. Instead, his remark that 'things engendred, are like the engendrers' expresses a commonplace: offspring tend to resemble their parents. Since Aristotle is known for elevating this observation to a natural principle, it is odd that Greene among other astute readers has overlooked his obvious meaning when considering the usury/sodomy analogy. But a likely cause is the strong explanatory force modern categories continue to exert on our understandings of earlier sexual practices. The prevailing logic seems to be: if homosexuality is like sodomy, and sodomy is like usury, then the unnatural quality of usury must have something to do with the concept of sameness that also defines homosexuality.[15] Yet neither Aristotle nor those who cited his authority thought this way.

If it was not the reproduction of sameness, what *did* Aristotle find unnatural about the breeding of money? Some early modern readers seem as perplexed by this question as today's. In his gloss of Aristotle, the 1598 translator of the *Politics* speculates,

As Plantes bring foorth like plants, and living creatures other living creatures, every one in his kind, commonly like their Parents, as a man, a horse, and a bull doe: so in usurie,

the engendrer, and the thing, is mony: which notwithstanding seemeth contary [*sic*] to nature, that a dead thing,
as mony, should engender.[16]

For this writer, the idea that like breeds like is so obvious
– supported by Genesis where God made each creature 'in
his kind' – that he is at a loss as to why, 'notwithstanding',
Aristotle would consider monetary reproduction unnatural.
He speculates that the problem must be for a 'dead thing' to
'engender'. Modern critics have seized on such statements to
postulate that usury was, like sodomy, a sin against nature
because it defied the mandate to be fruitful and multiply.
According to Will Fisher, 'The usurer's attempt to make barren
money breed is the equivalent of the sodomite's attempts
to make a non-reproductive sexual object or orifice breed.
The usurer and the sodomite thus commit the same crime in
different forms'.[17] Such formulations, plausible as they are,
seem not to have occurred to Renaissance writers. Scholars are
fond of quoting Miles Mosse's 1595 description of usury as
'a kind of Sodomie in nature' because 'it is against nature, for
money to begette money'; but they do so without noting that
Mosse raises this idea (which he attributes to medieval biblical
commentary) only to dismiss it as a poor explanation for why
Aristotle, and 'withal ... the writings of many learned men',
consider usury 'contrarie to the law of nature'. Instead, Mosse
stresses that usury is unnatural because 'it doth contrarie to the
verdit of the conscience'.[18] In a 1604 tract, Thomas Pie claims
that 'the Usurer maketh that breed, gender, and increase,
which by nature is barren and unapt to increase'. Yet he does
not connect this unnatural breeding to sodomy. Rather, Pie
invokes sodomy when considering a different argument for the
proposition that usury is 'against the law of Nature':

> The Usurer perverteth that end and use of money, which is
> ... agreeable to nature: namely commutation, for commu-
> tation was the end wherefore money was ordeined in
> humane societie; and is the use of it, which naturall use

the Usurer turneth into that which is against nature … .
Therefore it is called a kinde of Sodomie.[19]

Pie's claim that usury contradicts the purpose of money, which
is 'commutation' or equal exchange, accords perfectly with
Aristotle's assertion that

> engrossing and selling againe of commodities … [is]
> worthily blamed, because it is not agreeable to Nature,
> but rather to the end one might gaine and encroch upon
> another. Above all the rest, Usurie deserveth to bee hated,
> for that by it menne gaine and profite by money, not for
> that intent and purpose for which it was ordained, namely,
> for the exchaunging of commodities.[20]

When Aristotle described money as 'breeding', this was a
metaphor for what he actually considered unnatural: using
Nature's resources to 'gaine and encroch upon another'.

Once we clear away contemporary assumptions about
the relationship between sodomy and usury, we can perceive
that early modern writers compared these sins because they
violated not procreation, but 'commutation'. Thus sodomy
and usury converged as twinned antitheses to the virtue of
friendship. Lady Conscience in Robert Wilson's *The Three
Ladies of London* (1584) asks, 'if we lend for reward, how
can we say we are our neighbour's friend?'[21] Wilson's play
assimilates the biblical prohibition on charging interest to
'brothers' to the values of classical *amicitia*, an ideal of male
intimacy entailing selflessness. Drawing on this Greco-Roman
tradition, Michel de Montaigne explained in his essay 'Of
Friendship' that true friends, as 'one soule in two bodies, …
can neither lend or give ought to each other' because everything is 'by effect common betweene them'.[22] Yet, a speaker
in Thomas Wilson's 1572 dialogue *A Discourse on Usury*
lamented, 'God ordeyned lending for maintenaunce of amitye,
and declaration of love, betwixt man and man, wheras now
lending is used for private benefit and oppression, & so no

charitie is used at all'.[23] In *The Merchant of Venice*, Antonio makes the distinction between friendship and usury obvious: friends lend to each other 'gratis', avoiding Shylock's 'usances' (1.3.40; 104). A recent wealth of economic criticism has shown that in practice the distinction was far subtler. 'Interest' was a flexible term, allowing for types of loan arrangements that could earn profits while technically avoiding the label of usury. Wilson's *Discourse* warns that the usurer 'undoth as many as he dealeth with all under the color of amity and law'.[24] There is no sure way to distinguish gestures based on virtuous 'amity' from those motivated by sinful avarice. For in the Renaissance usury, as Hawkes observes, 'was first and foremost an attitude', a sin that 'occurred only in the mind'.[25] Usury was friendship's doppelganger.

Similarly, Bray demonstrates that although masculine friendship and sodomy might appear as the two extremes of male intimacy, the first representing the cornerstone of social order, the other its utter subversion, there had long been an 'uncanny' symmetry between them since the signs of each – kissing in public, being 'bedfellows' – were identical. Traditionally, what marked the distinction were certain assumptions: that the friends were of 'gentle' class and, for this reason, their relationship was 'personal, not mercenary'.[26] As these conventional guarantees were increasingly absent when wealth centred on wages and commodities rather than landed fealties, intimate male bonds were no longer protected from charges of sodomy, whose shadow 'was never far from the flower-strewn world of Elizabethan friendship and ... could never wholly be distinguished from it'.[27] The economic upheavals that made it difficult to tell friendship from sodomy also confused it with usury, and for the same reason: within this mercantile economy the generosity of giving that should appear a 'declaration of love' could easily be exposed as a means of extortion. Sodomy and usury were not simply analogous; they were on a continuum as sins that perverted the true course of male intimacy.

***

There is ample evidence of strain between the ideal and actual in the friendship at the centre of *The Merchant of Venice*. Bassanio asks for the loan by admitting, 'to you, Antonio, / I owe the most in money and in love' – a statement crassly mingling the financial with the emotional (1.1.130–1). Intensifying the mercenary undertones of the men's relationship is the difference in social class: 'Lord Bassanio' is a bankrupt aristocrat while Antonio is a wealthy merchant.[28] Once the men require a usurer to intervene in their dealings, the promiscuous breeding of his interest threatens to expose something sordid about their interest in each other. Shylock appears to remove this danger by offering, 'I would be friends with you and have your love, / ... / Supply your present wants, and take no doit / Of usance for my moneys' (1.3.134–7). He proposes a debt bond, an arrangement that, according to Amanda Bailey, was increasingly popular in Shakespeare's time 'because it offered an alternative to usury'.[29] However, since debt bonds prescribed a penalty if the money was not repaid in a fixed amount of time, they could be regarded as a form of usury. Wilson's *Discourse* offers an example in which one man lends another money for five months. If the creditor charges a cash penalty only to recoup the losses he would suffer with late payment, then this is 'reasonable usury' and he is a 'frend' who lends 'freely'. If, however, the creditor's motivation is profit, then he is a 'usurer'.[30] Shylock presents Antonio and Bassanio with a superficial gesture of friendship that, with a slight change in perspective, could be its opposite.

The nature of the penalty, which should clear this ambiguity, only intensifies it. In a 'merry sport' Shylock makes the suggestion of the forfeit with the assurance:

A pound of a man's flesh, taken from a man,
Is not so estimable, profitable neither,
As flesh of muttons, beefs or goats. I say
To buy his favour I extend this friendship[.]

(141; 161–4)

Because there would be no point in collecting such a penalty, the loan is, in effect, 'gratis'. Yet, as Bailey argues, by nominating a piece of Antonio's body as forfeit, the bond skips the penalty phase and proceeds directly to punishment. For in debt bonds, if 'the debtor was insolvent, then the creditor, unable to collect either the penal sum or principal, could lay claim to his debtor's person'.[31] According to Garrett, Shakespeare's audience would have been aware that creditors could harbour punitive fantasies under the guise of 'friendly' bonds. 'The creditor's right to imprison a debtor was easily abused', since it 'often meant relinquishing any hope of repayment in exchange for the satisfaction of bodily punishment'.[32] Wilson's *Discourse* warns that 'under the coloure of freindshippe, mennes throtes are cut'.[33]

This reality renders even more suspect not only Shylock's but the other men's motivations for entering, supposedly in the spirit of friendship, a contract brokered in flesh. Even before they strike the deal, Antonio has agreed to stand surety for Bassanio, who technically will owe the money to Shylock. Lars Engle points out that in England this arrangement would have been necessary because members of the nobility such as Bassanio could not be arrested for debt; therefore it was advantageous to have commoners stand surety who could bear the punishment on their behalf.[34] When Antonio offers his services to Bassanio in the play's first scene, he anticipates such corporeal sacrifice, claiming his credit shall be 'racked even to the uttermost', or stretched like a victim of torture (1.1.181). Antonio's willingness to be bound is the inverse of Bassanio's desire to 'come fairly off from [his] great debts', a bid for freedom foreign to the friendship code according to which, as Lorna Hutson explains, by 'overlooking his debts, … a lord ensured that his servant would be faithful to him'.[35] Rather than accepting the intimacy of owing his friend 'in money and in love', Bassanio expresses a wish to get clear of his debt, and so of Antonio. The extremes of bondage and liberty that characterize the men's relationship demonstrate its distance from friendship's traditional ties of mutual obligation.

The disparities between the men also cast a bawdy light on Antonio's offer to Bassanio, 'my purse, my person, my extremest means / Lie all unlocked to your occasions' (1.1.138–9). *Purse* was slang for the female genitals, while Antonio's metaphor of unlocking his 'person' is made explicit in the next scene when we learn that Portia's suitors must unlock the correct casket to gain access to her body. It is possible to assimilate Antonio's desire for penetration to the conventions of friendship; Montaigne describes how his friend 'having seized all my will, induced the same to plunge and loose it selfe in his, which likewise having seized all his will, brought it to loose and plunge it self in mine, with a mutuall greediness, and with a semblable concurrence'.[36] Noting that the English translation invites a pun on 'will' as erotic desire and organ, Jeffrey Masten comments: 'the essay figures a mutual interpenetration in which each friend's "will" acts as desire, penetrator, and receptacle' in an 'erotics of similitude'.[37] In contrast, by being 'bound' as Bassanio's surety, Antonio opens his person to penetration in a way his friend cannot reciprocate. When it is revealed in the courtroom scene that to claim his forfeit Shylock will pierce Antonio's flesh 'nearest the merchant's heart', what began as an erotic wish has transformed into a violent spectacle of emotional exposure.[38]

Given the ways Antonio and Bassanio breach the friendship code, *The Merchant of Venice* is ripe for the kind of interpretation Bray offers of Christopher Marlowe's *Edward II* which, he claims, places 'what could be a sodomitical relationship ... wholly within the incompatible conventions of Elizabethan friendship, in a tension which he never allows to be resolved'.[39] Like the relationship between Edward and his favorite Gaveston, that between Antonio and Bassanio involves: (1) men of different social classes; (2) one man bestowing considerable wealth on the other; (3) one man enabling the other's marriage; (4) a rivalry between one man and the other's wife; and (5) an act of violence that, in one case, involves anal penetration and, in the other, may evoke such an act. Yet critics who have used Bray's work to illuminate the tensions in

Merchant's central friendship have viewed Antonio as clinging, however tenuously, to the selfless behaviour expected of the friend. In the most influential of these interpretations, Steve Patterson ably documents how far the relationship between Antonio and Bassanio falls short of ideal amity. Nonetheless, Patterson claims that Antonio 'plays the standard part of devoted friend', though in his world 'only a radical staging of amity's power to secure bonds between men can reinvigorate its appeal'.[40] For this reason, Antonio does not simply enact but *performs* the part of the friend in a carefully choreographed 'radical staging' that begins with the letter he sends Bassanio in Belmont requesting his return to Venice: '*all debts are cleared between you and I if I but might see you at my death*' (3.2.316–18). Patterson comments: 'What might seem desperate or effeminate devices to ensnare a man are heroic actions in the friendship tradition' because they entail the public acknowledgment of amity's trials. 'To believe that his own society ... devalues the erotic possibilities of male friendship nearly to their vanishing point', Patterson adds, 'would not only nullify Antonio's love but turn the merchant himself into a kind of hapless, friendless "other"—possibly a sodomite but certainly a suspect character, since outside the bonds of amity and romance, his excessive behavior would seem useless or reckless'.[41] It is unclear whose belief Patterson is invoking here – it seems to be up to us to rescue Antonio from the taint of effeminacy and sodomy by shoring up his identity as friend, and hence hero.

If we relax our vigilance, however, we might ask whether a true friend would offer his life freely rather than using it as emotional blackmail. For we can contrast the tone of Antonio's letter with the assurances he made to Bassanio when he left for Belmont. Responding to Bassanio's promise to return with haste, Antonio answers,

> Do not so,
> Slubber not business for my sake, Bassanio,
> But stay the very riping of the time;

And for the Jew's bond, which he hath of me,
Let it not enter in your mind of love.
Be merry, and employ your chiefest thoughts
To courtship and such fair ostents of love
As shall conveniently become you there.

(2.8.38–45)

Here we have a completely standard expression of friendly caring in which Antonio puts aside his own needs for the sake of his friend's marital happiness. These sentiments, however, are reported by Salarino to Salanio, the Tweedledum and Tweedledee of Venetian conventionality. As such, they lack the mannerist distortions we hear from Antonio himself – as in the letter where he adds an emotional debt to Bassanio's financial one – or when, upon his friend's arrival in court, Antonio does not declare Bassanio's debt cleared as promised but instead grotesquely insists that he now pays it to Shylock:

Commend me to your honourable wife;
Tell her the process of Antonio's end,
Say how I loved you, speak me fair in death,
And, when the tale is told, bid her be judge
Whether Bassanio had not once a love.
Repent but you that you shall lose your friend
And he repents not that he pays your debt.
For if the Jew do cut but deep enough
I'll pay it instantly with all my heart.

(4.1.269–77)

Speaking what he believes will be his last words to Bassanio, Antonio frames his death not as the punishment for default but as the repayment of his friend's loan. Yet with this sacrifice, Bassanio's balance will not be empty; rather, he will owe an unending debt of guilt. Most critics have rightly seen Antonio as expressing rivalrous feelings toward Bassanio's 'honourable wife' in wanting to make sure that she knows Bassanio 'had …

once a love.' Some have also observed that by underscoring that he dies for Bassanio, Antonio makes his sacrifice a difficult act for Portia to follow. But no one to my knowledge has registered the full insidiousness of Antonio's farewell. For it is one thing to maintain a rivalry with your lover's spouse while you're alive; it is another to perpetuate that rivalry from beyond the grave. Antonio uses his last breath to frame his murder as a lasting reminder of his greater love and to cast its lingering pall over any future intimacy between Bassanio and his bride. We might measure the distance of such destructive desires from the selfless love expected of the friend by noting Antonio's use of the third-person: 'your friend ... / pays your debt.' Antonio can cite, but not embody, the name of friend.

I agree with Patterson that in this scene Antonio enacts a radical staging of amity – but, in its very extremity, this becomes a performance of usury/sodomy. In the courtroom Shylock and Antonio attempt to fulfill their agreement by violating its central, authorizing term: that of friendship. When Shylock offers, and Antonio accepts, the bond as a gesture of amity, the men's motivations are opaque. It is possible to portray both as sincerely believing this contract will set their relationship on a new footing. Likewise, it is possible to believe that Antonio stakes Bassanio in a sincere wish to see his friend happily married and cleared of his debts. Yet once Antonio defaults on the loan, it is impossible to read the bond as one of friendship. In the courtroom Shylock admits to 'a lodged hate and a certain loathing / I bear Antonio' (4.1.59–60). Poised with his knife to 'cut the forfeiture from that bankrupt', he is available to be read as the stereotypical usurer craving his *neshek* – the Hebrew word for interest, which (polemicists were fond of pointing out) meant 'to bite' (121). Though less obviously than Shylock, by this point Antonio is also actively and visibly violating the friendship ideal. Calling on Bassanio to witness his death as a sacrifice proving his unequalled love, Antonio reveals a desire for his own pound of flesh: the heart of his 'bosom lover' (3.4.17). Thus when Shylock is poised to cut into Antonio's flesh, the desires of usurer and merchant are oddly aligned: both wish to possess another human being. This is not to imply that the characters' motivations are simple; that is not my focus. Rather, they openly *articulate* motivations that, in their avarice, sinfully abrogate the code of friendship. In this way, Antonio engages in a form of dramatic inscription that is only possible when he acknowledges the taint of abjection he bears – and shares with the Jewish usurer.

* * *

In the courtroom, Antonio famously tells Bassanio, 'I am a tainted wether of the flock, / Meetest for death' (4.1.113–14). Since a 'wether' was a castrated ram, one line of criticism has read Antonio's pronouncement as an admission that he is a sinfully 'barren' breeder. Seymour Kleinberg stated the case most baldly in a 1983 article, where he read the phrase as Antonio's 'veiled admission that he deserves to die because he is a sodomite'. According to Kleinberg, the play upholds Antonio's self-assessment, since its 'happy ending' is 'the triumph of heterosexual marriage and the promise of generation over the romantic but sterile infatuation of homoeroticism'.[42] Thirty years later, Garrett similarly argues that Antonio is '"meetest for death" because of his place outside the play's affective economy of production—that is, marriage'.[43] While I agree that Antonio bears the mark of usury/sodomy, there is no more reason to believe he is literally impotent than that he thinks he is a sheep. Instead, we must read Antonio's self-characterization as the distortion of a discourse that celebrated amity as a love beyond social necessities and worldly ends. Montaigne rapturously claimed that 'friendship is enjoyed according as it is desired, it is neither bred, nor nourished, nor increaseth but in jouissance'.[44] Amity involves the pleasurable transcendence of a realm of purpose Montaigne tellingly associates with breeding, nourishing and increasing. At first the merchant Antonio attempts to gain access to this aristocratic discourse of ineffable homoerotic intimacy, but when by the courtroom scene he has descended to the status of an expendable human commodity, he dramatizes this abjectly useless position to enforce his claim of friendship on Bassanio. It is in this sense that he becomes, at *Merchant*'s climax, a figure for friendship in the form of its sodomitical violation. In doing so, he identifies with other categories of humans – aliens and women – who, because they are treated as commodities, are also vulnerable to being deemed 'not vendible', worthless flesh (1.1.112).

Jonathan Gil Harris observes that when Antonio calls himself a 'tainted wether' or stained sheep, this recalls when, upon asking Shylock for the loan, the usurer justified his profession by citing the biblical story of Jacob's long service for his uncle Laban:

> When Laban and himself were compromised
> That all the eanlings which were streaked and pied
> Should fall as Jacob's hire, the ewes, being rank,
> In end of autumn turned to the rams;
> And when the work of generation was
> Between these woolly breeders in the act,
> The skilful shepherd peeled me certain wands,
> And, in the doing of the deed of kind,
> He stuck them up before the fulsome ewes,
> Who, then conceiving, did in eaning time
> Fall parti-coloured lambs, and those were Jacob's.

> (1.3.74–84)

In the original tale Laban has agreed to give Jacob all of the 'streaked and pied' lambs born from the flock. Since he knows children tend to resemble their parents, Laban leaves the area with all the black and spotted sheep to prevent Jacob from collecting their similarly-coloured offspring. However, relying on the ancient belief that whatever the parents saw at the moment of conception could imprint its image onto the embryo, Jacob holds striped wands before the copulating sheep so that they bear 'parti-coloured lambs'.

As many critics have noted, this makes for a strange parable of usury: though at Antonio's prompting Shylock will claim that he makes money 'breed as fast' as Laban's ancient livestock, in fact Jacob does not increase the flock's fertility but instead changes its colour. If this is a story about usury, then what this practice scandalously multiplies is difference itself (1.3.92). Shylock implies as much when he describes the flock's 'work of generation' as the 'deed of kind'. 'Kind' could mean 'offspring', 'kin', or 'species', all of which the sheep's deed produces; but 'kind' also simply meant 'same'. Read this way, Jacob's intervention in the sheep's copulation appears unkind: interrupting the replication of white sheep from white, he introduces black marks that distinguish the parents from their young and separate him from his kind, his uncle. In the dialogue that follows, Shylock promises to reverse this differentiating process when, after Antonio responds with disgust at usury's 'barren' breeding, the moneylender counters:

Why, look you, how you storm.
I would be friends with you and have your love,
Forget the shames that you have stained me with,
Supply your present wants and take no doit
Of usance for my moneys, and you'll not hear me.
This is kind I offer.

(133–8)

Bassanio cautiously affirms, 'This were kindness', and Shylock echoes, 'This kindness will I show'; Antonio then declares 'I'll seal to such a bond / And say there is much kindness in the Jew' before marveling at how the 'Hebrew will turn Christian, he grows kind' (139; 148-49; 174). Given the references to religious conversion, 'kind' here means both 'generous' and 'of the same kind'.[45] By offering to accept payment in kind Shylock is treating the men as if they are brothers rather than strangers. He will 'forget the shames that you have stained me with' – the anti-Semitic abuses Antonio has hurled at him – initiating a process of whitening comparable to erasing the black marks Jacob's intervention imposed on the lambs (135). According to Harris, Shylock's biblical parable reflects the ways 'usury was repeatedly regarded as a stained and staining practice whose very condition was national and monetary hybridity'.[46] The bond promises 'kindness' as a homogenizing antidote to such unsettling mixture.

This promise has not just religious, national, and racial, but also gendered implications. Although the original story of Jacob and Laban's sheep reflected the ancient belief that whatever either parent saw at the moment of conception could influence the offspring, early modern commentators regularly cited Genesis 30 as evidence for the theory that the female in particular could transform her gestating embryo through the power of her imagination.[47] Shylock follows this trend by deviating from his source: Genesis recounts only that Jacob placed the rods before the 'shepe'; Shylock specifies that Jacob 'stuck them up before the fulsome Ewes' – a word capitalized in both the first Quarto and Folio.[48] While Shakespeare may have made this change for the ready pun Marc Shell points out between 'ewes' and 'use', Shylock's focus on the female sheep was in keeping with misogynist condemnations of usurious 'breeding'.[49]

Thomas Wilson's *Discourse* asks:

I pray you, what is more against nature, then that money should beget or bri[n]g forth money? Which was ordeined to be a pledge or right betwixt man & man, ... and not to encrease it selfe, as a woman dothe, that bringethe foorthe a childe, cleane contrarye to the firste institution of money? ... [M]oney which bringeth forth money is a swelling monster, waxing everye moneth bigger one then an other, and so horrible swelleth from time to time as no man by words is able to utter, contrary to nature, order, & al good reason.[50]

As Greene observes, Wilson's oddly parthenogenic image of usury increasing 'as a woman dothe, that bringethe foorthe a childe' endows the 'creature woman, like money, [with] a tendency to "increase it selfe" immoderately', monstrously intervening in homosocial bonding 'betwixt man & man'.[51]

While Wilson appears to oppose natural breeding to money's unnatural proliferation, his description has the effect of making procreation itself appear unnatural. In fact, such a conclusion follows logically from the theory of generation upon which the usurious breeding metaphor was based. Aristotle's claim that 'things engendred, are like the engendrers' was grounded in his belief that in the formation of offspring the semen provided the form and uterine lining the matter, meaning that 'natural' reproduction should result in children identical to the father. Yet since no child is actually identical to its father, in Aristotle's schema all sexual reproduction deviated to some degree from its natural *telos* and was on a trajectory toward monstrosity. Read through Wilson's Christian lens that condemned acts 'contrary to nature' this could imply that all sexual reproduction, because it involved female influence, was not only usurious but sodomitical. In this context, Antonio's response to Shylock's tale deserves scrutiny: 'Was this inserted to make interest good? / Or is your gold and silver ewes and rams?' (91–2). Antonio does not employ the standard Aristotelian metaphor of money breeding more of itself; instead he compares the joining of ewes and rams to the coupling of different metals.[52] Since he goes on to condemn the barren breeding of usury as antithetical to friendship, his attention to the sheep's sex difference suggests a particular disgust at the soiling contact of the feminine. Shylock capitalizes on this revulsion by framing his offer to forego interest as a gesture of friendship, in which 'kindness' expresses the generosity and likeness expected from an exclusively male exchange of intimacy.

Peggy Kamuf points out that in sealing the bond Shylock and Antonio have performed their own 'deed of kind, that is, their contract in kind, without interest'.[53] Yet the written document belies the lack of differentiation Shylock's 'kind offer' promises. Since debt bonds were executed on parchment, a material generally made from the skins of sheep, his description of Jacob's spotted flock eerily foretells the ink-stained surface of the deed the men will eventually sign. According to Harris, by the time Antonio is subject to this document's penalty, his self-description as a 'tainted wether' acknowledges that he has become 'property alienated to Shylock, legally comparable to the lambs that Jacob usuriously expropriated from Laban'.[54] The merchant's body is inscribed by the document that objectifies him, as is manifest when the characters use the terms 'bond', 'forfeit', and 'pound of flesh' interchangeably. Shylock defends his right to have his 'dearly bought' flesh by comparing it to the Venetians' 'purchased slave[s]', activating the association between Antonio's taint and the increasingly racialized skins of Africans who, as Bailey notes, served as domestics in England but, unlike native servants, were bought and sold.[55] The only times Shakespeare uses the concept of 'tainting' explicitly to denote blackening, however, are in reference to female sexual dishonour. In *Much Ado About Nothing*, Leonato condemns his daughter's apparent lewdness by lamenting,

> she is fallen
> Into a pit of ink, that the wide sea
> Hath drops too few to wash her clean again
> And salt too little which may season give
> To her foul-tainted flesh!

> (4.1.129–33)

As these lines indicate, in such moments Shakespeare links the taint of women's sexual impurity to the black marks of writing, a common trope connoting the public shame of unchastity (Othello asks of Desdemona, 'Was this fair paper, this most goodly book, / Made to write "whore" upon?').[56] In bearing such a taint, fictional women become dead letters, socially worthless and, too often, marked for slaughter. According to Kleinberg and Garrett, Antonio understands his own soiled condition as similarly casting him out from a normative economy of wedlock and procreation, from which his death will purge him once and for all.

Yet if this were true, after pointing to his taint one would expect Antonio to encourage Bassanio to move on and relish his life with his new bride. Instead he urges, 'You cannot better be employd Bassanio, / Than to live still and write mine epitaph!' (4.1.116–17). Antonio attempts to draw his friend into a ceaseless task of memorialization at which, apparently, he would be 'better employed' than in the enjoyment of his fresh marriage. As with many a fallen woman appearing on the early modern stage, Antonio's transformation into a text also potentially enables him to occupy a new, publicly expressive, role. Hutson explains the fact that women were 'articulated, characterized and given voice as never before' in Renaissance drama as reflective of fears surrounding the displacement of feudal pledges of friendship, including the homosocial exchange of female bodies, by humanism's 'emotionally persuasive communication, or the exchange of persuasive texts'.[57] This displacement enabled commoners such as Antonio to lay claim to amity's privileges – including what Jacques Derrida describes as the 'strange temporality opened up by the anticipated citation of some funeral oration'.[58] Such forms of public tribute were traditionally reserved for men of a higher class such as Etienne de la Boétie, the exemplary companion Montaigne commemorates in his essay on friendship. As a merchant, Antonio cannot rely on Bassanio's unspoken commitment to such eulogistic duties, so he turns the code of amity into a piece of persuasive rhetoric. Drawing a connection between 'tainted' and the legal term 'attainted', meaning 'proved guilty' or 'condemned', he suggests that as a defaulted debtor he is a commodity – or, as Shylock puts it, 'a weight of carrion flesh' – whose only value lies in being destroyed (4.1.40). Since as a self- proclaimed 'wether' or bankrupt he is equally impotent within a homosocial economy as a heterosexual one, he exists outside the realm of social obligation. Not only accepting but advertising his reduction to a textualized object, the merchant aligns himself with sexual incapacity and the stain of a worthless possession. In this way he paradoxically seeks to transform the illegible mark of the social outcast – the unchaste woman, the diseased slave – into the monumental sign of a love that transcends material necessity, including the cycle of birth and death. For Antonio, this becomes a strategy for enforcing amity as an eternally constraining commitment.

Thus Antonio may resemble Jacob's black-and-white sheep, but rather than being a young man's warrant to leave his stifling, even enslaving, service to his kinsman, his taint enjoins Bassanio to 'live still', frozen in a permanent state of emotional debt. This is not, however, the only possible application of Shylock's biblical parable. As Shell points out, the phrase 'fulsome ewes' anticipates Portia's reference to the 'full sum of me' – which, she tells Bassanio at their betrothal, is 'sum of something' (3.2.157–8). In referring to her 'full sum' Portia may be hinting that, like the ewes, she is fulsome in Shylock's sense of being pheromonally 'rank' and ready to make babies. But, as Shell notes, she and Bassanio never discuss having children. Instead, Portia frames her betrothal offer pedagogically, calling herself an 'unlessoned' girl eager to learn, where the pun on 'unlessened' continues the financial metaphor of the 'full sum' and suggests that she already has ample resources, both erotic and intellectual (159). In this she resembles the ewes' cognitive potential: as Thomas Browne would later explain, '*Jacobs* cattle became speckled, spotted and ring-straked ... by the Power and Efficacy of Imagination; which produceth effects in the conception correspondent unto the phancy of the Agents in generation; and sometimes assimilates the Idea of the Generator into a realty in the thing ingendred'.[59] Drawing upon the humanist ideal of *imitatio*, or inventive copying of sources, Browne emphasizes the mother's creative work in translating the information gathered though an 'intent view' into an 'Idea' realized in the 'thing ingendred'.

Portia comes to represent something like this humanist model of literary influence as opposed to Antonio's call for memorialization. So when these two characters present Bassanio with rival ways to use their full sum, it is only appropriate that they do so in writing.

***

As soon as Portia has betrothed herself to Bassanio, Salerio arrives with a letter from Antonio inked 'with a few of the unpleasant'st words / That ever blotted paper' (3.2.250–1). Bassanio explains:

> Here is a letter, lady,
> The paper as the body of my friend,
> And every word in it a gaping wound
> Issuing life-blood.

> (3.2.262–5)

Bassanio has just unlocked Portia's casket; now he beholds the letter as if it is Antonio's unlocked purse/person. Refusing to measure the distance between his friend's body and the text that predicts its violation, he seems already prepared to eternalize Antonio by penning his epitaph. Just before this, the play set up a different relationship between body and text when Bassanio opened the lead casket to discover 'Fair Portia's counterfeit' (115). 'Counterfeit' meant 'portrait', and Bassanio, after praising the lifelike detail of the painting, will dismiss it as a mere 'shadow' compared to the original (127–8). But in calling the image 'Portia's counterfeit', he ironically predicts that the next time he sees his wife, he will not recognize her as the lawyer who saves Antonio from Shylock's knife. Since Bassanio has just discovered Portia's false image by removing it from the additional covering of its casket, her doubly enwrapped state resembles the double cross-dressed boy actor who will soon appear.

This arrival also occurs in the form of a letter. Antonio has just commissioned Bassanio to write his epitaph when Portia's waiting woman Nerissa shows up in the guise of a page with a letter from the 'learned doctor' Bellario explaining that, though he is sick, he sends a 'young doctor of Rome' named Balthazar who was just with him in 'loving visitation':

> We turned o'er many books together; he is furnished with my opinion, which, bettered with his own learning, the greatness whereof I cannot enough commend, comes with him at my importunity to fill up your grace's request in my stead. I beseech you, let his lack of years be no impediment to let him lack a reverend estimation, for I never knew so young a body with so old a head.
>
> (4.1.154–60)

In place of Antonio's implication that Bassanio should devote all his energy to reproducing the image of his dead friend, Bellario instead presents a collaborative pedagogical exchange between the older man and his young colleague. This ideal scene of instruction takes on a different cast when, at the play's denouement, Portia produces another letter from Bellario revealing that 'Portia was the doctor, / Nerissa there her clerk' (5.1.269–70). Bassanio's relieved solicitation, 'Sweet doctor, you shall be my bedfellow. / When I am absent, then lie with my wife!' removes the Platonic patina from Bellario's earlier reference to the 'loving visitation' of his pupil with his 'young body', a comic deflation that continues when Nerissa's new husband Gratiano more crassly would 'wish it dark, / Till I were couching with the doctor's clerk!' (304–5). While it may seem that the play's one unambiguous reference to sodomitical desire – the husbands' gleeful anticipation of couching with boys – is protected as a heterosexual fantasy, the jokes call attention to the bodies of the boy actors playing the wives, multiplying rather than constraining the erotic possibilities created by the 'as if' world of the theater.

The lingering presence of Portia's 'Bathazar' persona at the end of the drama is open to both cynical and, I want to emphasize, fruitfully queer interpretation. The husbands' lascivious jokes about their wives' boyish alter-egos serve as a bridge leading the audience out of the play's fictional world and into the streets where boys would be available for such activities. Since, as Alan Sinfield points out, 'Traffic in boys occurs quite casually in *The Merchant*', the play also leaves open the possibility that Bassanio, like Ben Jonson's hypothetical man of pleasure, could have 'his ingle at home'. Indeed, Bassanio has access to two Balthazars, since Portia borrowed her name from a servant.[60] Bovilsky points out that this character could have been portrayed as an African, since 'Balthazar' was the name commonly attributed to the youngest of the biblical Magi who was in Shakespeare's day conventionally represented as from this continent.[61] Jonathan Goldberg speculates that if Balthazar were African this would be in keeping with the well-known phenomenon of giving slaves the names of famous kings and heroes as 'a way of pointing to their supposed utter incapacitation'.[62] Whatever the servant's status, by reducing Balthazar the great courtroom performer to a marital boy-toy, the drama appears to resolve the complex issues of oppression it has just raised by transforming the taint of difference into just another ironic pose donned by its elites as they blithely continue to buy and sell human flesh.

Alternatively, the brief reappearance of 'Balthazar' in the play's final scene could provide one last flicker of subaltern defiance, even though the aliens Morocco and Shylock have been banished from the stage. For 'Balthassar' was also the name given to the biblical Daniel when the Babylonians took him captive as part of their conquest of the 'children of Judah' (Dan. 2.27). The play reinforces this association when Shylock hails Portia/Balthazar as 'A Daniel come to judgement; yea, a Daniel!' (4.1.219). In the episode from the Book of Daniel that most directly bears on the courtroom scene, the Babylonian king is having a feast when a hand appears from thin air and writes an illegible phrase on the wall. Daniel is able to decipher this as *MENE, MENE, TEKEL, UPARSIN*, or 'Numbered, numbered, weighed, divided', which he reads as a prediction that the king's empire is about to be destroyed (Dan. 5.25–8). The phrase could also distill Portia's legal solution to Shylock's bond: the fact that, in order to get an exact pound, the flesh must, impossibly, be precisely weighed *before* it is divided from the body.[63] While this connection aligns Portia with the hero Daniel and reinforces her defeat of the Jewish villain Shylock, it happens that in the Bible story the Babylonian king is *also* named Baltassar, and Portia resembles him in sharing her name with a servant. The irony deepens when we understand that the first half of the Book of Daniel recounts how, as the child renamed 'Balthasar', Daniel will not 'defile himself with the portion of the King's meat, nor with the wine which he drank' and refuses to pray to his gods (Dan. 1.8). These actions resonate with Shylock's demurral early in the play, 'I will buy with you, sell with you, talk with you, walk with you and so following. But I will not eat with you, drink with you nor pray with you' (1.3.31–4). When Portia, as Balthazar, invokes a law against aliens to assist in the forced conversion of one of Daniel's tribe, are we sympathizing with the righteous Christian against the stubborn Jew, or the colonized subject against his tyrannical oppressor?

The story of the writing on the wall begins with the appearance of an alien hand tracing illegible script. I want to end by suggesting that such strange textual interruptions are the queer gestures of *The Merchant of Venice*. Their prototype is the moment when Jacob sticks up the rods before the ewes 'in the doing of the deed of kind' – a phrase that suggests the impossibility of doing this deed *without* the insertion of a wand, a pen, that gives the lie to the fantasy of sameness's self-perpetuation and instead allows for the inclusion of difference and so the possibility of generation, of movement, of life. Antonio's following question, 'Was this inserted to make interest good?' picks up on Jacob's act of insertion and highlights the way the biblical text itself feels inserted into the men's dialogue. Often cut from productions,

Shylock's speech interrupts an increasingly tense back-and-forth, inserting a long digression on a relatively obscure and logistically complex biblical episode with strained relevance to the matter at hand. Through these jagged and self-conscious insertions – ones that mimic the arrival of visitors and letters – the play disrupts the idealized forms of homosocial textual transmission found in the traditions of both classical friendship and humanist pedagogy.

One such moment of interruption occurs in the play's last scene, when Portia hands a paper to Antonio, declaring 'You shall not know by what strange accident / I chanced on this letter' (5.1.278–9). This random occurrence happens to provide Antonio with his happy ending, since the letter reports 'three of your argosies / Are richly come to harbour suddenly' (276–7). The specification of *three* argosies, combined with the letter's mysterious origin, make it a sly reference to the main source for Shakespeare's play, Fiorentino's *Il Pecorone*, in which the Antonio character, Anselmo, mires himself in debt to stake his godson Gianetto on three trading voyages. But Gianetto loses the merchant's goods to the Donna del Belmonte, the widowed ruler of a rich port, who challenges any man that if, upon spending the night, he can succeed in copulating with her, he wins her hand, the land and all its wealth. Gianetto twice fails the test and must cede his ships and cargo until he at last manages to bed and wed the Donna Del Belmonte – whose name is likely Fiorentino's joke about the path to success since, a period Italian-English dictionary explains, a 'Mónte de vénere' is '*a womans quaint*'.[64] Shakespeare gives this Lady of the Beautiful Mons a first name, Portia, that emphasizes her identity as the embodiment of a rich harbor. Since his play introduces a different test for the Lady's hand – Portia's suitors must open her casket rather than her body – there is no obvious reason why she would be the one to restore the merchant's wealth; hence the *deus ex machina* of Antonio's letter.

Shakespeare's intertextual insertion, via Portia, of this 'happy ending' may seem small compensation for Antonio, since it is evident by the end of the play that she has gained the upper hand in their competition for first place in Bassanio's loyalties. Interpreters sigh over Antonio's lonely fate in the last scene, a singleton among three married pairs. In contrast, in Fiorentino's story Gianetto gives Anselmo his wife's maid in marriage. This maid had helped Gianetto by tipping him off that her mistress put a sleeping draught in his wine, disabling him from passing her test. For her betrayal of her mistress for the sake of masculine conquest, the maid is rewarded by being traded among men. Antonio does not receive such a gift. In fact, Shakespeare goes out of his way to avoid this ending by inventing the character of Gratiano to marry Portia's maid instead of Antonio. Rather than the normative comedic resolution of marriage, Antonio gets his ships – a detail left out of Fiorentino's story. This ending leaves Antonio both independently wealthy and unmoored from any particular romantic script.

The letter, containing what was omitted from another text, arrives by a 'strange accident', making it appear foreign like Shylock, whose legal status as 'stranger' has just exiled him from the play (3.3.27; 4.1.345). Its accidental arrival is a near transparent ruse to tie up the plot's loose threads, but one that perhaps also reminds us of a procreative potential that exceeds the mere mechanical replication of Aristotelian repro-duction, be it of babies or money. 'The female is procreated by accident', Helikiah Crooke observed of Aristotle's theory of generation.[65] While for Aristotle such accidents occurred when the male seed was too weak to fully impose its form on feminine matter, Renaissance physiology credited instead the wayward meanderings of the imagination. In *The Merchant of Venice* Portia embodies this fulsome potentiality by acting as a gatekeeper – porteress, if you will – of the intertextual space between the play and its sources. This gap, like the one marking the insertion of Shylock's Jacob story or separating Portia from her alter-ego Balthazar, can make us aware of the other directions this story could take. Through this gap, Antonio could pursue some other, perhaps as yet unarticu-lated, version of queer intimacy. What do I think this might look like? Fie, fie.

11

Male femininity and male-to-female crossdressing in Shakespeare's plays and poems

Simone Chess

Shakespeare's queer resonance takes unexpected forms in modern popular culture: surprisingly, in 2016, the most popular Tumblr blog about 'male femininity' – a broad category that includes a range of feminine identifications in those assigned male-at-birth, including nonbinary, genderqueer, gender nonconforming and trans* femme presentations, as well as male-to-female crossdressing – is called *Shakespearean Male*.[1] The page's description explains, under an unremarked-upon picture of Henry Wriothesley:

> Shakespeare was the most androgynous of men. Throughout his plays, he objected to the extreme polarization of sex

roles and the contradictions underlying it. As an artist, he recognized the creative power of androgyny. Realizing that healthy men and women naturally display a variety of impulses, some masculine, some feminine, he equated androgyny with emotional balance. Shakespeare had an apparent delight in a complex mingling of masculine and feminine.[2]

What is perhaps most surprising about this internet invocation of Shakespeare is that, while it vaguely follows scholarly conversations in identifying androgyny and disguise as key to Shakespeare's work, it diverges from traditional feminist and queer academic approaches to Shakespeare and gender by focusing most on male femininity and male-to-female (MTF) crossdressing rather than female masculinity and female-to-male (FTM) crossdressing.[3] The bloggers, who besides this header and the prominent title naming Shakespeare make no obvious references to early modern drama or poetry, nevertheless associate Shakespeare with queer and femme masculinities, and locate his biographical queerness and the representations of queerness in his work in terms of gender, rather than sexuality. *Shakespearean Male*'s description concludes, 'You being a Woman or a Man yourself doesn't matter – once you have experienced the delights of a Feminized Male, your life will have changed forever – and there will be no way back'. Where are the feminized men and MTF crossdressers in Shakespeare? What language is used by and about them? If we pay more sustained attention to the queer 'delights' of male femininity in Shakespeare's work might we, in fact, find 'no way back'?

While it is my hope to prove *Shakespearean Male* right by recognizing and recentring Shakespeare's representations of male femininity, when it comes to MTF crossdressing Shakespeare's plays are a challenge. As I've shown elsewhere, there is an unsung canon of male-to-female crossdressers in early modern literary representation.[4] Many prominent sixteenth- and seventeenth-century playwrights like Lyly,

Jonson, Middleton, Fields, Chapman, Beaumont and Fletcher wrote and staged at least one major male-to-female cross-dressing plot each.[5] In contrast, in all of Shakespeare's plays I have identified only three main FTM examples, none of them central to the plot or sustained: Falstaff as the witch of Brainford in *Merry Wives of Windsor*, the double false marriage trick where Caius and Slender marry crossdressed boys thinking that they are Anne Page, also in *Merry Wives of Windsor*, and Christopher Sly's crossdressed 'wife' in the induction of *Taming of the Shrew*. One addition to this list would be Antony's possible crossdressing in the opening scene of *Antony and Cleopatra*, thought this instance has been the subject of some debate and is not explicit in the play's text. In addition to these, the plays include two boy-actor characters who perform female roles in plays-within-plays: the unnamed actor playing the role of Queen in *Hamlet*'s Mousetrap, and the actor Francis Flute playing Thisbe in *Midsummer Night's Dream*.[6] Compared to the sustained, complex and alluring queerness that Shakespeare depicts in his FTM crossdressing characters (Portia in *Merchant of Venice*, Rosalind in *As You Like It*, Viola in *Twelfth Night*, Julia in *Two Gentleman of Verona*, Imogen in *Cymbeline*), the few MTF plots super-ficially seem shallow, limited to the register of homophobic or even transmisogynistic sight gags. While these moments have been examined in passing, they have never been framed as potentially positive or as inherently queer rather than inher-ently queer-mocking.

Feminine/femme and transfeminine genders have been overlooked not only in Shakespeare, but more broadly in queer and gender studies. Where groundbreaking founda-tional work like Butler's *Gender Trouble* and Halberstam's *Female Masculinity* opened up new ways of thinking and talking about performances of gender, both focused almost exclusively on butch and drag king gender play, with limited sections on drag queens and even less on other forms of male feminine presentation; in the important inaugural 'keywords' issue of *Trans Studies Quarterly*, there is a definition for 'transbutch', but not 'transfemme'.[7] Gayle Salamon and others have written about the exclusion of trans studies, and especially transfeminist work from some Women's Studies programmes, and Julia Serano has named and defined this exclusion as transmisogyny.[8] Serano writes, 'those of us on the trans-female/feminine spectrum are culturally marked, not for failing to conform to gender norms, *per se*, but because of the specific direction of our gender transgression—that is, because of our feminine gender expression and/or our female gender identities'.[9] For this reason, she continues, 'I recoil from the idea of femme gender expression as "ironic and campy", as a form of drag or performance, because it plays into the popular assumption that femininity is artificial. I am particularly sensitive about this subject because, as I mention earlier, others often view me as doubly artificial because I am trans *and* because I am feminine'.[10] Drama is inherently artificial, but the types of characters, and genders, that it portrays don't have to be. This essay is an effort to take male femininity seriously, and to propose it as an unironic aspect of *Queer Shakespeare* by revisiting episodes of MTF crossdressing in Shakespeare's plays not just (or not only) as comedic farce but also as authentic experiments in gender presentation. In taking men in women's dresses more seriously, we stand to deepen and complicate the variety of expressions of genders and gendered desire in Shakespeare's plays.

Sonnet 20 and *Venus and Adonis*

If I am guilty of unabashed presentist queer optimism in my efforts to find merit and value embedded in MTF crossdressing episodes, and to read them as transfeminine and queer rather than farcical, I have been encouraged by Shakespeare himself, in his non-dramatic work. In the sonnets, most especially in Sonnet 20, Shakespeare overtly eroticizes and admires male effeminacy and androgyny, describing the perfect love object

as a master-mistress with the best of male and female characteristics. While the poem has been discussed richly in terms of
queer desire and male-male attraction, less attention has been
paid to the ways that the poem eroticizes not just same-sex
attraction but also queer-gender attraction.[11] The poem's
internal misogyny (its attention to women's false fashion
and rolling eyes) creates a scenario in which a feminine man,
a man 'first created for a woman', even, but then 'pricked
out for women's pleasure', is the most idealized love object,
more appealing than a cisgender (or not queer) woman or
man could be.[12] The poem further articulates the apparently
universal appeal of this queerly gendered master-mistress,
with 'all hues in his controlling', who 'much steals men's eyes
and women's souls amazeth'. In sharp contrast to the slapstick
and demeaning ways that MTF crossdressing plots are – at
least superficially – treated in the plays, this master-mistress is
elevated as the ideal Petrarchan love object, and is praised not
despite but *because* of his androgyny and femininity.

So too, in *Venus and Adonis*, Shakespeare goes out of his
way to detail and describe Adonis' androgyny and erotic
appeal – not just to lusty, masculinized Venus, but also to
the speaker, and through him, to the voyeuristic reader.[13]
'Thrice-fairer' than the sweaty goddess of love, Adonis is a
'Stain to all nymphs, more lovely than a man'. Just like the
master-mistress, he's a special favourite to Nature, who, in
making him, not only fell in love but considered him her best
work. Again and again throughout the poem, Shakespeare
draws special attention to Adonis' tenderness, his blushing, his
daintiness, 'the maiden burning of his cheeks'. But again, male
femininity is here praised and eroticized. Venus cannot control
herself, and even Adonis' death by boar tusk – itself a kind
of feminizing castration – is imagined as a kind of attraction
between the masculinized boar and the feminized boy. This
poem, like the fair youth sonnets, celebrates androgyny, queer
gender roles and a youth who, while not crossdressed, is
celebrated for his attractive, erotic, appealing feminine characteristics. In these poems and others, Shakespeare depicts

cross-gender MTF and queer-gender feminine presentations as potentially beneficial, attractive and appealing. While these positive depictions of male-femininity have certainly been noted, they have generally been subsumed by larger discussions about homosexuality, with male femininity read and coded as sexual immaturity and passivity.[14]

Attending to Adonis and the master-mistress not as immature men but as transfeminine ones – as *genderqueer* in addition to *sexually queer* – approaches the strategy that Susan Stryker describes as 'renarration', or 'transgender effects', in which 'foreground and background seem to flip and reverse, and the spectacle of an unexpected gender phenomenon illuminates the production of gender normativity in a startling new way. In doing so, the field [of transgender studies] begins to tell new stories about things many of us thought we already knew'.[15]

The language and imagery for Sonnet 20 and *Venus and Adonis* make it easy to renarrate their boy love-objects with a 'transgender effect'. Adonis and the fair youth are the sorts of characters that the bloggers of *Shakespearean Male* must have had in mind when they sought out Shakespeare (and Wriothesley) as an icon for male femininity. It is perhaps less intuitive to apply this 'transgender effect' to the episodes of male femininity, most of them MTF crossdressing, in the plays. And yet, because these episodes are short and self-contained, their role is inherently more philological than plot-driven. Male femininity is shown to be the product of self-manifesting language and rhetoric and of community reception and recognition. If we push past the joke, MTF crossdressing episodes showcase the work of making and maintaining gender, especially queer feminine gender. Read this way, admittedly against the conventional grain, the plays are in conversation with the poems – tonally different to be sure, but connected through an exploration of male femininity and its potential transgender effect.[16]

The Falstaff problem: The witch of Brainford

The most famous of Shakespeare's male-to-female cross-dressing moments is the scene in *The Merry Wives of Windsor* in which the wives dress Falstaff in the gown, hat and muffler of the aunt of Mistress Ford's maid, the old witch of Brainford. Though well-known, this episode is perhaps the least interesting – the least queer – of the FTM episodes, in part because it depends so heavily on diminishing, rather than eroticizing, crossdressing and crossgender feminine presentation. The scene has commonly been dismissed as slapstick or silly: a final humiliation for Falstaff, not a real effort to make him pass for a woman and certainly not an expression of Falstaff's own gender identity or femininity. Roger Moss, for instance, argues that the crossdressing trick is just another way to degrade Falstaff, but that it 'adds nothing to these comic twists, and makes them seem merely formulaic', lacking the 'surprise or energy' of the previous buckbasket trick.[17] Falstaff's crossdressing is generally seen to be motivated by his fear of being caught seducing Mistress Ford rather than by his own internal identity or interest, though some scholars, including W. H. Auden and Grace Tiffany, have focused on the sexual ambiguity of Falstaff crossdressed: Auden calls him 'a cross between a very young child and a pregnant mother', and Tiffany compares Falstaff's expression of sexuality to other crossdressing moments in the comedy of humours, concluding that 'Falstaff's disguise as the "fat woman of Brainford" during his final escape from Ford's house further muffles an already provisional sexual nature, adding to it another layer of sexual impossibility'.[18]

Already having withstood the buckbasket, Falstaff chooses crossdressing over a beating.[19] Yet, when he passes for the witch of Brainford, Falstaff makes himself more, not less, vulnerable to violence. Mistress Ford says, 'I would my husband would meet him in this shape. He cannot abide the

old woman of Brainford; he swears she is a witch, forbade her
my house, and hath threatened to beat her', to which Mistress
Page responds, 'Heaven guide my husband's cudgel, and the
devil guide his cudgel afterwards!' (4.2.80–3).[20] Already a fat
fool character, Falstaff's crossdressing makes him appear even
more ridiculous, which is the point of the joke. Mistresses
Ford and Page trick Falstaff into crossdressing to exploit their
husbands' misogyny toward old, fat and bearded women like
the widow of Brainford – for instance, Jonathan Goldberg
suggests that Falstaff's beating is grounded in the fact that he
becomes a masculine, bearded woman and is thus associated
with both witchcraft and with women who had sex with
women.[21] At the heart of the Brainford episode is the idea that
MTF crossdressing is humiliating, risks violence, generates
misogynistic disdain and, above all, is not desirable. The play
goes out of its way to explicitly link male femininity with
violent correction and shaming – Falstaff later reports that 'I
was beaten myself into all colors of the rainbow', 'the knave
constable had seyt me i' the stocks, i' the common stocks, for
a witch' (4.5.108; 113–14), and, of Master Ford, 'he beat me
grievously, in the shape of a woman; for in the shape of a man,
[...] I fear not Goliath with a weaver's beam' (5.1.19–22).
Bearded, fat, beaten, lecherous, ridiculous, Falstaff certainly
doesn't seem to show how queer feminine masculinity might
be a part of a *Queer Shakespeare* narrative.

For the purposes of this chapter, farcical crossdressed
Falstaff serves as a solid foil to both the erotic androgyny
of Shakespeare's poetry and the other, more open-ended
instances of MTF crossdressing in the plays. And yet, even in
this most incompetent episode of MTF crossdressing, there
is a queer residue. First, though the Brainford disguise seems
totally random, it is premediated in Falstaff's language in the
history plays. Well before he is tricked into playing the witch
of Brainford, Falstaff uses feminized self-descriptive language
in other plays, using a rhetoric of the female body to describe
himself. In *1 Henry IV*, he details his apparently ailing body,
'my skin hangs about me like an old lady's loose gown'

(3.3.3). Here, not only does his own flesh become a feminine dress, but he implies that the gown further feminizes him by hiding his penis under its flap; in the next line he further references his genital diminishment by describing himself as 'withered like an old apple-john' (3.3.4). In *2 Henry IV*, when Coleville recognizes Falstaff as he surrenders, Falstaff refers to his signature belly as 'my womb, my womb, my womb, my womb', triply feminizing his body through the repetition (4.3.22).

Preceding the witch of Brainford episode, Falstaff's self-feminizing speech gives context to the wives' pranks. It further deepens the possibility that, though brief, the Brainford episode may reveal an aspect of gendered queerness in Falstaff that he's hinted at in the Henriad moments. After the Brainford trick, after his beating, it is perhaps telling that Falstaff wears his Brainford disguise home, so that Simple, seeing him heading into his own room at the inn, tells the host 'There's an old woman, a fat woman, gone up into his chamber' (4.4.10–11). Even after the joke has run its course, Falstaff stays the witch of Brainford for a bit longer; when he emerges in his own clothing, he admits, 'There was, mine host, an old fat woman even now with me, but she's gone' (4.4.22–3). In the phrase 'even now with me', Falstaff leaves open the possibility that his disguise has been lastingly trans-formational, if only in a small way; in response to the host's question 'was there a wise woman with thee?' (4.455–6), Falstaff answers, 'Ay, that there was, mine host, one that hath taught me more wit than I ever learnt before in my life' (4.4.57–8). To imagine that Falstaff benefits from, internalizes or even takes seriously his brief presentation as the Witch of Brainford is to read against the grain of the play, but it is possible. Ford says that the real witch of Brainford 'works by charms, by spells, by the figure' (4.3.166); Falstaff later describes his experience as one of transformation, closer to magic than to a prank (4.5.88).

The Falstaff episode in *Merry Wives of Windsor* is almost certainly a joke that depends upon the assumed hilarity of male femininity and crossdressing. But Falstaff's descriptions of his experience, and the way that the language of the play lingers on the witch's presence even after the joke is over, hints at the possibility that the joke enables a brief and mostly veiled recognition of the transformational possibility and potential in male femininity, even against the backdrop of shaming and containment. In this way, while the plot forecloses on MTF crossdressing, Falstaff's language leaves room for further engagement.

The boy brides in *The Merry Wives of Windsor*

Setting the witch of Brainford aside, the remaining major instances of crossdressing are more conventional boy bride plots, in which the joke of crossdressing is, at the very least, reoriented away from the apparent hilarity of a man in a dress and toward the somewhat different joke of a man admiring, desiring or marrying a woman who turns out to be a man. In these boy bride episodes, the crossdressing comes at a moment where the play loses track of itself, pivots away from its primary plot and then reorients by ignoring the episode entirely in moving forward. While this context has generally caused the boy-bride moments to be underexamined as a sort of failed theatrical trick, the disjuncture that follows each episode might actually demonstrate Shakespeare's ambivalence and openness toward staging the kind of eroticized male femininity he explores in the poems.

Take, for example, the *other* crossdressing joke in *The Merry Wives of Windsor*, the one that comes at the play's carnivalesque near-conclusion. Both Slender and Dr Caius are tricked into running away with (and nearly marrying) boys who are dressed as Anne Page. Slender reports: 'I came yonder at Eton to marry Anne Page, and she's a great lubberly boy. If it had not been i' the church, I would have swinged him, or he would have swinged me' (5.5.180–3). When Page states the obvious, 'Upon my life, then, you took the wrong', he responds, 'What need you tell me that? I think so, when I took a boy for a girl. If I had been married to him, for all he was in woman's apparel, I would not have had him' (5.5.157–91). The reveal is repeated a second time as Dr Caius reports the same trick 'By gar, I am cozened, I ha' / married *un garçon*, a boy; *un paysan*, by gar! A boy it is not Anne Page' (5.5.201–3).

To be sure, both of the men's reactions are meant to be funny, especially because they highlight the characters' most comedic attibutes – Slender's stupidity and Caius's French accent. Certainly, a main part of the humour, just as in the earlier witch of Brainford moment, is about the special blend of homophobia and queer anxiety with misogyny and the policing of both male and female gender presentations. This aspect of the joke is highlighted by Slender's violent response to the postmaster's boy, whose crossdressing makes him both a threat ('he would have swinged me') and a target ('I would have swinged him') for violence. And still, the fact of the two boy bride's passing for female and the apparent ease with which they almost exchange themselves for cisgender women in marriage (with the implication that a similar replacement during sex is also possible), hits a different tone than the broad witch of Brainford joke. The joke is on the grooms, not the boys dressed as women whom they nearly marry. In nearly marrying Slender and Caius, these boy brides threaten boundaries of gender, sexuality and class. Though their boundary-crossing moment is short, it recalls the openness to transfeminine erotic allure found more often in Shakespeare's poems than in his plays.

The boy actor-characters in *Hamlet* and *A Midsummer Night's Dream*

In thinking about male femininity and MTF crossdressing in Shakespeare's plays, I have been cautious to draw a distinction between the boy actors who played the female roles (and, even more queerly, the FTM crossdressing roles); it is important, I think, to make clear that representations of crossdressing and queer gender, while informed by the bodies of the actors who performed them, retain their queer rhetoric and impact as separate from those performance conditions. But twice Shakespeare stages plays within plays which feature boys cast in female roles, and these instances permit a metatextual and metatheatrical opportunity to examine the overlap and boundaries of boyish androgyny and male femininity.

In *Hamlet*, the prince has a rare, if disjunctive, moment of clarity during his descent into madness when he pauses to greet the players who will later perform his 'Mousetrap'. In particular, he pays attention to the boys who've played female roles, noting a beard in one – 'O, old friend, why, thy face is valenced since I saw thee last. Com'st thou to beard me in Denmark?' (2.2.423–5) – and a growth spurt in another – 'What, my young lady and Mistress. By'r lady, your ladyship is nearer to heaven than when I saw you last by the altitude of a chopine. Pray God your voice, like a piece of uncurrent gold, be not cracked within the ring' (2.2.425–30). With these lines, Hamlet draws explicit attention to the queer gender position held by boy players, whose ability to play female roles depended upon their maintenance of androgyny. Hamlet's attention to the evidence of puberty in both of the actors whom he addresses directly reveals both the limited temporal space for erotic androgyny and the apparently acceptable scrutiny of male femininity, where androgynous boys can be openly examined for signs that they might be tipping from Adonis territory into witch of Brainford farce.

In addition to providing this metatheatrical demonstration of how boy actors might be received and evaluated, *Hamlet* also provides a brief demonstration of how one of those actors, once performing his female role (and, notably, performing it *after* the audience has seen him first in his male attire), can have substantial power and influence. Dressed as a queen, the player first performs a dumb show and then speaks. The player queen announces '*For women'n fear and love hold quantity, / In neither aught or in extremity*' (3.2.169–70), and '*Where love is great, the littlest doubts are fear: / Where little fears grow great, great love grows there*' (in folio: 3.2.173–4).[22] Finally, the player queen speaks the final words of the play-within-a-play, and it is in response to their speech that Gertrude makes her famous theatrical review, 'The lady doth protest too much, methinks' (3.2.232).

The key to the Mousetrap is that Gertrude must accept that the player queen is a lady, and must identify with her, in order for Hamlet's trick to work and the truth be revealed. And indeed, the player seems able to perform the role of queen convincingly, if perhaps too intensely. But by introducing the player first as a boy, drawing attention to his maleness, and only later showing him performing in his female role, Shakespeare highlights the fact that this powerful scene depends on queer gender performance, on a lady who is also a boy; when the player queen stands on stage before Queen Gertrude, both actually boys playing women, the play insists on a distinction between female verisimilitude (the audience should believe that Gertrude is a woman, and a mother, even if she is acted by a boy) and male femininity and crossdressing (the audience should, with Hamlet, be in the know about the performance and it's instability, and should admire how it hinges on a boy dressed as a queen, protesting too much).

In *A Midsummer Night's Dream*, the boy actor has both less skill and less importance to the plot than *Hamlet*'s player queen, but his performance of femininity is similar. Again, Shakespeare introduces us to the boy first, and draws attention to his position at the cusp of puberty; when Peter Quince assigns roles for *Pyramus and Thisbe* and calls on Peter Flute to 'take Thisbe on you', Flute optimistically hopes that Thisbe will be a male role, a 'wand'ring knight', and then protests taking the female part, 'let not me play a woman: I have a beard coming' (1.2.42, 45).[23]

When it comes time for the actual performance, though, Flute-as-Thisbe proves to be a solid actor, delivering her lines without the digressions that mark the other Mechanicals' performances and delivering the closing speech of *Pyramus and Thisbe*. While the speech begins in a comical way, with the forced rhyme of '*Asleep, my love? / What, dead, my dove?*', (5.1.319–20), it shifts to become more complex in form, tone, metaphor and emotional resonance toward the end:

> *Dead, dead? A tomb*
> *Must cover thy sweet eyes.*
> *These lily lips,*
> *This cherry nose,*
> *These yellow cowslip cheeks,*
> *Are gone, are gone!*

> (5.1.323–9)

In his 1999 film adaptation of the play, Michael Hoffman directs actor Sam Rockwell to emphasize this shift in the verse, having him abandon Thisbe's falsetto, remove her wig and deliver these lines as Flute, with feeling. This decision, perhaps the most favourably reviewed and most memorable moment in the film, draws attention the importance of the MTF crossdresser in the play; rather than remaining a farce, Flute has the potential, like the player queen, to perform with resonance and truth.[24] Like Adonis and the master mistress, and maybe even like Falstaff, Flute's Thisbe is not meant, ever, to pass for female. Instead, Flute's androgyny, his male performance of female emotion, can potentially override the generic limits of a mechanical in a play-within-a-comedy.

The Taming of the Shrew's induction

The strange, never-completed induction to *The Taming of the Shrew* is perhaps the strongest example of the potentially ambivalent depiction of erotic androgynous femininity in the plays. The episode brings together aspects of the MTF moments in *Merry Wives of Windsor*, *Hamlet* and *Midsummer Night's Dream* by staging a crossdresser who is a part of a trick and part of a performance, but who is not an actor or the butt of the joke. The crossdresser here is part of the Lord's elaborate trick on drunkard Christopher Sly. When he comes up with the plan, the Lord orders that his servants should tell Sly 'that his lady mourns at his disease', adding an imaginary noble lady wife to the list of valuable items that he uses to prank him. But when the lady is produced, of course, she's a crossdressed page, and actually a fairly large portion of the induction is dedicated to describing the mechanics of her presentation. The host instructs:

> Sirrah, go you to Barthol'mew my page,
> And see him dress'd in all suits like a lady.
> That done, conduct him to the drunkard's chamber,
> And call him 'madam', do him obeisance,
> Tell him from me, as he will win my love,
> He bear himself with honourable action,
> Such as he hath observ'd in noble ladies
> Unto their lords, by them accomplished.
> Such duty to the drunkard let him do,
> With soft low tongue and lowly courtesy

(Ind.1.104–13)

Here, part of the crossdressing trick is to have Bartholomew perform a convincing and appealing femininity, one that will entice Sly and draw him further into the trick. The behaviours and mannerisms that the page should perform reveal that such behaviours are performative whether they are enacted by actual courtly ladies or by a crossdressing mimic. The Lord's promise of love for his page, if the job is done well, implies that the job of playing the lady is one that is less shameful than admirable and perhaps homosocially bonding. And when the Lord is worried about his page being less than convincing, it's not because he doesn't think Bartholomew can pass for female; he only worries that his dutiful wifely tears might not be convincing without a 'woman's gift / To rain a shower of commanded tears', a direct echo of the master-mistress' eyes more bright than theirs, less false in rolling', and a problem apparently easily solved with an onion in a handkerchief (Ind.1.124–5).

In addition to the Lord's promise that, through crossdressing, the page might win his love, many aspects of the crossdressing episode are highly eroticized. As a lady, the page should approach Sly 'with kind embracements, tempting kisses, / And with declining head into his bosom' (Ind.1.117–18) and later, when Sly meets this wife, he immediately announces, 'Servants, leave me and her alone. / Madam, undress you and come now to bed' (Ind.1.121; here, Bartholomew smoothly announces that going to bed together would be against doctor's orders; apparently an improvisation outside the parameters originally outlined by the Lord). Sly's interest in the lady doesn't seem to be a joke that relies on her being unattractive or manly. The text also elaborates on this lady's beauty: she is 'a lady far more beautiful / Than any in this waning age', as having a 'lovely face', and as 'the fairest creature in the world […] inferior to none' (1.1.66–7). While the trick on Sly is satirical, the crossdressed lady need not be a joke; in the spirit of centring and admiring male feminity, we can perhaps take her beauty and allure at face value.

The induction's prank is never resolved, and the connection between the content of the induction and the content of the body of the play is never made explicit.[25] And yet despite the induction's marginal place in the play, there might just be some space for queer optimism in Bartholomew the page as Sly's wife. Beautiful, alluring, rhetorically skilled, capable of performing across both class and gender, the crossdressed boy bride is closer to an Adonis or master-mistress than to a witch of Brainford. At the end of the induction, Sly invites his lady to 'sit by my side, / And let the world slip' (1.1.144–5). Depending on the staging, the drunk in a lord's clothes and the page in a lady's dress sit at the periphery of the stage and watch the rest of the play. This final MTF crossdresser, then, potentially lingers on the stage, not a joke but an observer of the comedy, not a punchline but a point of identification for the audience more broadly.

This last example of male femininity through MTF crossdressing doesn't resolve the issue of why Shakespeare's FTM and queer feminine characters require so much rehabilitative optimism, but it does offer a glimpse of queer feminine potential where it's often been overlooked. Beyond lushly romantic descriptions of feminine boys in Sonnet 20 and *Venus and Adonis*, there are moments of feminine masculinity laced across Shakespeare's plays. Too often, queer and trans femininity is pushed aside as parody, slapstick, drag; in her call for a 'Femme Movement', Maura Ryan argues that 'Queers need to embrace femininity because queer femmes challenge the naturalness of gender and heterosexuality in unique ways'.[26] Shakespeare's MTF crossdressing moments are flawed, few and far between. But by offering them, and other instances of male femininity in Shakespeare's work, a truer place among the variety of expressions of gender, sexuality and desire in Shakespeare's work deepens, complicates and queers the canon.

12

Held in common: *Romeo and Juliet* and the promiscuous seductions of plague

Kathryn Schwarz

> *There is no end, no limit, measure, bound,*
> *In that word's death.*[1]

> *The plague-stricken town, traversed throughout with*
> *hierarchy, surveillance, observation, writing; the town*
> *immobilized by the functioning of an extensive power*
> *that bears in a distinct way over all individual bodies –*
> *this is the utopia of the perfectly governed city.*[2]

I begin with a proposition I do not mean to pursue: In Foucauldian terms, *Romeo and Juliet* is shaped by the spectacular power of the Prince.

One could make the case. The interdict Prince Escalus issues against the feud is affirmed (although not until the play's end); his prediction that lives will be forfeit is fulfilled (although they are not the lives he names); his edict of banishment is obeyed (although not for long); he has the last word (although it obscures more than it controls). I wonder, then, why the claim that identifies sovereignty as an efficient cause feels so odd. One obvious answer emerges from the pleasure of defiance: if the doomed love of Romeo and Juliet attaches beguiling mystique to undisciplined desire, then government shifts to the margins or slips beneath a more dominant force. The parenthetical qualifiers of my earlier sentence overshadow the clauses they modify. But mystique itself might redistribute and replicate the effects of centralized power, controlling unruly energies through the procedures that celebrate them; so Carla Freccero asks of the play's final, static memorials, 'Isn't this what "politics," by which here we understand a certain social order, wants?'[3] Collaborative idealization of a rebellious union absorbs idiosyncrasy into sociality. If you can't beat them, arrest and appropriate the forces that join them.

And yet, Freccero notes, 'Shakespeare is having it both ways', poising a legible public sign against 'the meaningless, absolute, irrational queer force' of the death drive.[4] Jonathan Goldberg instead argues that readers have it both ways, as he critiques transcendental and heterosexist readings of Romeo and Juliet: 'what makes their love so valuable is that it serves as a nexus for the social and can be mystified as outside the social'.[5] Goldberg and Freccero situate the twofold impulse differently, but these are cognate dualities. Each illuminates taxonomies of scale, which might conserve the individual at the expense of the communal or consume the individual in the service of the social. The disparate vectors of conservation and consumption matter less than the imperative that assigns proper objects to those drives. In the case of Romeo and Juliet, then, the question of how to value their desire-imbued bodies gives way to the question of what can be built on a symbolic carapace emptied of flesh. As synecdoche or sacrifice, as icon or caution, the merged corpus of the lovers promises a future purged of infectious excess.[6] Goldberg and Freccero resist the functional paradox that would have it both ways, pushing back against a double move which, as it subsumes compliance and deviance under the paradigm of use, fixes persons within social abstractions. Their readings recognize the queer force of itinerant desires, emphasizing drives and bonds that refuse to fit or fade or be still. Here I want to turn that project towards the seductive potential of contagion, and consider the lethal reciprocities that render subjects pervious to one another. More specifically, I want to think about plague.

In *The Posthuman*, Rosi Braidotti writes, 'We need to re-think death, the ultimate subtraction, as another phase in a generative process'. Braidotti contends that 'this life-death continuum' reveals the force of communion: 'It connects us trans-individually, trans-generationally and eco-philosophically'.[7] Her analysis resonates with other attempts to rethink community through death, and to recalibrate embodied personhood as a condition that traverses insular subjectivity.[8] Such arguments reach back, whether implicitly or explicitly, to Georges Bataille's influential formulation:

> I propose to admit, as a law, that human beings are only united with each other through rents or wounds; this notion has, in itself, a certain logical force. If elements are put together to form a whole, this can easily happen when each one loses, through a rip in its integrity, a part of its own being, which goes to benefit the communal being.[9]

Dis-integrated beings, whose wounds bleed beyond the bounds of functional sociality or autonomous personhood, pose an alternative to Michel Foucault's docile bodies and Louis Althusser's always-already subjects.[10] This alternative has a particular bite for *Romeo and Juliet*, in which dying is at once over-celebrated and curiously under-motivated. One could say that death, as ritual sacrifice, serves the needs of a disembodied social order; one could say that 'embodied subjects are interacting and inter-killing' to translate reckless actors into static signs.[11] Yet there is something insufficient about this account, if only because Romeo and Juliet themselves are insufficient to a sacrificial causality. Even Harold Bloom finds the aftermath of their deaths more bathetic than sublime: 'What is left on stage at the close of this tragedy is an absurd pathos'.[12] I suggest that the unhindered transfer of bodily fragilities points to something other than social parable or individuated pain. In a play that sequesters its privileged subjects first in a synoptic chorus and finally in an epitaphic couplet, the joint predicament of mortal, sexual bodies activates modes of communion that cause a stutter in social taxonomies. It is on these terms that we might understand infectious communion as queer.

Romeo and Juliet, like the plague writings with which it shares a linguistic preoccupation and a historical moment, theorizes the communities forged by contagion. This is not in itself a startling insight. 'From its first visitation in 1348 to well after its last in 1666, the bubonic plague inhabited England and the lives of her citizens', Rebecca Totaro writes. 'No one escaped its threat. No one could imagine immunity'.[13] Given the rapid cycle of outbreaks, any effect of widespread transmission, whether affective, corporeal or conceptual, metonymically extends towards epidemic potentialities. Still, I want to underscore a corollary effect: the dynamics of contagion cannot sustain hierarchical distinctions between the social and the individual. Neither rampant infections nor the strategies that oppose them divorce idiosyncrasy from sociality.

Plague explodes such discretions as it situates both threat and response within a collective frame, the logics of which do not entirely cohere with a disciplined public sphere. If, as the play's language insists, Romeo suffers a degenerative malady – 'I have lost myself, I am not here. / This is not Romeo' (1.1.197–8) – his condition of self-loss does not segregate him from others. When Mercutio draws him back into legible identities and affinities – 'Now art thou sociable, now art thou Romeo; now art thou what thou art' (2.4.89–90) – he embraces his own death: 'why the devil came you between us? I was hurt under your arm' (3.1.103–4). The 'you' who bears the mark of disease intervenes among the 'us' who constitute sociality; whether disowned or claimed, the touch is transferred. To read *Romeo and Juliet* as saturated with epidemic potential is to see affiliation as a welter of capricious indiscretions. Live bodies connect in deadly bonds that endanger privileged systems, even as dead bodies share spaces that breed lively fusions of flesh. Contagious in both life and death, communal intercourse blurs the line between transient persons and enduring structures, and expands propagation beyond generative descent. To put this in bare terms: Futurity cannot be sanitized when mass graves undergird the project of social survival. At the end of *Romeo and Juliet*, on what ground do those golden statues stand?

Words

This analytic trajectory has certain risks. I could define plague as crucial context, and veer towards historical determinism. I could cite the early modern fondness for analogies – or rather our retrospective notion of that fondness – and reduce the play to a microcosmic token perched atop a macrocosmic frame. I could trifle with equivalence, and apply the torque that renders textual formations identical with one another. In each case, I would anatomize contagion to provide something like diagnosis or cure. I want instead to highlight the play's own troubled, nonlinear relationship between prodigal bonds and systemic constraints, its oscillating, overlapping investments in contagion and quarantine. It intrigues me that the critical history of *Romeo and Juliet* often manifests awareness of forces that cannot be accommodated, even when the investment in closure runs deep; so Northrop Frye asks, 'But when we have a quite reasonable explanation for the tragedy,

the feud between the families, why do we need to bring
in the stars and such?' His answer – 'we shouldn't assume
that tragedy is something needing an explanation'[14] – circles
back to that question about *our* need. We may not need the
plague to understand the play, but we – even an unexpectedly
expansive 'we' – do seem to want more than sonnets or statues
or a flock of sacrificial lambs.

I suggested that the link between epidemic contagion
and anarchic communion is in part metonymic, an inexo-
rable, indecorous slide from idea to idea and from word to
thing.[15] I would add that the link is also in some odd sense
homonymic. This intuition is difficult to unpack, but it
attempts to describe a shift across registers, through which
structural resemblance at the level of expression becomes
conceptual correspondence at the level of effect. Interrelation
may fuse with pestilence because they sound the same in their
articulation of signs: 'Affliction is enamour'd of thy parts
/ And thou art wedded to calamity' (3.3.2–3). Such messy
compounds recall Freccero's description of queer forces in
language: '*queer* can also be a grammatical perversion, a
misplaced pronoun, the wrong proper name.'[16] For *Romeo
and Juliet*, of course, wrong proper names are much to
the point, and a grammatical perversion can be a sentence
of death: 'Then "banished" / Is death, misterm'd', Romeo
declares (3.3.20–1).[17] What I want to get at here is a
relationship between communion and contagion that is
intimate and correlative but not unidirectional or causal.
While it only echoes the play to say that love is a plague, it
introduces a different dimension to say that plague, through
the sheer ruthlessness of perilous association, has a great
deal to do with love. It is after all in the context of plague
that Théodore de Bèze invokes 'that general band especially,
wherwith man is bounde unto man, and that which without
the taking away of humanity it selfe, cannot be broken'.[18]
In pandemic time, when the social world seems as fragile as
the bodies that inhabit it, narrow protocols of coalition open
outward to more volatile terms and forms.

The path along which I approach *Romeo and Juliet* is laid out by Mercutio's thrice-repeated curse: 'A plague o' both your houses' (3.1.92; 100–1; 107). The fame of the line tends to obscure its commonness. Shakespeare uses at least thirty versions of the curse, giving it voices famous (Richard III, Falstaff) and obscure (the Third Fisherman in *Pericles*), valences vitriolic ('A plague upon your epileptic visage') and comic ('a plague o' these pickle-herring!').[19] It is this quality of the common – common as quotidian, common as shared – that I want to press. For *Romeo and Juliet*, plague binds the literal disease that quarantines Friar John to the conceptual disease of deadly passion, mobilizing a rhetoric of morbidity inseparable from the rhetoric of desire. In its commonness and its commonality, the cliché that equates desire with disease resists the artifacts of exceptionalism. Contagion, as irrefusable connection, yokes flesh acts to speech acts, intermingles valued subjects with disposable persons, and locates intimate attachment not in a fixed relationship to social forms but in a supple, capacious lexicon of ways in which all mortal bodies might touch.

In a brief 2005 essay, Matthew J. Bolton proposes that we understand Mercutio's curse as a speech act. 'Mercutio's dying words may possess more than rhetorical power, for it is a plague on a house that impedes Friar Laurence's messenger and that hence leads to the deaths of Romeo and Juliet', Bolton notes, and concludes, 'Friar John's internment in the sick-house may therefore be attributable neither to accident nor to fate, but to the dying Mercutio's occult revenge upon the families that have killed him'.[20] Whatever Mercutio's witchy mad skills, *Romeo and Juliet* surely links a material causality – a friar's encounter with 'the infectious pestilence' (5.2.10) – to an imagistic preoccupation with communion as disease. Here I am inclined to understand the curse not as necromantic nor even as performative, but rather as indicative of a bridge between the contagion of bodies and the contagion of ideas, across which words migrate into bodies and bodies into words. Thomas Dekker models this interpenetration in his appeal to plague victims: 'with your bodies cast a ring about me: let me behold your ghastly vizages, that my paper may receive their true pictures: *Eccho* forth your grones through the hollow truncke of my pen, and raine downe your gummy teares into mine Incke'.[21] Within the idiom of plague, language is interlaced with flesh. And if this is merely coherent with early modern theories of porosity, it is nonetheless worth noting that some words are more communicable than others.

I do not dismiss the speech act; I find it useful to consider the Prince's edict and Mercutio's curse as locutions that aspire to inherent realization. 'Throw your mistemper'd weapons to the ground / And hear the sentence of your moved prince' (1.1.87–8): this is strong stuff, immediate as a ruler's word should be. One might wonder why Escalus doesn't stop the bloodshed earlier, but cynicism whispers that it could prove politic – a delicate balance of dangerous powers – until it kills too many useful subjects. From this angle the feud has a preservative effect, isolating each family in the static exactitude of sanctioned self-replication. When Capulet tells Juliet, 'And you be mine I'll give you to my friend; / And you be not, hang! Beg! Starve! Die in the streets!', his violent chastisement may not oppose the priorities of his monarch (3.5.192–3). If we follow the thought farther, we arrive at a linguistic rivalry between Escalus and Mercutio. Where Escalus's decree mandates separation, Mercutio's curse demands union: the phrase 'a plague on' is a commonplace, but the word 'both' makes plague itself a common place, a site at which warring factions meet. The feud, well-regulated by the sovereign, conserves through quarantine; the curse, ill-conceived by a subject, destroys through contagion; people die; plague wins.

Yet I do not think this is what happens at all. A different line of thought might begin with skepticism about the Prince's efficacy. 'Rebellious subjects, enemies to peace, / Profaners of this neighbour-stained steel – / Will they not hear?' (1.1.81–3): the question hints that quarantine fails because no one listens to the man who speaks it. In his long poem *The Triumph of Death*, John Davies, like most writers of plague treatises, argues that an epidemic reduces civil authority either to culpable neglect or to profound irrelevance: 'The Magistrates did flie, or if they staid, / They staid to pray, for if they did command, / Hardly, or never should they be obaid'.[22] But people do listen to Escalus, and recur to his words: 'The Prince expressly hath / Forbid this bandying in Verona streets' (3.1.87–8); 'The Prince will doom thee death / If thou art taken' (3.1.135–6); 'What less than doomsday is the Prince's doom?' (3.3.9). The problem is rather that sovereign will circulates amidst a generalized awareness of deadly possibilities. In a broad sense such awareness is characteristic of discipline; we glimpse the panopticon when Benvolio warns, 'Here all eyes gaze on us' (3.1.52). But the vectored precision of discipline becomes indiscriminate and diffuse when law is just another word for nothing left to lose. Before the Prince speaks, we hear the citizens: 'Clubs, bills and partisans! Strike! Beat them down! Down with the Capulets! Down with the Montagues!' (1.1.72–4). This reveals not only that the feud's infection has spread, but that it has suffused its constituents with sameness. 'Two households both alike in dignity' have become symptoms of a general condition rather than discrete objects of sovereign control (Prologue, 1). 'If ever you disturb our streets again / Your lives shall pay the forfeit of the peace' (1.1.96–7): those words 'if' and 'again' capture the mix of belatedness and deferral that disaggregates the speech act. When the ruler suspends power in a counterfactual 'if', the spectre of that power travels into a common place, where subjects amalgamate and forfeiture becomes enfolded within the larger contagion of ideas. One word for that place might be 'doom', with its manifold definitions: 'A statute, law, enactment'; 'The last day of one's life'; 'The action or process of judging'; 'Final fate, destruction, ruin, death'.[23] Each meaning circulates in the late sixteenth century. How then can one separate the curse from the law, or the plague from the Prince?

Both Escalus and Mercutio set out to prescribe violent revisions of the relationship between the individual and the social; both are caught in the time trap that renders their words descriptive of a communal endemic state. The infection first appears in the prefatory sonnet, carried by the word 'alike'; it travels across discipline and desire, law and rebellion, rivalry and alliance, so lines of distinction instead weave a web. 'Some shall be pardon'd, and some punished', the Prince promises in his faintly epilogic speech, but these amorphous groups and equivocal acts take no shape (5.3.308). This is the last gasp of a taxonomic system that has ceased to bear its own weight. Quarantine and contagion reveal their intricate interdependence as bodies and ideas converge to coincidence. The unbounded ardor that spreads from Juliet's 'borrow'd likeness of shrunk death' (4.1.104) to the fatal crossings of Juliet, Romeo and Paris originates in the methodical confinement of Friar John: 'the searchers of the town, / Suspecting that we both were in a house / Where the infectious pestilence did reign, / Seal'd up the doors and would not let us forth' (5.2.8–11). The letter returns to Friar Laurence – 'I could not send it — here it is again — / Nor get a messenger to bring it thee, / So fearful were they of infection' (5.2.14–16) – who must read the transposition of his intent. 'The sender, we tell you, receives from the receiver his own message in reverse form', Jacques Lacan writes, and concludes, 'a letter always arrives at its destination'.[24] We might find that destination in the last line of Davies' quatrain: 'Death dares all Authority withstand'.

In the final scene, the Prince asserts a proper, if improbable, recuperation of government: 'Seal up the mouth of outrage for a while / Till we can clear these ambiguities / And know their spring, their head, their true descent' (5.3.216–18). But the speech pivots on a point of implication, for the Prince has already admitted he has skin in this game: 'I have an interest in your hearts' proceeding; / My blood for your rude brawls doth lie a-bleeding' (3.1.189–90). The fall from dispassion into kinship twists the end of the later speech: 'And then will I be general of your woes / And lead you, even to death' (5.3.219–20). This pledge invites attention. We could note that it remains unfulfilled within the scope of the play; we could confine the moveable, mutable dead within the *cordon sanitaire* of a sonnet and a couplet.[25] We could let the last scene manufacture eternization and certainty, individuation and iconicity, whether we commend or condemn these products. But we would ignore the ephemeral, interrelational, seductive perils with which the play is so deeply concerned. This is where I do think *Romeo and Juliet* is shaped by the Prince: not by his invincible power of decree, but by his helpless openness to contact. The epidemic consummation he anticipates – 'even unto death' – does not happen in our view, but its appearance as a deferred subjunctive reminds us that any separation between the actual and the counterfactual dead is only a matter of time. We do not just inherit symbols from this play; we inherit sharp questions about the discrete boxes that populate symbolic systems and the imbricated spaces in which people live. Even as the play indulges in clichés of exceptionalism and immortality, it foregrounds that other, collective truism voiced by Capulet: 'Well, we were born to die' (3.4.4).

Graves

If anyone approximates a speech act, it might be Juliet: 'I should kill thee with much cherishing' (2.2.183). Yet here again I read the locution as descriptive, and indeed I would describe all those heavy-handed ironies – 'My grave is like to be my wedding bed' (1.5.135); 'Alas poor Romeo, he is already dead' (2.4.14); 'I dreamt my lady came and found me dead' (5.1.6) – as the verbal tics of an infected world. All bonds can prove deadly in such a world. We could listen to Mercutio: 'Nay, and there were two such, we should have none shortly, for one would kill the other' (3.1.15–16). We could listen to E. K. Chambers: 'Love comes into life like a sword, touching here a man and there a woman, and scorching them with a terrible flame'.[26] We could listen to Alan Sinfield: 'The processes of desire were uneven and risky and, pursued under pressure, might be threatening to the psyche and, at least in the drama, to life'.[27] And we could listen to plague writers: 'It was confusion but a friend to greet, / For, like a Fiend, he baned with his breath'.[28] Vocabularies within and around the play speak a shared conviction: the ties that hold persons in common create lethal contiguities, so that any touch might kill.

My question, still, is how this kind of affiliation – intimate, indiscriminate, fecund, fatal – intersects social imperatives. Those imperatives persist in *Romeo and Juliet*; to think otherwise would be to imagine that desire and death could exempt subjects from ideological inscription. 'Love, from the start of the play, is implicated in the social, not separate from it', Goldberg writes; more than two decades later, Crystal Bartolovich stresses 'the social interdependence on which all life, all "individuals" – indeed all love – depends'.[29] I can only agree; the escape from social subjectivity is precisely as easy to fantasize as it is difficult to achieve, for radical individualism is an illusion calibrated to serve corporate ends. But I wonder whether an unquantified multiple of persons might become, at least to a degree, socially unintelligible through being individual in that other sense of indivisible.[30] What if love and death attach not to unique beings or dyadic units, but to messy heaps? What might such cumulations mean for identity and sociality?

Bèze calls on 'that general band' to argue that citizens should risk infection to preserve communion. *Romeo and Juliet*, like early modern plague writing, flatly asserts that anyone might die, and neither obscures nor evades the consequent proposition that everyone might die. The explicitness of ubiquitous mortality creates situational ideologies, systems of valuation and intersection that interrupt dominant orthodoxies. Situational ideologies remain ideological – they represent 'the imaginary relationship of individuals to their real conditions of existence'[31] – but the terms of imagination and existence change. So categories, in *Romeo and Juliet*, lose crystal distinction to confused overlap as events press towards death. Marriage shifts from structured reparation – 'For this alliance may so happy prove / To turn your households' rancour to pure love' (2.3.87–8) – to mutual annihilation: 'These violent delights have violent ends / And in their triumph die, like fire and powder, / Which as they kiss consume' (2.6.9–11). The feud provides a formula for action based in distinction – 'Now by the stock and honour of my kin, / To strike him dead I hold it not a sin' (1.5.58–9) – until it condenses too many debts of kind: 'My very friend, hath got this mortal hurt / In my behalf — my reputation stain'd / With Tybalt's slander — Tybalt that an hour / Hath been my cousin' (3.1.111–14). The clear utility of affiliation and partition yields to the apparent disarray of condensation and consumption, a move not from order to chaos but from a socially legible logic to one that is more urgent and more obscure. For Juliet, that second logic undoes the difference between eradication and survival. When she believes Tybalt and Romeo are dead, she recognizes an apocalyptic moment: 'Then dreadful trumpet sound the general doom, / For who is living if those two are gone?' (3.2.67–8). When she knows Romeo is alive, the cataclysm expands: 'to speak that word / Is father, mother, Tybalt, Romeo, Juliet, / All slain, all dead. Romeo is banished, / There is no end, no limit, measure, bound, / In that word's death' (3.2.122–6). This is irrational only by familiar metrics, and Juliet already inhabits strange norms. Her series of deaths – imagined, feigned, consummated – is less progression than reiteration. When Friar Laurence says, 'Lady, come from that nest / Of death, contagion, and unnatural sleep' (5.3.151–2), he attempts to unravel strands that have fused. 'Sovereign, here lies the County Paris slain, / And Romeo dead, and Juliet, dead before, / Warm, and new kill'd' (5.3.195–7): this is where we end, in a tangle of bodies and timelines and names and bonds.[32]

When no one is immune, more flexible if also more terrible ways of being in common appear: 'Friends here kill'd friends,

womb-fellowes Kill their Brothers / Fathers their Sons, and
Daughters kill their Mothers: / By one another (strange!) so
many di'de / And yet no murder here, no Homicide'.[33] Units
of kinship and alliance do not succumb to barrenness; they
explode into generation, but their creation is the teeming
promiscuity of mass graves. In an epidemic context, Andrew
Marvell's famous claim – 'The grave's a fine and private place,
/ But none, I think, do there embrace' – has the feel of arrant
fantasy. When Juliet consents to her death trick, she pictures
'a vault, an ancient receptacle / Where for this many hundred
years the bones / Of all my buried ancestors are pack'd'
(4.3.39–41). That crowded space drives her to predict a riot
of dissolute intercourse:

> O, if I wake, shall I not be distraught,
> Environed with all these hideous fears,
> And madly play with my forefathers' joints,
> And pluck the mangled Tybalt from his shroud,
> And, in this rage, with some great kinsman's bone
> As with a club dash out my desperate brains?
>
> (4.3.49–54)

Romeo, too, finds little privacy in a grave where his embrace
has been pre-empted: 'Ah, dear Juliet, / Why art thou yet so
fair?' he asks; 'Shall I believe / That unsubstantial Death is
amorous, / And that the lean abhorred monster keeps / Thee
here in dark to be his paramour?' (5.3.101–5). Whatever
death's desires may be, the collection of corpses exerts
a magnetic pull on everyone else: 'Hide me nightly in a
charnel-house / O'ercover'd quite with dead men's rattling
bones' (Juliet, 4.1.81–2); 'Well, Juliet, I will lie with thee
tonight. / Let's see for means' (Romeo, 5.1.34–5); 'O, I am
slain! If thou be merciful, / Open the tomb, lay me with
Juliet' (Paris, 5.3.72–3). The tomb that should assure a final
segregation – only Capulets rot here – becomes a catholic
destination. Lady Capulet observes that the public has joined

the rush: 'O, the people in the street cry "Romeo", / Some "Juliet", and some "Paris", and all run / With open outcry toward our monument' (5.3.191–3). If *Romeo and Juliet* must give us a monument, golden statues could give way to this: a tomb bursting with deviant desires, intermingling friends and enemies and beauty and bones, entwining and ending family lines, erasing distinctions between vitality and mortality, and drawing all subjects into an unseemly confusion of persons and passions that will not stop for death.

For a plague-stricken populace, the mass grave is a constant preoccupation defined as improper union. Dekker chastises London for indifferent, indecent funerals: 'thou tumbledst them into their everlasting lodgings (ten in one heape, and twenty in another) as if all the roomes upon earth had bin full. The gallant and the begger lay together; the scholler and the carter in one bed: the husband saw his wife, and his deadly enemy whom he hated, within a paire of sheetes'.[34] His vivid apostrophe to a prospective victim concludes, 'If thou art in love with thy selfe, this cannot choose but possesse thee with frenzie'.[35] Loss of separateness becomes loss of self, a drastic uncoupling both from individual autonomy and from ordered sociality. And that uncoupling facilitates unlimited re-couplings, consummated in a postmortem orgy of overpopulated sheets. One need only glance at John Donne to see how sexual proscription and social discretion fall to the same coalescent force: 'Miserable incest, when I must bee maried to my mother and my sister, and bee both father and mother to my owne mother and sister ... when the ambitious man shall have no satisfaction, if the poorest alive tread upon him, nor the poorest receive any contentment in being made equall to Princes, for they shall bee equall but in dust'. Like Dekker, Donne concludes his passage with the utter vitiation of self: 'This is the most inglorious and contemptible vilification, the most deadly and peremptory nullification of man, that wee can consider'.[36]

The problem is less annulment than permeability, a contiguous diffusion troubled by knowledge of the borders it violates. In *Corpus*, Jean-Luc Nancy writes, 'The cadavers in a mass grave aren't the dead, they aren't our dead: they are wounds heaped up, stuck in, flowing into one another … Through another concentration, bodies are only signs annulled'.[37] This is a trenchant critique of how we discard persons whose classification has shifted from worth to waste. Yet the wounds that flow towards coalescence also define Bataille's account of communion. Mass graves lay bare the ambivalence of inter-implication within an epidemic of bonds. When communion becomes a contagion that slides into dissolution, on what grounds does one choose between a desire for isolate security and an acceptance of unsafe intimacy? Plague is, by early modern definition, an event that disables elective faculties; few decide to fall ill, and many remain in spaces of danger out of necessity rather than choice. At the same time, however, the very vastness of its scale establishes an interrelational system of local choices, at once alternative to and operative within established social structures. If we can imagine a decision to engage made under the coercive imposition of proximity, a meaningful determination that confounds agential and fatalistic states, we might glimpse affinities and pluralities that unsquare the box of social subjectivity.

I find contagion a useful fulcrum for ideas about how queer methodologies continue to expand, reaching beyond the identities and acts privileged either by their historical situation or by our historical knowledge. It is, at least arguably, difficult for sexuality to escape taxonomies of social value when it is seen through the lens of particular persons and procedures. Can an infinitely multiplicative interpenetration transect boundaries with enough force to challenge instrumental dispositions? While this question does not lend itself to a simple 'yes', it does illuminate a synthesis of action and passion that neither idealizes a subject nor disposes of an object. For those cumulated persons who neither escape contagion nor choose it, the shared dilemma of presentness might beget reciprocities of recognition and desire. And if such bonds are precarious, contingent, mutable, elastic, ambivalent, unexpected, opportunistic or transient – if they occur at an angle to orthodox patterns of connection – it is perhaps in this sense that they resonate as queer. Still, I want to conclude by stressing the limits of the model I have proposed. To draw out the epidemic interrelations in *Romeo and Juliet* is not to conjure a queer utopian future; inextricable from the nexus of contagion and communion is an awareness that there may be no viable future at all. Nor does this sort of 'no future' license its implicated persons to abjure sociality. Contagion actuates annihilation rather than nihilism, negation rather than abnegation; it lacks the explosive grandeur of self-shattering or the implosive splendor of *jouissance*. If the intimacies I trace have heterodox force, such force inheres in a communion that reveals something intrinsic to sociality itself. Symbolic systems are contingent on bodies that do more than fuel a machine. The interdependence of abstract structures and transitory persons becomes visible at moments of common risk, when desirous, porous, blighted, conjoint and moribund bodies fill the space of social subjects. This is what we might see if we refuse to sheathe fickle flesh in constant gold.

13

Antisocial procreation in
Measure for Measure

Melissa E. Sanchez

Procreation – particularly that which results from sex between 'man and woman, after this downright way of creation' – would seem to be one of the least queer topics that one could discuss (*Measure for Measure*, 3.2.100–1).[1] The modern Christian Right has repeatedly invoked the 'facts' of human reproduction to justify the persecution of sexual minorities and the criminalization of practices that are not heterosexual and procreative. Given that procreative heterosex has been so effectively normalized, it is unsurprising and appropriate that queer and feminist scholars have focused on affirming the ethical and political value of practices that refuse the injunction to 'bring forth fruit and multiply' – most prominently, same-sex desire and attachment but also celibacy, masturbation, BDSM, prostitution and pornography. Perhaps most provocatively, Lee Edelman argues that the Christian Right might have a point in equating abortion with homosexuality, for it is precisely that equation which illuminates the pernicious effects of a 'culture of life'. Pondering the 'ideological truth' revealed by the 'common stake in the

militant right's opposition to abortion and to queer sexualities', Edelman asks 'Who *would*, after all, come out *for*
abortion or stand *against* reproduction, *against* futurity, and
so against life?' The answer, of course, is the queer, who must
demand not mere toleration or inclusion within the existing
social order, but rather 'must insist on disturbing, on queering,
social organization as such'.[2] The queer, that is, faces up to the
fact that the refusal to procreate does in fact threaten a social
order built on an ideal of present self-sacrifice in service of a
greater, always deferred good – one demanded above all of
the pregnant woman whose body has ceased to be 'her own'
and whose forfeiture of pleasure and autonomy is the logical
conclusion of reproductive futurism.

In direct opposition to this 'romance' of reproductive
futurism, Edelman celebrates in the *sinthom*osexual 'something
truly inhuman, something meaningless and mechanistic, that
replaces volition and agency with subjection to the drive',
insisting that the 'ethical task for which queers are singled
out' is 'to embrace the impossibility, the inhumanity of the
*sinthom*osexual'.[3] Edelman brilliantly and rightly calls out the
smug morality – expressed above all in political rhetoric that
idealizes capitulation to 'the fascism of the baby's face' – which
has legitimated so much violence against sexual minorities.[4]
But, as Jennifer Doyle has noted, at times 'Edelman comes
awfully close to speaking from exactly the reproductive
position he so forcefully challenges – speaking as Child cut
from the body of the mother', and '[t]hat subject position
– generated via the separation of child from mother and the
fantasy of autonomy generated in the cutting of that cord – is
not anti-reproductive. It is the very gesture through which
heteronormative patriarchal authority manufactures itself'.[5]
This is the fantasy of declaring the freedom of form from
matter, mind from body, that, as feminist philosophers have
long noted, has historically been framed in gendered terms.[6]

In this chapter, I want to place Edelman's important
challenge to reproductive futurism in conversation with recent
new materialist work that stresses what Jane Bennett calls the

'vitality' of matter in order to 'dissipate the onto-theological binaries of life/matter, human/animal, will/determinant, and organic/inorganic'.[7] As Bennett argues in her discussion of stem-cell research, the 'free and undetermined agency' of matter – including that which eventually will become human 'life' – reminds 'secular modernists that while we can surely intervene in the material world, we are not in charge of it, for there are "foreign" powers about'.[8] Awareness of these 'foreign powers' allows us to reject a view of matter as inert stuff distinct from and subject to human rationality and autonomy. It also opens the way to revising a definition of nature as passive and inert, a view that has prompted many feminist theorists to privilege the virgin and the lesbian separatist as figures for the emancipation from the 'nature' to which women's reproductive bodies have traditionally been consigned.[9] As numerous queer, materialist and ecofeminist scholars have pointed out, a more productive path would be 'to undertake the transformation of gendered dualisms – nature/culture, body/mind, object/subject, resource/agency, and others – that have been cultivated to denigrate and silence certain groups of human as well as nonhuman life'.[10] This refusal of (post)modern disenchantment, as Bruno Latour has argued, entails a reparative relation not just to the material and technological worlds, but also to one's situation in time: '"No future": this is the [postmodern] slogan added to the moderns' motto "No past"'. An acceptance of hybridity, Latour contends, entails 'a rereading of our history' by which 'we discover that we have never begun to enter the modern era' in which 'nature' and 'culture', self and other, past and future can be neatly distinguished.[11]

Accordingly, returning to past worlds may allow us to challenge many of the categories, both sexual and ontological, that we now take for granted. In recent years, medieval and early modern scholars have shown that a premodern archive makes available a range of perspectives that challenge the human exceptionalism upon which heteronormativity rests: Aristotle's ensouled nature, Epicurus's and Lucretius's atoms, and Spinoza's substance are but a few.[12] In this chapter, I examine the materialist view of 'life' in *Measure for Measure*, a play which reminds us that modern sexual ideologies are built on a Cartesian split between passive body and active mind, intentional human subject and determined non-human object, that did not yet operate in early modern thought and that continues to be inadequate to address the complexity of 'life' today.[13] In this notoriously troubling problem play, sex is relentlessly tied to the unintentional production of bare life (*zoē*) rather than the considered perpetuation of socio-political life (*bios*).[14] As Mario DiGangi, drawing on Bennett's concept of impersonal affect, has observed, the early modern period saw not only language and behaviour as 'bawdy', but also things, including bodily substances like blood, 'which seems to operate independently of human appetite or subjectivity'.[15] Building on these insights, I attend to sex, pregnancy and gestation, even more mysterious material events in the early modern world than they are now, which involve organs, substances and processes that act independently of conscious intent. The 'rebellion of a codpiece' is not only the act of fornication, but also the unpredictable activity of fleshly and fluid matter that continues after the sex act itself is complete (*Measure for Measure*, 3.2.110). Moreover, as Lucio's sardonic speculation that Angelo is the offspring of 'a sea-maid' or 'two stockfishes' indicates, reproduction without sex could in fact be imagined as *more* conducive to a normative social order – one based on intentional, conjugal procreation – than 'the downright way of creation' (3.2.103–4, 101).[16]

Indeed, the 'fundamental discomfort with the facts of human conception' that Janet Adelman has identified in *Measure for Measure* may be at least as much a visceral reaction against the inscrutable formation of 'life' as a moral anxiety about sin or a socio-economic anxiety about lines of inheritance.[17] The fleshly human is immune to the ideals and chronologies we would impose on it, and pregnancy is only one instance of a '*congealing of agency*' across, inside and outside individual bodies that challenges the gendered, sexual and ontological hierarchies that modern thought takes for granted.[18] This is not to argue that *Measure for Measure* endorses an exuberant 'zoe-egalitarianism' that acknowledges the 'generative power that flows across all species' and therefore 'opens up unexpected possibilities for the recomposition of communities, for the very idea of humanity and for ethical forms of belonging'.[19] Instead, the play's depiction of procreation reminds us that, as Noreen Giffney and Myra Hird argue, 'Recognizing the nonhuman in every trace of the Human also means being cognizant of the exclusive and excluding economy of discourses relating to what it means to be, live, act or occupy the category of the Human'.[20] In this light, the deep pessimism about 'human nature' – its resistance to transcending or redeeming heterosex and its unintentional progeny – that we find in *Measure for Measure* can be instructive for a queer project of challenging 'natural' hierarchies and ontologies.

Despite its well-documented biblical references, *Measure for Measure* consistently desacralizes human life, depicting the human creature as little better than the inanimate matter – the dust – from which she or he came and to which she or he will return. In his guise as Friar Lodowick, the Duke expresses a materialist view of life as something dispersed and impersonal, counselling Claudio: 'Thou art not thyself, / For thou exists on many a thousand grains / That issue out of dust' (3.1.19–21). Humanity and dirt, organic and inorganic matter, are only momentarily distinguishable; the illusions of transcendence that the human creature entertains are shockingly temporary.[21] This grim view of life is voiced in the postlapsarian punishment that 'In the sweat of thy face shalt thou eat bread, till thou return to the earth, for out of it wast thou taken, because thou art dust, and to dust shalt thou return' (Gen. 3.19) and the incantatory 'Earth to earth, asshes to asshes, dust to dust' from the burial service in the *English Book of Common Prayer*.[22] Critically, however, the Duke leaves out the service's subsequent assurance that material existence is not all, that we return to the earth 'in sure and

certayne hope of resurreccion to eternal lyfe'.[23] In excluding
this Christian consolation, the Duke does not so much suggest
that there is no future beyond death as insist on an endless,
irresistible future as matter.

Nor does the Duke's surprisingly desacralized view of life
(surprising given that in this scene he impersonates Friar
Lodowick, 'a man divine and holy' [5.1.146]) hint at any
miracle of birth or procreation. Generation and disease are
equally uncontrollable processes:

> thine own bowels which do call thee sire,
> The mere effusion of thy proper loins,
> Do curse the gout, serpigo, and the rheum
> For ending thee no sooner.

(3.1.28–32)

Here, it is difficult to distinguish not only between the human
and the non-human, activity and passivity, but also between
interiority and exteriority. What is inside the body (cells,
tissue, blood, organs, instincts, diseases, embryos, fetuses) and
what is outside (the loving kinsfolk that might help us, the
hostile forces that might destroy us) are hard to distinguish.
'Bowels' and 'loins' are both the interior of the body, its
entrails and reproductive organs, and the independent lives
that emerge from their 'effusion', or excretion of fluids from
their 'proper' origin – generation evokes the tumescence
and leakiness of gout and rheum. 'Life', itself erratically
personified in the Duke's speech, consists of an assemblage
of organs, fluids and infections that act apart from human
intention. In the initiation as well as the ending of life, this
speech suggests, 'there are "foreign" powers about', within
and beyond the individual body.

The Duke's emphatically materialist vision of human
life as itself inextricable from an indeterminate network
of substances – food, flesh, disease, offspring – reminds
us that generation, no less than sex, may break down the

social taxonomies we associate with human life even as it
questions the borders between life and death. In both plot
and structure, *Measure for Measure* depicts its various
characters as part of a single network. These intricate
relations are particularly evident in the non-human processes
of pregnancy and disease with which individual human life
begins and ends. By tracing representations of pregnancy in
Measure for Measure, we can see that social spheres usually
understood to be separate – marriage and procreation, on the
one hand, prostitution and disease, on the other – overlap
and inhabit one another.

Early on in *Measure for Measure*, the brothel is depicted
as a source of contagion that connects persons of a range of
social classes, along with the sexual mores that would appear
to separate them. Lucio huddles with the two Gentlemen,
joking about the 'diseases' they have 'purchased' in Mistress
Overdone's establishment, a conversation cut short by the
news that Claudio is to be executed 'for getting Madam
Julietta with child' (1.2.45, 71). Not only Lucio, but also the
Gentlemen and Mistress Overdone appear to know Claudio
well. Mistress Overdone is at once a widow who has been
married nine times and a 'bawd of eleven years' continuance'
who 'has worn [her] eyes out in the service' (2.1.197–8,
3.2.190, 1.2.109–10). Elbow's wife, 'great with child' and
craving stewed prunes, turns up in a brothel where she is either
propositioned or assaulted – we can't tell – by the wealthy heir
Froth.[24] The 'bawd born' Pompey (3.2.66) is conscripted to
assist the hangman Abhorson, a partnership that brings into
focus the ideological significance of the triple pun that constitutes Abhorson's name: conventional morality 'abhors' the
'whoreson' as a misformed life – one early modern meaning
of abortion – that brings *bios* into uncomfortable proximity
with *zoē*, political life with social death.[25] And at the play's
conclusion Lucio is compelled to marry Kate Keep-down, a
prostitute whose child he has fathered.

This last example has received little attention, with all
critics that I know of accepting Lucio's description of Kate as a

'whore' and a 'punk' as simple statements of longstanding fact (5.1.512, 518). I propose instead that what we can infer of Kate's circumstances troubles the boundaries of this category. If Kate's marriage to Lucio transforms her from 'punk' to 'wife', her pregnancy may have turned her from 'maid' to 'punk' (5.1.178–81). For Kate's actual status – maid or punk? – at the time she conceived Lucio's child is never clearly stated. Mistress Overdone claims that Lucio 'promised her marriage' (3.2.194–5). And in Lucio's own account, he was brought before the Duke 'for getting a wench with child', paternity that he privately admits ('marry, I did') but publicly denies ('I was fain to forswear it; / they would else have married me to the rotten medlar' [4.3.170–1]). It seems unlikely that a paying client would promise a prostitute marriage: the whole point of prostitution is that men can have sex *without* marriage, commitment or progeny. It also seems unlikely, given the public shaming and harsh corporeal, carceral and economic penalties imposed on prostitutes, that a prostitute would take a client who has impregnated her to court in hopes of compelling him to marry her, more unlikely still that the court would rule in her favour if he acknowledged paternity.[26] At the very least, Mistress Overdone's account, along with Lucio's own certainty that he would have been forced to marry Kate had he told the truth, suggests two things: 1) Kate did not have sex with Lucio as a prostitute – that is, in exchange for money, and 2) she had not slept with other men, as a prostitute or otherwise, for enough time before and after her encounter with Lucio that his paternity is unquestionable.

It is clear that Mistress Overdone has been taking care of Kate's child, suggesting Kate's own residence in her brothel, and nothing in *Measure for Measure* contradicts Lucio's assertion that Kate is a 'whore' in the present tense of the play's action, which takes place over a year after the child was born, probably about two after it was conceived (5.1.512).[27] But it seems more likely that this status followed than preceeded her encounter with Lucio. In an early modern economy that afforded very few legitimate employment prospects to women, prostitution might very well have been the only option for sustaining Kate's own life and that of the child that Mistress Overdone had been keeping.[28] As Mairead Sullivan points out, 'The Child, for radical feminists, cannot be simply rejected or refused, the child, itself, is already the figuration of a thwarted future'.[29] Not every child is a Child, or a symbol of a new and better tomorrow. This is particularly true in the socio-economic world of *Measure for Measure*, where the creation of new life may subject women to literal disease and social and literal death. As bare lives to be preserved rather than political lives to be promoted, the play's prostitutes and their offspring silently exist at the cusp of the human and the non-human in this play. Typically, these border figures have been read according to the comforting taxonomy of the 'outbreak narrative' described by Priscilla Wald, in which the 'villains' are women, homosexuals, the working classes, immigrants and inhabitants of the Third World, all figured as uniquely, ignorantly open to infection.[30] Yet the shards of information that *Measure for Measure* provides about Kate's history indicate the permeability of these modern epistemological and biological borders. At once marginal and central, spectral and insistently real, Kate – mother and prostitute, carrier of both life and death – registers the futility of a model of sexual hygiene that would definitely quarantine sex from love, health from disease, those who have futures from those who do not. Abject and dehumanized, the prostitute is one of those who, in Audre Lorde's words, 'were never meant to survive' – but who persist in the traces (textual, biological) left by their contagious, unbounded bodies.[31]

Rather than accept Kate's status as prostitute as inevitable, and the marginal lives of prostitutes as the natural outcome of illicit sex, I have sought to reconstruct the circumstances of the procreative sex that appears to have doomed her to the slow death of those outside the protective category of *bios*.[32] What we can glean of Kate's encounter suggests that attention to the processes, timelines and practicalities of procreation can trouble the normative definitions of healthy, virtuous sex that we bring to our encounters with past texts as well as present worlds. This is equally true of the one couple in the play usually understood to have practiced the loving, procreative sex that can be euphemized as reproductive futurism: Claudio and Juliet.

It is the very fact of Juliet's untimely pregnancy – the presence, not the absence, of procreation – that not only reveals her relationship with Claudio but also threatens to sustain its illegitimacy. And not, as critics have tended to assume, because Angelo's excessive zeal has divided a couple virtually en route to the altar.[33] Rather, when we consider the advanced date of Juliet's pregnancy, we can see that this procreative union, no less than that of Kate and Lucio, may have been inspired by inhuman appetite rather than 'human' love. As in that decidedly unromantic pair, the pregnancy resulting from the encounter between Claudio and Juliet is cause for shame and dismay, not joy in having unwittingly brought forth fruit, as we see in Claudio's own account:

> LUCIO   Is lechery so look'd after?
> CLAUDIO   Thus stands it with me: upon a true contract
>   I got possession of Julietta's bed.
>   You know the lady; she is fast my wife,
>   Save that we do the denunciation lack
>   Of outward order. This we came not to
>   Only for propagation of a dower
>   Remaining in the coffer of her friends,
>   From whom we thought it meet to hide our love
>   Till time had made them for us. But it chances
>   The stealth of our most mutual entertainment
>   With character too gross is writ on Juliet.
> LUCIO   With child, perhaps?
> CLAUDIO   Unhappily, even so.
>
>   (1.2.142–53)

Like Lucio, who 'promised' Kate marriage then 'was fain to forswear it' to avoid marriage to 'the rotten medlar' (3.2.171), or like Angelo, who 'swallowed his vows whole, pretending in [Mariana] discoveries of dishonor' (3.1.225–6), Claudio has offered marriage in exchange for something else: he confesses both Lucio's desire for sex and Angelo's desire for a dowry.

Claudio may have 'got possession of Julietta's bed' in return for 'a true contract', or promise of marriage, but this promise was kept secret in hopes of 'propagation of a dower' – no one, including Isabel, seems to have heard of it. Unfortunately ('unhappily'), Claudio and Juliet have propagated a child instead of a dowry. Now that 'the stealth of [their] most mutual enjoyment' has become legible pregnancy, writ large (or 'gross') on Juliet's body, there may be little hope that more 'time' will bring Juliet's relatives to favour the match. In fact, any time the couple has to legitimate their offspring – to parent a child rather than a bastard – has nearly run out by the start of the play. Claudio's emphasis on Juliet's size, along with the Provost's reports that Juliet is 'groaning' in labour and 'very near her hour' and Angelo's order that she be moved 'To some more fitter place; and that with speed' should turn our attention to the time that has passed between the procreative act and the present tense of the play (2.2.15–17). If Juliet's pregnancy is far enough along that it is not only visibly obvious but also close to the moment of birth, then Claudio has had many months between his initial knowledge of the pregnancy and his arrest to honour the terms of his 'true contract'.

One might object that it is silly to treat Juliet's pregnancy as 'real' enough to count the months in which marriage might have taken place. After all, this is a fictional character. But the play gives us more evidence for this technical attention to her bodily state than for the romanticized past and present that are usually projected onto this couple. Given that Angelo was able to extricate himself from a more secure contract, one for which the dowry was determined and 'the nuptial appointed' (3.1.213), and given that Lucio successfully denied both paternity and promise of marriage in court, the overwhelming critical belief that Claudio will marry

Juliet out of love responds less to what the play tells us of
their relationship and more to the desire to isolate healthy
from unhealthy sex. Isabella's immediate response to the
news of Juliet's pregnancy – 'O let him marry her!' – accen-
tuates Claudio's foot-dragging even as it treats marriage as a
pragmatic arrangement rather than an expression of love or
virtue (1.4.49). In this light, the Duke's order that Claudio
'restore' the woman he has 'wrong'd' is neither superfluous
nor sublimating (5.1.520). The command aligns Claudio with
the impersonal, anonymous desires of Angelo and Lucio, the
other figures compelled to marry women they have 'wronged'
– that is, to 'restore' these women to the human and political
world of *rights* (3.1.199, 239, 5.1.505).

Claudio's initial account of the cause for his arrest describes
his and Juliet's 'most mutual enjoyment' in the inhuman terms
of appetite and disease that we have witnessed elsewhere in
the play's representations of sex. When Lucio initially asks
him 'whence comes this restraint?' Claudio replies

> From too much liberty, my Lucio. Liberty,
> As surfeit, is the father of much fast;
> So every scope by the immoderate use
> Turns to restraint. Our natures do pursue,
> Like rats that ravin down their proper bane,
> A thirsty evil, and when we drink, we die.

(1.2.125–30)

Claudio's emphasis on excess here – 'too much liberty',
'surfeit', 'immoderate use' – suggests that he may already have
had more than enough of Juliet, whose body is here compared
to the 'proper bane' of rat poison. To 'ravin' is to devour
voraciously, but also to plunder or prey. Juliet's pregnancy
does not so much redeem as expose this excess: the 'teeming
foison' of her 'plenteous womb / Expresseth his full tilth and
husbandry' (1.3.43–4). The redundancy of the metaphors
with which Lucio describes Juliet's pregnancy ('teeming',

'foison', 'plenteous', 'full') echoes the language of superfluity
in Claudio's own description, bringing life and death into close
proximity through an impersonal, agricultural 'husbandry' in
which procreation is natural but not sacred.

Yet to simplify this relation (or those of Lucio and Kate,
Angelo and Mariana) as one of predatory male appetite and
victimized female innocence would be to restore a moral
order that is absent from *Measure for Measure*. Rather than
blame Claudio for taking advantage of her youth or credulity,
Juliet describes their relationship as one of shared creaturely
corruption that is not the opposite of human 'love' but an
inextricable part of it:

DUKE   Repent you, fair one, of the sin you carry?
JULIET I do; and bear the shame most patiently.
...
DUKE   Love you the man that wronged you?
JULIET Yes, as I love the woman that wronged him.
DUKE   So then it seems your most offenceful act
        Was mutually committed.
JULIET   Mutually.
DUKE   Then was your sin of heavier kind than his.
JULIET I do confess it, and repent it, father.

                                        (2.3.19–29)

Critics have tended to focus on the Duke's misogynistic
charge of female guilt and his insistence on original sin to the
exclusion of the rest of the conversation.[34] What is significant
about this passage, however, is not the Duke's misogyny
(though that is both undeniable and indefensible) but Juliet's
refusal to claim that she has been uniquely 'wronged' by
sex. Like Claudio, she affirms the mutuality of their 'most
offenceful act': she has 'wronged' Claudio insofar as she has
participated in the illegal act of fornication. Whatever 'love'
they feel for each other (and this is itself a loaded word, given
Angelo's proclamations of 'love' for Isabella and Mariana's

'violent and unruly' – and humiliating – love for Angelo [3.1.251]) cannot be separated from the 'injurious' progeny that 'respites [Juliet] a life, whose very comfort / Is still a dying horror' (2.3.40–2).[35] If Juliet's 'sin' is 'of heavier kind' than Claudio's it is because she literally bears its consequence: the progeny that far from sustaining her own (and Claudio's) place in Vienna's socioeconomic order, threatens to bring literal and social death to both of them through execution, through childbirth, through poverty, through ostracization. Juliet expresses no romantic ideal of the baby she is about to deliver as a child; it is a 'sin' and a 'shame' that exposes rather than redeems the inhuman appetite that created it. What Carol Thomas Neely has noted of Claudio and Lucio may be more generally true of human generation in *Measure for Measure*: it is 'a grotesque embarrassment'.[36] Procreation, in this sense, may be irreducibly antisocial insofar as it resists the meanings that humanity would impose on it. But what Adelman laments as a view of this new life as, in her artful phrase, 'stinkingly dependent' (or in Juliet's words, 'a dying horror') may also offer a valuable challenge to the violent imposition of meaning that is reproductive futurism – and humanism more largely.[37]

In their introduction to a recent volume of *GLQ* on 'Queer Inhumanisms', Dana Luciano and Mel Y. Chen pose the question of the ethics of new materialist and posthuman theoretical perspectives: 'why look away from the already overlooked or advantage the inanimate over the dehumanized?'[38] One answer that they come to is that 'Many of queer theory's foundational texts interrogate, implicitly or explicitly, the nature of the "human" in its relation to the queer, both in their attention to how sexual norms themselves constitute and regulate hierarchies of humanness, and as they work to unsettle those norms and the default forms of humanness they uphold'.[39] The non- or inhuman, that is to say, is useful to think with because it reminds us of the consequences of violent exclusion even as it evokes generative possibility.[40] A materialist perspective on the reproduction of *Measure for Measure* can expand our understanding of queerness beyond a disembodied universality that refuses 'every substantialization of identity'.[41] Belonging to neither a 'culture of life' allegorized by the Child nor a death drive allegorized by the *sinthom*osexual, unwanted lives and the women who bear them do not so much refuse the future as underscore its extra-human dimensions. In accentuating the material, inhuman dimension of reproduction, *Measure for Measure* allows us to appreciate the difficulty of drawing a line between virtuous and shameful sex, even as it reveals the limitations of a queerness that would speak of sex, and of 'life', only in the present tense. Matter in the biological, ecological and evolutionary senses has its own history and its future, though not one that can be understood in teleological terms that privilege a normative version of the human.

Rather, 'human' 'life' is caught up in a material future, one of which procreation is only one manifestation – and one to which we cannot say 'no'. Ashes to ashes, dust to dust, earth to earth.

Afterword

Vin Nardizzi

I'll put a girdle round about the earth /
In forty minutes

(2.1.175–6)[1]

At the start of *Queer Shakespeare*, Goran Stanivukovic
spotlights the queer effects that contemporary Shakespeare
performance can generate. Despite such prominence, this
moment is rare, though not unprecedented, in the volume:
a contributor briefly expands its remit to include a 'queer
reading […] of stage performance and of popular film and
music' (23). The subject of this introductory analysis is
director Emma Rice's *A Midsummer Night's Dream* for the
Globe Theatre, which was the talk of the theatrical town in
summer 2016. In Stanivukovic's formulation, the decision to
reconfigure the 'sex-gender distinction and the gender politics
of Shakespeare's text' (Helena is Helenus in this production)
leads, at play's end, to a positive representation of publicly
affectionate married men: the audience 'witnesses' in Ncuti
Gatwa's Demetrius 'a moving moment of public acceptance
of one's own queer desire' and then celebrates a same-sex
union between him and Ankur Bahl's Helenus. Stanivukovic,
for his part, highlights an earlier exchange between Demetrius
and Helenus that is less mainstream than is gay marriage:
in it, Helenus, as Helena had used to do,[2] imagines himself
as Demetrius's 'spaniel' (2.1.205) and so offers 'a proposal

for S/M submission within the male same-sex economy of power and desire' (2). Stanivukovic's main point is that, when reassigned to Helenus, the lines express 'the complexity and diversity of desire and sexuality produced by Rice's intervention' (1). They do so precisely because they tap into 'the queer resourcefulness of Shakespeare's text' (2). In different registers, this is a central concern of *Queer Shakespeare*.

As does Stanivukovic, I also cannot imagine 'queer Shakespeare' right now without thinking about the Globe's *Midsummer*, which I saw as a matinee in June 2016 and again as a recording in September 2016. Likewise, I cannot imagine queerness in this *Midsummer* without recourse to the production's (updated) erotic languages. But whereas, for Stanivukovic, the Globe's *Midsummer* mines 'Shakespeare's text' for its 'queer resourcefulness', I attend to the decision to inject into the playtext a suite of musical resources (Bowie, Beyonce, sitar rhythms, a music-hall song and dance number, camp opera and lines snatched from Renaissance poems) that newly charge it with erotic energy. Tellingly, in the context of this volume, the soundtrack to Globe's *Midsummer* made me feel the most tingly – months later, I still have no more sophisticated term for it – when I realized that I was *not* listening to actors recite from Shakespeare. Instead, listening to lines adapted from John Donne's Elegy 19, which is alternately called 'To his Mistris going to Bed', produced for me a queer effect, in that the complex erotic and sexual conditions of their performance at the Globe estranged my sense of what Donne's poem could mean. Characters in the production sing lines plucked from it at two different points in the same scene, and I figured out that Donne's poem had been grafted into Shakespeare's playtext when I picked out these famous lines: 'License my roving hands, and let them go, / Before, behind, between, betwixt, above, below'.[3] In what follows, then, I elaborate responses to some questions that I take to be condensed in my reaction: How does Donne help this *Midsummer* articulate a 'queer Shakespeare'? And how does the inclusion of lines from this poem inflect the play's erotic

and environmental entanglements (its queer ecology), specifically its representation of desire in the woods located outside
London (not Athens) in this production? In pursuing such
questions, I contribute to conversations in *Queer Shakespeare*
initiated by scholars who study gender and (anti-)homophobia
in *Midsummer* (Simone Chess and Kirk Quinsland) and
who explore relations between desire and environmentality,
broadly construed (Melissa E. Sanchez, Kathryn Schwarz and
Christine Varnado).

Donne's Elegy 19 is a naughty, ironic and aggressive poem.[4]
Its speaker, after all, spends most of it trying to convince
a woman to disrobe so as to achieve a state that he names
'Full nakedness' (l.33).[5] In doing so, the speaker employs a
series of imperatives that imaginatively strip the woman. He
commands, 'Off with that girdle', which is likely a belt that
wraps around the waist and to which 'household keys or a
purse, pair of scissors or other small personal items'[6] might
have been attached (l.5). He also commands her to 'Unpin that
spangled breastplate' (l.7), tells her to 'Unlace yourself' (l.9),
and then he directs her to take off other articles of clothing
and ornament, including her 'happy busk' (l.11), her 'gown'
(l.13), her hair pieces (ll.15–16), her 'white lynnen' (l.45)
and even her 'shooes' (l.17). But at the end of the poem, the
speaker changes tack, making one final, outrageous move in
an effort to view – and presumably to ravish – the woman's
body. 'To teach thee, I am naked first', he self-reports; 'why
then,' he reasons, 'What needst thou have more covering than
a man' (ll.47–8). The poem thus concludes with the speaker
completely starkers, casting himself as the butt of a joke: he's
naked, and she's probably not. His persuasions, which have
been forceful so far in their articulation, now feel comic and
impotent.

By these lights, Donne's poem is an inspired accompa-
niment for the Globe's *Midsummer*. It captures especially
well the erotic temperature of an early woodland scene that
features eloping lovers. Exhausted from the journey into the
woods around London, the couple prepares to rest for the

night, and Edmund Derrington's Lysander has decided on a
particularly intimate sleeping arrangement: 'One turf shall
serve as pillow for both of us; / One heart, one bed, two
bosoms, and one troth' (2.2.40–1). Perhaps Lysander's plans
are innocuous – and he insists that they are in the playtext, up
to a point (2.2.44–51) – but Anjana Vasan's Hermia construes
them as invitations to close bodily contact, if not outright
sex. However hot Hermia is for Lysander in this production,
she tells him twice to 'Lie further off' (2.2.43, 56). 'Such
separation', she explains, 'Becomes a virtuous bachelor and a
maid' (2.2.57–8). Just before they turn in separately, Lysander
sings the opening lines of Donne's poem as Hermia changes
into her pajamas:

> Come, Madam, come, all rest my powers defy,
> Until I labour, I in labour lie.
> The foe oft-times having the foe in sight,
> Is tir'd with standing though he never fight.

Lysander rounds off this part of the song, for which Hermia
has begun to provide background vocals, with a couplet that
rewrites and adapts more verse from Donne's poem: 'In this
wondrous woodland full of sprites, / That set our hairs, I
find my flesh upright'. The sweetness of Lysander's musical
performance might lead some of us to regard the song as
a lullaby that we would not mind having the dreamy actor
playing Lysander sing for us. And yet its lyrics also contain a
standard Renaissance sex joke ('Until I labour') and a reference
to an erection ('I find my flesh upright'). In incorporating
these lines from Donne's poem, the Globe *Midsummer* forges
a strong link between Lysander and Donne's speaker: both
are sexually frustrated at this moment, and so their sexual
dissatisfaction is observable and possibly comic. (Indeed, just
moments earlier Lysander, wearing only a leather jacket and
hipster underpants, crawled uncomfortably across the stage
on his belly, trying to hide an erection; the audience giggles.)
Even so, the sublimation of Lysander's erotic energy produces

an artful script – the script of Donne's speaker – that takes as its subject unfulfilled desire.

The artful sublimation, in fact, is mutual. After Lysander's alludes to the physical effects of fear and desire on his body ('That set our hairs, I find my flesh upright'), he and Hermia momentarily sing as a duet a haunting and sexy line adapted from Donne's poem. Lysander begins, 'License my roving hands and let them go', and then the couple jointly sings the next line: 'Before, behind, between, betwixt, above, below'. Hermia will again provide strong background vocals, as Lysander extends the Donne-inspired song: he directs her to 'Unlace yourself' so that he can 'start to mine your precious stones. / For now it's bedtime. / Off with your girdle; cast all white linen hence. / There is no penance due to innocence'. At this point, they kiss. Lysander walks Hermia to her tent, zips her into it, as his passionate ode comes full circle: 'Come, Madam, come, all rest my powers defy; / Until I labour, I in labour lie'. The last words on their lips are a parting 'Love you'.

Lullabies are soothing, perhaps, but, as is true of Lysander's, they also possess a kernel of unpleasantness. 'Rock-a-bye baby', after all, ends with the baby, 'cradle and all' falling out of the tree. Poor Hermia wakes up from the sleep into which Lysander's lullaby has lulled her in the throes of a terrible vision: 'Help me, Lysander, help me! Do thy best / To pluck this crawling serpent from my breast! / Ay me, for pity! What a dream was here' (2.2.144–6). I half suspect that the image of Lysander's crawling on the woodland floor, in combination with the spooky air of his song ('woodland full of sprites / That set our hairs … upright'), serves as source material for Hermia's nightmare. After she is jolted back to consciousness, Hermia finds no comfort in her future husband's arms. Lysander has begun to pursue affection and delight somewhere else in the woods and has left poor Hermia to fend for herself.

While Hermia sleeps onstage enduring a night terror, two significant things have happened to Lysander: Katy Owen's Puck has mistakenly placed on Lysander's eyes the

extract from the flower love-in-idleness, and Helenus has
stirred him awake. Since, as Puck says, 'the flower's force'
is 'in stirring love' (2.2.68), Lysander falls hard for Helenus,
setting into motion the production's bold same-sex revision
of Shakespeare's love plot. Tellingly, the Globe's *Midsummer*
continues in this plot to mine Donne's poem for its erotic
vocabulary. The flower extract may have altered Lysander's
affection, but it has not affected the content of his lover's
discourse. Shortly after he wakes, Lysander sings a Donne-
inspired song to Helenus, part of which he had earlier
performed for and with Hermia. But this time, no doubt to
signal the coercive force of the flower, there is no duet, and the
Globe's musical arrangement for Lysander's song proves more
aggressive, edgier, frenzied and sexier:

> License my roving hands, and let them go,
> Before, behind, between, betwixt, above, below.
> Oh my America, my new found land.
> My kingdom safely'st with one man band.

As he had done earlier, Lysander adds a final couplet to
these lines that loosely adapts other parts of Donne's Elegy
19: 'Off with your girdle!', he exclaims, 'Cast white linen
hence, / There is no penance due to innocence'. During
this scene, Helenus, intermittently effeminate, but reliably
delivering prissy camp, wears a hopelessly unfashionable and
utterly practical hip pack (also a 'bum bag' in UK parlance;
a 'fanny pack' in North American terms) when he enters the
woods in the Globe *Midsummer*. It reads 'First Aid', but he
does not unfasten this 'girdle' at Lysander's command. (If only
Helenus had done so at this moment, then he would have
added a sight gag to the scene.)

Despite (if not because of) its erotic charge, the second
performance of Donne in the Globe's *Midsummer* articulates complex gender politics and erotic arrangements. In
marking the transfer of affection from Hermia to Helenus by
means of lyrics just shared between Hermia and Lysander,

the second song's performance works to cast Hermia and
Helenus, her gay best friend, as nearly structurally equivalent
in terms of gender and race (both characters are played by
actors of colour): early in the production, they celebrate
the planned elopement by dancing, in unison, to Beyonce's
'Single Ladies', and later, as Helena does in Shakespeare's
text, Helenus compares himself to Daphne, the woman who
fails to escape Apollo's unwanted sexual pursuit in classical
myth (2.1.231). In a way that Lysander's first song had not,
in large measure because that theatrical moment strove to
highlight the mutuality of eloping heterosexual lovers, the
second performance of Donne in the Globe's *Midsummer*
also significantly reconfigures the gender dynamics of Elegy
19. In Donne's poem, the female body is 'America', a 'new
found land' over which the speaker fantasizes that he has
been granted possession – or license – by the very woman
he is addressing. He effectively commands her to consent
to her own sexual domination, and, in this way, he comes
across as kin to Zubin Varla's Theseus, who informs Meow
Meow's prisoner-of-war Hippolyta at the start of the Globe
performance that he 'woo'd thee with my sword' (1.1.16). In
the idiom of sixteenth-century colonialist discourse, Donne's
speaker would play Columbus to the so-called virgin territory
of 'America', an idea that we can observe more concretely in
lines of verse from Donne directly following those that have
been incorporated into Lysander's song to Helenus. In them,
Donne's speaker refers to the woman as 'My Myne of precious
stones: My Emperie' and then congratulates himself on his
Columbus-like success: 'How blest am I in this discovering
thee!' (29–30).

Lysander, then, is less explicit in the second song than is
Donne's speaker about the link connecting extractive coloni-
alism and eroticism, for he does not sing these lines to
Helenus. Instead, as you recall, he desires to 'mine' Hermia's
'precious stones', not Helenus's (if I can presume he has them).
The Globe's *Midsummer* would seem to work to code Hermia
and Helenus as structurally similar (perhaps so that a switch

in Lysander's affection from one to the other is conceivable), but it also seems to scramble such structural similarity in the way it distributes (and adapts) lines from the poem across Hermia's and Helenus's bodies. In retrospect, I would have expected Lysander to sing about Helenus's 'precious stones,' which, in turn, prompts me to wonder about Hermia's body (what are her stones?) and how, exactly, Lysander imagines he would enjoy Helenus's body.

Even so, if we follow the song's lyrics, it is perfectly clear that what Lysander wants from Helenus is exactly what he wanted from Hermia. He tells both objects of his affection: 'Off with your girdle! Cast white linen hence, / There is no penance due to innocence'. Cast off – or *dis*cover, in a different sense of the word – your white shirt, Lysander presses, as he nearly succeeds in removing Helenus's white top; and he urges that there is no better time than the present to unlatch that hip pack. (Helenus only does so near play's end, when he changes onstage into a wedding outfit.) Thus far, I have been interpreting *Midsummer*'s 'girdle' as a joke about sex and bad fashion, but it is literally way bigger than this. In Donne's poem, the speaker imagines this precise article of clothing in celestial terms. He says, 'Off with that girdle, like heavens Zone glittering, / But a far fairer world incompassing' (ll.5–6). According to the scholarly notes for these lines in the poem, 'girdle' is likened here to the Milky Way, but it does not contain and envelop the stars and planets. Instead, it encompasses a 'far fairer world', which is presumably the woman's body imagined as a more beautiful terrestrial globe. The 'girdle' is thus a 'glittering' and even 'glistening' atmosphere that enshrouds the female form. It is the 'world' below or behind or underneath this atmospheric veil that Donne's speaker wishes to discover. This arrangement would seem to translate less easily to Helenus's body than to Hermia's, but he (not she) wears the girdle in this production.

I argue that the image's associations in Donne's poem also attach retrospectively to Puck's use of the word 'girdle' to name the shape that he will create when he goes off to locate the flower love-in-idleness. In response to Oberon's command to fetch the flower, as detailed in the epigraph, Puck boasts, 'I'll put a girdle round about the earth / In forty minutes' (2.1.175–6). The 'earth' – or the Globe, our planet – is less extensive than is the Milky Way, which is likely why Puck can make the journey in so short a span of time. (In fact, it takes Puck little time, since audiences do not wait forty minutes for the fairy to arrive back onstage.) Daniel Vitkus has recently cited Puck's response to Oberon to argue that Shakespeare's play figures a 'circumscribable planet'.[7] In Vitkus's formulation, the 'imagined fairy flight around the world, to the Indies and back in search of a rare "herb", is only one example of the way that Shakespeare associated the magical potency of his theatre with the new sense of global mobility that seemed to bring the world's commodities within reach'.[8] Vitkus casts Puck's 'girdle' as an aerial circumnavigation akin to Ferdinand Magellan's sea voyage, which began in 1519 and ended in 1522 without Magellan onboard, and to Sir Francis Drake's return sailing in 1580.[9] I cannot help but imagine Vitkus as picturing Puck, as if Puck were a cartoon character, trailing behind him a cloud of smoke or mist that forms an atmospheric circle around the globe that he has travelled. I would add to Vitkus's compelling reading the idea that the Globe's *Midsummer* spotlights the eroticism implicit in Puck's act of girdling the earth by aligning it with the 'girdle' in Donne's Elegy 19. What Puck retrieves, after all, is a flower that 'Will make or man or woman madly dote / Upon the next live creature that is sees' (2.1.171–2). It is a foreign entity that distills the essence of desire and that, when applied to the eye, generates otherwise unimaginable desire.

Common to both Donne and Shakespeare and inventively made adjacent with one another in the Globe's *Midsummer*, the 'girdle', in my analysis, functions as a hinge word that establishes, unwittingly or not, a novel intertextual relation between Shakespeare's playtext and Donne's poem. The girdle proves an object that has erotic (and comic) valences, and Puck's creation of one around a more global body, the body of the earth, articulates for it a more planetary, perhaps even galactic, association. This new intertextuality thus cross-hatches erotic with environmental matters. One of these matters, I propose, is the figure of a global environment, and so I now change course, moving from explicitly erotic contexts to ecological ones, in an effort to pursue the environmental co-ordinates of the 'girdle' that Puck fashions around the world in this twenty-first-century *Midsummer* at the Globe.

Daniel Vitkus can help us in this project, too. He gestures toward these environmental co-ordinates when he locates in the title of his book chapter the circumnavigations of Magellan, Drake and Puck as near (or at) 'the Origins of Globalization'. These circumnavigations exemplify an 'emergent globalization': 'The globe', Vitkus further observes about its status at the turn of the seventeenth century, 'had become something to be *encompassed* by imperial and commercial enterprise'. In this origin story, which, according to Vitkus, 'began in 1492', historical and literary examples of early European global trade and imperialism anticipate a 'global capitalism' that 'has [now] achieved its dark telos, the catastrophe of our Anthropocene end times'.[10] Along the way and in the process, the forces of global capitalism have not only swept up in its currents peoples, animals and plants that have been relocated and/or have died in enormous numbers, but it has also inequitably redistributed sources of labour and wealth around the world. In the nearly Shakespearean words of ecocritic Steve Mentz, such 'catastrophic clashes of cultures, peoples, viruses, and ecosystems' resulted from overseas journeys that 'put ... wooden girdles round about the globe'.[11] These 'wooden girdles', of course, are the European vessels of international trade and empire-building.

There is a name for the economic and environmental narrative that I've just elaborated and that Vitkus places at 'the Origins of Globalization', even though he does not cite it. It is the Columbian Exchange, which, of course, nods to the effects of Christopher Columbus's so-called 'discovery' of the New World. According to the geographers Simon L. Lewis

and Mark A. Maslin, 'One biological result of the exchange
was the globalization of human foodstuffs'. Following the
scholarship of the environmental historian Alfred W. Crosby,
whose book *The Columbian Exchange* was first published in
1972,[12] Lewis and Maslin describe how 'The New World crops
maize/corn, potatoes and the tropical staple manioc/cassava
were subsequently grown across Europe, Asia and Africa.
Meanwhile, Old World crops such as sugarcane and wheat
were planted in the New World'. In their telling of this history
of biological and environmental contact that could not have
occurred without ships, 'The cross-continental movement of
dozens of other food species (such as the common bean, to the
New World), domesticated animals (such as the horse, cow,
goat and pig, all to the Americas) and human commensals (the
black rat, to the Americas), plus accidental transfers (many
species of earth worms, to North America; American mink
to Europe) contributed to a swift, ongoing, radical reorgani-
zation of life on Earth without geological precedent'.[13] The
Columbian Exchange not only altered human agriculture
and dietary regimes, but it also – and more profoundly –
changed and rearranged the fossil record. The appearance in
the next 100 years of 'New World plant species in Old World
sediments – and vice versa – may provide', Lewis and Maslin
suggest, 'a common marker' for the new geological epoch that
scientists have dubbed the Anthropocene. They have assigned
the year 1610 'as the beginning of the Anthropocene'.[14] In
this narrative about planetary history,[15] events unfolding in
the wake of the Columbian Exchange and as a result of early
globalization are literally *epochal*.

Vitkus's thumbnail history of globalization associated the
Anthropocene with 'catastrophe' and the rhetoric of 'end
times'. If there is a hand-wringing fatalism, a sense of gloom
and doom, linked to the Anthropocene Epoch in less scientific
writings, then it might be because the Anthropocene, as the
term's etymology indicates, concerns what man – *anthropos*
– has done to affect for the worse the Earth's ecosystemic
health. As Lewis and Maslin observe, 'The onward effects

of the arrival of Europeans in the Americas also highlights a long-term and large-scale example of human actions unleashing processes that are difficult to predict or manage'.[16] Two modern instances will suffice to demonstrate the adverse effects that human action has had and continues to have on the planet. The first concerns nuclear energy, especially the proliferation and detonation of nuclear weapons in the twentieth-century, as well as the ongoing potential risk of accident at nuclear power plants and radiation fallout.[17] And the second is the measurement in 2013 at Mauna Loa, Hawaii of CO_2 (carbon dioxide) concentrations at 400 parts per million (ppm), when, according to the scientific community, the benchmark for safe levels of carbon dioxide in the Earth's atmosphere is 350 ppm. This second effect is more familiar to us as global warming. This is the story of how burning fossil fuels increases carbon dioxide in the atmosphere, which could have been sequestered in the trees of the global forest,[18] but is no longer so sequestered there because of mass defor- estation; a rise in atmospheric carbon increases the global temperature, which, in turn, melts glaciers at the poles and, in turn, raises the sea levels, thus endangering, among other things, population centres that are coastal, such as Miami, New York, Amsterdam, and that are tidal, like London. It is perhaps little wonder that invocations of the Anthropocene are often couched in a rhetoric that conjoins alarm and hubris. We wring our hands because 'we' – human beings, but really not all human beings and really not in the same way, at the same time and at the same rate – are responsible for our current 'end times'.[19]

It should go without saying that Earth's health is different for us now than it was in Shakespeare's day. The geological timeline would place Shakespeare's culture at the start of the Anthropocene Epoch and ours (perhaps?) closer to its end. The idea of the Anthropocene frames in a new way my previous research,[20] which focussed on English Renaissance drama and its relation to the popular sentiment in sixteenth- and seven- teenth-century England that there was not enough timber and wood to be had to meet people's basic needs, especially for fuel and building purposes. This perceived shortage of timber was undoubtedly more local than 'national' in its nature, and it engendered fantasies and nightmares about scarcity and plenitude in court proclamations, in cheaply printed pamphlets, and in plays, like *The Tempest*, which dates from around 1610, that featured wood and woodland settings. This body of literature helped me to draw comparisons between that rhetoric of scarcity and more contemporary discussions about the ongoing and uneven shift from fossil fuels to renewable energy. Anxiety is at the heart of the environmental literary history I told. But Shakespeare's culture also imagined colonial enterprises, especially in early Virginia, as a possible solution to its home-grown energy crisis and so to this anxiety. By a logic that, as we shall see, is deeply unsettling, the effects of the Columbian Exchange had the potential to mitigate environmental health in England.

What I only know now, after reading new histories of the Anthropocene, is that there was more woodland in North America in the wake of the Columbian Exchange precisely because there were fewer people living there. In Lewis and Maslin's narration, 'Regional population estimates sum to a total of 54 million people in the Americas in 1492, with recent population modeling estimates of 61 million people. Numbers rapidly declined to a minimum of about 6 million people by 1650 via exposure to diseases carried by Europeans, plus war, enslavement and famine'. My readings in early colonial history of the Americas have taught me that so-called New World 'discovery' massively attenuated indigenous populations and cultures.[21] In a disquieting twist, it turns out that genocide also had other environmental consequences, most notably, a net increase in the number of trees rooted in the global forest. According to Lewis and Maslin, 'The accompanying near-cessation of farming and reduction in fire use [among indigenous populations] resulted in the regeneration of over 50 million hectares of forest, woody savanna and grassland', and this regeneration, in turn, sequestered carbon dioxide from the atmosphere so that the amount of CO_2 in it declined 7–10 ppm between 1570 and 1620. 'This dip in atmospheric CO_2', the geographers continue, 'is the most prominent feature, in terms of both rate of change and magnitude, in pre-industrial atmospheric CO_2 records over the past 2,000 years'. In lay terms, we can say that the Anthropocene Epoch commenced at an unpredictably low point in 'preindustrial' carbon history. Lewis and Maslin 'suggest naming the dip in atmospheric CO_2 the "Orbis spike" and the suite of changes marking 1610 as the beginning of the Anthropocene the "Orbis hypothesis", from the Latin [word] for world'.[22] The globality that inheres in such scientific nomenclature is apt.

In pursuing this moment in the environmental history of 'early globalization' (that's an economist's phrase), of the Columbian Exchange (an environmental historian's phrase) and of the early Anthropocene Epoch (that's a geologist's term), I would seem to have strayed from the Globe's *Midsummer*. My excuse and model is Puck. Upon arriving to the stage after having 'put a girdle round about the earth', Puck returns, in Oberon's words, a 'wanderer' (2.1.247). I, too, have wandered, and am trying to come full circle, as Puck did, with a purpose. In light of this environmental history, I linger, in closing, on the 'little western flower' that Puck has fetched from afar (2.1.166) and that initiates in the play a series of presumably long-lasting effects. After all, its introduction into *Midsummer*'s ecology magically fixes two of the play's three love plots.

My aim is not to interpret Puck's global flight as a ready allegory for what we would today call emergent globalization, the Columbian Exchange or even the Anthropocene. In the strictest terms, fairies are not human agents, although they were imagined, as we shall soon see, to have some power over human affairs. There is no sense that Puck decimated biotic populations during his voyage. The fairy brings into the play's woodland only one flower and does not treat it as botanical stock to be planted and propagated. As a scholar working primarily in the field of historical ecocriticism (and also sometimes in the history of sexuality), I should not expect, in other words, that literary texts from the past anticipate with precision the account of environmental (or sexual) history that is accepted as today's standard narrative. Instead, in the case of *Midsummer*, I am more interested in spotlighting for the telling of environmental history the fantasies of desire and power that the play's flower condenses. It is a desire for the stabilization of domestic relations through the receipt and application of a foreign botanical agent. The flower promises a quick fix to problems about love, sex and family, and its effects, of course, go wildly awry. And the botanical extract does eventually succeed in settling in a fabulous way two points of real contention and hostility in the Globe's *Midsummer*: Demetrius's homophobic rejection of Helenus and the foster care of the Indian boy.[23]

But along with Puck's girdling the earth, which makes newly accessible the flower's powers, does it also mitigate the widespread consequence for humanity of Titania and Oberon's feud over the Indian boy's fosterage? In a long speech near the start of the play, Titania reminds Oberon that they are the 'parents and original' of what now appears to scholars' eyes as a literary allusion to a series of devastating weather – and so agricultural – events that were experienced in early 1590s England and that have been linked to the effects of the Little Ice Age.[24] Titania reports that there has been an unexpected surge in rain; crops have failed; farm animals are diseased and dying; footpaths, those avenues of human civilization, are proving less passable than they used to be; human beings are becoming increasingly sick; and, most amazingly, 'The seasons [have] alter[ed]' so that 'The spring, the summer, / The childing autumn, angry winter, change / Their wonted liveries, and the mazed world / … now knows not which is which' (2.1.107, 111–14). The seasons are in such disarray, according to Titania, because of a 'distemperature' (2.1.106).

I wonder what Puck saw of such climate change when he 'put a girdle round about the earth.' There's no way to know, as there's no way to answer the questions that thinking environmentally about Puck's girdle have prompted for me: do the seasons return to a state of regularity at play's end?[25] If they do, is the reversion instantaneous or incremental? Does climate even matter to inhabitants of the world, both to newly married humans and to the reunited fairies,[26] at it is depicted at the end of *Midsummer* in the way that, according to Titania, it clearly once mattered to humans? And what are the side-effects, if any, of easy solutions in human affairs? Maybe we cannot answer such questions on behalf of Shakespeare's *Midsummer*, but, on this side of the Anthropocene and after having twice watched the Globe's *Midsummer* during the hottest summer (most distempered?) in recorded history, I think we should persist in imagining them.

NOTES

Introduction

1   At the time when this book was ready to go to press, Emma
    Rice's departure as the Artistic Director of the Globe Theatre
    has ignited a brief but heated debate in press and social media
    about the radical manner in which she treated Shakespeare's
    text as performance on the Globe's stage. Her production of *A
    Midsummer Night's Dream* was taken up as as an example of
    Rice's intervention in the text that, apparently, did not suit the
    Globe's purpose.

2   Bruce Smith, 'Queer Goings-On', *A Midsummer Night's
    Dream*, production programme (The Globe Theatre, 2016),
    n.p.

3   Melissa E. Sanchez, '"Use Me But as Your Spaniel": Feminism,
    Queer Theory, and Early Modern Sexualities', *PMLA* 127 (3)
    (May 2012): 493–511; 505. Emphasis in the original.

4   In an online blog, the actor Ankur Bahl, who plays Helenus,
    makes the point about Demetrius's coming out at this moment.

5   Michael Taylor, *Shakespeare Criticism in the Twentieth
    Century* (Oxford: Oxford University Press, 2001).

6   Alan Sinfield, 'Cultural Materialism and Intertextuality: The
    Limits of Queer Reading in *A Midsummer Night's Dream* and
    The Two Noble Kinsmen', *Shakespeare Survey* 56 (2003):
    67–78; 68.

7   Daniel Juan Gil, *Before Intimacy: Asocial Sexuality in Early
    Modern England* (Minneapolis and London: University of
    Minnesota Press, 2006), esp. 77–101.

8   Madhavi Menon, *Indifference to Difference: On Queer
    Universalism* (Minneapolis: University of Minnesota Press,
    2015), 69.

9   Christopher Castiglia and Christopher Reed, 'Introduction: In
     the Interest of Time', in *If Memory Serves: Gay Men, AIDS,
     and the Promise of the Queer Past* (Minneapolis and London:
     University of Minnesota Press, 2012), 1–37; 23.

10   A similar point is also made in *Same-Sex Desire in Early
     Modern England, 1550–1735: An Anthology of Literary Texts
     and Contexts*, ed. Marie H. Loughlin (Manchester and New
     York: Manchester University Press, 2014), 3. The groundwork
     on male same-sex desire and sodomy, as a term that captured
     the type that market both a type of man engaged in sex with
     another man (anally or not), or a broader term of slander rooted
     in religious, racial and ethnic difference, was explored, among
     others, by Jonathan Goldberg, *Sodometries: Renaissance Texts,
     Modern Sexualities* (Stanford: Stanford University Press, 1992);
     Bruce R. Smith, *Homosexual Desire in Shakespeare's England:
     A Cultural Poetics* (Chicago: The University of Chicago Press,
     1994). Alan Stewart writes in detail about the sodomite as
     a type in humanist writing. See *Close Readers: Humanist
     and Sodomy in Early Modern England* (Princeton: Princeton
     University Press, 1997). Valerie Traub has provided a nuanced
     interpretation about the distinction between the 'tribade', a
     woman who pleasures other women sexually, and 'lesbian',
     as an image used to describe representations and discourses
     of female same-sex desire. See Traub, *The Renaissance of
     Lesbianism in Early Modern England* (Cambridge: Cambridge
     University Press, 2002). Representation of female homoeroticism
     in Shakespeare and early modern drama is the subject of Denice
     A. Walen, *Constructions of Female Homoeroticism in Early
     Modern Drama* (New York: Palgrave-Macmillan, 2005).

11   Menon, *Indifference to Difference*, 21.

12   Elizabeth Freeman, *Time Binds: Queer Temporalities, Queer
     Histories* (Durham and London: Duke University Press, 2010),
     xiii.

13   Freeman, *Time Binds*, 16.

14   Mario DiGangi, *The Homoerotics of Early Modern Drama*
     (Cambridge: Cambridge University Press, 1997), 51.

15   Carla Freccero, *Queer/Early/Modern* (Durham and London:
     Duke University Press, 2006), 15.

16 *Shakesqueer: A Queer Companion to the Complete Works of Shakespeare*, ed. Madhavi Menon (Durham and London: Duke University Press, 2011).

17 Madhavi Menon, 'Queer Shakes', introduction to *Shakesqueer: A Queer Companion to the Complete Works of Shakespeare*, ed. Menon (Durham and London: Duke University Press, 2011), 1–27; 12.

18 I thank John Garrison for a productive discussion that led to this formulation.

19 See James Saslow, *Ganymede in the Renaissance: Homosexuality in Art and Society* (New Haven: Yale University Press, 1986).

20 On Calisto and early modern 'lesbianism', see Traub, *The Renaissance of Lesbianism in Early Modern England* (Cambridge: Cambridge University Press, 2002), 228–75; 'The Perversion of "Lesbian" Desire', *History Workshop Journal* 41 (Spring 1996): 23–49.

21 See Jonathan Goldberg, 'The Anus in *Coriolanus*', in *Shakespeare's Hand* (Minneapolis and London: University of Minnesota Press, 2003), 176–85.

22 Joseph Pequigney, 'The Two Antonios and Same-Sex Love in *Twelfth Night* and *The Merchant of Venice*', *ELR* 22 (2) (Spring 1992): 201–21.

23 Stephen Guy-Bray, *Against Reproduction: Where Renaissance Texts Come From* (Toronto: University of Toronto Press, 2009), xiv.

24 DiGangi, 'Queering the Shakespearean Family', *Shakespeare Quarterly* 47 (3) (Fall 1996): 269–90; 270.

25 Freccero, *Queer/Early/Modern*, 20.

26 Eve Kosofsky Sedwick, 'Swan in Love: the Example of Shakespeare's Sonnets', in *Between Men and Male Homosocial Desire* (New York: Columbia University Press, 1985), 29.

27 Paul Hammond, 'Reading the Sonnet Tradition', in *Shakespeare's Sonnets: An Original-Spelling Text*, ed. P. Hammond (Oxford: Oxford University Press, 2012), 43. Hammond elaborates on the versions and valences of homoerotic desire in the sonnets in his book *Figuring Sex*

between Men from Shakespeare to Rochester (Oxford: Clarendon Press, 2002).

28 Hammond, 'Reading the Sonnet Tradition', 46.

29 Queer early modern scholars, who have written about queerness in the Sonnets, formulate their arguments on the topic related to that explored by Hammond in terms that are more transparently aligned with the critical practice of deconstruction in queer theory. See Brue R. Smith, 'I, You, He, She, and We: On the Sexual Politics of Shakespeare's Sonnets', in *Shakespeare's Sonnets: Critical Essays*, ed. James Schiffer (New York and London: Garland Publishing, 2000), 411–29; Traub, 'Sex Without Issue: Sodomy, Reproduction, and Signification in Shakespeare's Sonnets', in *Shakespeare's Sonnets: Critical Essays*, ed. Schiffer, 431–52.

30 *Queering the Renaissance,* ed. Jonathan Goldberg (Durham and London: Duke University Press), 1994.

31 Goldberg, 'Romeo and Juliet's *Open Rs*', in *Queering the Renaissance*, 218–35; 227.

32 Jonathan Goldberg and Madhavi Menon, 'Queering History', *PMLA* 120 (5) (October 2005): 1608–17; 1610.

33 Jonathan Goldberg, *The Seeds of Things: Theorizing Sexuality and Materiality in Renaissance Representations* (New York: Fordham University Press, 2009), 3.

34 Kaja Silverman, 'Looking With Leo', *PMLA* 125 (2) (March 2010): 410–13; 412.

35 *Sex before Sex: Figuring the Act in Early Modern England*, eds James M. Bromley and William Stockton (Minneapolis and London: University of Minnesota Press, 2013), 9.

36 Jeffrey Masten, *Textual Intercourse: Collaboration, authorship, and sexualities in Renaissance drama* (Cambridge: Cambridge University Press, 1997), 49.

37 Jeffrey Masten, 'Toward a Queer Address: The Taste of Letters and Early Modern Male Friendship', *GLQ* 10 (3) (2004): 367–84; 370.

38 Will Tosh, *Male Friendship and Testimonies of Love in Shakespeare's England* (London: Palgrave Macmillan, 2016), 7.

39 See Valerie Traub, 'Desire and the Differences it Makes', in *The*

Matter of Difference: Materialist Criticism of Shakespeare, ed. Valerie Wayne (New York and London: Harvester Wheatsheaf, 1991), 81–114; 85.

40 Recently, excellent accounts of how queer theory illuminates discourses of friendship and of the affective exchanges between men have been the subject of the following two studies, respectively: John S. Garrison, *Friendship and Queer Theory in the Renaissance: Gender and Sexuality in Early Modern England* (New York and London: Routledge, 2014) and Will Tosh, *Male Friendship and Testimonies of Love in Shakespeare's England* (New York: Palgrave-Macmillan, 2016).

41 See Peter Mack, *Elizabethan Rhetoric: Theory and Practice* (Cambridge: Cambridge University Press, 2002).

42 N. F. Blake, *The Language of Shakespeare* (Houndmills and London: Macmillan, 1985), 18.

43 Richard Waswo, *Language and Meaning in the Renaissance* (Princeton: Princeton University Press, 1987), 8–82. Charles Barber, *Early Modern English* (London: Andre Deutsch, 1981), 143–95.

44 Jeffrey Masten, *Queer Philology: Sex, Language, and Affect in Shakespeare's Time* (Philadelphia: University of Pennsylvania Press), 2016.

45 I owe this phrase to Madhavi Menon in a private correspondence.

46 John S. Garrison, *Friendship and Queer Theory in the Renaissance: Gender and Sexuality in Early Modern England* (New York and London: Routledge and Taylor Francis, 2014).

47 David Orvis, 'Cross-Dressing, Queerness, and the Early Modern Stage', in *The Cambridge History of Gay and Lesbian Literature*, eds E. L. Maccallum and Mikko Tuhkanen (Cambridge: Cambridge University Press, 2014), 197–217; 199.

48 Valerie Traub, *Thinking Sex with the Early Moderns* (Philadelphia: Pennsylvania University Press, 2016), 4.

49 Mario DiGangi, *Sexual Types: Embodiment, Agency, and*

Dramatic Character from Shakespeare to Shirley (Philadelphia: Pennsylvania University Press, 2011), 6.

50 At the SAA conference in New Orleans in 2016, the seminar, 'Shakespeare and his contemporaries in the 18th and the 19th centuries', led by Ivan Lupić, addressed these issues in an extended discussion in the context of Huw Griffiths's paper '"And all this passion for a boy?": Anachronistic Homoeroticism in Eighteenth-Century Adaptations of *Philaster*', whose aim was to use historicism in order to intervene in the debates around 'anachronism' which have affected critical discussions in queer Shakespeare studies and the histories of early modern sexuality.

51 The popular American composer and singer, Rufus Wainwright, has recently released a CD featuring his music to nine sonnets from Shakespeare's collection, exploiting the subtlety of sexual ambiguities in them, in a way that can call his music queer. Rufust Wainwright, *Take All My Loves: 9 Shakespeare Sonnets*, released by Deutsche Grammophon GmbH, 2016.

52 Kate Chedgzoy has exemplified some of the uses of 'queer' Shakespeare in contemporary popular film, literature and fringe theatre, employing mostly feminist and psychoanalytic theory. See *Shakespeare's Queer Children: Sexual Politics and Contemporary Culture* (Manchester and New York: Manchester University Press, 1995).

53 Giuseppe Marcocci, 'Matrimoni omosessuali nella Roma del tardo cinquecento', *Quaderni storici* 45 (133) (2010): 107–37; and Marina Baldassari, *Bande giovanili e 'vizio nefando': violenza e sessualità nella Roma barocca* (Roma: Viella, 2005). I am grateful to Jonathon Hunt for drawing my attention to these Italian sources and for helping me clarify thoughts on the comparative aspect of engaging with Italian and English manifestations of homoerotic and homosexual realities, in culture and literature respectively.

54 Traub, *Thinking Sex with the Early Moderns*, 13.

55 Giuseppe Marcocci, 'Is This Love? Same-Sex Marriage in Renaissance Rome', *Historical Reflections* 41 (2) (Summer 2015): 37–51; 37.

56 Stephen Greenblatt, 'Fiction and Friction', in *Shakespearean Negotiations: The Circulation of Social Energy in Renaissnce England* (Oxford: Clarendon Press, 1992), 66–93; 77.

57 The absence of Shakespeare in Goldberg's recent overview of that history makes *Queer Shakespeare* timely. See 'English Renaissance Literature in the History of Sexuality', in *The Cambridge History of Homosexuality*, 164–78.

Chapter 1: 'Which is worthiest love' in *The Two Gentlemen of Verona*?

1 Citations to act, scene, and line number hereafter appear in text.

2 Jeffrey Masten, *Textual Intercourse: Collaboration, Authorship, and Sexualities in Renaissance Drama* (Cambridge: Cambridge University Press, 1997), 39, 48. In a more recent essay, Masten, '*The Two Gentlemen of Verona*', in *A Companion to Shakespeare's Works: The Comedies*, eds Richard Dutton and Jean E. Howard (Malden, MA: Blackwell Publishing, 2003), 266–88, 275–6, identifies Lance's speeches to Crab and Julia's employment of cross-dressing as possible sites of resistance to elevated male friendship.

3 Stephen Guy-Bray, 'Shakespeare and the Invention of the Heterosexual', *Early Modern Literary Studies* 13 (2) (2007) / Special Issue 16: 12.1–28, 12.6. Available online: http://extra. shu.ac.uk/emls/si-16/brayshks.htm (accessed 15 June 2016).

4 Elizabeth Rivlin, 'Mimetic Service in *The Two Gentlemen of Verona*', *ELH* 72 (1) (2005): 105–28; 105–6.

5 Masten, '*The Two Gentlemen*', 270.

6 According to J. L. Simmons, 'Coming Out in Shakespeare's *The Two Gentlemen of Verona*', *ELH* 60 (4) (1993): 857–77; 858, 'The disturbances in Shakespeare's greenest text reveal a fearful "coming out," a nervous debut, marking both the narrative and the narrator as thwarted by uncertainties of desire'. These 'uncertainties of desire', I want to suggest, serve as both cause and effect in the playtext's interrogation of love.

7   The 210 instances of 'love' break down as follows: 'love' (166),
    'loved' (10), 'loves' (8), 'lovest' (6), 'lover' (5), 'beloved' (3),
    'love's' (5), 'lovers' (3), 'lover's' (2) and 'lovely' (2). This tally
    is based on analysis of William Shakespeare, *Mr. VVilliam
    Shakespeares comedies, histories, & tragedies* (London:
    1623), cross-checked with 'Concordance of Shakespeare's
    Complete Works', *Open Source Shakespeare*, http://www.
    opensourceshakespeare.org/concordance/ (accessed 15 June
    2016), and with the Arden Shakespeare edition (3rd series)
    of *Two Gentlemen*. Due to considerable variability among
    editions of *Two Gentlemen*, the tally does not separate out
    'Love' and 'love' or 'Love's' and 'love's'.

8   See Jonathan Goldberg, *Voice Terminal Echo: Postmodernism
    and English Renaissance Texts* (New York: Methuen, 1986),
    68–100; Masten, *Textual Intercourse*, 40–5; and Guy-Bray,
    'Shakespeare and the Invention of the Heterosexual'.

9   Masten, *Queer Philologies*, 77–8. Emphasis in original.

10 Ibid., 74, 72. Emphasis in original.

11 Ibid., 72. Emphasis in original.

12 On the Ovidian ideology of male possession that underwrites
    this particular instance of traffic in women, see William C.
    Carroll, '"And love you 'gainst the nature of love": Ovid,
    Rape, and *The Two Gentlemen of Verona*', in *Shakespeare's
    Ovid: The Metamorphoses in the Plays and Poems*, ed. A. B.
    Taylor (Cambridge: Cambridge University Press, 2000), 49–65.
    On further Latin sources for the play's discomforting ending,
    see Betsy Bowden, 'Latin Pedagogical Plays and the Rape Scene
    in *The Two Gentlemen of Verona*', *English Language Notes*
    41 (2) (2003): 18–32.

13 Julie Crawford, 'The Homoerotics of Shakespeare's Elizabethan
    Comedies', in *A Companion to Shakespeare's Works: The
    Comedies*, eds Richard Dutton and Jean E. Howard (Malden,
    MA: Blackwell Publishing, 2003), 135–58; 150.

14 James M. Bromley, *Intimacy and Sexuality in the Age of
    Shakespeare* (Cambridge: Cambridge University Press, 2011).

15 Melissa E. Sanchez, '"Use Me But as Your Spaniel": Feminism,
    Queer Theory, and Early Modern Sexualities', *PMLA* 127 (3)
    (2012): 493–511.

16 On male friendship and/as early modern homonormativity, see
    Laurie Shannon, 'Nature's Bias: Renaissance Homonormativity
    and Elizabethan Comic Likeness,' *Modern Philology* 98 (2)
    (2000): 183–210; and Shannon, *Sovereign Amity: Figures of
    Friendship in Shakespearean Contexts* (Chicago: University of
    Chicago Press, 2002), 1–14, 64–8.

17 Masten, *Textual Intercourse*, 39.

18 Elizabeth Willamson, 'Dismembering Rhetoric and Lively
    Action', in *The Two Gentlemen of Verona*', in *Staging the
    Blazon in Early Modern English Theater*, eds Deborah Uman
    and Sara Morrison (Burlington, VT: Ashgate, 2013), 37–49;
    38.

19 Guy-Bray, 'Shakespeare and the Invention of the
    Heterosexual', 14.

20 See John D. Cox, 'Shakespeare and the Ethics of Friendship',
    Religion and Literature 40 (3) (2008): 1–29, esp. 14–18;
    Tom MacFaul, *Male Friendship in Shakespeare and his
    Contemporaries* (Cambridge: Cambridge University Press,
    2007), 72–5; Robert Stretter, 'Cicero on Stage: Damon
    and Pithias and the Fate of Classical Friendship in English
    Renaissance Drama', *Texas Studies in Literature and Language*
    47 (4) (2005): 345–65, esp. 346.

21 Valerie Traub, *The Renaissance of Lesbianism in Early
    Modern England* (Cambridge: Cambridge University Press,
    2002), 19.

22 In the version of *Two Gentlemen* included in Shakespeare, *Mr.
    VVilliam Shakespeares comedies, histories, & tragedies*, 22,
    'Loue wounded' appears in place of 'love-wounded', perhaps
    underscoring Cupid's agency.

23 Kingsley-Smith, *Cupid in Early Modern Literature and
    Culture*, 2. See also Catherine Belsey, 'Cleopatra's Seduction',
    in *Alternative Shakespeares 2*, ed. Terence Hawkes (London:
    Routledge, 1988), 38–62; Kate Chedgzoy, 'Playing with
    Cupid: Gender, Sexuality and Adolescence', in *Alternative
    Shakespeares 3*, ed. Diana E. Henderson (London: Routledge,
    2007), 138–57.

24 On the Cupid/Puck connection, see Alan Lewis, 'Reading
    Shakespeare's Cupid', *Criticism* 47 (2) (2005): 177–213.

25 In 1 John 4(8).16, the evangelist twice makes the assertion
    'God is love'.

26 Barbara Newman, 'Love's Arrows: Christ as Cupid in Late
    Medieval Art and Devotion', in *The Mind's Eye: Art and
    Theological Argument in the Middle Ages*, eds Jeffrey F.
    Hamburger and Anne-Marie Bouché (Princeton, NJ: Princeton
    University Press, 2006), 263–86; 263–4.

27 Richard Rambuss, *Closet Devotions* (Durham, NC: Duke
    University Press, 1998), 74.

28 Mario DiGangi, *The Homoerotics of Early Modern Drama*
    (Cambridge: Cambridge University Press, 1997), 20, writes,
    'Like David, St. Sebastian is often depicted as a beautiful,
    androgynous young man. In Italian Renaissance paintings, this
    saint who sacrificed himself for the love of Christ is commonly
    portrayed as a naked Apollonian figure suggestively penetrated
    by arrows'. See also Merrill Cole, *The Other Orpheus: A
    Poetics of Modern Homosexuality* (New York: Routledge,
    2003), 96–7; James M. Saslow, *Pictures and Passions: A History
    of Homosexuality in the Visual Arts* (New York: Viking, 1999),
    98–9; and Saslow, 'The Tenderest Lover: Saint Sebastian in
    Renaissance Painting: a Proposed Homoerotic Iconology for
    North Italian Art, 1450–1550', *Gai Saber* 1 (1) (1977): 58–66.

29 According to Stephen Hamrick, *The Catholic Imaginary and
    the Cults of Elizabeth, 1558–1582* (Burlington, VT: Ashgate,
    2009), 'Widespread in this period, such a connection [between
    Venus, Cupid, and Catholic religious practice] points to the
    saturation of the Catholic imaginary within Elizabeth culture',
    75. See also Jane Kingsley-Smith, *Cupid in Early Modern
    Literature and Culture* (Cambridge: Cambridge University
    Press, 2010), esp. 1–23; and Newman, 'Love's Arrows'.

30 Barbara Newman, *God and the Goddesses: Vision, Poetry,
    and Belief in the Middle Ages* (Philadelphia: University of
    Pennsylvania Press, 2003), 149.

31 Gary Kuchar, '"Loves Best Habit": Eros, Agape, and the
    Psychotheology of *Shakespeare's Sonnets*', in *The Return of
    Theory in Early Modern English Studies: Tarrying with the
    Subjunctive*, eds Paul Cefalu and Bryan Reynolds (New York:
    Palgrave Macmillan, 2011), 211–34; 221.

32 Thomas Hyde, *The Poetic Theology of Love: Cupid in Renaissance Literature* (Newark: University of Delaware Press, 1986), 18.

33 Ibid., 28.

34 Maurice Hunt, 'Catholicism, Protestant Reformation, and *The Two Gentlemen of Verona*', in *Shakespeare's Religious Allusiveness: Its Play and Tolerance* (Aldershot: Ashgate, 2004), 1–17, 12–13, notes the 'uneasy coexistence of Protestant and Catholic motifs' and the 'syncretism of Shakespeare's Catholic/Protestant artistry' in *Two Gentlemen*.

35 Erwin Panofsky, 'Blind Cupid', in *Studies in Iconology: Humanistic Themes in the Art of the Renaissance* (1939; rpt. New York: Harper & Row, 1972), 95–128.

36 On Blind Cupid as the embodiment of carnal love, see Panofsky, 'Blind Cupid'. On his metonymic status for transcendent love, see Edgar Wind, 'Orpheus in Praise of Blind Love', in *Pagan Mysteries in the Renaissance* (New York: W. W. Norton, 1968), 53–80.

37 Hunt, 'Catholicism, Protestant Reformation, and *The Two Gentlemen of Verona*', 9.

38 Ibid., 11. See also Peter Lindenbaum, 'Education in *The Two Gentlemen of Verona*', *Studies in English Literature* 15 (1975): 229–44; 240.

39 Hunt, *Shakespeare's Religious Allusiveness*, 12. Although it was much more common in Renaissance England for sodomy to be associated with Catholicism, Alan Stewart, 'A Society of Sodomites: Religion and Homosexuality in Renaissance England', in *Love, Friendship and Faith in Europe, 1300–1800*, eds Laura Gowing, Michael Hunter and Miri Rubin (New York: Palgrave Macmillan, 2014), 88–109, uncovers incidents of and contexts for Puritanism being identified with sodomitical practices and societies.

Chapter 2: Glass: The Sonnets' desiring object

1   See Herbert Grabes, *The Mutable Glass: Mirror-Imagery in Titles and Texts of the Middle Ages and English Renaissance,* trans. Gordon Collier (Cambridge: Cambridge University Press, 1928) and Margaret J. M. Ezell, 'Looking Glass Histories', *Journal of British Studies* 43 (3) (July 2004): 317–38.

2   Kalas offers a wonderful discussion of the sonnets in the sixth chapter of *Frame, Glass, Verse: The Technology of Poetic Invention in the English Renaissance* (Ithaca and London: Cornell University Press, 2007), 166–98.

3   I wish to extend thanks to Stephen Guy-Bray, Margaret Ferguson, Kyle Pivetti, Goran Stanivukovic, Will Stockton, Christine Varnardo and Jeffrey Masten for helpful comments and conversations as I developed this essay. The discussion throughout builds upon initial thinking articulated in my book *Glass* (London and New York: Bloomsbury, 2015).

4   I acknowledge that the sonnets might neither be in a sequence nor be cleanly divided between a singular 'young man' and a singular 'dark lady'. However, I would posit that the particular sonnets examined in this essay have a male addressee in mind. For a good starting point about debates regarding the number and gender of addressees in the sonnets, see William Nelles, 'Sexing Shakespeare's Sonnets: Reading Beyond Sonnet 20', *ELR* 39 (1) (2009): 128–40, and Valerie Traub, 'The Sonnets: Sequence, Sexuality, and Shakespeare's Two Loves', in *A Companion to Shakespeare's Works, Vol. 4: The Poems, Problem Comedies, and Late Plays,* ed. Richard Dutton and Jean E. Howard (Malden: Blackwell, 2003), 275–301.

5   In his incisive study of the operations and politics of same-sex desire in contemporary African-American culture, C. Riley Snorton puts it nicely, 'the concept of glass [demonstrates] the complex and even contradictory ways visuality structures our perceptions of others and ourselves'. C. Riley Snorton, *Nobody is Supposed to Know: Black Sexuality on the Down Low* (Minneapolis: University of Minnesota Press, 2014), 17.

6 Quotations from the sonnets are drawn from William Shakespeare, *The Arden Shakespeare Complete Works*, ed. Richard Proudfoot, Ann Thompson and David Scott Kastan (New York and London: Bloomsbury, 2011).

7 André Greene, *The Chains of Eros: The Sexual in Psychoanalysis*, trans. Luke Thurston (London: Karnac Books, 2000), 117.

8 Blondie, 'Heart of Glass', writ. Debbie Harry and Chris Stein, *Parallel Lines* (Chrysalis, 1978).

9 Text for the poem is drawn from John Donne, *The Complete English Poems*, ed. A. J. Smith (New York: Penguin, 1977), 46–7.

10 Samuel Daniel, 'A Defence of Ryme', in *Elizabethan Critical Essays*, ed. G. Gregory Smith, vol. 2 (Oxford: Oxford University Press, 1904), 356–84; 359, and Kalas, 59.

11 Tristan Garcia, *Form and Object: A Treatise on Things*, trans. Jon Cogburn and Mark Allan Ohm (Edinburgh: University of Edinburgh Press, 2014), 238.

12 All discussions of word meanings and origins in this book cite the *Oxford English Dictionary* online, available at www.oed.com (accessed 15 June 2016).

13 Garcia, *Form and Object*, 124.

14 Aranye Fradenburg, 'Momma's Boys', in *Shakesqueer: A Queer Companion to the Complete Works of Shakespeare*, ed. Madhavi Menon (Durham and London: Duke University Press, 2011), 319–27; 320.

15 Melissa Sanchez, 'The Poetics of Feminine Subjectivity in Shakespeare's Sonnets and "A Lover's Complaint"', in *The Oxford Handbook Shakespeare's Poetry*, ed. Jonathan Post (Oxford: Oxford University Press, 2013), 505–21; 509.

16 The *OED* notes that, since the fifteenth century, the term 'comely' has been used to describe persons who are 'Fair, pretty, 'nice-looking' and 'pleasing', and 'comeliness' has been used for those who exhibit 'Pleasing appearance; gracefulness or beauty of form; handsomeness'. George Puttenham, *The arte of English poesie. Contrived into three bookes: the first of poets and poesie, the second of proportion, the third of*

ornament (London: Richard Field, 1589), 168; and Henry Peacham, *The Garden of Eloquence, conteining the most excellent ornaments, exornations, lightes, flowers, and formes of speech, commonly called the figures of rhetorike* (London: H. Jackson, 1577), sig. Hiiii^v.

17 Henry Peacham, *The Garden of Eloquence, conteining the most excellent ornaments, exornations, lightes, flowers, and formes of speech, commonly called the figures of rhetorike,* (London: Richard Field, 1593), 45, 47.

18 Peacham, *Garden of Eloquence,* 55, 48.

19 Derrida claims that there exists a 'friendship of rhyme', where the presence of 'alliance, harmony, assonance, chime' in language function as 'traffic signals' for the presence of friendship. Jacques Derrida, *Politics of Friendship*, trans. George Collins (London: Verso, 2005), 166–7; and Peacham, *Garden of Eloquence,* 50. For an extensive discussion of repetition in poetry, especially within early modern treatises on poetry, see Brian Vickers, 'Repetition and Emphasis in Rhetoric: Theory and Practice', in *Repetition* 7 (SPELL: Swiss Papers in English Language and Literature), ed. Andreas Fischer (Tübingen: Gunter Narr Verlag, 1994), 85–114.

20 Peacham, *Garden of Eloquence,* 46, and Jeffrey Masten, *Queer Philologies: Sex, Language, and Affect in Shakespeare's Time* (Philadelphia: University of Pennsylvania Press, 2016), 69–82.

21 Maurice Charney, *Wrinkled Deep in Time: Aging in Shakespeare* (New York: Columbia University Press, 2009), 42. On aging in Shakespeare, see also Naomi Conn Liebler, '"The oldest hath borne most": The Burdens of Aging and the Morality of Uselessness in *King Lear*', in *Shakespeare and Moral Agency*, ed. Michael D. Bristol (London: Continuum, 2010), 111–26.

22 Kalas opens the possibility that Sonnet 5 'describes the poet's deflowering of the young man' and indeed the homoerotic charge is strong here, as the speaker must penetrate the addressee in order to know and accumulate his interiority later trapped in glass (173).

23 Stephen Guy-Bray, 'Remembering to Forget: Shakespeare's

Sonnet 35 and Sigo's "XXXV"', in *Sexuality and Memory in Early Modern England*, ed. John S. Garrison and Kyle Pivetti (New York and London: Routledge, 2016), 43–50; 47.

24 Guy-Bray, 'Remembering to Forget', 47.

25 Holly Dugan, *The Ephemeral History of Perfume: Scent and Sense in Early Modern England* (Baltimore: Johns Hopkins University Press, 2001), 19.

26 Garrett A. Sullivan, Jr., 'Afterword: "A Prescript Order of Life": Memory, Sexuality, Selfhood', in *Sexuality and Memory in Early Modern England*, ed. John S. Garrison and Kyle Pivetti (New York and London: Routledge, 2016), 237–44; 239.

27 Jane Bennett, *Vibrant Matter: A Political Ecology of Things* (Durham and London: Duke University Press, 2010), 4.

28 Leo Bersani, 'The Power of Evil and the Power of Love', in Leo Bersani and Adam Phillips, *Intimacies* (Chicago and London: University of Chicago Press, 2008), 57–88; 67.

29 Levi Bryant describes a point of view that embraces what he has termed an 'onticology', where 'being itself is composed of objects', as well as relations between objects, rendering visible how subjects themselves are inevitably objects. Levi Bryant, *The Democracy of Objects* (Ann Arbor: University of Michigan Library, 2011), 50.

30 Deborah Shuger, 'The "I" of the Beholder: Renaissance Mirrors and the Reflexive Mind', in *Renaissance Culture and the Everyday*, ed. Patricia Fumerton and Simon Hunt (Philadelphia: University of Pennsylvania Press, 1999), 21–41.

31 Medieval and Renaissance innovations around glass played a critical role in speculation – both in terms of improving human sight and in terms of positing new ideas about abstract concepts. For a terrific read that tracks this argument in detail, see Alan Macfarlane and Gerry Martin, *Glass: A World History* (Chicago: University of Chicago Press, 2002).

32 Sara Ahmed, *Queer Phenomenology: Orientations, Objects, Others* (Durham, NC: Duke University Press, 2006), 1.

33 Ahmed, *Queer Phenomenology*, 1.

34 Jonathan Culler, *Theory of the Lyric* (Cambridge: Harvard University Press, 2015), 350.

35 George Gascoigne, *The steele glas. A satyre co[m]piled by George Gascoigne Esquire. Togither with The complainte of Phylomene. An elegie deuised by the same author* (London: Richard Smith, 1576), I.ii.

36 John Dee, 'To the Vnfained Lover of truth, and constant Studentes of Noble *Sciences*', in *The elements of geometrie of the most auncient philosopher Euclide*, trans. Sir Henry Billingsley (London, 1570), sig. bjᵛ.

37 Adam Phillips, *On Balance* (New York: Picador, 2011), 23.

38 Adam Philips, 'On a More Impersonal Note', in Leo Bersani and Adam Philips, *Intimacies* (Chicago: University of Chicago Press, 2010), 89–118; 103.

39 Just as Žižek concludes that *Richard II* 'proves beyond any doubt that Shakespeare had read Lacan', it seems here as if Shakespeare has been reading his Barthes. Slavoj Žižek, *Looking Awry: An Introduction to Jacques Lacan through Popular Culture* (Cambridge, MA: MIT Press, 1992), 9.

40 Michel Foucault, 'Of Other Spaces', trans. Jay Miskowiec, *Diacritics* 16 (1) (Spring 1986): 22–7; 24.

41 José Esteban Muñoz. *Cruising Utopia: The Then and There of Queer Futurity* (New York: New York University Press, 2009), 187.

42 Muñoz, *Cruising Utopia*, 186. For another perspective on the linkages between the etymology of 'ecstasy' as enabling a mode of being dispossessed or standing outside of hegemonic ontological systems, see Judith Butler, *Undoing Gender* (London and New York: Routledge, 2004), 131–52; 151–2.

Chapter 3: The sport of asses: *A Midsummer Night's Dream*

I am grateful to Goran Stanivukovic for putting together this collection and inviting me to join it; to Mario DiGangi, Will Stockton and the other participants in the 2015 SAA seminar that produced much of the work in this volume; and to Stephanie Pietros, Tony D'Agostino and Mary Bly for offering feedback and support at critical moments. This essay would not exist at all if not for Corey McEleney, who generously allowed me to sit in on his graduate seminar, 'The Queer Renaissance', at Fordham University, and who offered innumerable suggestions for fixing the essay's numerous faults. Any that stubbornly remain are my own.

1   Eve Kosofsky Sedgwick, 'Preface to the 2008 Edition', in *Epistemology of the Closet*, updated edn (Berkeley: University of California Press, 2008), xvi.

2   Stephen Guy-Bray, Vin Nardizzi and Will Stockton, 'Queer Renaissance Historiography: Backward Gaze', in *Queer Renaissance Historiography: Backward Gaze*, ed. Stephen Guy-Bray, Vin Nardizzi and Will Stockton (Farnham: Ashgate, 2009), 1.

3   For such readings of *Midsummer*, see Mario DiGangi's discussion in *Sexual Types: Embodiment, Agency, and Dramatic Character from Shakespeare to Shirley* (Philadelphia: University of Pennsylvania Press, 2011) of the potential for Titania's homoerotic desire for the votaress. Helena's relationship with Hermia occupies Melissa Sanchez's '"Use me but as your Spaniel": Feminism, Queer Theory, and Early Modern Sexualities', *PMLA* 127 (3) (2012): 493–511. Like Sanchez, Richard Rambuss declares 'Its vectors of same-sex attraction – the usual touchstone for queer readings of Shakespeare – no longer strike me as what's queerest about this comedy [...] This play's generic homoeroticism is routine for the form'. Instead, Rambuss prefers to look at the cross-species relations of the play, both human/fairy and human/animal. 'Shakespeare's Ass Play', in *Shakesqueer*, ed. Madhavi Menon (Durham and London: Duke University Press, 2011), 234–44; 235.

4 See, for example, Carla Freccero, *Queer/Early/Modern*
      (Durham: Duke University Press, 2006). Picking up Freccero's
      thread of taking issue with New Historicist arguments about
      the necessity of avoiding the word 'homosexual' when
      discussing the early modern period, Madhavi Menon argues
      that 'heterohistory' stands in opposition to 'homohistory',
      which becomes a tool for dismantling historicist engagement
      with texts. The *homo* in homohistory, she writes, 'challenges
      the historicist investment in a progressive chronology according
      to which the stable present becomes the point from which to
      map an unstable past (whose instability is fixed under the mark
      of its pastness)'. Heterohistory, then, is invested in teleology
      and fixedness, concerned primarily with establishing the
      present as one thing and the past as another entirely. She later
      concedes that the split between homo- and hetero-histories is
      not quite so neat: 'an anti-teleological argument can respect
      the possibility of historical difference while simultaneously
      embracing inconsequence and instability – it can accept that
      no two ages will behave in an identical manner while resisting
      the argument that one (fluid) age always sets the stage for a
      later (stable) one'. *Unhistorical Shakespeare: Queer Theory
      in Shakespearean Literature and Film* (New York: Palgrave
      Macmillan, 2008), 3, 33.

5 It is not universally the case that critics enforce such a
      distinction. Valerie Traub, for example, has blended the terms
      when writing that 'once the hierarchy between the homoerotic
      and heterosexual is dissolved within the critical enterprise,
      homoerotic significations are everywhere'. *Desire and Anxiety:
      Circulations of Sexuality in Shakespearean Drama* (London:
      Routledge, 1992), 113. More recently, Traub slides freely
      between the terminology of 'female homoeroticism' and
      'early modern lesbianism'. 'Setting the Stage Behind the Seen:
      Performing Lesbian History', in *The Queerest Art: Essays
      on Lesbian and Gay Theater*, ed. Alisa Solomon and Framji
      Minwalla (New York: New York University Press, 2002a),
      56–7.

6 David Orvis, 'Cross-Dressing, Queerness, and the Early
      Modern Stage', in *The Cambridge History of Gay and
      Lesbian Literature*, ed. E. L. McCallum and Mikko Tuhkanen
      (Cambridge: Cambridge University Press, 2014), 199.

7   Yet as Iain Morland notes, particularly focusing on the desensitized intersex body, bodily conceptions of the queer are built on normative bodies and tend to exclude alternatives. See 'What Can Queer Theory Do for Intersex?', *GLQ* 15 (2) (2009): 285–312.

8   Elizabeth Freeman, *Time Binds: Queer Temporalities, Queer Histories* (Durham and London: Duke University Press, 2010), xviii. Freeman elsewhere in the book discusses the importance of recentralizing the body erotic: 'The temporal orders on which heteronormativity depends for its meanings and power, themselves imbricated with the whole system of production and consumption, can be contested only with an equally forceful commitment to thinking queer pleasures' (58).

9   Carla Freccero, 'Queer Times', *South Atlantic Quarterly* 106 (3) (2007): 485–94; 485.

10 Madhavi Menon, 'Queer Shakes', in *Shakesqueer* (Durham and London: Duke University Press, 2011), 1–27; 7.

11 As Alisa Solomon puts it, 'That homophobic panic throbs at the heart of the age-old antitheatrical prejudice hardly needs documenting', though she goes on to provide a thorough overview of the dangers that antitheatrical writing believes that drama poses to the sex/gender system. Alisa Solomon, 'Great Sparkles of Lust: Homophobia and the Antitheatrical Tradition', in *The Queerest Art: Essays on Lesbian and Gay Theater*, ed. Alisa Solomon and Framji Minwalla (New York: New York University Press, 2002), 9–20; 10.

12 Lee Edelman, *No Future: Queer Theory and the Death Drive* (Durham and London: Duke University Press, 2006), 24.

13 Ibid., 4.

14 This is something of a throwaway rhetorical question, largely because it is one that I do not have an easy answer to. Even for a theory like Edelman's, even a touch of the queer is enough to position a figure as being queer. Yet I am not entirely comfortable with the absolutism of the split between not-queer/queer because of the impossibility of bifurcating the world into two such neat categories, the open question of who gets to identify or name what counts as queer, and the possibility for individuals or bodies to slide between (or simultaneously occupy) the two positions based on behaviour or perception.

15 Sedgwick, *Epistemology of the Closet*, 9–10.

16 As Alan Sinfield rather tartly observes, 'To be interesting, a
    reading against the grain will invoke diverse nuances in the
    text, but it will recognize nonetheless that the text has an
    ideological project, to which other inferences will always be
    marginal. [...] Of course, this is not a reliable procedure. But
    on this the deconstructionists are right: language isn't going
    to afford a reliable procedure. If we were to wait until we had
    achieved an unambiguous utterance, we would starve to death'.
    'Cultural Materialism and Intertextuality: The Limits of Queer
    Reading in *A Midsummer Night's Dream* and *The Two Noble
    Kinsmen*', *Shakespeare Survey* 56 (2003): 67–78; 77.

17 For a fairly extensive catalogue of antitheatrical references
    to sodomy, see Ellen MacKay, *Persecution, Plague, and Fire*
    (Chicago: University of Chicago Press, 2011), 149–53.

18 Tanya Pollard notes, 'scholarly convention has taken to referring
    to [the author] as John Greene'. See *Shakespeare's Theater: A
    Sourcebook* (Hoboken, NJ: Wiley-Blackwell, 2008), 255.

19 I. G., *A Refutation of the Apology for Actors* (London:
    W. White, 1615), 61.

20 See especially Laura Levine, *Men in Women's Clothing:
    Anti-theatricality and Effeminization, 1579–1642* (Cambridge:
    Cambridge University Press, 1994); Stephen Orgel,
    *Impersonations: The Performance of Gender in Shakespeare's
    England* (Cambridge: Cambridge University Press, 1996).

21 Reprinted in Pollard, *Shakespeare's Theater: A Sourcebook*,
    172. Emphasis added.

22 Reprinted in Pollard, *Shakespeare's Theater: A Sourcebook*, 20.

23 Reprinted in Pollard, *Shakespeare's Theater: A Sourcebook*, 34.

24 All quotations from *A Midsummer Night's Dream* refer to the
    individual Arden edition of the play.

25 Much of the criticism that focuses on the Mechanicals and
    their play has thought about them as class outsiders and artistic
    interlopers. See, for example, Barbara Freedman's argument
    that 'By punishing those who make unlawful comparisons
    between themselves and others, *A Midsummer Night's Dream*
    seeks to preserve a rigidly hierarchical social order against the
    threats of encroaching bourgeois individualism'. 'Dis/Figuring

Power: Censorship and Representation in *A Midsummer Night's Dream*', in *A Midsummer Night's Dream: Critical Essays*, ed. Dorothea Kehler (New York and London: Garland, 1998), 179–215; 184. Kehler's bibliographical essay in the same volume runs through the long history of this particular kind of criticism (see esp. 42–5).

26 This is the most uses in any of Shakespeare's plays. It occurs ten times in *Merry Wives*, again almost exclusively in the context of playing tricks to publicly humiliate Falstaff, and nine times in *Love's Labour's Lost*, where it is also used in the context of marking an inset play – the masque of the Nine Worthies – as an inferior entertainment.

27 As Harold Brooks notes, 'stand upon points' means '(1) take much stock in punctuation; (2) stick at trifles'. David Bevington notes that the phrase means 'pay attention to punctuation in his reading. (Thus the humor of Quince's speech is in the blunders of its punctuation)', which problematically presupposes that speech blunders in its punctuation. David Bevington (ed.), *The Complete Works of Shakespeare* (New York: Longman, 1997), 174.

28 Traub takes this reference as indicating 'cross-sex fellatio' because Flute is dressed as Thisbe. The gender/sexuality signification of the allusion is almost certainly not purely cross-sex, since Flute is male, but as Rainolds claims, putting on the dress would turn Flute female. Traub, *Thinking Sex with the Early Moderns* (Philadelphia: University of Pennsylvania Press, 2016), 363 n.105.

29 This claim opposes a critical tradition that reads the inset play as supporting *Midsummer*'s marriage telos. As Tom Pettitt notes, 'There is much about the play which would have made it appropriate for performance at wedding revels, so much so that a number of specific weddings have been suggested as its original auspices'. '"Perchance you wonder at this show": Dramaturgical Machinery in *A Midsummer Night's Dream* and 'Pyramus and Thisbe', in *The Narrator, the Expositor, and the Prompter in European Medieval Theatre*, ed. Philip Butterworth (Turnhout: Brepols, 2007), 215. Patricia Parker associates the Mechanicals 'with *joinery* and *joining* in particular, in ways that suggest links between the artisanal,

material, or artefactual and the joinings in matrimony that form its close'. *Shakespeare from the Margins: Language, Culture, Context* (Chicago: University of Chicago Press, 1996), 88. Even Alan Sinfield observes that the potential disruptions to patriarchy, and by extension heteronormativity, in *Midsummer* are 'less marked [...] than might be expected,' though he also believes that the play is open to the reading that 'love and marriage will turn out all right, so long as we do as we are told and don't ask too many questions'. 'Cultural Materialism and Intertextuality', 72, 76. Bruce Boherer also explores the text's complicated interplay between embracing and rejecting non-heteronormative relationships. 'Economies of Desire in *A Midsummer Night's Dream*', *Shakespeare Studies* 32 (2004): 99–117.

30 Hugh Grady, 'Shakespeare and Impure Aesthetics: The Case of *A Midsummer Night's Dream*', *Shakespeare Quarterly* 59 (3) (2008): 274–302; 301.

31 Brooks regards the inset play in a similar manner, writing that it provides 'specially good opportunity for burlesque' (lxxxvi).

32 Parker also points out the extent to which the play seems to subvert its own ends in *Shakespeare from the Margins*, esp. 109–12.

33 It is, of course, quite funny, particularly in performance. I am not saying that the scene isn't funny, but rather I want to point out that it can be funny *and* serve another end simultaneously.

Chapter 4: As You Like It or What You Will: Shakespeare's Sonnets and Beccadelli's *Hermaphroditus*

1 On queer historiography, see Vin Nardizzi and Stephen Guy-Bray, *Queer Interventions: Queer Renaissance Historiography: Backward Gaze* (Farnham: Routledge, 2016). See also Jonathan Goldberg (ed.), *Queering the Renaissance* (Durham: Duke University Press, 1994); Carla Freccero, *Queer/*

Early/Modern (Durham: Duke University Press, 2006), James M. Bromley and Will Stockton (eds), *Sex before Sex: Figuring the Act in Early Modern England* (Minneapolis: University of Minnesota Press, 2103), and Valerie Traub, *Thinking Sex with the Early Moderns* (Philadelphia: University of Pennsylvania Press, 2015).

2   There is a massive secondary literature on gender ambiguity in Shakespeare. For an overview of queer studies in Shakespeare see Madhavi Menon (ed.), *Shakesqueer: A Queer Companion to the Complete Works of Shakespeare* (Durham: Duke University Press, 2011).

3   All references to the works of Shakespeare are to *The Arden Shakespeare Complete Works*, 2nd edn, ed. Richard Proudfoot, Ann Thompson and David Scott Kastan (London: Bloomsbury, 2011). On issues of gender ambiguity and queer desire in Sonnet 20, see Natasha Distiller, 'Shakespeare's Perversion: A Reading of Sonnet 20', *Shakespeare* 8 (2) (June 2012): 137–53, which reviews much of the scholarship on the topic.

4   Ovid, *Metamorphoses*, 4.383. All references to the Latin text of the *Metamorphoses* are to the Oxford Classical Texts edition, ed. R. J. Tarrant (New York: Oxford University Press, 2004).

5   *OED* cites from 1398, J. Trevisa, trans. Bartholomew de Glanville, *De Proprietatibus Rerum* (1495), xviii. li. 811: 'In harmofroditus is founde bothe sexus male and female: but alway vnperfyte'.

6   Jenny C. Mann, 'How to Look at a Hermaphrodite in Early Modern England,' *Studies in English Literature, 1500–1900* 46 (1) (Winter 2006): 67–91.

7   'Nec femina dici / nec puer ut possit, neutrumque et utrumque videntur,' Ovid, *Metamorphoses*, 4.379–379. My translation.

8   'tactis subito mollescat in undis,' Ovid, *Metamorphoses*, 4.386. My translation.

9   Thomas Peend, *The pleasant fable of Hermaphroditus and Salmacis* (London, 1565). STC 18971.

10   The poem, *Salmacis and Hermaphroditus,* ascribed to Francis Beaumont (London, 1602) also reads the hermaphrodite as an

effeminized, weakened man rather than an ideal union of male and female. The concluding lines are 'who in that fountaine swimmes, / A mayden smoothnesse seyzeth halfe his limmes,' (sig. E4^r). STC 18972.

11 Genesis 2.24.

12 Edmund Spenser, *The Faerie Queene* (London: 1590), sig. Oo8^r. Book 3, canto 12, stanzas 45–7.

13 Lauren Silberman, *The Transformations of Desire: Erotic Knowledge in Books III and IV of the Faerie Queene* (Berkeley, CA: University of California Press, 1994), 68.

14 Despite much effort, no convincing source has been found for Spenser's 'rich Romane'. Some ancient statues of hermaphrodites survive, but there is no evidence that Spenser had any direct knowledge of them. See Donald Cheney, 'Spenser's Hermaphrodite and the 1590 *Faerie Queene*', *PMLA* 87 (2) (March 1972): 192–200; 194–5.

15 Thomas Nashe, *Strange Newes* (London: 1592), sig. B4^r–B4^v.

16 Poem 1.42 'To the Noble Cosimo on the Division of his Book', in Antonio Beccadelli, *The Hermaphrodite*, ed. and trans. Holt Parker (Cambridge, MA: Harvard University Press, 2010), 53. All quotes from *Hermaphroditus* are from this edition.

17 Boccaccio, *Genealogie deorum gentilium*, 3.21; see Parker's edition of Beccadelli, *Hermaphrodite*, xxii–xxiii.

18 For examples of the genre, see *Poeti giocosi del tempo di Dante*, ed. P. Cudini (Milan: Rizzoli, 1956).

19 References to poems in *Hermaphroditus* are by book and poem number, corresponding to those in Parker's text.

20 See poems 1.35, 2.3, 2.4, 2.5.

21 Thomas Hobbes, 'To the Reader', from *Philosophical Rudiments concerning Government and Society* (London, 1651), sig. B2^r.

22 For an overview of male sexual mores under the Roman Empire, see Kyle Harper, *From Shame to Sin: The Christian Transformation of Sexual Morality in Late Antiquity* (Cambridge, MA: Harvard University Press, 2013), 22–37 (on same-sex eros) and 52–61 (on the ideal of moderation).

23 Parker notes of this passage that although Beccadelli's expression is a bit muddled (men piss too) his general meaning is clear (*Hermphrodite*, 215 n.27). Significantly, both men and women are seen here solely as differing holes to be penetrated.

24 Poems in praise of the Emperor include 1.4, 1.6, 1.14, etc. Poems on oral sex include 3.82, 3.96, 11.46, 11.85, etc. Poems on anal sex include 1.24, 11.78, etc. Poems lamenting the death of children include 7.96, 10.61, 11.91, etc.

25 From the Latin name of Palermo (Panormus), Beccadelli's birthplace.

26 Parker's edition of Beccadelli, *Hermaphrodite*, xv.

27 Beccadelli's recantation may be found in Parker's edition of Beccadelli, *Hermaphrodite*, 124–7.

28 Parker's edition of Beccadelli, *Hermaphrodite*, xiv.

29 On Nashe as an English Aretine, see Ian Frederick Moulton, *Before Pornography: Erotic Writing in Early Modern England* (New York: Oxford, 2000), 158–93.

30 Ludwig Pastor, *History of the Popes*, 3rd edn (London: 1906), I:23–4. Quoted in Parker's edition of Beccadelli, *Hermaphrodite*, vii.

31 Frances Meres, *Palladis Tamia* (London: 1598), sig. Oo1ᵛ–Oo2ʳ. STC 17834.

32 Only twenty-four manuscript copies of individual sonnets survive from the early modern period (none in Shakespeare's hand of course). None seem to predate the publication of the sonnets in 1609. See Peter Beal (ed.), *Index of English Literary Manuscripts*, vol. 1.2 (New York: R. R. Bowker, 1980), 449–54.

33 For details, see Parker's edition of Beccadelli, *Hermaphrodite*, ix.

34 On the controversy, see Parker's edition of Beccadelli, *Hermaphrodite*, xiii–xvi.

35 See for example *Martialis castus, ab omni obscoenitate perpurgatis* (Paris, 1554), and *M. Valerij Martialis Epigrammaton libri omnes* (Ingolstadt: 1602), edited by Matthaeo Radero, a Jesuit.

36 Martial, *M. Val. Martialis epigrammaton libri Animaduersi, emendati et commentariolis luculenter explicati.* (London: 1615). STC 17492.

37 Alastair Bellany, 'Killigrew, Sir Robert (1579/80–1633)', *Oxford Dictionary of National Biography*, Oxford University Press, 2004; online edition, January 2008. Available online: http://www.oxforddnb.com.ezproxy1.lib.asu.edu/view/article/15537 (accessed 18 June 2016).

38 STC 17493.

39 George Parfitt, in his edition of Jonson's poems, writes: 'Jonson was aiming at achieving in English what Martial had achieved with the Latin epigram, and Jonson's collection is the first set of English epigrams showing genuine understanding of what Martial's poems were like'. Ben Jonson, *The Complete Poems*, ed. George Parfitt (New York: Penguin, 1975), 482.

40 Besides the English edition of 1615, Jonson also owned a Paris 1617 edition and another published in Leyden in 1619. See David McPherson, 'Ben Jonson's Library and Marginalia: An Annotated Catalogue', *Studies in Philology* 71 (5) (December 1974): 1–106; 68–70. Since some of Jonson's own epigrams were written prior to 1615, it is likely he owned earlier editions as well, but many of his books were destroyed in a fire in 1623. See McPherson, 'Ben Jonson's Library', 5–6.

41 Ibid., 69. The volume annotated is Martial, *M. Val. Martialis Nova Editio Ex Museo Petri Scriverii* (Leyden, 1619).

42 Attitudes expressed in the rare early modern references to oral sex tend to be those found in Classical poetry. Romans generally thought oral sex the most degrading of all sex acts because it brought the mouth in contact with the genitals. Marilyn B. Skinner, *Sexuality in Greek and Roman Culture* (Malden, MA: Blackwell, 2005), 18.

43 A partial translation by Thomas May was published in 1629 (STC 17494). Another by R. Fletcher appeared in 1656 (Wing M831).

44 Wing M825A.

45 Editions include, Wing M825C, M825D, M826, M826A, M827, M828, M829.

46 Martial, *Epigrams*, trans. James Mitchie (New York: Penguin, 1973) republished in the Modern Library series 2002; Martial, *Epigrams: With Parallel Latin Text*, trans. Gideon Nisbet, Oxford World's Classics (New York: Oxford University Press, 2015). Both editions number the epigrams correctly, so that readers can see that some are missing, but neither volume advertises itself as a selection.

47 sed hi libelli,
tamquam coniugibus suis mariti
non possunt sine mentula placere.
...
lex haec carminibus data est iocosis
ne possint, nisi pruriant, placere. (Martial 1.35)

All quotations from Martial are from Martial, *Epigrams*, 3 volumes, ed. and trans. D. R. Shackleton-Bailey, Loeb Classical Library (Cambridge, MA: Harvard University Press, 1993).

48 The identity of Mino is unclear, but Beccadelli's friend and fellow humanist Poggio Bracciolini, did advise him to write less provocative poems. See Parker's edition of Beccadelli, *Hermaphrodite*, ix.

Chapter 5: The queer language of size in *Love's Labour's Lost*

1 Madhavi Menon, 'The L Words', in *Shakesqueer: A Queer Companion to the Complete Works of Shakespeare*, ed. M. Menon (Durham: Duke University Press, 2011), 187–93; 187.

2 For arguments that the Princess and her three ladies mock and reject the men's efforts to impress them with Petrarchan clichés, see Kathryn M. Moncrief, '"Teach us, sweet madam": Masculinity, Femininity, and Gendered Instruction in *Love's Labour's Lost*', in *Performing Pedagogy in Early Modern England: Gender, Instruction, and Performance*, ed. K. M. Moncrief and K. R. McPherson (Burlington, VT: Ashgate, 2011), 113–27; Jane Kingsley-Smith, 'Aristotelian Shame and Christian Mortification in *Love's Labour's Lost*', in

Shakespeare and Renaissance Ethics, ed. P. Gray and J. D. Cox (New York: Cambridge University Press, 2014), 76–97; Peter B. Erickson, 'The Failure of Relationship Between Men and Women in *Love's Labour's Lost*', in *Love's Labour's Lost: Critical Essays*, ed. F. H. Londré (New York: Garland Publishing, 1997), 243–56; and Mark Breitenberg, 'The Anatomy of Masculine Desire in *Love's Labor's Lost*', *Shakespeare Quarterly* 43 (4) (1992): 430–49.

3   Breitenberg, 'The Anatomy of Masculine Desire', 433, 435. Breitenberg draws on Nancy Vickers, 'Diana Described: Scattered Woman and Scattered Rhyme', *Critical Inquiry* 8 (1981): 265–79.

4   Ibid., 435.

5   William Shakespeare, *Love's Labour's Lost*, ed. H. R. Woudhuysen, The Arden Shakespeare, Third Series (New York: Bloomsbury, 1998). I follow the naming conventions in this edition, which are based on the 1598 Quarto.

6   Jeffrey Masten, 'Towards a Queer Address: The Taste of Letters and Early Modern Male Friendship', *GLQ: A Journal of Gay and Lesbian Studies* 10 (3) (2004): 367–84. Masten both calls attention to and resists the conventionality of the word 'sweet' in particular, arguing that the word communicates an intense male intimacy in early modern texts that modern readers tend to gloss over as mere convention (370).

7   See Patricia Fumerton, *Cultural Aesthetics: Renaissance Literature and the Practice of Social Ornament* (Chicago: University of Chicago Press, 1991).

8   Susan Stewart, *On Longing: Narratives of the Miniature, the Gigantic, the Souvenir, the Collection* (Baltimore: Johns Hopkins University Press, 1984), 56.

9   Ruth Stevenson, '"This Senior-Junior, Giant-Dwarf Dan Cupid": Generations of Eros in Shakespeare's *Love's Labour's Lost*', *Renaissance Papers* (2009): 75–84; 81. Stevenson also likens Armado and Boyet to alternative versions of Cupid.

10   Jeffrey Masten, 'Editing Boys: The Performance of Gender in Print', in *From Performance to Print in Shakespeare's England*, ed. P. Holland and S. Orgel (New York: Palgrave, 2006), 113–34; 117.

11 Masten, 'Toward a Queer Address', 372. Emphasis in original.

12 The erotic appeal of boy actors has been well documented. See especially Masten, 'Editing'; Lisa Jardine, 'Boy Actors, Female Roles, and Elizabethan Eroticism', in *Staging the Renaissance: Reinterpretations of Elizabethan and Jacobean Drama*, ed. D. S. Kastan and P. Stallybrass (New York: Routledge, 1991), 57–67; Stephen Orgel, *Impersonations: The Performance of Gender in Shakespeare's England* (New York: Cambridge University Press, 1996); Valerie Traub, *Desire and Anxiety: Circulations of Sexuality in Shakespearean Drama* (New York: Routledge, 1992).

13 Patricia Parker, 'Preposterous Reversals: *Love's Labour's Lost*', *Modern Language Quarterly* 54 (4) (1993): 435–82; 436–9.

14 The first definition cited comes from 'excrement, n.2'. *OED Online*, June 2016. The *OED* cites *Love's Labour's Lost* as the first use of this meaning, and it cites the final use as occurring in 1705. The second definition cited comes from 'excrement, n.1'. *OED Online*, June 2016. Available online: www.oed.com (both accessed 30 June 2016). This meaning had developed by the mid-sixteenth century.

15 Christine Varnado, '"Invisible Sex!" What Looks Like the Act in Early Modern Drama?', in *Sex Before Sex: Figuring the Act in Early Modern England*, ed. J. M. Bromley and W. Stockton (Minneapolis: University of Minnesota Press, 2013), 25–52; 32.

16 Parker, 'Preposterous Reversals: *Love's Labour's Lost*', *Modern Language Quarterly* 54 (4) (1993): 479. For influential studies of the early modern legal category of sodomy, see Alan Bray, *Homosexuality in Renaissance England* (London: Gay Men's Press, 1982); and Jonathan Goldberg, *Sodometries* (Stanford: Stanford University Press, 1992).

17 Valerie Traub, *Thinking Sex with the Early Moderns* (Philadelphia: University of Pennsylvania Press, 2016); 158, 112.

18 Ibid., 112.

19 Dorothea Kehler, 'Jaquenetta's Baby's Father', in *Love's Labour's Lost: Critical Essays*, ed. F. H. Londré (New York: Garland Publishing, 1997), 305–12; 306.

Chapter 6: Locating queerness in *Cymbeline*

1   Amanda Berry, 'Cymbeline: desire vomit emptiness: *Cymbeline*'s Marriage Time', in *Shakesqueer: A Queer Companion to the Works of Shakespeare*, ed. Madhavi Menon (Durham NC: Duke University Press, 2011), 90.

2   Ros King, *Cymbeline: Constructions of Empire* (Farnham: Ashgate, 2005), 1.

3   Ibid, 93. For King's larger discussion of troubled masculinity in the play, see 93–104.

4   Edelman discusses this topic in various places; see especially R. King, *No Future: Queer Theory and the Death Drive* (Durham: Duke University Press, 2004), 1–31.

5   N. Simpson-Younger, '"The Garments of Posthumus": Identifying the Non-Responsive Body in *Cymbeline*', in *Staging the Blazon in Early Modern English Theater*, ed. Deborah Uman and Sara Morrison (New York: Routledge, 2016), 177.

6   Berry, 'Cymbeline: desire vomit emptiness', 92.

7   H. Love, 'Milk', in *Shakesqueer: A Queer Companion to the Works of Shakespeare*, ed. Madhavi Menon (Durham: Duke University Press, 2011), 201.

8   For an interesting discussion of the importance of clothing to the play, see Paola Colaiacomo, 'Other from the Body: Sartorial Metatheatre in Shakespeare's *Cymbeline*', in *Identity, Otherness and Empire in Shakespeare's Rome*, ed. Maria del Sapio Gabero (Farnham: Ashgate, 2009), 61–74. For a discussion of the gendering of legibility and plausibility in the final scene, see Patricia Walsh, 'Reading Women: Chastity and Fictionality in *Cymbeline*', *Renaissance Papers* (2013): 131–45.

9   All quotations will appear parenthetically.

10 See Simpson-Younger, 'The Garments of Posthumus', 178–80 for a discussion of the corpse in the play.

11 K. Gillen, 'Chaste Treasure: Protestant Chastity and the Creation of a Notational Economic Sphere in *The Rape of Lucrece* and *Cymbeline*', *Early English Studies* 4 (2011): n.p.

12 B. R. Smith, 'Eyeing and Wording in *Cymbeline*', in *Knowing Shakespeare: Senses, Embodiment and Cognition*, ed. Lowell Gallagher and Shankar Raman (New York: Palgrave Macmillan, 2010), 51.

13 Ibid, 63.

14 J. Lopez, *Theatrical Convention and Audience Response in Early Modern Drama* (Cambridge: Cambridge University Press, 2003), 128. For his discussion of the exposition at the beginning of *Cymbeline*, see 89–94.

15 For my earlier discussion of the relationship between what we see and what we hear with reference to *Pericles*, see S. Guy-Bray, 'Sources', in *Early Modern Theatricality*, ed. Henry S. Turner (Oxford: Oxford University Press, 2013), 145–9. In *Pericles*, however, the issue is of much less importance to the play as a whole. For another discussion of seeing in *Cymbeline* (particularly in the final scene), see Paul Yachnin, 'The Publicity of the Look', in *Shakespeare in our Time: A Shakespeare Association of America Collection*, ed. Dympna Callaghan and Suzanne Gossett (London: Bloomsbury, 2015), 277–85.

16 For a good discussion of the different terms and what they mean, see Smith, 'Eyeing and Wording in *Cymbeline*', 54–5.

17 S. Wall-Randell, 'Reading the Book of the Self in Shakespeare's *Cymbeline* and Wroth's *Urania*', in *Staging Early Modern Romance: Prose Fiction, Dramatic Romance, and Shakespeare*, ed. Mary Ellen Lamb and Valerie Wayne (New York: Routledge, 2009), 111. For her discussion of the scene as a whole, see 'Reading the Book', 109–12.

18 An excellent discussion of the final scene (very different from mine) is Sarah Beckwith, *Shakespeare and the Grammar of Forgiveness* (Ithaca, NY: Cornell University Press, 2012), 122–6.

Chapter 7: Desiring H: *Much Ado About Nothing* and the sound of women's desire

1   'H, n.,' *OED Online*. Available online: http://www.oed.com.
    proxygw.wrlc.org/view/Entry/82936?rskey=peqgts&result=1
    (accessed 22 July 2016).

2   In the Arden third series, Claire McEachorn glosses H as:
    'Both the letter and the word "ache" were pronounced in the
    same way, as "aitch"', citing Heywood's proverbs. See 3.4.50,
    288. The *Norton,* which prints the minuscule, glosses it as
    'punningly: "ache" was pronounced in the same way.' See
    William Shakespeare, *Much Ado About Nothing*, ed. Stephen
    Greenblatt et al. (New York: W. W. Norton, 2016), 3.4. 46,
    447 n.9.

3   See, for instance, Jeffrey Masten's 'prolegomenon' for a larger
    project on 'Boys in Print' – a study of 'an archive of images of
    male children and adolescent that adorn Renaissance printed
    texts.' Jeffrey Masten, *Queer Philologies: Sex, Language and
    Affect in Shakespeare's Time* (Philadelphia: University of
    Pennsylvania Press, 2016), 130–49.

4   See Joel Fineman, 'The Sound of O in *Othello:* the Real of
    the Tragedy of Desire', *October* 45 (Summer 1988): 76–96;
    Bruce Smith, *Acoustic Worlds of Early Modern England*
    (Chicago: University of Chicago Press, 1999). See also Miriam
    Jacobson, *Barbarous Antiquities: Reorienting the Past in the
    Poetry of Early Modern England* (Philadelphia: University of
    Pennsylvania Press, 2015), 93–4.

5   Masten, *Queer Philologies,* 16.

6   Valerie Traub, *Thinking Sex with the Early Moderns*
    (Philadelphia: University of Pennsylvania Press, 2015), 173.

7   See Fleury, cited in Masten, *Queer Philologies.*

8   See David Sacks, *Letter Perfect* (New York: Vintage, 2007); see
    also Kökeritz, *Shakespeare's Pronunciation,* 90.

9   See B. I., *The Workes of Benjamin Jonson*, 2nd edn (London,
    1641), 48.

10 For more on the link between Shakespeare's corpus and orthography, particularly in terms of *Much Ado About Nothing*, see Jeffrey Masten, *Queer Phililogies*, 43.

11 John Heywood, *An Hundred Epigrams* (London, 1556), sig. C2ʳ, Early English Books Online.

12 See 'pike, v.1', *OED Online*. Available online: http://www.oed.com.proxygw.wrlc.org/view/Entry/143773?rskey=IQ4uRQ&result=11&i sAdvanced=false (accessed 22 July 2016).

13 See John Taylor, *The World Runs on Wheels* (London, 1635), sig. B1ᵛ, Early English Books Online. Available online: http://gateway.proquest.com.proxygw.wrlc.org/openurl?ctx_ver=Z39.88-2003&res_id=xri:eebo&rft_id=xri:eebo:image:23550:10 (accessed 23 July 2016). The line about H, curiously, is missing from the 1623 edition.

14 John Mennes, *Recreation for ingenious head-peeces, or, a pleasant walk in of epigrams* (London, 1654), sig. E3ᵛ, Early English Books Online. Available online: http://gateway.proquest.com.proxygw.wrlc.org/openurl?ctx_ver=Z39.88-2003&res_id=xri:eebo&rft_id=xri:eebo:citation:12272443 (accessed 19 July 2016). See also H. Parrot, *Cures for the Itch: Characters, Epigrams, Epitaphs* (London, 1626), sig. B6ᵛ, Early English Books Online. Available online: http://gateway.proquest.com.proxygw.wrlc.org/openurl?ctx_ver=Z39.88-2003&res_id=xri:eebo&rft_id=xri:eebo:image:20619:26 (accessed 19 July 2016.)

15 Susan Butler, *The Aitch Factor: Adventures in Australian English* (Sydney: Pan Macmillan, 2014), Kindle edn (location 153).

16 'F, n.', *OED Online*. Available online: http://www.oed.com.proxygw.wrlc.org/view/Entry/67372?rskey=dbD3dv&result=1 (accessed 22 July 2016).

17 Carol Cook, in 1986, notes that the 'pun on *nothing* and *noting* in the play has frequently been remarked …'. See her article, 'Reading Gender Difference in *Much Ado About Nothing*', *PMLA* 101 (2) (1986): 186–202.

18 See David Crystal, *Pronouncing Shakespeare: The Globe Experiment* (New York: Cambridge University Press, 2005), 65–70.

19 Helge Kökeritz, *Shakespeare's Pronunciation* (New Haven: Yale University Press, 1953), 309.

20 On the metaphorical significance of this phrase, see Daniel Vitkus, *Turning Turk: English Theater and the Multicultural Mediterranean, 1570–1630* (New York: Palgrave-Macmillan, 2003); see also Jonathan Burton, 'English Anxiety and the Muslim Power of Conversion: Five Perspectives on "Turning Turk" in Early Modern Texts', *JEMCS* 2 (1) (2002): 35–67.

21 On the role of travel, print history and poetic tropes, particularly around barbarousness in the early modern period, see Miriam Jacobson, *Barbarous Antiquity: Reorienting the Past in the Poetry of Early Modern England* (Philadelphia: University of Pennsylvania Press, 2015), esp. 7.

22 Pietro Anghiera, *The Decades of the new worlde or west India conteynyng the nauigations and conquests of the Spanyards* (London: 1555), sig. Jjiv^r.

23 On Herod and histrionic performance, see Jonathan Gil Harris, *Untimely Matter in the Time of Shakespeare* (Philadelphia: University of Pennsylvania Press, 2012), 83.

24 So, too, does Falstaff. As Gina Bloom argues, Falstaff's pronunciation emphasizes that 'honor' is 'insensible' and as a result 'Falstaff's impossible social aspirations are neatly captured by [its] unaspirated "h"'. See *Voice in Motion: Staging Gender, Shaping Sound in Early Modern England* (Philadelphia: University of Pennsylvania Press, 2007), 67.

25 Stanley Wells, 'Editorial Treatment of the Foul-Paper Texts: *Much Ado About Nothing* as a Test Case', *Review of English Studies* 31 (121) (1980): 1–16; see also James Mardock and Eric Rasmussen, 'What Does Textual Evidence Reveal About the Author', in *Shakespeare Beyond Doubt: Evidence, Argument, Controversy,* ed. Paul Edmondson and Stanley Wells (Cambridge: Cambridge University Press, 2013), 111–20.

26 See Wells, 'Editorial Treatment of the Foul-Papers'.

27 Ibid., 3.

28 Ibid., 4.

29 Their entrance is more complicated than it may seem: it does not make sense for them to enter with the revellers, since they

are part of Leonato's household, but nor does it make sense for them to enter with him and sit silently until the dance. See Wells, 'Editorial Treatment', 5.

30   Allan Gilbert, 'Two Margarets: The Composition of *Much Ado About Nothing*', *Philological Quarterly* 151 (1) (1962): 61–71; 61.

31   Michelle Dowd, 'Desiring Subjects: Staging the Female Servant in Early Modern Tragedy', in *Working Subjects in Early Modern English Drama*, ed. Michelle Dowd and Natasha Korda (New York: Routledge, 2011): 131–44; 140.

32   Lee Salinger, 'Borachio's Indiscretion: Some Noting About Much Ado', in *The Italian World of English Renaissance Drama: Cultural Exchange and Intertextuality*, ed. Michee Marrapodi and A. J. Hoenselaars (Newark, DE: University of Delaware Press, 1998), 225–39; 225.

33   Claire McEarchern, 'Introduction', in William Shakespeare, *Much Ado About Nothing*, 3rd edn (London: Bloomsbury, 2016): 1–181, 4–45.

34   Alwin Thaler, 'Spenser and "Much Ado About Nothing"', *Studies in Philology* 37 (2) (1940): 225–35; 233.

35   David Bevington, *Shakespeare's Ideas: More Things in Heaven and Earth* (Oxford: Wiley-Blackwell, 2009), 30.

36   Thaler, 'Spenser and "Much Ado About Nothing"', 235.

37   *Shakespeare's Comedy of Love* (London: Methuen, [1974]), 158, cited in Philip Collington, '"Stuffed with all honourable virutes": Much Ado About Nothing and the Book of the Courtier', *Studies in Philology* 103 (3) (2006): 281–312; 302 n.32.

38   See Booth, 'Who Doesn't Listen in Shakespeare', in *Who Hears in Shakespeare? Auditory Worlds on Stage and Screen*, ed. Laury Magnus and Walter Cannon (Teaneck, NJ: Farleigh Dickenson University Press, 2012), 235–46; 247.

39   See Diana Henderson, 'Mind the Gaps: The Ear, The Eye, and the Senses of a Woman in *Much Ado About Nothing*', in *Knowing Shakespeare*, ed. Lowell Gallagher and Shankar Raman (New York and Houndsmills: Palgrave-Macmillan, 2010), 192–215.

40   See Henderson, 'Mind the Gaps', 209.

41 Ibid, 211.

42 Ann Pellegrini, 'Closing Ranks, Keeping Company: Marriage Plots and the Will to Be Single', in *Shakesqueer*, ed. Madhavi Menon (Durham: Duke University Press, 2011), 243–53; 250.

Chapter 8: 'Two lips, indifferent red': Queer styles in *Twelfth Night*

1 E. H. Gombrich, *Art and Illusion: A Study in the Psychology of Pictorial Representation* (Oxford: Phaidon Press, 1988), 17.

2 Russ McDonald, *Shakespeare and the Arts of Language* (Oxford: Oxford University Press, 2001), 8.

3 William Scott, *The Model of Poesy*, ed. Gavin Alexander (Cambridge: Cambridge University Press, 2013), 46.

4 Cicero, *De Oratore*, trans. H. Rackham (Cambridge, MA and London: Harvard University Press, 1992), 99.

5 *The Art of English Poesy by George Puttenham: A Critical Edition*, ed. Frank Whigham and Wayne A. Rebhorn (Ithaca, NY and London: Cornell University Press, 2007), 233.

6 See James Turner, *Philology: The Forgotten Origins of the Modern Humanities* (Princeton and Oxford: Princeton University Press, 2014), 36.

7 Carla Freccero, *Queer/Early/Modern* (Durham and London: Duke University Press, 2006), 20.

8 Kevin Ohi, *Henry James and the Queerness of Style* (Minneapolis and London: University of Minnesota Press, 2011).

9 Jeffrey Masten, *Queer Philology: Sex, Language, and Affect in Shakespeare's Time* (Philadelphia: University of Pennsylvania Press, 2016), 15.

10 Bruce R. Smith, '"His fancy's queen:" Sensing Sexual Strangeness in *Twelfth Night*', in *Twelfth Night: New Critical Essays*, ed. James Schiffer (London and New York: Routledge, 2011), 64–79; 79.

11 Diversity of desire and the sexual politics produced by the transvestite plot of *Twelfth Night* have been the subject of David L. Orvis, 'Cross-Dressing, Queerness, and the Early Modern Stage', in *The Cambridge History of Gay and Lesbian Literature*, ed. E. L. McCallum and Mikko Tuhkanen (Cambrdige: Cambridge University Press, 2014), 197–217; Arthur L. Little, '"A Social Habitation and a Name": Presence, Witnessing, and Queer Marriage in Shakespeare's Romantic Comedies', in *Presentism, Gender, and Sexuality in Shakespeare*, ed. Evelyn Gajowski (New York: Palgrave, 2009), 207–36; Stephen Orgel, *Impersonations: The Performance of Gender in Shakespeare's England* (Cambridge: Cambridge University Press, 1996); Phyllis Rackin, 'Androgyny, Mimesis, and the Marriage of the Body Heroine on the English Renaissance Stage', *PMLA* 102 (2) (1987): 29–41; Valerie Traub, *Desire and Anxiety: Circulation of Sexuality in Shakespearean Drama* (London: Routledge, 1992).

12 Stephen Greenblatt, Introduction to *Twelfth Night*, in *The Norton Shakespeare*, ed. Stephen Greenblatt et al., 3rd edn (New York and London: W. W. Norton, 2016), 1907.

13 Valerie Traub, *The Renaissance of Lesbianism in Early Modern England* (Cambridge: Cambridge University Press, 2002), 56.

14 Orvis, 'Cross-Dressing, Queerness, and the Early Modern Stage', 203.

15 Paul Edmondson, *Twelfth Night: A Guide to the Text and its Theatrical Life* (Houndsmills and New York: Palgrave Macmillan, 2005), 104–5.

16 Quentin Skinner, *Forensic Shakespeare* (Oxford: Oxford University Press, 2014), 27.

17 Samuel Schoenbaum, *William Shakespeare: A Compact Documentary Life* (Oxford: Oxford University Press, 1987), 213.

18 David Crystal and Ben Crystal, *Shakespeare's Words: A Glossary & Language Companion* (London: Penguin Books, 2002), 90.

19 In Arden 3, Elam's gloss follows the *OED*, as do *The Norton Shakespeare*, 3rd edn (ed. Greenblatt et al., 2016) and the RSC *Complete Works*, ed. Jonathan Bate and Eric Rasmussen (New York: The Modern Library, 2007), 624; Roger Warren

and Stanley Wells suggest 'countable (as in 'accountable'),
i.e. sensitive. *Twelfth Night, or What You Will* (Oxford and
New York: Oxford University Press, 1995), 111; Elizabeth
Story Donno retains 'comptible', glosses it as 'sensitive',
and describes it as 'a nonce use'. *Twelfth Night*, The New
Cambridge Shakespeare (Cambridge: Cambridge University
Press, 1985), 64.

20 *Twelfe Night, or, What You Will*, ed. Horace Howard Furness,
A New Variorum Shakespeare (Philadelphia and London: J. B.
Lippincott Company, 1901), 80.

21 Stanley Wells and Gary Taylor with John Jowett and William
Montgomery, *William Shakespeare: A Textual Companion*
(Oxford: Clarendon Press, 1987), 421. There is no quarto
edition of the play. That a 'theatrical' manuscript of the play
which was used in the playhouse for the purpose of performance
was a 'possible printer's copy' cannot be ruled out, argues Paul
Werstine in *Early Modern Playhouse Manuscripts and the
Editing of Shakespeare* (Cambridge: Cambridge University Press,
2013), 226. The theatrical copy would have been prepared for
the theatre by a scribe, but in the absence of material evidence of
such a copy for *Twelfth Night*, it is 'impossible to be confident',
Wells and Taylor argue, about what the scribe's copy was like.
Wells and Taylor et al., *William Shakespeare*, 421.

22 The phrase is used by Ohi in his delineation of the linguistic
properties of Henry James's writing. Ohi, *Henry James and the
Queerness of Style*, 1.

23 This idea draws on the writing about the signification of
language within the philological practice of reading delineated
in Leo Spitzer's project of stylistic study, especially in
Stilstudien (München: Hueber, 1928) and *Linguistics and
Literary History* (Princeton: Princeton University Press, 1948).

24 Lorna Hutson, 'On Not Being Deceived: Rhetoric and the Body
in *Twelfth Night*', *Texas Studies in Literature and Language*
38 (2) (Summer 1996): 140–74; 140.

25 Ibid., 147.

26 Arthur F. Marotti, '"Love is not Love": Elizabethan Sonnet
Sequences and the Social Order', *ELH* 49 (2) (Summer 1982):
396–428; 416.

27 I borrow the term from Russ McDonald, *Shakespeare and the Arts of Language* (Oxford: Oxford University Press, 2001), 176.

28 Keir Elam (ed.), *Twelfth Night* (London: Bloomsbury, 2008), 83.

29 Aristotle, *The 'Art' of Rhetoric*, trans. John Henry Freese (Cambridge, MA and London: Harvard University Press, 1991), III.xi.15.

30 Henry Peacham, *The Garden of Eloquence* (London, 1577; STC 19497), *A Scolar Press Facsimile* (Menston: The Scolar Press, 1971), D4ᵛ.

31 *The Art of English Poesy*, ed. Whigham and Rebhorn, 276.

32 John Hoskins, *Directions for Speech and Style* (Harleian MSS 4604 and 850), ed. Hoyt H. Hudson (Princeton: Princeton University Press, 1935), 29.

33 Some of the information in this regard is available in David F. Greenberg, *The Construction of Homosexuality* (Chicago and London: The University of Chicago Press, 1988).

34 Traub, *The Renaissance of Lesbianism*, 57.

35 Carla Freccero, *Queer/Early/Modern* (Durham and London: Duke University Press, 2006), 21.

36 Catherine Bates, *Masculinity, Gender and Identity in The English Renaissance Lyric* (Cambridge: Cambridge University Press, 2007), 117.

37 I drew on some of Bates' vocabulary at this point.

38 This is how Janet Clare describes it in *Shakespeare's Stage Traffic: Imitation, Borrowing and Competition in Renaissance Theatre* (Cambridge: Cambridge University Press, 2014), 135.

39 Bruce R. Smith (ed.), *Twelfth Night: Texts and Contexts* (Boston and New York: Bedford/St. Martin's, 2001), 203.

40 The one-sex model in the early modern period was presented in detail by Thomas Laqueur, *Making Sex: Body and Gender from the Greeks to Freud* (Cambridge, MA and London: Harvard University Press, 1992). For a critique of the one-sex model, especially as it was applied to Shakespeare, see Janet Adelman, 'Making Defect Perfection: Shakespeare and the One-Sex

Model', in *Enacting Gender on the English Renaissance Stage*, ed. Viviana Comensoli and Anne Russell (Urbana and Chicago: University of Illinois Press, 1992), 23–52.

41 Mark Breitenberg, *Anxious Masculinity in Early Modern England* (Cambridge: Cambridge University Press, 1996), 133.

42 Smith, *Twelfth Night*, 202.

43 *The Art of English Poesy by George Puttenham*, 176.

44 See Derek Attridge, *Moving Words: Forms of English Poetry* (Oxford: Oxford University Press, 2005), 29.

45 Lukas Erne addresses this difference and provides ample evidence for Shakespeare's text being as important in print and intended for reading, as they were meant for performance, in *Shakespeare as Literary Dramatist* (Cambridge: Cambridge University Press, 2005).

46 The feminine that is here made both an aspect of versification and of the theme in this passage may also be seen, in abstract terms, as in fact fitting in the theatre as feminine, as Alain Badiou, writing in the shadow of Lacan here, speculates when he says that 'If theatre is of the order of the not-all, it is essentially feminine'. See *Rhapsody for the Theatre*, trans. Bruno Bosteels with the assistance of Martin Puchner (London and New York: Verso, 2013), 47.

47 Smith, *Twelfth Night*, 205.

48 Lori Maguire addresses the methodology in source studies in her 'Editor's Introduction' to the part on sources in *How to Do Things With Shakespeare: New Approaches, New Essays*, ed. Laurie Maguire (Malden, MA and Oxford: Blackwell, 2008), 8–10.

49 For an extensive discussion of Shakespeare's use of 'style', see Stuart Sillars, 'Style, rhetoric, and identity in Shakespearean soliloquy', in *Style in Theory: Between Literature and Philosophy*, ed. Ivan Callus, James Corby and Gloria Lauri-Lucente (London: Bloomsbury, 2013), 50.

50 Sharon Holland, 'Is There an Audience for My Play?', in *Shakesqueer: a queer companion to the complete works of Shakespeare* (Durham, NC: Duke Univeristy Press, 2011), 385–93; 386.

Chapter 9: Queer nature, or the weather in *Macbeth*

1   *The Indistinct Human in Renaissance Literature*, ed. Jean E.
    Ferrick and Vin Nardizzi (New York: Palgrave Macmillan,
    2012); Jonathan Goldberg, *The Seeds of Things: Theorizing
    Sexuality and Materiality in Renaissance Representations*
    (New York: Fordham University Press, 2009); Laurie Shannon,
    'Nature's Bias: Renaissance Homonormativity and Elizabethan
    Comic Likeness', *Modern Philology* 98 (2) (2000): 183–210;
    and Lorraine Daston, 'The Nature of Nature in Early Modern
    Europe', *Configurations* 6 (2) (1998): 149–72.

2   Karen Barad, *Meeting the Universe Halfway: Quantum Physics
    and the Entanglement of Matter and Meaning* (Durham:
    Duke University Press, 2007); Barad, 'Nature's Queer
    Performativity', *Qui Parle: Critical Humanities and Social
    Sciences* 19 (2) (2011): 121–58; Jane Bennett, *Vibrant Matter:
    A Political Ecology of Things* (Durham and London: Duke
    University Press, 2010); Mel Y. Chen, *Animacies: Biopolitics,
    Racial Mattering, and Queer Affect* (Durham and London:
    Duke University Press, 2012).

3   See the recent essay collections *Object Oriented Environs*,
    ed. Jeffrey Jerome Cohen and Julian Yates (Earth: punctum
    books, 2016); *Inhuman Nature*, ed. J. J. Cohen (Washington,
    DC: Oliphaunt Books, 2014); and *Animal, Vegetable,
    Mineral: Ethics and Objects*, ed. J. J. Cohen (Washington, DC:
    Oliphaunt Books, 2012).

4   Janet Halley and Andrew Parker provocatively ask contributors
    what is un-queer or least-queer about their work in the
    introduction to 'After Sex? Writing Since Queer Theory', *South
    Atlantic Quarterly* 106 (3) (2007): 421–32.

5   Chen, *Animacies: Biopolitics, Racial Mattering, and Queer
    Affect*, 2.

6   Chen, *Animacies: Biopolitics, Racial Mattering, and Queer
    Affect*, 2.

7   Chen, *Animacies: Biopolitics, Racial Mattering, and Queer
    Affect*, 1–6.

8   Yahoo! Answers, 'How is the weather used as a symbol in
    Shakespeare's "Macbeth"?', https://answers.yahoo.com/question/
    index?qid=20090220183819AAedngh (accessed 30 June 2016).

9   Two recent examples are Tom MacFaul's *Shakespeare and
    the Natural World* (Cambridge: Cambridge University
    Press, 2015); and Gabriel Egan's *Green Shakespeare: From
    Ecopolitics to Ecocriticism* (London and New York: Routledge,
    2006), both of which interrogate how the human interacts
    with, and can act against, something understood as non-human
    nature in early modern cosmology.

10 E. M. W. Tillyard, *The Elizabethan World Picture* (New York:
    Vintage Books, 1959 [1943]), 83.

11 E. M. W. Tillyard, *Shakespeare's History Plays*
    (Harmondsworth: Penguin Books, 1991 [1944]), 24–5.

12 See J. Halberstam, *The Queer Art of Failure* (Durham and
    London: Duke University Press, 2011).

13 Eve Kosofsky Sedgwick, 'The Weather in Proust', in *The
    Weather in Proust*, ed. Jonathan Goldberg (Durham and
    London: Duke University Press, 2011), 6. Hereafter cited
    parenthetically in the text.

14 Barad, *Meeting the Universe Halfway*, 179.

15 Barad, *Meeting the Universe Halfway*, 180–1.

16 Barad, *Meeting the Universe Halfway*, 181.

17 See Deleuze and Guattari's notion of the rhizome, and the
    inter-dependent co-becoming of rhizomatic assemblages, in *A
    Thousand Plateaus: Capitalism and Schizophrenia*, trans. Brian
    Massumi (Minneapolis: University of Minnesota Press, 1987),
    7–10.

18 Heather Love, '*Macbeth:* Milk', in *Shakesqueer: A Queer
    Companion to the Complete Works of Shakespeare*, ed.
    Madhavi Menon (Durham and London: Duke University Press,
    2011), 201–8.

19 Diane Purkiss, 'The All-singing, All-dancing Plays of the
    Jacobean Witch Vogue', in *The Witch in History: Early
    Modern and Twentieth-Century Representations* (London:
    Routledge, 1996), 207–14.

20 Purkiss, 'The All-singing, All-dancing Plays', 207.

21 My thinking here intersects with Julian Yates', who in a talk entitled 'Macbeth's Bubbles' at the Shakespeare Association of America annual meeting in New Orleans in 2016 pondered the work of bubbles in the play, but with a focus on the ontology of the bubble as a figure for the political and ethical problem of differentiating between inside and outside, self and other.

22 I am indebted to Adam Hooks (personal communication) for talking through the implications of this scene's textual indeterminacy with me.

23 Purkiss, 'The All-singing, All-dancing Plays', 214.

24 Chen, *Animacies*, 2–3.

25 Deleuze and Guattari, *A Thousand Plateaus*, 10.

26 Barad, *Meeting the Universe Halfway*; 'What if queerness were understood to reside not in the breach of nature/culture *per se*, but in the very nature of spacetimemattering?' ('Nature's Queer Performativity', 29).

Chapter 10: Strange insertions in *The Merchant of Venice*

1 W. H. Auden offered a similar reading in 1962, though he did not connect sodomy with unnatural breeding, instead pointing out Shakespeare's association of usury with sexual reproduction; see *The Dyer's Hand and Other Essays* (New York: Random House, 1962), 230–1.

2 Arthur L. Little, Jr., 'The Rites of Queer Marriage in *The Merchant of Venice*', in *Shakesqueer: A Queer Companion to the Complete Works of Shakespeare*, ed. Madhavi Menon (Durham: Duke University Press, 2011), 220.

3 Lauren Garrett, 'True Interest and the Affections: The Dangers of Lawful Lending in *The Merchant of Venice*', *Journal for Early Modern Cultural Studies* 14 (1) (2014): 43.

4 See Alan Bray, 'Homosexuality and the Signs of Male Friendship in Early Modern England', in *Queering the*

Renaissance, ed. Jonathan Goldberg, Series Q (Durham: Duke University Press, 1994), 40–61.

5   For a fuller discussion of effeminacy, see the first chapter of Amy Greenstadt, *Rape and the Rise of the Author: Gendering Intention in Early Modern England*, Women and Gender in the Early Modern World (Farnham: Ashgate, 2009), 29–56.

6   Lara Bovilsky, '"Racked to the Uttermost": The Verges of Love and Subjecthood in *The Merchant of Venice*', in *This Distracted Globe: Worldmaking in Early Modern Literature*, ed. Marcie Frank, Jonathan Goldberg and Karen Newman (New York: Fordham University Press, 2016), 119. I am grateful to Lara for patiently and encouragingly talking me through some of my ideas for this project.

7   The other recent interpretation that stresses Antonio's desire to be hurt is Drew Daniel, '"Let Me Have Judgment, and the Jew His Will": Melancholy Epistemology and Masochistic Fantasy in *The Merchant of Venice*', *Shakespeare Quarterly* 61 (2) (Summer 2010): 206–34. As Bovilsky observes, critics prior to the 1980s were more likely to view Antonio's behaviour in extreme terms. See, e.g. John Hurrell, 'Love and Friendship in *The Merchant of Venice*', *Texas Studies in Literature and Language* 3 (3) (1961): 328–41; Lawrence W. Hyman, 'The Rival Lovers in *The Merchant of Venice*', *Shakespeare Quarterly* 21 (2) (1970): 109–16.

8   For some of many versions of this argument see, e.g. Steve Patterson, 'The Bankruptcy of Homoerotic Amity in Shakespeare's *Merchant of Venice*', *Shakespeare Quarterly* 50 (1) (1999): 9–32, Alan Sinfield, 'How to Read *The Merchant of Venice* Without Being Heterosexist', in *Alternative Shakespeares II*, ed. Terence Hawkes and John Drakakis, (London: Routledge, 1996), 122–39; Bruce R. Smith, *Shakespeare and Masculinity*, Oxford Shakespeare Topics (Oxford and New York: Oxford University Press, 2000a), 87–8.

9   Little, 'The Rites of Queer Marriage', 217, 220, 218.

10 David Hawkes, 'Sodomy, Usury, and the Narrative of Shakespeare's Sonnets', *Renaissance Studies* 14 (3) (2000): 346.

11 Peter C. Herman, 'What's the Use? Or, the Problematic

of Economy in Shakespeare's Procreation Sonnets', in *Shakespeare's Sonnets: Critical Essays*, ed. James Schiffer (New York: Routledge, 2000), 275. We see a similar logic in Joel Fineman, *Shakespeare's Perjured Eye: The Invention of Poetic Subjectivity in the Sonnets* (Berkeley: University of California Press, 1986), 256.

12 On sodomy the definitive sources remain Mark D. Jordan, *The Invention of Sodomy in Christian Theology*, Chicago Series on Sexuality, History, and Society (Chicago: University of Chicago Press, 1997) and Alan Bray, *Homosexuality in Renaissance England* (New York: Columbia University Press, 1995).

13 Aristotle, *Aristotles Politiques, or Discourses of Government*, trans. Loys Le Roy (London, 1598), 49.

14 Jody Greene, '"You Must Eat Men": The Sodomitic Economy of Renaissance Patronage', *GLQ* 1 (1994): 171.

15 Herman and Greene use 'sodomy' and 'homoeroticsm'/ 'homosexuality' interchangeably. Herman contends that 'numerous critics have noted' that 'Elizabethans made Aristotle's repugnance at the concept of like breeding with like a central element in their polemics against usury' (274); yet this claim is absent from the authorities he cites.

16 Le Roy's translation in Aristotle, *Aristotles Politiques*, 52.

17 Will Fisher, 'Queer Money,' *ELH* 66 (1) (1999): 11.

18 Miles Mosse, *The Arraignment and Conviction of Usurie* (London, 1595), 110. Fisher omits Mosse's qualifying language, which undermines his claim that Mosse equates usury and sodomy (see 11); Garrett similarly reads Mosse out of context (43).

19 Thomas Pie, *Usuries Spright Conjured: Or a Scholasticall Determination of Usury* (London, 1604), 19.

20 Aristotle, *Aristotles Politiques*, 49.

21 Robert Wilson, *Three Ladies of London* (1584) in *Three Usury Plays*, ed. Lloyd Edward Kermode (Manchester: Manchester University Press, 2009), 10.28.

22 Michel de Montaigne, *The Essayes or Morall, Politike and Millitarie Discourses of Lo: Michaell de Montaigne*, trans. John Florio, vol. 1 (London, 1603), I.93–4.

23 Thomas Wilson, *A Discourse Uppon Usurye* (London, 1572), fol. 95r.

24 Ibid., fol. 96^r.

25 David Hawkes, *The Culture of Usury in Renaissance England* (New York: Palgrave 2010), 23.

26 Bray, 'Homosexuality', 40; 50.

27 Ibid., 57.

28 The character is referred to with this title ten times in the play, with the first occurrence at 1.1.69. For discussions of the men's class difference, see Lars Eagle Patterson, '"Thrift Is Blessing": Exchange and Explanation in *The Merchant of Venice*', *Shakespeare Quarterly* 37 (1) (Spring 1986): 20–37; and Walter S. H. Lim, 'Surety and Spiritual Commercialism in *The Merchant of Venice*', *Studies in English Literature, 1500–1900* 50 (2) (2010): 355–81.

29 Amanda Bailey, *Of Bondage: Debt, Property, and Personhood in Early Modern England* (Philadelphia: University of Pennsylvania Press, 2013), 10.

30 Wilson, *A Discourse Uppon Usurye*, fol. 128^v–9^r.

31 Bailey, *Of Bondage*, 6.

32 Garrett, 'True Interest and the Affections', 47.

33 Wilson, *A Discourse Uppon Usurye*, fol. 37^v.

34 Engle, 'Thrift Is Blessing', 27.

35 *Merchant* 1.1.127; Lorna Hutson, *The Usurer's Daughter: Male Friendship and Fictions of Women in Sixteenth-Century England* (London: Routledge, 1994), 3.

36 Montaigne, *The Essayes*, I.93.

37 Jeffrey Masten, *Textual Intercourse: Collaboration, Authorship, and Sexualities in Renaissance Drama*, vol. 14, Cambridge Studies in Renaissance Literature and Culture (Cambridge: Cambridge University Press, 1997), 35.

38 4.1.229; Janet Adelman views Antonio as wishing to 'be known inwardly by Bassanio'; *Blood Relations: Christian and Jew in* The Merchant of Venice (Chicago: University of Chicago Press, 2008), 119.

39 Bray, 'Homosexuality', 49.

40 Patterson, 'Thrift Is Blessing', 16, 24. Other interpretations
    that view Antonio as an exemplary friend include Little and
    Edward J. Geisweidt, 'Antonio's Claim: Triangulated Desire
    and Queer Kinship in Shakespeare's *The Merchant of Venice*',
    Shakespeare 5 (4) (2009): 338–54.

41 Ibid., 23. Interestingly, the other interpretation that draws
    heavily on Bray comes to the conclusion Patterson fears. James
    O'Rourke argues that 'Antonio's showering of gifts, or bribes,
    on Bassanio creates precisely' the ambiguity between friendship
    and sodomy that Bray identifies in Edward II; 'Racism and
    Homophobia in *The Merchant of Venice*', *ELH* 70 (2) (Summer
    2003): 380. Yet O'Rourke also critiques Bray's Foucaultian
    approach and argues that Antonio would have been perceived
    as having a recognizable sexual orientation as a 'sodomite'. This
    causes O'Rourke's bracing discussion to return to the well-worn
    argument that Antonio is an outcast homosexual 'stigmatized
    and compelled to live the role of an internal exile' (392).

42 Seymour Kleinberg, '*The Merchant of Venice*: The
    Homosexual as Anti-Semite in Nascent Capitalism', *Journal of
    Homosexuality* 8 (3–4) (1983): 124.

43 Garrett, 'True Interest and the Affections', 54.

44 Montaigne, *The Essayes*, I.91.

45 I discuss the complexities of 'kind' in Amy Greenstadt, 'The
    Kindest Cut: Circumcision and Queer Kinship in The Merchant
    of Venice', *ELH* 80 (4) (2013): 945–80. There, however, I do
    not address the appearance of the word in Shylock's story; the
    present discussion should be considered to complement that
    earlier reading.

46 Jonathan Gil Harris, *Sick Economies: Drama, Mercantilism,
    and Disease in Shakespeare's England* (Philadelphia: University
    of Pennsylvania Press, 2004), 78.

47 See Elizabeth A. Spiller, 'From Imagination to Miscegenation:
    Race and Romance in Shakespeare's *The Merchant of Venice*',
    Renaissance Drama 29 (1998): 141–2. Jenny Davidson, 'Why
    Girls Look Like Their Mothers: David Garrick's *The Winter's
    Tale*,' in *Shakespeare and the Eighteenth Century*, ed. Peter
    Sabor and Paul Edward Yachnin (Aldershot: Ashgate, 2008),
    172.

48 *The Geneva Bible: A Facsimile of the 1560 Edition*, ed. Lloyd E. F. Berry (Peabody: Hendrickson Publishers, 2007), 30:38–41. All future biblical references are from this edition. William Shakespeare, *The Most Excellent Historie of the Merchant of Venice* (London, 1600), sig. B3ʳ and *Mr William Shakespeares Comedies Histories & Tragedies* (London, 1623), 166.

49 See Marc Shell, 'The Wether and the Ewe: Verbal Usury in *The Merchant of Venice*', *The Kenyon Review* 1 (4) (1979): 65–92.

50 Wilson, *A Discourse Uppon Usurye*, fol. 97ʳ⁻ᵛ.

51 Greene, 'You Must Eat Men', 172.

52 The only other use of this formulation I have found is the oft-quoted passage from Francis Meres: 'As *Paederastice* is unlawfull, because it is against kinde: so usurie and encrease by gold and silver is unlawful, because against nature; nature hath made them sterill and barren, & usurie makes them procreative'; *Palladis Tamia, Or, Wits Treasury Being the Second Part of Wits Commonwealth*, ed. Nicholas Ling, vol. 2 (London, 1598), 322r. Fisher comments, 'The argument here works by analogy ... : just as pederasty could be understood as an attempt to breed two things of the same "kinde" (meaning both "gender" and "nature"), so usury is an attempt to breed money with itself (to make money from money)' (11). Yet Meres describes *Paederastice* not as an act between 'two things of the same "kinde"' but as *against* 'kinde', presumably because, as Montaigne explained, it involved 'disparitie of ages, and diference of offices betweene lovers' (I.92). This accounts for Meres's comparison of this sin to the usurer's 'encrease' by the coupling of disparate metals, 'gold and silver'. *Palladis Tamia* happens to be the first text to mention *Merchant*, and I continue to research the question of influence.

53 Peggy Kamuf, '"This Were Kindness": Economies of Differance in *The Merchant of Venice*', *Oxford Literary Review* 34 (1) (29 June 2012): 83.

54 Harris, *Sick Economies*, 78.

55 *Merchant* 1.4.99; 89. Bailey, *Of Bondage*, 63.

56 William Shakespeare, *Othello*, ed. E. A. J. Honigmann, 3rd edn (London: Arden, 2006), 4.2.72–3. The narrator also describes Lucrece's blood as tainted in Shakespeare's poem. In Chapter

2 of *Rape and the Rise of the Author* I discuss how, in ways similar to Antonio, Lucrece uses such marks to memorialize herself. See 57–82.

57 Hutson, *The Usurer's Daughter*, 7, 3.

58 Jacques Derrida, *The Politics of Friendship* (London: Verso, 1997), 5.

59 Sir Thomas Browne, *Pseudodoxia Epidemica, Or, Enquiries into Very Many Received Tenents, and Commonly Presumed Truths* (London, 1646), 6.10.275.

60 Sinfield, 'How to Read *The Merchant of Venice*', 133; Ben Jonson, *Epicoene or the Silent Woman*, ed. Roger Holdsworth (London: Bloomsbury, 1979), 1.1.23.

61 Lara Bovilsky, *Barbarous Play: Race on the English Renaissance Stage* (Minneapolis: University of Minnesota Press, 2008), 103.

62 Jonathan Goldberg, 'Carnival in *The Merchant of Venice*', *Postmedieval: A Journal of Medieval Cultural Studies* 4 (4) (Winter 2013): 432.

63 To my knowledge no one has connected the writing on the wall to Portia-as-Balthazar. Most treat Shylock's reference to Daniel in terms of this character's appearance as judge in the Book of Susannah. Barbara Lewalski briefly discusses the link of Balthazar to Daniel in 'Biblical Allusion and Allegory in *The Merchant of Venice*', *Shakespeare Quarterly* 13 (3) (Summer 1962): 327–43. Thomas Luxon claims that the play refers to Daniel's role as prophet of Jesus Christ; however, in the Book of Daniel's prophetic section the name 'Balthazar' is mentioned once, whereas it is significant in the book's first half, which chronicles Daniel's defiance of his Babylonian captors; see 'A Second Daniel: The Jew and the "True Jew" in *The Merchant of Venice*', *Early Modern Literary Studies: A Journal of Sixteenth- and Seventeenth-Century English Literature* 4 (3) (January 1999): 1–37.

64 John Florio, *Queen Anna's New World of Words* (London, 1611), 321. On sources for *Merchant* see Geoffrey Bullough (ed.), *Narrative and Dramatic Sources of Shakespeare*, vol. 2 (London: New York: Routledge and Kegan Paul; Columbia University Press, 1957).

65 Helkiah Crooke, *Mikrokosmographia: A Description of the Body of Man* (London, 1618), 271.

Chapter 11: Male femininity and male-to-female crossdressing in Shakespeare's plays and poems

1 Tumblr blog, *Shakespearean Male*, http://shakespeareanman. tumblr.com/ (accessed 7 July 2016); please note that the site contains pornographic images. Tumblr is a short-format-blog social media platform where users post images, writing and links. As far as I know, Tumblr had its queer Shakespeare debut at the 2016 meeting of the Shakespeare Association of America, where outgoing SAA president Mario DiGangi and incoming president Heather James performed a dramatic reading from the Tumblr blog *Fuck Yeah Queer Shakespeare* (http:// fuckyeahqueershakespeare.tumblr.com/ [accessed 7 July 2016]). Both *Shakespearean Male* and *Fuck Yeah Queer Shakespeare* show the ways that online non-academic communities are investing in and reinterpreting queer readings of Shakespeare, and both further show that queer Shakespeare still matters as an emblem and example to some modern queers.

2 'In Praise of the Feminine Man', in Tumblr blog *Shakespearean Male*.

3 A small sample of influential works on FTM crossdressing includes the following: Michael Shapiro, *Gender in Play on the Shakespearean Stage: Boy Heroines and Female Pages* (Ann Arbor: University of Michigan Press, 1994); M. Garber, *Vested Interests: Crossdressing and Cultural Anxiety* (New York: Routledge, 1992); Catherine Belsey, 'Disrupting Sexual Difference', in *Alternative Shakespeares*, ed. John Drakakis (London: Methuen, 1985), 166–90; Karen Newman, 'Portia's Ring: Unruly Women and Structures of Exchange in *The Merchant of Venice*', *Shakespeare Quarterly* 38 (1987): 19–33; Stephen Greenblatt, 'Fiction and Friction', in *Shakespearean Negotiations* (Berkeley: University of

California Press, 1988), 66–94; Mary Beth Rose, 'Women in Men's Clothing: Apparel and Social Stability in *The Roaring Girl*', *ELR* 14 (1984): 367–91; Juliet Dusinbere, *Shakespeare and the Nature of Women* (New York: Macmillan, 1975); David Cressy, 'Gender Trouble and Cross-Dressing in Early Modern England', *Journal of British Studies* 35 (4) (October 1996): 438–65; Jean E. Howard, 'Crossdressing, the Theater, and Gender Struggle in Early Modern England', *Shakespeare Quarterly* 39 (4) (Winter 1998): 418–40; Lisa Jardine, *Still Harping on Daughters: Women and Drama in the Age of Shakespeare* (Towata, NJ: Harvester, 1983; reprinted New York: Columbia University Press, 1989), 9–36; Phyllis Rackin, 'Androgyny, Mimesis, and the Marriage of the Boy Heroine on the English Renaissance Stage, *PMLA* 102 (1987): 29–41; Linda Bamber, *Comic Women, Tragic Men: A Study of Genre and Gender in Shakespeare* (Stanford: Stanford University Press, 1982); Valerie Traub, *Desire and Anxiety: Circulations of Sexuality in Shakespearean Drama* (New York: Routledge, 1992); and Clare Everett, 'Venus in Drag: Female Transvestism and the Construction of Sex Difference in Renaissance England', in *Venus and Mars: Engendering Love and War in Early Modern Europe*, ed. Andrew Lynch and Phillippa C. Madden (Nedlands: University of Western Australia Press, 1995), 191–212. Male-to-female (MTF) crossdressing, has generally been discussed in terms of boy actors in female costume, rather than on male characters disguised as female. On boy actors, see the following: Levine, 1–25; Shapiro, *Gender in Play*; and Rose. See also: Kathleen McLuskie, 'The Act, the Role, and the Actor: Boy Actresses on the Elizabethan Stage', *New Theatre Quarterly* 3 (1987): 120–30; Peter Stallybrass, 'Transvestism and the "Body Beneath": Speculating on the Boy Actor', in *Erotic Politics: Desire on the Renaissance Stage*, ed. Susan Zimmerman (New York: Routledge, 1992), 64–83; Lisa Jardine, 'Boy Actors, Female Roles, and Elizabethan Eroticism', in *Staging the Renaissance: Reinterpretations of Elizabethan and Jacobean Drama*, ed. David Scott Kastan and Peter Stallybrass (New York: Routledge, 1991), 57–67; Sedinger, '"If Sight and Shape be True:" The Epistemology of Crossdressing on the London Stage', *Shakespeare Quarterly* 48 (1) (1997): 63–79; Stephen

Orgel, 'Nobody's Perfect: or, Why Did the English Stage Take Boys for Women?', *South Atlantic Quarterly* 88 (1989): 7–29; Katherine E. Kelly, 'The Queen's Two Bodies: Shakespeare's Boy Actress in Breeches', *Theatre Journal* 42 (1990): 81–93; Steve Brown, 'The Boyhood of Shakespeare's Heroines: Notes on Gender Ambiguity in the Sixteenth Century', *Studies in English Literature, 1500–1900* 30 (1990): 243–63; Ursula K. Heise, 'Transvestism and the Stage Controversy in Spain and England, 1580-1680', *Theatre Journal* 44 (1992): 357–74.

4   For work on MTF crossdressing, see Simone Chess, *Male-to-Female Crossdressing in Early Modern English Literature* (New York: Routledge, 2016); Howard, 'Crossdressing', an essay upon which she expands in *The Stage and Social Struggle in Early Modern England* (New York: Routledge, 1994); Other foundational MTF crossdressing scholarship includes Winfried Schleiner, 'Male Cross-Dressing and Transvestism in Renaissance Romances', *Sixteenth Century Journal* 19 (4) (Winter 1988): 605–19; Steven Mentz, 'The Thigh and the Sword: Gender, Genre, and Sexy Dressing in Sidney's *New Arcadia*', in *Prose Fiction and Early Modern Sexualities in England, 1570–1640* (New York: Palgrave MacMillan, 2003), 77–92; David Cressy, 'Cross-Dressing in the Birth Room: Gender Trouble and Cultural Boundaries', in *Travesties and Transgressions in Tudor and Stuart England: Tales of Discord and Dissension* (Oxford: Oxford University Press, 1999); and Laura Levine, *Men in Women's Clothing: Anti-theatricality and Effeminization 1579–1642* (Cambridge: Cambridge University Press, 1994). In her expansive coverage of crossdressing in *Vested Interests*, Garber considers both male-to-female and female- to-male crossdressing. Victor Oscar Freeburg's thorough chapter on 'The Boy Bride' in *Disguise Plots in Renaissance Drama* (New York: Columbia University Press, 1915) is an incredible resource for locating and comparing MTF crossdressing plots.

5   Well-known plays that include MTF crossdressing include Ben Jonson (*Epicoene* and *The Devil is an Ass*), Thomas Middleton (*A Mad World My Masters*), Nathan Fields (*Amends for Ladies*), Beaumont and John Fletcher (*The Scornful Lady)*, John Fletcher on his own (*Monseiur Thomas*), John Lyly (*Woman*

in the Moon, Cupid in *Gallathea*), and George Chapman (*May Day*). It is worth mentioning that many of these playwrights wrote for boys companies, and that therefore they had comparatively more androgynous actors available to play male, female, male-to-female and female-to-male characters all in the same play, while Shakespeare, working with adult companies, would have had to use a more limited group of boy actors to play all female roles and also any male-to-female crossdressing roles. See especially Lucy Munro, *Children of the Queen's Revels: A Jacobean Theatre Repertory* (Cambridge: Cambridge University Press, 2005) and Michael Shapiro, *Gender in Play on the Shakespearean Stage: Boy Heroines and Female Pages* (Ann Arbor: University of Michigan Press, 1994).

6   See Gordon P. Jones, 'The "Strumpet's Fool" in *Antony and Cleopatra*', *Shakespeare Quarterly* 34 (1) (Spring 1983): 62–8. Also in *Antony and Cleopatra*, Mardian the eunuch offers a model of feminized masculinity, though he is never crossdressed.

7   Judith Butler, *Gender Trouble: Feminism and the Subversion of Identity*, 2nd edn (New York: Routledge, 1999); J. Halberstam, *Female Masculinity* (Durham: Duke University Press, 1998); Jen Manion, 'Transbutch', *TSQ: Transgender Studies Quarterly* 1 (1–2) (May 2014): 230–1.

8   Gayle Salamon, *Assuming a Body: Transgender and Rhetorics of Materiality* (New York: Columbia University Press, 2010); see also Stephen Whittle, 'Forward', in *The Transgender Studies Reader*, ed. Susan Stryker and Steven Whittle (New York: Routledge, 2006). Julia Serano first defines and popularizes the term 'transmisogyny' in *Whipping Girl: A Transsexual Woman on Sexism and the Scapegoating of Femininity* (Emeryville, CA: Seal Press, 2007).

9   Julia Serano, 'Reclaiming Femininity', in *Transfeminist Perspectives in and Beyond Transgender and Gender Studies*, ed. Anne Enke (Philadelphia: Temple University Press), 170–83; 170.

10 Ibid., 180.

11 The recently-coined term 'scoliosexual' describes attraction to queer gender, rather than same- or opposite-sex orientations.

For a thorough summary of editing and scholarship of the
sonnets, especially in terms of the 'scandal' of the fair youth
and the poems potential 'homosexuality', see Margreta De
Grazia, 'The Scandal of Shakespeare's Sonnets', *Shakespeare
Survey* 46 (1993), which argues for a greater scandal
surrounding the dark lady, and Robert Matz, 'The Scandals
of the Shakespeare's Sonnets', *ELH* 77 (2) (Summer 2010):
477–508. Natasha Distiller similarly summarizes the critical
debate, while arguing for a perverse, rather than queer,
Shakespeare in 'Shakespeare's Perversion: A Reading of Sonnet
20', *Shakespeare* 8 (2) (June, 2012): 137–53. See also Heather
Dubrow, 'Incertainties Now Crown Themselves Assur'd:
The Politics of Plotting Shakespeare's Sonnets', *Shakespeare
Quarterly* 47 (1996): 291–305; Peter Stallybrass, 'Editing as
Cultural Formation: The Sexing of Shakespeare's Sonnets',
Modern Language Quarterly 54 (1993): 91–103. Other work
on sexuality and the sonnet includes Valerie Traub, 'Sex
without Issue: Sodomy, Reproduction, and Signification in
Shakespeare's Sonnets', in *Shakespeare's Sonnets: Critical
Essays*, ed. James Schiffer (New York: Garland, 2000) 431–54;
Eve Kosofsky Sedgwick, 'Swan in Love: The Example of
Shakespeare's Sonnets', in *Between Men: English Literature
and Male Homosocial Desire* (New York: Columbia University
Press, 1985), 28–47.

12   Joshua Cohen hints at a trans narrative for the master-
mistress in exploring the connection between Sonnet 20 and
Ovid's story of Iphis and Ianthe in metamorphoses, in 'Ovid
Inverted: Shakespeare's Sonnet 20 and the Metamorphosis
of a Metamorphosis', *Shakespeare Newsletter* 58 (3) (Winter
2008): 93.

13   The queerest reading of the poem that I know of is Goran
Stanivukovic's in '"Kissing the Boar:" Queer Adonis and
Critical Practice', in *Straight with a Twist: Queer Theory and
the Subject of Heterosexuality*, ed. Calvin Thomas (Urbana:
University of Illinois Press, 1999), 87–108. See also Richard
Rambuss, 'What it Feels Like for a Boy: Shakespeare's *Venus
and Adonis*', in *A Companion to Shakespeare's Works*, ed.
Richard Dutton and Jean Howard (Malden, MA: Blackwell,
2013), 240–58; Catherine Belsey, 'Love as Trompe-L'oeil:

Taxonimies of Desire in *Venus and Adonis'*, in *Venus and Adonis: New Essays*, ed. Philip Kolin (New York: Routledge, 1997), 261–86.

14 A notable example of this kind of reading occurs in Alan Sinfield's 'Coming on to Shakespeare: Offstage Action and Sonnet 20' (in *Shakespeare* 3 [1–3] [April–December 2007]: 108–25), where he suggests that the problem of Sonnet 20 is that both the speaker and the object 'want to be tops', and that the poet's 'insistence on the boy's femininity occurs because the Boy has claimed the "active" role' (122).

15 Susan Stryker, '(De)Subjugated Knowledges: An Introduction to Transgender Studies', in *The Transgender Studies Reader*, ed. Susan Stryker and Steven Whittle (New York: Routledge, 2006), 1–17; 13.

16 Jenny C. Mann gives an example of this productive approach when she reads Sonnet 20 against another MTF crossdressing play, Jonson's *Epicoene*, in terms of grammatical case and gendered rhetoric in 'The "Figure of Exchange": Shakespeare's Master-Mistress, Jonson's *Epicene*, and the English Art of Rhetoric', *Renaissance Drama* 38 (2010): 173–98.

17 Roger Moss, 'Falstaff as a Woman', *Journal of Dramatic Theory and Criticism* 10 (1) (Fall 1995): 31–41.

18 W. H. Auden, 'The Prince's Dog', in *The Dyer's Hand and Other Essays* (New York: Random House, 1948); Grace Tiffany, 'Falstaff's False Staff: "Jonsonian" Asexuality in *The Merry Wives of Windsor*', *Comparative Drama* 26 (3) (Fall 1992): 254–70.

19 On the significance of Falstaff's buckbasket ride, see Richard Helgerson, 'The Buck Basket, the Witch, and the Queen of Faeries: The Women's World of Shakespeare's Windsor', in *Renaissance Culture and the Everyday*, ed. Patricia Fumerton and Simon Hunt (Philadelphia: University of Pennsylvania Press, 1998), 162–82.

20 This and all quotations from Shakespeare's work are quoted from *The Arden Shakespeare Complete Works* (rev. edn), ed. Richard Proudfoot, Ann Thompson and David Scott Kastan (London: Bloomsbury, 2011).

21 Jonathan Goldberg, 'What Do Women Want?: The Merry

Wives of Windsor', *Criticism* 51 (3) (Summer 2009): 225–33. Scholars have focused on Falstaff's beard, and especially on Caius's exclamation, 'I like not when a 'oman has a great peard' (4.2.193). See, for example, David Landreth's argument that other men in the play are emasculated by Falstaff's crossdressing because of their failure to recognize that he is male despite evidence like his beard in 'Once More into the Preech: The Merry Wives' English Pedagogy', *Shakespeare Quarterly* 55 (4) (2004): 420–49.

22 The final couplet of this speech is in Q2 but omitted in the Folio; of three instances where the Folio and Q2 of *Hamlet* diverge, two are in the player queen's lines about what it means to be a woman and to love.

23 Though Quince's answer is that Flute will wear a mask and speak in a forced falsetto, it nevertheless seems crucial that the Thisbe role be played by a young, androgynous man; when Bottom auditions for the role, he is rejected (1.2.36–45). Interestingly, Robin Starveling is assigned the role of Thisbe's mother, but we don't see this staged in the final performance.

24 For example, Sarah Moss claims that with this performance from Flute, the entire play 'is transformed from comedy to pathos' ('A Shakespeare for the People?', *Textual Practice* 17 [2] [2003]: 295–315; 296).

25 'The Frolicksome Duke: Or, the Tinker's Good Fortune' (Pepys, 4.235), attempts to rehabilitate the induction, making the frame of the play into the primary material of the song and resolving the induction's lack of conclusion by supplying the missing ending to the story. The ballad carefully ignores the queer content of the induction, making the Sly character (here a tinker) forget who he is, but not that he has a wife named Joan. I have also discussed this ballad in 'Shakespeare's Plays and Broadside Ballads', *Literature Compass* 7 (2010): 772–85.

26 Maura Ryan, 'The Femme Movement: Why We're Here, Why We're (So Damn and Beautifully) Queer, and Why You're Gonna Get Used to it', *Visible: A Femmethology*, vol. 2 (Ypsilanti, MI: Homofactus Press, 2009), 60–3; 63.

Chapter 12: Held in common: *Romeo and Juliet* and the promiscuous seductions of plague

1   William Shakespeare, *Romeo and Juliet*, ed. Brian Gibbons. In *The Arden Shakespeare Complete Works*, ed. Richard Proudfoot, Ann Thompson and David Scott Kastan (London: Bloomsbury Arden Shakespeare, 2011), 3.2.125–6. Subsequent quotations from Shakespeare's plays follow this edition.

2   Michel Foucault, *Discipline and Punish: The Birth of the Prison*, trans. Alan Sheridan (New York: Vintage Books, 1979), 198.

3   Carla Freccero, 'Romeo and Juliet Love Death', in *Shakesqueer: A Queer Companion to the Complete Works of Shakespeare*, ed. Madhavi Menon (Durham, NC: Duke University Press, 2011), 302–8; 306.

4   Ibid, 306; 305. For a reading that instead focuses on 'the life-driven notes of caution and patience', see Will Stockton, 'The Fierce Urgency of Now: Queer Theory, Presentism, and *Romeo and Juliet*', in *The Oxford Handbook of Shakespeare and Embodiment: Gender, Sexuality, and Race*, ed. Valerie Traub (New York: Oxford University Press, 2016), 287–301; 290.

5   Jonathan Goldberg, '*Romeo and Juliet*'s Open Rs', in *Queering the Renaissance*, ed. Jonathan Goldberg (Durham: Duke University Press, 1994), 218–35; 220.

6   I am indebted to Lee Edelman's account of 'the regressive fantasy to which all futurism clings'; see *No Future: Queer Theory and the Death Drive* (Durham, NC: Duke University Press, 2004), 60.

7   Rosi Braidotti, *The Posthuman* (Cambridge: Polity Press, 2013), 121, 135.

8   On the relationship between community and death, see for example Jean-Luc Nancy, *The Inoperative Community*, trans. Peter Connor et al. (Minneapolis and London: University of Minnesota Press, 1991); and Roberto Esposito, *Communitas: The Origin and Destiny of Community*, trans. Timothy

Campbell (Stanford, CA: Stanford University Press, 2010). On the relationship between community and vulnerable embodiment, see for example Judith Butler, *Precarious Life: The Powers of Mourning and Violence* (London and New York: Verso, 2004), and Isabell Lorey, *State of Insecurity: Government of the Precarious* (London and New York: Verso, 2015).

9   Georges Bataille, 'The College of Sociology', in *Visions of Excess: Selected Writings, 1927– 1939*, ed. and trans. Allan Stoekl (Minneapolis: University of Minnesota Press, 1985), 246–53; 251.

10 Foucault, *Discipline and Punish*, 135–69; Louis Althusser, 'Ideology and Ideological State Apparatuses', in *Lenin and Philosophy and Other Essays*, trans. Ben Brewster (London: New Left Books, 1971), 121–73.

11 Braidotti, *The Posthuman*, 130–1.

12 Harold Bloom, *Shakespeare: The Invention of the Human* (New York: Riverhead Books, 1998), 103.

13 Rebecca Totaro, *Suffering in Paradise: The Bubonic Plague in English Literature from More to Milton* (Pittsburgh, PA: Duquesne University Press, 2005), 1. See also F. P. Wilson, *The Plague in Shakespeare's London* (Oxford: Oxford University Press, 1999 [1927]). Carl James Grindley reads plague in *Romeo and Juliet* as furthering 'a sort of nebulous apocalypticism'; see 'The Plague in Filmed Versions of *Romeo and Juliet* and *Twelfth Night*', in *Apocalyptic Shakespeare: Essays on Visions of Chaos and Revelation in Recent Film Adaptations*, ed. Melissa Croteau and Carolyn Jess-Cooke (Jefferson, NC: McFarland, 2009), 148–65; 149. For a remarkable analysis of 'the theater as infection', see Ellen MacKay, *Persecution, Plague, and Fire: Fugitive Histories of the Stage in Early Modern England* (Chicago and London: University of Chicago Press, 2011), 81–104.

14 Northrop Frye, *Northrop Frye on Shakespeare*, ed. Robert Sandler (New Haven and London: Yale University Press, 1986), 31. See also Bloom, *The Invention of the Human*, 102; and E. K. Chambers, *Shakespeare: A Survey* (London: Penguin Books, 1923, 1964), 61–2.

15 On early modern perceptions of metonymy as improper association, see for example Madhavi Menon, *Wanton Words: Rhetoric and Sexuality in English Renaissance Drama* (Toronto: University of Toronto Press, 2004), Ch. 2; Sylvia Adamson, Gavin Alexander, and Katrin Ettenhuber (eds), *Renaissance Figures of Speech* (Cambridge: Cambridge University Press, 2007), Chs 5 and 12; and Kathryn Schwarz, *What You Will: Gender, Contract, and Shakespearean Social Space* (Philadelphia: University of Pennsylvania Press, 2011), Ch. 2.

16 Carla Freccero, *Queer/Early/Modern* (Durham, NC: Duke University Press, 2006), 18. Emphasis original.

17 On the problem of proper names in *Romeo and Juliet*, see Lisa Freinkel's astute discussion of nominalism and catachresis, in *Reading Shakespeare's Will: The Theology of Figure from Augustine to the Sonnets* (New York: Columbia Univ. Press, 2002), 204–5.

18 Théodore de Bèze, *A shorte learned and pithie Treatize of the Plague*, trans. John Stockwood (London: Thomas Dawson for George Bishop, 1580), sig. D2.

19 *Richard III*, 1.3.58; *1 Henry IV*, 2.2.20; *Pericles*, 2.1.25; *King Lear*, 2.2.82; *Twelfth Night*, 1.5.117–18.

20 Matthew J. Bolton, 'Shakespeare's *Romeo and Juliet*', *The Explicator* 63 (4) (2005): 208–9; 208, 209.

21 Thomas Dekker, *The Wonderfull Yeare* (London: Thomas Creede, 1603), sig. C3v.

22 John Davies of Hereford, *Humours Heav'n on Earth* (London: A. I., 1609), 223.

23 *The Oxford English Dictionary*, s.v. 'doom' (n.), 1, 7b, 5, 4b.

24 Jacques Lacan, 'Seminar on "The Purloined Letter"', trans. Jeffrey Mehlman, in *The Purloined Poe: Lacan, Derrida, and Psychoanalytic Reading*, ed. John P. Muller and William J. Richardson (Baltimore: Johns Hopkins University Press, 1988), 28–54; 52–3.

25 Christine Varnado gives this idealized memorialization an intriguingly queer twist; see '"Invisible Sex!": What Looks Like the Act in Early Modern Drama?', in *Sex Before Sex: Figuring the Act in Early Modern England*, ed. James M. Bromley

and Will Stockton (Minneapolis and London: University of Minnesota Press, 2013), 25–52; 34.

26 Chambers, *Shakespeare: A Survey*, 58.

27 Alan Sinfield, *Shakespeare, Authority, Sexuality: Unfinished Business in Cultural Materialism* (London and New York: Routledge, 2006), 86.

28 Davies, *Humours Heav'n on Earth*, 233.

29 Goldberg, '*Romeo and Juliet*'s Open Rs', 223; Crystal Bartolovich, '"First as Tragedy, then as ...": Gender, Genre, History, and *Romeo and Juliet*', in *Rethinking Feminism in Early Modern Studies: Gender, Race, and Sexuality*, ed. Ania Loomba and Melissa E. Sanchez (London and New York: Routledge, 2016), 75–91; 86.

30 On the dual meaning of 'individual', see Raymond Williams, *Keywords: A Vocabulary of Culture and Society*, rev. edn (New York: Oxford University Press, 1985), 161–5; Peter Stallybrass, 'Shakespeare, the Individual, and the Text', in *Cultural Studies*, ed. Lawrence Grossberg, Cary Nelson and Paula A. Treichler (New York: Routledge, 1992), 593–610; and Jeffrey Masten, *Textual Intercourse: Collaboration, Authorship, and Sexualities in Renaissance Drama* (Cambridge: Cambridge University Press, 1997), esp. Ch. 2.

31 Althusser, 'Ideology and Ideological State Apparatuses', 153.

32 For a theological reading of joint burial as a posthumous extension of spousal intimacy, and of *Romeo and Juliet* as a repudiation of this ideal, see Ramie Targoff, 'Mortal Love: Shakespeare's *Romeo and Juliet* and the Practice of Joint Burial', *Representations* 120 (1) (2012): 17–38.

33 Abraham Holland, *Hollandi Post-huma* (Cantabrigiae: Impensis Henrici Holland, 1626), sig. G1.

34 Thomas Dekker, *The Seven Deadly Sinnes of London* (London: E. A. for Nathaniel Butter, 1606), 32. On the use of 'pest-pits' during plague outbreaks, see Wilson, *The Plague in Shakespeare's London*, esp. 40–8.

35 Dekker, *The Wonderfull Yeare*, sig. C4v.

36 John Donne, *Deaths Duell* (London: Printed by Thomas Harper for Richard Redmer and Benjamin Fisher, 1632), 20–2. I have removed italics from this passage.

37 Jean-Luc Nancy, *Corpus*, trans. Richard A. Rand (New York: Fordham University Press, 2008), 77.

Chapter 13: Antisocial procreation in *Measure for Measure*

1   *Measure for Measure*, in *The Arden Shakespeare: Complete Works*, rev. edn, ed. Richard Proudfoot, Ann Thompson, David Scott Kastan and H. R. Woudhuysen (London: Bloomsbury, 2014).

2   Lee Edelman, *No Future: Queer Theory and the Death Drive* (Durham: Duke University Press, 2006), 15–17.

3   Edelman, *No Future*, 132, 56, 109.

4   Edelman, *No Future*, 75.

5   Doyle, 'Blind Spots and Failed Performance: Abortion, Feminism, and Queer Theory', *Qui Parle* 18 (1) (2009): 25–52; 35–6. Jack (Judith) Halberstam offers a similar critique, observing that 'Edelman always runs the risk of linking heteronormativity in some essential way to women, and, perhaps unwittingly, woman becomes the site of the unqueer: she offers life, while queerness links up with the death drive; she is aligned sentimentally with the child and with "goodness", while the gay man in particular leads the way to "something better" while "promising absolutely nothing"' (*The Queer Art of Failure* [Durham: Duke University Press, 2011], 118).

6   Work in this vein is copious, but just a few well-known examples are Simone de Beauvoir, *The Second Sex*, trans. Constance Borde and Sheila Malovany-Chevallier (New York: Vintage, 2011); Luce Irigaray, *Speculum of the Other Woman*, trans. Gillian C. Gill (Ithaca, NY: Cornell University Press, 1985); Elizabeth Grosz, *Volatile Bodies: Toward a Corporeal Feminism* (Bloomington: Indiana University Press, 1994); and Stacy Alaimo, *Undomesticated Ground: Recasting Nature as Feminist Space* (Ithaca, NY: Cornell University Press, 2000).

7   Bennett, *Vibrant Matter: A Political Ecology of Things* (Durham: Duke University Press, 2010), x. Along with

Bennett's concept of 'vitality' as 'the capacity of things ...
not only to impede or block the will and designs of humans
but also to act as quasi agents or forces with trajectories,
propensities, or tendencies of their own' (viii), I have in mind
what Bruno Latour variously refers to as 'actants', 'hybrids',
'networks' and, following Michel Serres, 'quasi-objects' (*We
Have Never Been Modern* [1991], trans. Catherine Porter
[Cambridge: Harvard University Press, 1993], esp. 10–12, 47,
55, 114–16; and *Reassembling the Social: An Introduction
to Actor- Network Theory* [New York: Oxford University
Press, 2005], esp. 63–86); Gilles Deleuze and Felix Guattari's
assemblages of objects and affects (*A Thousand Plateaus:
Capitalism and Schizophrenia* [1980], trans. and Foreword
by Brian Massumi [London and New York: Continuum,
1987]), 3–28; 25); Stacy Alaimo's 'transcorporeality' that
blurs the borders of the human individual and the human
species (*Bodily Natures: Science, Environment, and the
Material Self* [Bloomington: Indiana University Press, 2010]);
Rosi Braidotti's endorsement of a '*zoe*-egalitarianism' that
would 'by-pass the metaphysics of substance and its corollary,
the dialectics of otherness' (*The Posthuman* [Cambridge:
Polity Press, 2013], 71); and Mel Chen's 'animacy' as a
'veering-away from dominant ontologies and the normativities
they promulgate' (Mel Y. Chen, *Animacies: Biopolitics, Racial
Mattering, and Queer Affect* [Durham: Duke University Press,
2012], 11).

8   Bennett, *Vibrant Matter*, 82, 90.

9   Early modern critics who have seen Isabella's celibacy as a
     bid for freedom from the sex- gender system of patriarchy
     include Barbara J. Baines, 'Assaying the Power of Chastity in
     Measure for Measure', *Studies in English Literature* 30 (1990):
     283–300; Laura Lunger Knoppers, '(En)gendering Shame:
     Measure for Measure and the Spectacles of Power', *ELR* 23
     (1993): 450–71; Theodora Jankowski, *Pure Resistance: Queer
     Virginity in Early Modern English Drama* (Philadelphia:
     University of Pennsylvania Press, 2000). Darryl F. Gless
     critiques the 'sterile bondage' of Isabella's virginity and
     breathes a sigh of relief at the Duke's proposal in *Measure
     for Measure, the Law, and the Convent* (Princeton: Princeton

University Press, 1970), 212. On the figure of the lesbian separatist as an even more deadly enemy of the family than the (male) *sinthom*osexual, see Mairead Sullivan, 'Kill Daddy: Reproduction, Futurity, and the Survival of the Radical Feminist', *Women's Studies Quarterly* 44 (2016): 268–82.

10 Stacy Alaimo, *Bodily Natures*, 5; see also 141–58 on genetics and evolution in science fiction. For more detailed discussion of feminism and nature, see Alaimo, *Undomesticated Ground*, 1– 23; Grosz, *Volatile Bodies*, 187–210; and the essays in *Materialist Feminisms*, ed. Stacy Alaimo and Susan Heckman (Bloomington: Indiana University Press, 2008), especially Karen Barad, 'Posthumanist Performativity: Toward an Understanding of How Matter Comes to Matter', 120–54, and Tobin Siebers, 'Disability Experience on Trial', 291–307. For discussions of the queerness of nature, see Lynda Birke, 'Bodies and Biology,' in *Feminist Theory and the Body: A Reader*, ed. Janet Price and Margrit Shildrick (New York: Routledge, 1999), 42–9; and Myra J. Hird, 'Naturally Queer', *Feminist Theory* 5 (1) (2004): 85–9.

11 Latour, 'We Have Never Been Modern', 46, 47.

12 Just a few examples include Jonathan Goldberg, *The Seeds of Things: Theorizing Sexuality and Materiality in Renaissance Representations* (New York: Fordham, 2009); Vin Nardizzi and Jean E. Feerick (eds), *The Indistinct Human in Renaissance Literature* (New York: Palgrave 2012); Andrew Cole, 'The Call of Things: A Critique of Object-Oriented Ontologies', *minnesota review* 80 (2013): 106–18; Laurie Shannon, T*he Accommodated Animal: Cosmopolity in Shakespearean Locales* (Chicago: University of Chicago Press, 2013); Jeffrey Jerome Cohen, *Stone: An Ecology of the Inhuman* (Minneapolis: University of Minnesota Press, 2015); and Tiffany Werth (ed.), 'Shakespeare and the Human', Special Issue of *The Shakespearean International Yearbook* 15 (2015); and Ayesha Ramachandran and Melissa E. Sanchez (eds), 'Spenser and "the Human"', Special Issue of *Spenser Studies* 30 (2015).

13 This point has been carefully illuminated by the scholars cited in note 12. Sylvia Adamson has shown that the uncertainty of the animate-inanimate contrast was registered in interrogative

pronouns, with 'what' at least as likely as 'who' to designate a human subject ('Questions of Identity in Renaissance Drama: New Historicism Meets Old Philology', *Shakespeare Quarterly* 61 (1) [2010]: 56–77). For a discussion of two productions of *Measure for Measure* that underscore the dissolution of human exceptionalism in the figure of Barnardine, see Huw Griffiths, 'Hotel Rooms and Bodily Fluids in Two Recent Productions of *Measure for Measure*, Or, Why Barnardine is Still Important', *Shakespeare Bulletin* 32 (4) (2014): 559–83.

14 Drawing on Foucault, Giorgio Agamben has influentially argued that 'the entry of *zoē* into the sphere of the polis – the politicization of bare life as such – constitutes the decisive event of modernity and signals a radical transformation of political/philosophical categories of classical thought' in which the sovereign response to natural life had no part. See *Homo Sacer: Sovereign Power and Bare Life*, trans. Daniel Heller-Roazen [1995] (Stanford: Stanford University Press, 1998), 4.

15 'Forum: Methodology and Queer Historiography', *Journal of Early Modern Cultural Studies (JEMCS)* 16 (2) (2016): 107–30; 110–11.

16 On the queerness of asexual reproduction, see Marjorie Swann, 'Vegetable Love: Botany and Sexuality in Seventeenth-Century England', in Nardizzi and Feerick, *The Indistinct Human in Renaissance Literature*, 139–58.

17 Janet Adelman, 'Bed Tricks: On Marriage as the End of Comedy in *All's Well That Ends Well* and *Measure for Measure*"', in *Shakespeare's Personality*, ed. Norman N. Holland, Sidney Homan and Bernard J. Paris (Berkeley and Los Angeles: University of California Press, 1989): 151–74; 163.

18 Karen Barad, *Meeting the Universe Halfway: Quantum Physics and the Entanglement of Matter and Meaning* (Durham: Duke University Press, 2007), 151. Barad's emphasis.

19 Braidotti, *The Posthuman*, 103.

20 Noreen Giffney and Myra Hird (eds), 'Introduction: Queering the Non/Human', in *Queering the Non/Human* (Burlington, VT: Ashgate, 2008), 7–8.

21 On humanity's ontological and social relations to earth, see Jean E. Feerick, 'Groveling with Earth in Kyd and

Shakespeare's Historical Tragedies' and Ian MacInnes, 'The Politic Worm: Invertebrate Life in the Early Modern English Body', in Nardizzi and Feerick, *The Indistinct Human in Renaissance Literature*, 231–52, 253–73.

22 Geneva Bible (1599). Available online: http://www.genevabible.org/files/Geneva_Bible/Old_Testament/Genesis_F.pdf; and 'The Ordre for the Buriall of the Dead', *The Boke of Common Prayer* (1552). Available online: http://justus.anglican.org/resources/bcp/1552/Burial_1552.htm (accessed 15 June 2016).

23 Geneva Bible, 'The Ordre for the Buriall of the Dead'.

24 On the gendered and social implications of the confusion surrounding Elbow's wife, see Mario DiGangi, 'Pleasure and Danger: Measuring Female Sexuality in *Measure for Measure*', *ELH* 60 (3) (1993): 589–609.

25 DiGangi was the first to notice that 'abhorson' is a 'virtual homonym for abortion' ('Pleasure and Danger', 600). Along with the miscarriage or destruction of a pregnancy (or, in a figurative sense, any endeavour), the *OED* also gives as one early modern meaning 'a person or thing not fully or properly formed; an ill-conceived or badly executed action or undertaking; a monstrosity' (s. v. 'abortion'). Angelo invokes this view in his equation of murder with the production of bastards (2.3.42–9).

26 On the punishment of prostitutes in the context of public shaming for fornication and adultery more generally, see Knoppers, '(En)gendering Shame'.

27 Mistress Overdone asserts that the child of Kate and Lucio 'is a year and a quarter old come Philip and Jacob' (3.2.195–6). Knoppers cites an example of a bawd known to have delivered the offspring of women with no where else to go: 'Margaret Rutt is summoned "for thatt she is a comon harborer of light weemen great with child and suffring them to be brought to bedd in her house"' (Middlesex County Records [Old Series], 4 vols, ed. John Cordy Jeaffreson [London, 1886- 92], II: 46; quoted by Knoppers, '(En)gendering Shame', 457).

28 Jonathan Dollimore notes that 'poverty drove [most prostitutes] to the brothels and after a relatively short stay in which they had to run the hazards of disease, violence, and contempt, most were driven back to it' ('Transgression and

Surveillance in *Measure for Measure*', in *Political Shakespeare: Essays in Cultural Materialism*, ed. Jonathan Dollimore and Alan Sinfield, 2nd edn [Ithaca, NY: Cornell University Press, 1994], 72–87).

29   Sullivan, 'Kill Daddy', 276.

30   The 'heroes', in this scenario, are the (white, male) scientists and doctors who identify and contain disease. Wald, *Contagious: Cultures, Carriers, and the Outbreak Narrative* (Durham: Duke University Press, 2008), 1–28.

31   Lorde, 'The Transformation of Silence into Language and Action', in *Sister Outsider: Essays and Speeches* (New York: Ten Speed Press, 2012), 42. As Wald reminds us, 'the word *contagion* means literally "to touch together" and one of its earliest uses in the fourteenth century referred to the circulation of ideas and attitudes', often those deemed dangerous (12). The fragmentary textual persistence of Kate throughout *Measure for Measure* makes her a figure of contagion insofar as she brings into contact concepts that conservative morality would prefer to keep from touching.

32   I draw here on Lauren Berlant's description of 'slow death' as 'the physical wearing out of a population in a way that points to its deterioration as a defining condition of its experience and historical existence' (*Cruel Optimism* [Durham: Duke University Press, 2011], 95).

33   Richard A. Levin comments that '[a]s for Juliet and Claudio, we cannot help thinking that they would have found their way to the church without the duke's intervention' ('Duke Vincentio and Angelo: Would "A Feather Turn the Scale?"', *Studies in English Literature* 22 [2] [1982]: 257–70; 269); Janet Adelman sees them as 'the one potentially happy couple' in the play (171); Julia Lupton celebrates their relationship as a 'civil experiment' that 'harmonizes affective and economic interests' (*Citizen-Saints: Shakespeare and Political Theology* [Chicago: University of Chicago Press, 2005], 148); Pascale Aebischer calls Claudio and Juliet 'the play's most unambiguous example of a mutual affection that finds its fulfilment in sexual union and pregnancy' ('Silence, Rape and Politics in *Measure for Measure*: Close Readings in Theatre History', *Shakespeare Bulletin* 26 [4] [2008]: 1–23; 14).

34 See, for instance, Adelman, 'Bed Tricks', 162–3, and Aebischer, 'Silence, Rape and Politics', 14–15.

35 The overdetermined meaning of 'love' in *Measure for Measure* is particularly visible in Angelo's proposition to Isabella:

> ANGELO   Plainly conceive, I love you.
> ISABELLA My brother did love Juliet,
>   And you tell me he shall die for't.
> ANGELO   He shall not, Isabel, if you give me love.
>   (2.4.140–3)

36 Neely, *Broken Nuptials in Shakespeare's Plays* (New Haven: Yale University Press, 1985), 100.

37 Adelman, 'Bed Tricks', 163.

38 Luciano and Chen, 'Introduction: Has the Queer Ever Been Human?', *GLQ* 21 (2–3) (2015): 183–207; 184.

39 Luciano and Chen, 'Introduction', 186.

40 Luciano and Chen, 'Introduction', 196.

41 This refusal, Edelman argues, is the ethical duty of the queer (Edelman, *No Future*, 4).

Afterword

I am grateful to the students enrolled in the Globe Education Summer Programme 'Into the Woods' for their feedback on an earlier version of this Afterword.

1   By act, scene and line number, I cite all passages from *A Midsummer Night's Dream* from *The Norton Shakespeare: Early Plays and Poems*, gen. ed. Stephen Greenblatt, 3rd edn (New York: W. W. Norton, 2016). With thanks to Will Tosh and Keziah Serreau of the Globe Theatre, I have been able to compare dialogue as it appears in *The Norton* with the script that was adapted for performance as part of the 2016 season at the Globe. In referring to this script, I nonetheless always key passages to their place in *The Norton*. I also screened the recording of the production, which was made available

through the BBC (http://www.bbc.co.uk/programmes/p0471ccz [accessed 18 September 2016]), to confirm and to correct my memorial reconstruction of the performance, knowing full well, of course, that a show in September would differ in some respects from one in June.

2   On the queerness of Helena's desire in this moment, see Richard Rambuss, 'Shakespeare's Ass Play', in *Shakesqueer: A Queer Companion to the Complete Works of Shakespeare*, ed. Madhavi Menon (Durham: Duke University Press, 2011), 234–44, and Melissa E. Sanchez, '"Use Me But As Your Spaniel": Feminism, Queer Theory, and Early Modern Sexualities', *PMLA* 127 (3) (2012): 493–511.

3   Here and throughout this account, I take lines from 'Donne's poem' to the September performance of the play. Although useful, the Globe script seems to both shorthand cues for actors and prove inconsistent (to non-actors): the lines that begin 'License my roving hands' appears in the script only to be sung to Helenus, when, in fact, the performance also calls for Lysander to sing these lyrics to (and with) Hermia, and the performance of the song on both occasions adds a 'betwixt' to the line 'before, behind, between, above, below', which is not marked in the script (and is not included in standard printings of the poem).

4   My guides for engaging this poem are Thomas M. Greene, 'The Poetics of Discovery: A Reading of Donne's Elegy 19', *Yale Journal of Criticism* 2 (2) (1989): 129–43, and Albert C. Labriola, 'Painting and Poetry of the Cult of Elizabeth I: The Ditchley Portrait and Donne's "Elegie: Going to Bed"', *Studies in Philology* 93 (1) (1996): 42–63.

5   I have consulted the version of this poem in *John Donne: The Complete English Poems*, ed. C. A. Patrides (London: Everyman, 1999), 122–4. When I refer to it, I cite by line number.

6   I take this description of the uses of a Renaissance girdle from the 'Summary' provided for a silver girdle in the collections of the Victoria and Albert Museum (http://collections.vam. ac.uk/item/O115439/girdle-unknown/ [accessed 20 September 2016]).

7   Daniel Vitkus, 'Circumnavigation, Shakespeare, and the
     Origins of Globalization', in *Shakespeare in Our Time: A
     Shakespeare Association of America Collection*, ed. Dympna
     Callahan and Suzanne Gossett (London: Bloomsbury, 2016),
     167. On the early history of globalization in relation to early
     modern sea travel and colonialism, see also Peter Sloterdijk,
     Globes: Macrospherology, trans. Wieland Hoban (South
     Pasadena, CA: Semiotext(e), 2014).

8   Vitkus, 'Circumnavigation', 170.

9   Ibid., 167–8.

10   Ibid., 168, 170.

11   Steve Mentz, *Shipwreck Modernity: Ecologies of Globalization,
     1550–1719* (Minneapolis: University of Minnesota Press,
     2015), xxvii.

12   Alfred W. Crosby, *The Columbian Exchange: Biological and
     Cultural Consequences of 1492* (Westport, CT: Praeger, 2003).

13   Simon L. Lewis and Mark A. Maslin, 'Defining the
     Anthropocene', *Nature* 519 (12 March 2015): 174.

14   Ibid., 175.

15   On the Anthropocene and narrativity, especially in
     relation to Lewis and Maslin, see Dana Luciano, 'The
     Inhuman Anthropocene' (http://avidly.lareviewofbooks.
     org/2015/03/22/the-inhuman-anthropocene/ [accessed 19
     September 2016]).

16   Lewis and Maslin, 'Defining the Anthropocene', 177.

17   In 2016 the Working Group on the Anthropocene (WGA)
     announced that it would recommend 1950 as the start for the
     Anthropocene. See 'The Anthropocene epoch: scientists declare
     dawn of human influenced-age' (https://www.theguardian.com/
     environment/2016/aug/29/declare-anthropocene-epoch-experts-
     urge-geological-congress-human-impact-earth [accessed 19
     September 2016]).

18   On this nomenclature, see Diana Beresford-Kroeger, *The
     Global Forest* (New York: Viking, 2010).

19   My thinking here has been influenced by Rob Nixon, *Slow
     Violence and the Environmentalism of the Poor* (Cambridge,
     MA: Harvard University Press, 2011).

20 Vin Nardizzi, *Wooden Os: Shakespeare's Theatres and England's Trees* (Toronto: University of Toronto Press, 2013), esp. Intro. and Ch. 4.

21 For period reportage on genocide, see Bartolomé De Las Casas, *A Short Account of the Destruction of the Indies*, ed. and trans. Nigel Griffin (London: Penguin Books, 1992).

22 Lewis and Maslin, 'Defining the Anthropocene', 175.

23 For a provocative reading of the Indian boy in relation to a desire that has no explicit bodily sign in Shakespeare's play, see Madhavi Menon, 'Desire', in *Early Modern Theatricality*, ed. Henry S. Turner (Oxford: Oxford University Press, 2013), 327–45.

24 Randall Martin, *Shakespeare & Ecology* (Oxford: Oxford University Press, 2015), 10.

25 On how the fairy dance at play's end '*attempts* an imaginative intervention in a perceived ecological crisis', see Todd A. Borlik, *Ecocriticism and Early Modern English Literature* (New York: Routledge, 2011), 124. Emphasis mine.

26 On the fact that, at play's end, these 'cataclysmic weather anomalies' seem not to matter to human characters and for the related argument that Titania's speech signals the reach of 'the fairies' hubris', see Jeffrey S. Theis, *Writing the Forest in Early Modern England: A Sylvan Pastoral Nation* (Pittsburgh: Duquesne University Press, 2009), 105.

BIBLIOGRAPHY

A Midsummer Night's Dream. BBC. Available online: http://www.
bbc.co.uk/programmes/p0471ccz (last accessed 18 September
2016).

Adamson, S. (2007), 'Questions of Identity in Renaissance Drama:
New Historicism Meets Old', in S. Adamson, G. Alexander
and K. Ettenhuber (eds) (2007), *Renaissance Figures of Speech*.
Cambridge: Cambridge University Press.

Adelman, J. (1989), 'Bed Tricks: On Marriage as the End of Comedy
in *All's Well That Ends Well* and *Measure for Measure*,' in
N. N. Holland, S. Homan and B. J. Paris (eds), *Shakespeare's
Personality*. Berkeley and Los Angeles: University of California
Press.

Adelman, J. (1992), 'Making Defect Perfection: Shakespeare and
the One-Sex Model,' in V. Comensoli and A. Russell (eds),
Enacting Gender on the English Renaissance Stage. Urbana and
Chicago: University of Illinois Press.

Adelman, J. (2008), *Blood Relations: Christian and Jew in
The Merchant of Venice*. Chicago: University of Chicago Press.

Aebischer, P. (2008), 'Silence, Rape and Politics in *Measure for
Measure*: Close Readings in Theatre History,' *Shakespeare
Bulletin* 26 (4).

Agamben, G. (1998), *Homo Sacer: Sovereign Power and Bare Life*,
trans. D. Heller-Roazen. Stanford: Stanford University Press.

Ahmed, S. (2006), *Queer Phenomenology: Orientations, Objects,
Others*. Durham: Duke University Press.

Alaimo, S. (2000), *Undomesticated Ground: Recasting Nature as
Feminist Space*. Ithaca, NY: Cornell University Press.

Alaimo, S. (2010), *Bodily Natures: Science, Environment, and the
Material Self*. Bloomington: Indiana University Press.

Althusser, L. (1971), 'Ideology and Ideological State Apparatuses',
in *Lenin and Philosophy and Other Essays*, trans. B. Brewster.
London: New Left Books.

Anghiera, P. (1555), *The Decades of the new worlde or west India conteynyng the nauigations and conquests of the Spanyards.* London: n.p.

Aristotle (1598), *Aristotles Politiques, or Discourses of Government,* trans. L. Le Roy. London: n.p.

Aristotle (1991), *The 'Art' of Rhetoric,* trans. J. H. Freese. Cambridge, MA and London: Harvard University Press.

Attridge, D. (2005), *Moving Words: Forms of English Poetry.* Oxford: Oxford University Press.

Auden, W. H. (1948), 'The Prince's Dog', in *The Dyer's Hand and Other Essays.* New York: Random House.

Auden, W. H. (1962), *The Dyer's Hand and Other Essays.* New York: Random House.

Badiou, A. (2013), *Rhapsody for the Theatre,* trans. B. Bosteels with M. Puchner. London and New York: Verso.

Bailey, A. (2013), *Of Bondage: Debt, Property, and Personhood in Early Modern England.* Philadelphia: University of Pennsylvania Press.

Baines, B. J. (1990), 'Assaying the Power of Chastity in *Measure for Measure*', *Studies in English Literature* 30.

Baldassari, M. (2005), *Bande giovanili e 'vizio nefando': violenza e sessualità nella Roma barocca.* Roma: Viella.

Bamber, L. (1982), *Comic Women, Tragic Men: A Study of Genre and Gender in Shakespeare.* Stanford: Stanford University Press.

Barad, K. (2007), *Meeting the Universe Halfway: Quantum Physics and the Entanglement of Matter and Meaning.* Durham: Duke University Press.

Barad, K. (2011), 'Nature's Queer Performativity', *Qui Parle: Critical Humanities and Social Sciences* 19 (2).

Barber, C. (1981), *Early Modern English.* London: Andre Deutsch.

Bartolovich, C. (2016), '"First as Tragedy, then as …": Gender, Genre, History, and *Romeo and Juliet*', in A. Loomba and M. E. Sanchez (eds), *Rethinking Feminism in Early Modern Studies: Gender, Race, and Sexuality.* Farnham and New York: Ashgate.

Bataille, G. (1985), 'The College of Sociology', in *Visions of Excess: Selected Writings, 1927–1939,* ed. and trans. A. Stoekl. Minneapolis: University of Minnesota Press.

Bates, C. (2007), *Masculinity, Gender and Identity in The English Renaissance Lyric.* Cambridge: Cambridge University Press.

Beal, P. (ed.) (1980), *Index of English Literary Manuscripts*, vol. 1.2. New York: R. R. Bowker.

Beaumont, F. (1602), *Salmacis and Hermaphroditus* (Poem). London.

Beauvoir, S. de (2011), *The Second Sex*, trans. C. Borde and S. Malovany-Chevallier. New York: Vintage.

Beccadelli, A. (2010), 'To the Noble Cosimo on the Division of his Book,' in *The Hermaphrodite*, ed. and trans. H. Parker. Cambridge, MA: Harvard University Press.

Beckwith, S. (2012), *Shakespeare and the Grammar of Forgiveness*. Ithaca, NY: Cornell University Press.

Bellany, A. 'Killigrew, Sir Robert (1579/80–1633)', *Oxford Dictionary of National Biography*. Oxford: Oxford University Press, 2004; online edn, January 2008. Available online: http://www.oxforddnb.com.ezproxy1.lib.asu.edu/view/article/15537 (accessed 18 June 2016).

Belsey, C. (1985), 'Disrupting Sexual Difference', in J. Drakakis (ed.), *Alternative Shakespeares*. London: Methuen.

Belsey, C. (1988), 'Cleopatra's Seduction', in T. Hawkes (ed.), *Alternative Shakespeares 2*. London: Routledge.

Belsey, C. (1997), 'Love as Trompe-L'oeil: Taxonimies of Desire in *Venus and Adonis*', in P. Kolin (ed.), *Venus and Adonis: New Essays*. New York: Routledge.

Bennett, J. (2010), *Vibrant Matter: A Political Ecology of Things*. Durham and London: Duke University Press.

Beresford-Kroeger, D. (2010), *The Global Forest*. New York: Viking.

Berlant, L. (2011), *Cruel Optimism*. Durham: Duke University Press.

Berry, L. E. F. (ed.) (2007), *The Geneva Bible: A Facsimile of the 1560 Edition*. Peabody: Hendrickson Publishers.

Bersani, L. (2008), 'The Power of Evil and the Power of Love', in L. Bersani and A. Phillips, *Intimacies*. Chicago and London: University of Chicago Press.

Bevington, D. (ed.) (1997), *The Complete Works of Shakespeare*. New York: Longman.

Bevington, D. (2009), *Shakespeare's Ideas: More Things in Heaven and Earth*. Oxford: Wiley-Blackwell.

Bèze, T. de (1580), *A shorte learned and pithie Treatize of the Plague*, trans. J. Stockwood. London: Thomas Dawson for George Bishop.

B. I. (1641), *The Workes of Benjamin Jonson*, 2nd edn. London: Richard Bishop.

Birke, L. (1999), 'Bodies and Biology,' in J. Price and M. Shildrick (eds), *Feminist Theory and the Body: A Reader*. New York: Routledge.

Blake, N. F. (1985), *The Language of Shakespeare*. Houndmills and London: Macmillan.

Bloom, G. (2007), *Voice in Motion: Staging Gender, Shaping Sound in Early Modern England*. Philadelphia: University of Pennsylvania Press.

Bloom, H. (1998), *Shakespeare: The Invention of the Human*. New York: Riverhead Books.

Blondie (1978), 'Heart of Glass', writ. D. Harry and C. Stein, *Parallel Lines*. Chrysalis.

Boccaccio, G. (1951) *Genealogie deorum gentilium*, ed. Vincenzo Romano. Bari: G. Laterza.

Boherer, B. (2004), 'Economies of Desire in *A Midsummer Night's Dream*', *Shakespeare Studies* 32.

Bolton, M. J. (2005) 'Shakespeare's *Romeo and Juliet*', *The Explicator* 63 (4).

Booth, S. (2012), 'Who Doesn't Listen in Shakespeare', in L. Magnus and W. Cannon (eds), *Who Hears in Shakespeare? Auditory Worlds on Stage and Screen*. Teaneck, NJ: Farleigh Dickenson University Press.

Borlik, T. A. (2011), *Ecocriticism and Early Modern English Literature*. New York: Routledge.

Bovilsky, L. (2008), *Barbarous Play: Race on the English Renaissance Stage*. Minneapolis: University of Minnesota Press.

Bovilsky, L. (2016), '"Racked to the Uttermost": The Verges of Love and Subjecthood in *The Merchant of Venice*', in M. Frank, J. Goldberg and K. Newman (eds), *This Distracted Globe: Worldmaking in Early Modern Literature*. New York: Fordham University Press.

Bowden, B. (2003), 'Latin Pedagogical Plays and the Rape Scene in *The Two Gentlemen of Verona*', *English Language Notes* 41 (2).

Braidotti, R. (2013), *The Posthuman*. Cambridge: Polity Press.

Bray, A. (1982), *Homosexuality in Renaissance England*. London: Gay Men's Press.

Bray, A. (1994), 'Homosexuality and the Signs of Male Friendship in Early Modern England,' in J. Goldberg (ed.), *Queering the Renaissance*. Series Q. Durham: Duke University Press.

Bray, A. (Summer 2003), 'Racism and Homophobia in *The Merchant of Venice*,' *ELH* 70 (2).

Breitenberg, M. (1992), 'The Anatomy of Masculine Desire in *Love's Labor's Lost*', *Shakespeare Quarterly* 43 (4).

Breitenberg, M. (1996), *Anxious Masculinity in Early Modern England*. Cambridge: Cambridge University Press.

Bromley, J. M. (2011), *Intimacy and Sexuality in the Age of Shakespeare*. Cambridge: Cambridge University Press.

Bromely, J. M. and W. Stockton (eds) (2013), *Sex before Sex: Figuring the Act in Early Modern England*. Minneapolis and London: University of Minnesota Press.

Brown, S. (1990), 'The Boyhood of Shakespeare's Heroines: Notes on Gender Ambiguity in the Sixteenth Century', *Studies in English Literature, 1500–1900* 30.

Browne, T. (1646), *Pseudodoxia Epidemica, Or, Enquiries into Very Many Received Tenents, and Commonly Presumed Truths*. London: n.p.

Bryant, L. (2011), *The Democracy of Objects*. Ann Arbor: University of Michigan Library.

Bullough, G. (ed.) (1957), *Narrative and Dramatic Sources of Shakespeare*, vol. 2. London and New York: Routledge and Kegan Paul and Columbia University Press.

Burton, J. (2002), 'English Anxiety and the Muslim Power of Conversion: Five Perspectives on "Turning Turk" in Early Modern Texts', *JEMCS* 2 (1).

Butler, J. (1999), *Gender Trouble: Feminism and the Subversion of Identity*, 2nd edn. New York: Routledge.

Butler, J. (2004), *Precarious Life: The Powers of Mourning and Violence*. London and New York: Verso.

Butler, J. (2004), *Undoing Gender*. London and New York: Routledge.

Butler, S. (2014), *The Aitch Factor: Adventures in Australian English*. Sydney: Pan Macmillan.

Carroll, W. C. (2000), '"And love you 'gainst the nature of love": Ovid, Rape, and *The Two Gentlemen of Verona*', in A. B. Taylor (ed.), *Shakespeare's Ovid: The Metamorphoses in the Plays and Poems*. Cambridge: Cambridge University Press.

Castiglia, C. and C. Reed (2012), 'Introduction: In the Interest of Time', in *If Memory Serves: Gay Men, AIDS, and the Promise of the Queer Past*. Minneapolis and London: University of Minnesota Press.

Chambers, E. K. (1964 [1923]), *Shakespeare: A Survey*. London: Penguin Books.

Charney, M. (2009), *Wrinkled Deep in Time: Aging in Shakespeare*. New York: Columbia University Press.

Chedgzoy, K. (1995), *Shakespeare's Queer Children: Sexual Politics and Contemporary Culture*. Manchester and New York: Manchester University Press.

Chedgzoy, K. (2007), 'Playing with Cupid: Gender, Sexuality and Adolescence', in D. E. Henderson (ed.), *Alternative Shakespeares 3*. London: Routledge.

Chen, M. Y. (2012), *Animacies: Biopolitics, Racial Mattering, and Queer Affect*. Durham: Duke University Press.

Cheney, D. (March 1972), 'Spenser's Hermaphrodite and the 1590 *Faerie Queene*', *PMLA* 87 (2).

Chess, S. (2010), 'Shakespeare's Plays and Broadside Ballads', *Literature Compass* 7.

Chess, S. (2016), *Male-to-Female Crossdressing in Early Modern English Literature*. New York: Routledge.

Cicero (1992), *De Oratore*, trans. H. Rackham. Cambridge, MA and London: Harvard University Press.

Clare, J. (2014), *Shakespeare's Stage Traffic: Imitation, Borrowing and Competition in Renaissance Theatre*. Cambridge: Cambridge University Press.

Cohen, J. (Winter 2008), 'Ovid Inverted: Shakespeare's Sonnet 20 and the Metamorphosis of a Metamorphosis', *Shakespeare Newsletter* 58 (3).

Cohen, J. J. (ed.) (2012), *Animal, Vegetable, Mineral: Ethics and Objects*. Washington, DC: Oliphaunt Books.

Cohen, J. J. (2015), *Stone: An Ecology of the Inhuman*. Minneapolis: University of Minnesota Press.

Cohen, J. J. and J. Yates (eds) (2016), *Object Oriented Environs*. Earth: Punctum Books.

Colaiacomo, P. (2009), 'Other from the Body: Sartorial Metatheatre in Shakespeare's *Cymbeline*', in M. del Sapio Gabero (ed.), *Identity, Otherness and Empire in Shakespeare's Rome*. Farnham: Ashgate.

Cole, A. (2013), 'The Call of Things: A Critique of Object-Oriented Ontologies', *Minnesota Review* 80.

Cole, M. (2003), *The Other Orpheus: A Poetics of Modern Homosexuality*. New York: Routledge.

Collington, P. (2006), '"Stuffed with all Honourable Virutes": Much Ado About Nothing and the Book of the Courtier', *Studies in Philology* 103 (3).

Cook, C. (1986), 'Reading Gender Difference in *Much Ado About Nothing*', *PMLA* 101 (2).

Conn Liebler, N. (2010), 'The oldest hath borne most': The Burdens of Aging and the Morality of Uselessness in *King Lear*', in M. D. Bristol (ed.), *Shakespeare and Moral Agency*. London: Continuum.

Cox, J. D. (2008), 'Shakespeare and the Ethics of Friendship', *Religion and Literature* 40 (3).

Crawford, J. (2003), 'The Homoerotics of Shakespeare's Elizabethan Comedies', in R. Dutton and J. E. Howard (eds), *A Companion to Shakespeare's Works: The Comedies*. Malden, MA: Blackwell Publishing.

Cressy, D. (October 1996), 'Gender Trouble and Cross-Dressing in Early Modern England', *Journal of British Studies* 35 (4).

Cressy, D. (1999), 'Cross-Dressing in the Birth Room: Gender Trouble and Cultural Boundaries', in *Travesties and Transgressions in Tudor and Stuart England: Tales of Discord and Dissension*. Oxford: Oxford University Press.

Crooke, H. (1618), *Mikrokosmographia: A Description of the Body of Man*. London: n.p.

Crosby, A. W. (2003), *The Columbian Exchange: Biological and Cultural Consequences of 1492*. Westport, CT: Praeger.

Crystal, D. (2005), *Pronouncing Shakespeare: The Globe Experiment*. New York: Cambridge University Press.

Crystal, D. and B. Crystal (2002), *Shakespeare's Words: A Glossary & Language Companion*. London: Penguin Books.

Cudini, P. (ed.) (1956), *Poeti giocosi del tempo di Dante*. Milan: Rizzoli.

Culler, J. (2015), *Theory of the Lyric*. Cambridge, MA: Harvard University Press.

Daniel, D. (Summer 2010), '"Let Me Have Judgment, and the Jew His Will": Melancholy Epistemology and Masochistic Fantasy in *The Merchant of Venice*', *Shakespeare Quarterly* 61 (2).

Daniel, S. (1904), 'A Defence of Ryme', in G. Smith (ed.),

Elizabethan Critical Essays, vol. 2. Oxford: Oxford University Press.

Daston, L. (1998), 'The Nature of Nature in Early Modern Europe', *Configurations* 6 (2).

Davidson, J. (2008), 'Why Girls Look Like Their Mothers: David Garrick's *The Winter's Tale*', in P. Sabor and P. E. Yachnin (eds), *Shakespeare and the Eighteenth Century*. Aldershot: Ashgate.

Davies, J. of Hereford (1609), *Humours Heav'n on Earth*. London: A. I.

Dekker, T. (1603), *The Wonderfull Yeare*. London: Thomas Creede.

Dekker, T. (1606), *The Seven Deadly Sinnes of London*. London: E. A. for Nathaniel Butter.

De Grazia, M. (1993), 'The Scandal of Shakespeare's Sonnets', *Shakespeare Survey* 46.

De Las Casas, B. (1992), *A Short Account of the Destruction of the Indies*, ed. and trans. N. Griffin. London: Penguin Books.

Dee, J. (1570), 'To the Vnfained Lover of truth, and constant Studentes of Noble *Sciences*', in *The elements of geometrie of the most auncient philosopher Euclide*, trans. Sir Henry Billingsley. London: n.p.

Deleuze, G. and F. Guattari (1987 [1980]). *A Thousand Plateaus: Capitalism and Schizophrenia*, trans. and Foreword Brian Massumi. London and New York: Continuum.

Derrida, J. (20050, *Politics of Friendship*, trans. G. Collins. London: Verso.

DiGangi, M. (1993), 'Pleasure and Danger: Measuring Female Sexuality in *Measure for Measure*', *ELH* 60 (3).

DiGangi, M. (Fall 1996), 'Queering the Shakespearean Family', *Shakespeare Quarterly* 47 (3).

DiGangi, M. (1997), *The Homoerotics of Early Modern Drama*. Cambridge: Cambridge University Press.

DiGangi, M. (2011), *Sexual Types: Embodiment, Agency, and Dramatic Character from Shakespeare to Shirley*. Philadelphia: Pennsylvania University Press.

Distiller, N. (June 2012), 'Shakespeare's Perversion: A Reading of Sonnet 20', *Shakespeare* 8 (2).

Dollimore, J. (1994), 'Transgression and Surveillance in *Measure for Measure*', in J. Dollimore and A. Sinfield (eds), *Political Shakespeare: Essays in Cultural Materialism*, 2nd edn. Ithaca: Cornell University Press.

Donne, J. (1632), *Deaths Duell*. London: Printed by Thomas Harper for Richard Redmer and Benjamin Fisher.

Donne, J. (1977), *The Complete English Poems*, ed. A. J. Smith. New York: Penguin.

Dowd, M. (2011), 'Desiring Subjects: Staging the Female Servant in Early Modern Tragedy', in M. Dowd and N. Korda (eds), *Working Subjects in Early Modern English Drama*. New York: Routledge.

Doyle, J. (2009), 'Blind Spots and Failed Performance: Abortion, Feminism, and Queer Theory', *Qui Parle* 18 (1).

Dubrow, H. (1996), 'Incertainties Now Crown Themselves Assur'd: The Politics of Plotting Shakespeare's Sonnets', *Shakespeare Quarterly* 47.

Dugan, H. (2001), *The Ephemeral History of Perfume: Scent and Sense in Early Modern England*. Baltimore: Johns Hopkins University Press.

Dusinbere, J. (1975), *Shakespeare and the Nature of Women*. New York: Macmillan.

Edelman, L. (2006), *No Future: Queer Theory and the Death Drive*. Durham and London: Duke University Press.

Edmondson, P. (2005), *Twelfth Night: A Guide to the Text and Its Theatrical Life*. Houndsmills and New York: Palgrave Macmillan.

Egan, G. (2006), *Green Shakespeare: From Ecopolitics to Ecocriticism*. London and New York: Routledge.

Elam, K. (ed.) (2008), *Twelfth Night*. London: Bloomsbury.

Erickson, P. B. (1997). 'The Failure of Relationship Between Men and Women in *Love's Labour's Lost*', in F. H. Londre (ed.), *Love's Labour's Lost: Critical Essays*. New York: Garland Publishing.

Erne, L. (2010), *Shakespeare as Literary Dramatist*. Cambridge: Cambridge University Press.

Esposito, R. (2010), *Communitas: The Origin and Destiny of Community*, trans. T. Campbell. Stanford: Stanford University Press.

Everett, C. (1995), 'Venus in Drag: Female Transvestism and the Construction of Sex Difference in Renaissance England' in A. Lynch and P. C. Madden (eds), *Venus and Mars: Engendering Love and War in Early Modern Europe*. Nedlands: University of Western Australia Press.

Ezell, E. J. M. (July 2004), 'Looking Glass Histories', *Journal of British Studies* 43 (3).

Ferrick, J. E. and V. Nardizzi (eds) (2012), *The Indistinct Human in Renaissance Literature*. New York: Palgrave Macmillan.

Fineman, J. (1986), *Shakespeare's Perjured Eye: The Invention of Poetic Subjectivity in the Sonnets*. Berkeley: University of California Press.

Fineman, J. (Summer 1988), 'The Sound of O in *Othello:* the Real of the Tragedy of Desire', *October* 45.

Fisher, W. (1999), 'Queer Money', *ELH* 66 (1).

Florio, J. (1611), *Queen Anna's New World of Words*. London: n.p.

Foucault, M. (1979), *Discipline and Punish: The Birth of the Prison*, trans. A. Sheridan. New York: Vintage Books.

Foucault, M. (Spring 1986), 'Of Other Spaces', trans. J. Miskowiec, *Diacritics* 16 (1).

Fradenburg, A. (2011), 'Momma's Boys', in M. Menon (ed.), *Shakesqueer: A Queer Companion to the Complete Works of Shakespeare*. Durham and London: Duke University Press.

Freeburg, V. O. (1915), 'The Boy Bride' in *Disguise Plots in Renaissance Drama*. New York: Columbia University Press.

Freeman, E. (2010), *Time Binds: Queer Temporalities, Queer Histories*. Durham and London: Duke University Press.

Freccero, C. (2006), *Queer/Early/Modern*. Durham and London: Duke University Press.

Freccero, C. (2007), 'Queer Times', *South Atlantic Quarterly* 106 (3).

Freccero, C. (2011), 'Romeo and Juliet Love Death', in M. Menon (ed.), *Shakesequeer: A Queer Companion to the Complete Works of Shakespeare*. Durham: Duke University Press.

Freedman, B. (1998), 'Dis/Figuring Power: Censorship and Representation in *A Midsummer Night's Dream*', in D. Kehler (ed.), *A Midsummer Night's Dream: Critical Essays*. New York and London: Garland.

Freinkel, L. (2002), *Reading Shakespeare's Will: The Theology of Form from Augustine to the Sonnets*. New York: Columbia University Press.

Frye, N. (1986), *Northrop Frye on Shakespeare*, ed. Robert Sandler. New Haven and London: Yale University Press.

Fumerton, P. (1991), *Cultural Aesthetics: Renaissance Literature and the Practice of Social Ornament*. Chicago: University of Chicago Press.

Garber, M. (1992), *Vested Interests: Crossdressing and Cultural Anxiety*. New York: Routledge.

Garcia, T. (2014), *Form and Object: A Treatise on Things*, trans. J. Cogburn and M. A. Ohm. Edinburgh: University of Edinburgh Press.

Garrett, L. (2014), 'True Interest and the Affections: The Dangers of Lawful Lending in *The Merchant of Venice*', *Journal for Early Modern Cultural Studies* 14 (1).

Garrison, J. S. (2014), *Friendship and Queer Theory in the Renaissance: Gender and Sexuality in Early Modern England*. New York and London: Routledge.

Garrison, J. S. (1999), '"Kissing the Boar:" Queer Adonis and Critical Practice', in C. Thomas (ed.), *Straight with a Twist: Queer Theory and the Subject of Heterosexuality*. Urbana: University of Illinois Press.

Garrison, J. S. (2015), *Glass*. London and New York: Bloomsbury.

Gascoigne, G. (1576), *The steele glas. A satyre co[m]piled by George Gascoigne Esquire. Togither with The complainte of Phylomene. An elegie deuised by the same author*. London: Richard Smith.

Geisweidt, E. J. (2009), 'Antonio's Claim: Triangulated Desire and Queer Kinship in Shakespeare's *The Merchant of Venice*', *Shakespeare* 5 (4).

Geneva Bible (1599). Available online: http://www.genevabible.org/files/Geneva_Bible/Old_Testament/Genesis_F.pdf (accessed 15 June 2016).

Giffney, N. and M. J. Hird (2008), 'Introduction: Queering the Non/Human', in N. Giffney and M. J. Hird (eds), *Queering the Non/Human*. Burlington, VT: Ashgate.

Gil, D. J. (2006), *Before Intimacy: Asocial Sexuality in Early Modern England*. Minneapolis and London: University of Minnesota Press.

Gilbert, A. (1962), 'Two Margarets: The Composition of *Much Ado About Nothing*', *Philological Quarterly* 151 (1).

Gillen, K. (2011), 'Chaste Treasure: Protestant Chastity and the Creation of a Notational Economic Sphere in *The Rape of Lucrece* and *Cymbeline*,' *Early English Studies* 4.

Gless, D. F. (1970), *Measure for Measure, the Law, and the Convent*. Princeton: Princeton University Press.

Goldberg, J. (1986), *Voice Terminal Echo: Postmodernism and English Renaissance Texts*. New York: Methuen.

Goldberg, J. (1992), *Sodometries: Renaissance Texts, Modern Sexualities*. Stanford: Stanford University Press.

Goldberg, J. (ed.) (1994), *Queering the Renaissance*. Durham and London: Duke University Press.

Goldberg, J. (2003), 'The Anus in *Coriolanus*', in *Shakespeare's Hand*. Minneapolis and London: University of Minnesota Press.

Goldberg, J. (2009), *The Seeds of Things: Theorizing Sexuality and Materiality in Renaissance Representations*. New York: Fordham University Press.

Goldberg, J. (Summer 2009), 'What Do Women Want?: The Merry Wives of Windsor', *Criticism* 51 (3).

Goldberg, J. (Winter 2013), 'Carnival in *The Merchant of Venice*', *Postmedieval: A Journal of Medieval Cultural Studies* 4 (4).

Goldberg, J. (2014), 'English Renaissance Literature in the History of Sexuality', in *The Cambridge History of Gay and Lesbian Literature*. Cambridge: Cambridge University Press.

Goldberg, J. and M. Menon (October 2005) 'Queering History', *PMLA* 120 (5).

Gombrich, E. H. (1988), *Art and Illusion: A Study in the Psychology of Pictorial Representation*. Oxford: Phaidon Press.

Grabes, H. (1928), *The Mutable Glass: Mirror-Imagery in Titles and Texts of the Middle Ages and English Renaissance*, trans. G. Collier. Cambridge: Cambridge University Press.

Grady, H. (2008), 'Shakespeare and Impure Aesthetics: The Case of *A Midsummer Night's Dream*', *Shakespeare Quarterly* 59 (3).

Greenblatt, S. (1992), 'Fiction and Friction,' in *Shakespearean Negotiations: The Circulation of Social Energy in Renaissance England*. Oxford: Clarendon Press.

Greenblatt, S. (gen. ed.) (2016), *The Norton Shakespeare: Early Plays and Poems*, 3rd edn. New York: W. W. Norton.

Greenberg, D. F. (1988), *The Construction of Homosexuality*. Chicago and London: University of Chicago Press.

Greene, A. (2000), *The Chains of Eros: The Sexual in Psychoanalysis*, trans. L. Thurston. London: Karnac Books.

Greene, J. (1994), '"You Must Eat Men": The Sodomitic Economy of Renaissance Patronage,' *GLQ* 1.

Greene, T. M. (1989), 'The Poetics of Discovery: A Reading of Donne's Elegy 19', *Yale Journal of Criticism* 2 (2).

Greenstadt, A. (2009), *Rape and the Rise of the Author: Gendering Intention in Early Modern England*. Women and Gender in the Early Modern World. Farnham: Ashgate.

Greenstadt, A. (2013), 'The Kindest Cut: Circumcision and Queer Kinship in The Merchant of Venice', *ELH* 80 (4).

Griffiths, H. (2014), 'Hotel Rooms and Bodily Fluids in Two Recent Productions of *Measure for Measure*, Or, Why Barnardine is Still Important', *Shakespeare Bulletin* 32 (4).

Grindley, C. J. (2009), 'The Plague in Filmed Versions of *Romeo and Juliet* and *Twelfth Night*', in M. Croteau and C. Jess-Cooke (eds), *Apocalyptic Shakespeare: Essays on Visions of Chaos and Revelation in Recent Film Adaptations*. Jefferson, NC: McFarland.

Grosz, E. (1994), *Volatile Bodies: Toward a Corporeal Feminism*. Bloomington: Indiana University Press.

Guy-Bray, S. (2009), *Against Reproduction: Where Renaissance Texts Come From*. Toronto: University of Toronto Press.

Guy-Bray, S. (2013), 'Sources,' in *Early Modern Theatricality*, ed. H. S. Turner. Oxford: Oxford University Press.

Guy-Bray, S. (2016), 'Remembering to Forget: Shakespeare's Sonnet 35 and Sigo's "XXXV"', in J. S. Garrison and K. Pivetti (eds), *Sexuality and Memory in Early Modern England*. New York and London: Routledge.

Guy-Bray, S. (2017), 'Shakespeare and the Invention of the Heterosexual', *Early Modern Literary Studies* 13 (2); Special Issue 16 (12) (1–28), 12 (6). Available online: http://extra.shu.ac.uk/emls/si-16/brayshks.htm (accessed 15 June 2016).

Guy-Bray, S., V. Nardizzi and W. Stockton (eds) (2009), 'Queer Renaissance Historiography: Backward Gaze', in *Queer Renaissance Historiography: Backward Gaze*. Farnham: Ashgate.

Halberstam, J. (1998), *Female Masculinity*. Durham: Duke University Press.

Halberstam, J. (2011), *The Queer Art of Failure*. Durham: Duke University Press.

Halley, J. and A. Parker. (2007), 'After Sex? Writing Since Queer Theory', *South Atlantic Quarterly* 106 (3).

Hammond, P. (2002), *Figuring Sex between Men from Shakespeare to Rochester*. Oxford: Clarendon Press.

Hammond, P. (ed.) (2012), 'Reading the Sonnet Tradition,' *Shakespeare's Sonnets: An Original-Spelling Text*. Oxford: Oxford University Press.

Hamrick, S. (2009), *The Catholic Imaginary and the Cults of Elizabeth, 1558–1582*. Burlington, VT: Ashgate.

Harper, K. (2013), *From Shame to Sin: The Christian Transformation of Sexual Morality in Late Antiquity*. Cambridge, MA: Harvard University Press.

Harris, J. G. (2004), *Sick Economies: Drama, Mercantilism, and Disease in Shakespeare's England*. Philadelphia: University of Pennsylvania Press.

Harris, J. G. (2012), *Untimely Matter in the Time of Shakespeare*. Philadelphia: University of Pennsylvania Press.

Hawkes, D. (2000), 'Sodomy, Usury, and the Narrative of Shakespeare's Sonnets', *Renaissance Studies* 14 (3).

Hawkes, D. (2010), *The Culture of Usury in Renaissance England*. New York: Palgrave.

Heise, U. K. (1992), 'Transvestism and the Stage Controversy in Spain and England, 1580–1680', *Theatre Journal* 44.

Helgerson, R. (1998), 'The Buck Basket, the Witch, and the Queen of Faeries: The Women's World of Shakespeare's Windsor', in P. Fumerton and S. Hunt (eds), *Renaissance Culture and the Everyday*. Philadelphia: University of Pennsylvania Press.

Henderson, D. (2010), 'Mind the Gaps: The Ear, The Eye, and the Senses of a Woman in *Much Ado About Nothing*', in L. Gallagher and S. Raman (eds), *Knowing Shakespeare*. New York and Houndsmills: Palgrave-Macmillan.

Herman, P. C. (2000), 'What's the Use? Or, the Problematic of Economy in Shakespeare's Procreation Sonnets,' in J. Schiffer (ed.), *Shakespeare's Sonnets: Critical Essays*. New York: Routledge.

Heywood, J. (1556), *An Hundred* Epigrams. London: n.p.

Hird, M. J. (2004), 'Naturally Queer' *Feminist Theory* 5 (1).

Hobbes, T. (1651), 'To the Reader,' in *Philosophical Rudiments concerning Government and Society*. London: n.p.

Hoskins, J. (1935), *Directions for Speech and Style*, ed. H. H. Hudson. Princeton: Princeton University Press.

Howard, J. E. (1994), *The Stage and Social Struggle in Early Modern England*. New York: Routledge.

Howard, J. E. (Winter 1998), 'Crossdressing, the Theater, and Gender Struggle in Early Modern England', *Shakespeare Quarterly* 39 (4).

Hunt, M. (2004), 'Catholicism, Protestant Reformation, and *The Two Gentlemen of Verona*', in *Shakespeare's Religious Allusiveness: Its Play and Tolerance*. Farnham: Ashgate.

Hurrell, J. (1961), 'Love and Friendship in *The Merchant of Venice*,' *Texas Studies in Literature and Language* 3 (3).

Hutson, L. (1994), *The Usurer's Daughter: Male Friendship and Fictions of Women in Sixteenth-Century England*. London: Routledge.

Hutson, L. (Summer 1996), 'On Not Being Deceived: Rhetoric and the Body in *Twelfth Night*', *Texas Studies in Literature and Language* 38 (2).

Hyde, T. (1986), *The Poetic Theology of Love: Cupid in Renaissance Literature*. Newark: University of Delaware Press.

Hyman, L. W. (1970), 'The Rival Lovers in *The Merchant of Venice*,' *Shakespeare Quarterly* 21 (2).

I. G. (1615), *A Refutation of the Apology for Actors*. London: W. White.

Irigaray, L. (1985), *Speculum of the Other Woman*, trans. G. C. Gill. Ithaca, NY: Cornell University Press.

Jacobson, M. (2105), *Barbarous Antiquities: Reorienting the Past in the Poetry of Early Modern England*. Philadelphia: University of Pennsylvania Press.

Jankowski, T. (2000), *Pure Resistance: Queer Virginity in Early Modern English Drama*. Philadelphia: University of Pennsylvania Press.

Jardine, L. (1989 [1983]), *Still Harping on Daughters: Women and Drama in the Age of Shakespeare*. Towata, NJ: Harvester; repr. New York: Columbia University Press.

Jardine, L. (1991), 'Boy Actors, Female Roles, and Elizabethan Eroticism', in D. S. Kastan and P. Stallybrass (eds), *Staging the Renaissance: Reinterpretations of Elizabethan and Jacobean Drama*. New York: Routledge.

Jeaffreson, J. C. (ed.) (1886–92), Middlesex County Records [Old Series], 2 vols, vol II. London: n.p.

Jones, G. P. (Spring 1983), 'The "Strumpet's Fool" in *Antony and Cleopatra*', *Shakespeare Quarterly* 34 (1).

Jonson, B. (1975), *The Complete Poems*, ed. George Parfitt. New York: Penguin.

Jonson, B. (1979), *Epicoene or the Silent Woman*, ed. R. Holdsworth. London: Bloomsbury.

Jordan, M. D. (1997), *The Invention of Sodomy in Christian Theology*. Chicago Series on Sexuality, History, and Society. Chicago: University of Chicago Press.

Kalas, R. (2007), *Frame, Glass, Verse: The Technology of Poetic*

Invention in the English Renaissance. Ithaca and London: Cornell University Press.

Kamuf, P. (June 2012), '"This Were Kindness": Economies of Différance in *The Merchant of Venice*', *Oxford Literary Review* 34 (1).

Kehler, D. (1997), 'Jaquenetta's Baby's Father', in F. H. Londré (ed.), *Love's Labour's Lost: Critical Essays*. New York: Garland Publishing.

Kelly, K. E. (1990), 'The Queen's Two Bodies: Shakespeare's Boy Actress in Breeches', *Theatre Journal* 42.

King, R. (2004), *No Future: Queer Theory and the Death Drive*. Durham: Duke University Press.

King, R. (2005), *Cymbeline: Constructions of Empire*. Farnham: Ashgate.

Kingsley-Smith, J. (2010), *Cupid in Early Modern Literature and Culture*. Cambridge: Cambridge University Press.

Kingsley-Smith, J. (2014), 'Aristotelian Shame and Christian Mortification in *Love's Labour's Lost*', in P. Gray and J. D. Cox (eds), *Shakespeare and Renaissance Ethics*. New York: Cambridge University Press.

Kleinberg, S. (1983), '*The Merchant of Venice*: The Homosexual as Anti-Semite in Nascent Capitalism', *Journal of Homosexuality* 8 (3–4).

Kökeritz, H. (1953), *Shakespeare's Pronunciation*. New Haven: Yale University Press.

Kosofsky Sedgwick, E. (1985), 'Swan in Love: The Example of Shakespeare's Sonnets', in *Between Men: English Literature and Male Homosocial Desire*. New York: Columbia University Press.

Kosofsky Sedgwick, E. (2008), 'Preface to the 2008 Edition', in *Epistemology of the Closet*, updated edn. Berkeley: University of California Press.

Kosofsky Sedgwick, E. (2011), 'The Weather in Proust', in Jonathan Goldberg (ed.), *The Weather in Proust*. Durham and London: Duke University Press.

Kuchar, G. (2011), '"Loves Best Habit": Eros, Agape, and the Psychotheology of *Shakespeare's Sonnets*', in P. Cefalu and B. Reynolds (eds), *The Return of Theory in Early Modern English Studies: Tarrying with the Subjunctive*. New York: Palgrave Macmillan.

Labriola, A. C. (1996), 'Painting and Poetry of the Cult of Elizabeth

I: The Ditchley Portrait and Donne's "Elegie: Going to Bed"',
    Studies in Philology 93 (1).
Lacan, J. (1988), 'Seminar on "The Purloined Letter"', trans.
    J. Mehlman (trans.), in J. P. Muller and W. J. Richardson
    (eds), *The Purloined Poe: Lacan, Derrida, and Psychoanalytic
    Reading*. Baltimore: Johns Hopkins University Press.
Landreth, D. (2004), 'Once More into the Preech: The Merry
    Wives' English Pedagogy', *Shakespeare Quarterly* 55 (4).
Laqueur, T. (1992), *Making Sex: Body and Gender from the Greeks
    to Freud*. Cambridge, MA and London: Harvard University
    Press.
Latour, B. (2005), *Reassembling the Social: An Introduction to
    Actor-Network Theory*. New York: Oxford University Press.
Levin, R. A. (1982), 'Duke Vincentio and Angelo: Would "A
    Feather Turn the Scale?"', *Studies in English Literature* 22 (2).
Levine, L. (1994), *Men in Women's Clothing: Anti-theatricality and
    Effeminization, 1579–1642*. Cambridge: Cambridge University
    Press.
Lewalski, B. (Summer 1962), 'Biblical Allusion and Allegory in *The
    Merchant of Venice*,' *Shakespeare Quarterly* 13 (3).
Lewis, A. (2005), 'Reading Shakespeare's Cupid', *Criticism* 47 (2).
Lewis, S. L. and M. A. Maslin (March 2015), 'Defining the
    Anthropocene', *Nature* 519.
Lim, W. S. H. (2010), 'Surety and Spiritual Commercialism in *The
    Merchant of Venice*,' *Studies in English Literature, 1500–1900*
    50 (2).
Lindenbaum, P. (1975), 'Education in *The Two Gentlemen of
    Verona*', *Studies in English Literature* 15.
Little, A. L. (2009), '"A Social Habitation and a Name": Presence,
    Witnessing, and Queer Marriage in Shakespeare's Romantic
    Comedies', in E. Gajowski (ed.), *Presentism, Gender, and
    Sexuality in Shakespeare*. New York: Palgrave.
Little, A. L. (2011), 'The Rites of Queer Marriage in *The Merchant
    of Venice*' in M. Menon (ed.), *Shakesqueer: A Queer Companion
    to the Complete Works of Shakespeare*. Durham: Duke
    University Press.
Lopez, J. (2003), *Theatrical Convention and Audience Response
    in Early Modern Drama*. Cambridge: Cambridge University
    Press.
Lorde, A. (2012), 'The Transformation of Silence into Language

and Action', in *Sister Outsider: Essays and Speeches*. New York: Ten Speed Press.

Lorey, I. (2015), *State of Insecurity: Government of the Precarious*. London and New York: Verso.

Loughlin, M. H. (ed.) (2014), *Same-Sex Desire in Early Modern England, 1550–1735: An Anthology of Literary Texts and Contexts*. Manchester and New York: Manchester University Press.

Love, H. (2011), 'Milk', in M. Menon (ed.), *Shakesqueer: A Queer Companion to the Works of Shakespeare*. Durham: Duke University Press.

Luciano, D. (2016), 'The Inhuman Anthropocene'. Available online: http://avidly.lareviewofbooks.org/2015/03/22/the-inhuman-anthropocene/) (accessed 19 September 2016).

Luciano, D. and M. Y. Chen (2015), 'Introduction: Has the Queer Ever Been Human?', *GLQ* 21 (2–3).

Lunger Knoppers, L. (1993), '(En)gendering Shame: *Measure for Measure* and the Spectacles of Power', *ELR* 23.

Lupton, J. (2005), *Citizen-Saints: Shakespeare and Political Theology*. Chicago: University of Chicago Press.

Luxton, T. (January 1999), 'A Second Daniel: The Jew and the "True Jew" in *The Merchant of Venice*', *Early Modern Literary Studies: A Journal of Sixteenth- and Seventeenth-Century English Literature* 4 (3).

Macfarlane, A. and G. Martin (2002), *Glass: A World History*. Chicago: University of Chicago Press.

MacFaul, T. (2007), *Male Friendship in Shakespeare and his Contemporaries*. Cambridge: Cambridge University Press.

MacFaul, T. (2015), *Shakespeare and the Natural World*. Cambridge: Cambridge University Press.

Mack, P. (2002), *Elizabethan Rhetoric: Theory and Practice*. Cambridge: Cambridge University Press.

Mackay, E. (2011), *Persecution, Plague, and Fire: Fugitive Histories of the Stage in Early Modern England*. Chicago and London: The University of Chicago Press.

Maguire, L. (2008), *How to Do Things with Shakespeare: New Approaches, New Essays*, ed. L. Maguire. Malden, MA and Oxford: Blackwell.

Manion, J. (May 2014), 'Transbutch', *TSQ: Transgender Studies Quarterly* 1 (1–2).

Mann, J. C. (Winter 2006), 'How to Look at a Hermaphrodite

in Early Modern England,' *Studies in English Literature, 1500–1900* 46 (1).

Mann, J. C. (2010), 'The "Figure of Exchange:" Shakespeare's Master-Mistress, Jonson's *Epicene*, and the English Art of Rhetoric', *Renaissance Drama* 38.

Marcocci, G. (2010), 'Matrimoni omosessuali nella Roma del tardo cinquecento', *Quaderni storici* 45 (133).

Marcocci, G. (Summer 2015), 'Is This Love? Same-Sex Marriage in Renaissance Rome', *Historical Reflections* 41 (2).

Mardock, J. and E. Rasmussen (2013), 'What Does Textual Evidence Reveal About the Author', in P. Edmondson and S. Wells (eds), *Shakespeare Beyond Doubt: Evidence, Argument, Controversy*. Cambridge: Cambridge University Press.

Marotti, A. F. (Summer 1982), '"Love is not Love": Elizabethan Sonnet Sequences and the Social Order', *ELH* 49 (2).

Martial (1619), *M. Val. Martialis epigrammaton libri Animaduersi, emendati et commentariolis luculenter explicati*. London: n.p.

Martial (1619), *M. Val. Martialis Nova Editio Ex Museo Petri Scriverii*. Leyden: n.p.

Martial (1993), *Epigrams*, ed. and trans. D. R. Shackleton-Bailey, 3 vols. Loeb Classical Library. Cambridge, MA: Harvard University Press.

Martial (2002 [1973]), *Epigrams*, trans. J. Mitchie. New York: Penguin.

Martial (2015), *Epigrams: With Parallel Latin Text*, trans. G. Nisbet. Oxford World's Classics. New York: Oxford University Press.

Martin, R. (2015), *Shakespeare & Ecology*. Oxford: Oxford University Press.

Masten, J. (1997), *Textual Intercourse: Collaboration, Authorship, and Sexualities in Renaissance Drama*. Cambridge: Cambridge University Press.

Masten, J. (2003), '*The Two Gentlemen of Verona*', in R. Dutton and J. E. Howard (eds), *A Companion to Shakespeare's Works: The Comedies*. Malden, MA: Blackwell Publishing.

Masten, J. (2004), 'Toward a Queer Address: The Taste of Letters and Early Modern Male Friendship', *GLQ* 10 (3).

Masten, J. (2006), 'Editing Boys: The Performance of Gender in

Print', in P. Holland and S. Orgel (eds), *From Performance to Print in Shakespeare's England*. New York: Palgrave.

Masten, J. (2016), *Queer Philologies: Sex, Language, and Affect in Shakespeare's Time*. Philadelphia: University of Pennsylvania Press.

Matz, R. (Summer 2010), 'The Scandals of the Shakespeare's Sonnets', *ELH* 77 (2).

McDonald, R. (2001), *Shakespeare and the Arts of Language*. Oxford: Oxford University Press.

McLuskie, K. (1987), 'The Act, the Role, and the Actor: Boy Actresses on the Elizabethan Stage', *New Theatre Quarterly* 3.

McPherson, D. (December 1974), 'Ben Jonson's Library and Marginalia: An Annotated Catalogue,' *Studies in Philology* 71 (5).

Menon, M. (2004), *Wanton Words: Rhetoric and Sexuality in English Renaissance Drama*. Toronto: University of Toronto Press.

Menon, M. (2008), *Unhistorical Shakespeare: Queer Theory in Shakespearean Literature and Film*. New York: Palgrave Macmillan.

Menon, M. (ed.) (2011), *Shakesqueer: A Queer Companion to the Complete Works of Shakespeare*. Durham and London: Duke University Press.

Menon, M. (2013), 'Desire', in Henry S. Turner (ed.), *Early Modern Theatricality*. Oxford: Oxford University Press.

Menon, M. (2015), *Indifference to Difference: On Queer Universalism*. Minneapolis: University of Minnesota Press.

Mennes, J. (1654), *Recreation for ingenious head-peeces, or, a pleasant walk in of epigrams*. London: n.p. Available online: Early English Books Online, http://gateway.proquest.com. proxygw.wrlc.org/openurl?ctx_ver=Z39.88-2003&res_ id=xri:eebo&rft_id=xri:eebo:citation:12272443 (accessed 19 July 2016).

Mentz, S. (2003), 'The Thigh and the Sword: Gender, Genre, and Sexy Dressing in Sidney's *New Arcadia*', in *Prose Fiction and Early Modern Sexualities in England, 1570–1640*. New York: Palgrave MacMillan.

Mentz, S. (2015), *Shipwreck Modernity: Ecologies of Globalization, 1550–1719*. Minneapolis: University of Minnesota Press.

Meres, F. (1598), *Palladis Tamia, Or, Wits Treasury Being the Second Part of Wits Commonwealth*, ed. N. Ling, vol. 2. London: n.p.

Moncrief, K. M. (2011), '"Teach us, sweet madam": Masculinity, Femininity, and Gendered Instruction in *Love's Labour's Lost*', in M. M. Kathryn and K. R. McPherson (eds), *Performing Pedagogy in Early Modern England: Gender, Instruction, and Performance*. Burlington, VT: Ashgate.

Montaigne, M. de (1603), *The Essayes or Morall, Politike and Millitarie Discourses of Lo: Michaell de Montaigne*, trans. J. Florio, vol. 1. London: n.p.

Morland, I. (2009), 'What Can Queer Theory Do for Intersex?', *GLQ* 15 (2).

Moss, R. (Fall 1995), 'Falstaff as a Woman', *Journal of Dramatic Theory and Criticism* 10 (1).

Moss. S. (2003), 'A Shakespeare for the People?', *Textual Practice*, 17 (2).

Mosse, M. (1595), *The Arraignment and Conviction of Usurie*. London: n.p.

Moulton, I. F. (2000), *Before Pornography: Erotic Writing in Early Modern England*. New York: Oxford.

Muñoz, J. E. (2009), *Cruising Utopia: The Then and There of Queer Futurity*. New York: New York University Press.

Munro, L. (2005), *Children of the Queen's Revels: A Jacobean Theatre Repertory*. Cambridge: Cambridge University Press.

Nancy, J.-L. (1991), *The Inoperative Community*, trans. Peter Connor et al. Minneapolis and London: University of Minnesota Press.

Nancy, J.-L. (2008), *Corpus*, trans. Richard A. Rand. New York: Fordham University Press.

Nardizzi, V. (2013), *Wooden Os: Shakespeare's Theatres and England's Trees*. Toronto: University of Toronto Press.

Nardizzi, V. and J. E. Feerick (eds) (2012), *The Indistinct Human in Renaissance Literature*. New York: Palgrave.

Nardizzi, V., S. Guy-Bray and W. Stockton (2016), *Queer Renaissance Historiography: Backward Gaze*. Farnham: Routledge.

Nashe, T. (1592), *Strange Newes*. London n.p.

Neely, C. T. (1985), *Broken Nuptials in Shakespeare's Plays*. New Haven: Yale University Press.

Nelles, W. (2009), 'Sexing Shakespeare's Sonnets: Reading Beyond Sonnet 20', *ELR* 39 (1).

Newman, B. (2003), *God and the Goddesses: Vision, Poetry,*

and Belief in the Middle Ages. Philadelphia: University of
Pennsylvania Press.

Newman, B. (2006), 'Love's Arrows: Christ as Cupid in Late
Medieval Art and Devotion', in J. F. Hamburger and A-M.
Bouché (eds), *The Mind's Eye: Art and Theological Argument in
the Middle Ages*, Princeton, NJ: Princeton University Press.

Newman, K. (1987), 'Portia's Ring: Unruly Women and Structures
of Exchange in *The Merchant of Venice*', *Shakespeare Quarterly*
38.

Nixon, R. (2011), *Slow Violence and the Environmentalism of the
Poor*. Cambridge, MA: Harvard University Press.

Ohi, K. (2011), *Henry James and the Queerness of Style*.
Minneapolis and London: University of Minnesota Press.

Orgel, S. (1989), 'Nobody's Perfect: Or, Why Did the English Stage
Take Boys for Women?', *South Atlantic Quarterly* 88.

Orgel, S. (1996), *Impersonations: The Performance of Gender in
Shakespeare's England*. Cambridge: Cambridge University Press.

Orvis, D. (2014), 'Cross-Dressing, Queerness, and the Early
Modern Stage', in E. L. Maccallum and Mikko Tuhkanen
(eds), *The Cambridge History of Gay and Lesbian Literature*.
Cambridge: Cambridge University Press.

Ovid (2004), *Metamorphoses*, ed. R. J. Tarrant. Oxford Classical
Texts; New York: Oxford University Press.

Oxford English Dictionary. Available online: http://www.oed.com
(accessed 15 June 2016).

Panofsky, E. (1972 [1932]), 'Blind Cupid', in *Studies in Iconology:
Humanistic Themes in the Art of the Renaissance*. New York:
Harper & Row.

Parker, P. (1993), 'Preposterous Reversals: *Love's Labour's Lost*',
Modern Language Quarterly 54 (4).

Parker, P. (1996), *Shakespeare from the Margins: Language,
Culture, Context*. Chicago: University of Chicago Press.

Parrot, H. (1626), *Cures for the Itch: Characters, Epigrams,
Epitaphs*. London: n.p. Early English Books Online.
Available online: http://gateway.proquest.com.proxygw.wrlc.
org/openurl?ctx_ver=Z39.88-2003&res_id=xri:eebo&rft_
id=xri:eebo:image:20619:26 (accessed 9 July 2016).

Pastor, L. (1906), *History of the Popes*, 3rd edn. London: n.p.

Patrides, C. A. (ed.) (1999), *John Donne: The Complete English
Poems*. London: Everyman.

Patterson, L. E. (Spring 1986), '"Thrift Is Blessing": Exchange and
    Explanation in *The Merchant of Venice*', *Shakespeare Quarterly*
    37 (1).
Patterson, S. (1999), 'The Bankruptcy of Homoerotic Amity
    in Shakespeare's *Merchant of Venice*', *Shakespeare Quarterly*
    50 (1).
Peacham, H. (1577), *The Garden of Eloquence, conteining the
    most excellent ornaments, exornations, lightes, flowers, and
    formes of speech, commonly called the figures of rhetorike.*
    London: H. Jackson.
Peacham, H. (1593), *The Garden of Eloquence, conteining the
    most excellent ornaments, exornations, lightes, flowers, and
    formes of speech, commonly called the figures of rhetorike.*
    London: Richard Field.
Peend, T. (1565), *The pleasant fable of Hermaphroditus and
    Salmacis.* London: n.p.
Pellegrini, A. (2011), 'Closing Ranks, Keeping Company: Marriage
    Plots and the Will to Be Single', in M. Menon (ed.), *Shakesqueer*.
    Durham: Duke University Press.
Pequigney, J. (Spring 1992), 'The Two Antonios and Same-Sex Love
    in *Twelfth Night* and *The Merchant of Venice*', *ELR* 22 (2).
Pettitt, T. (2007), '"Perchance you wonder at this show":
    Dramaturgical Machinery in *A Midsummer Night's Dream* and
    "Pyramus and Thisb"', in P. Butterworth (ed.), *The Narrator,
    the Expositor, and the Prompter in European Medieval Theatre*.
    Turnhout: Brepols.
Philips, A. (2010), 'On a More Impersonal Note', in L. Bersani and
    A. Philips, *Intimacies*. Chicago: University of Chicago Press.
Phillips, A. (2011), *On Balance*. New York: Picador.
Pie, T. (1604), *Usuries Spright Conjured: Or a Scholasticall
    Determination of Usury*. London: n.p.
Pollard, T. (2008), *Shakespeare's Theater*. Hoboken, NJ:
    Wiley-Blackwell.
Proudfoot, R., A. Thompson, D. Scott Kastan and H. R.
    Woudhuysen (eds) (2011), *The Arden Shakespeare Complete
    Works*, 2nd edn. London: Bloomsbury.
Proudfoot, R., A. Thompson, D. Scott Kastan and H. R.
    Woudhuysen (eds) (2014), '*Measure for Measure*', in *The Arden
    Shakespeare: Complete Works*, rev. edn. London: Bloomsbury.
Purkiss, D. (1996), 'The All-singing, All-dancing Plays of the

Jacobean Witch Vogue', in *The Witch in History: Early Modern and Twentieth-Century Representations*. London: Routledge.

Puttenham, G. (1589), *The arte of English poesie. Contrived into three bookes: the first of poets and poesie, the second of proportion, the third of ornament*. London: Richard Field.

Rackin, P. (1987), 'Androgyny, Mimesis, and the Marriage of the Body Heroine on the English Renaissance Stage.' *PMLA* 102 (2).

Radero, M. (ed.) (1554), *Martialis castus, ab omni obscoenitate perpurgatis*. Paris: n.p.

Radero, M. (ed.). (1602), *M. Valerij Martialis Epigrammaton libri omnes*. Ingolstadt: n.p.

Ramachandran, A. and M. E. Sanchez (eds) (2105), 'Spenser and "the Human"', *Spenser Studies* 30 (Special Issue).

Rambuss, R. (1998), *Closet Devotions*. Durham: Duke University Press.

Rambuss, R. (2011), 'Shakespeare's Ass Play', in M. Menon (ed.), *Shakesqueer*. Durham and London: Duke University Press.

Rambuss, R. (2013), 'What it Feels Like for a Boy: Shakespeare's *Venus and Adonis*', in R. Dutton and J. Howard (eds), *A Companion to Shakespeare's Works*. Malden, MA: Blackwell.

Riley Snorton, C. (2014), *Nobody is Supposed to Know: Black Sexuality on the Down Low*. Minneapolis: University of Minnesota Press.

Rivlin, E. (2005), 'Mimetic Service in *The Two Gentlemen of Verona*', *ELH* 72 (1).

Rose, M. B. (1984), 'Women in Men's Clothing: Apparel and Social Stability in *The Roaring Girl*', *ELR* 14.

Royal Shakespeare Company (RSC) (2007), *Complete Works*, ed. J. Bate and E. Rasmussen. New York: The Modern Library.

Ryan, M. (2010), 'The Femme Movement: Why We're Here, Why We're (So Damn and Beautifully) Queer, and Why You're Gonna Get Used to it', in *Visible: A Femmethology*, vol. 2. Ypsilanti, MI: Homofactus Press.

Sacks, D. (2007), *Letter Perfect*. New York: Vintage.

Salamon, G. (2010), *Assuming a Body: Transgender and Rhetorics of Materiality*. New York: Columbia University Press.

Salinger, L. (1998), 'Borachio's Indiscretion: Some Noting About Much Ado', in M. Marrapodi and A. J. Hoenselaars (eds), *The Italian World of English Renaissance Drama: Cultural*

Exchange and Intertextuality. Newark, DE: University of Delaware Press.

Sanchez, M. (May 2012), '"Use Me but as Your Spaniel": Feminism, Queer Theory, and Early Modern Sexualities', *PMLA* 127 (3).

Sanchez, M. (2013), 'The Poetics of Feminine Subjectivity in Shakespeare's Sonnets and "A Lover's Complaint"', in J. Post (ed.), *The Oxford Handbook Shakespeare's Poetry*. Oxford: Oxford University Press.

Saslow, J. (1977), 'The Tenderest Lover: Saint Sebastian in Renaissance Painting: A Proposed Homoerotic Iconology for North Italian Art, 1450–1550', *Gai Saber* 1 (1).

Saslow, J. (1986), *Ganymede in the Renaissance: Homosexuality in Art and Society*. New Haven: Yale University Press.

Saslow, J. (1999), *Pictures and Passions: A History of Homosexuality in the Visual Arts*. New York: Viking.

Schleiner, W. (Winter 1988), 'Male Cross-Dressing and Transvestism in Renaissance Romances', *Sixteenth Century Journal* 19 (4).

Schoenbaum, S. (1987), *William Shakespeare: A Compact Documentary Life*. Oxford: Oxford University Press.

Schwarz, K. (2011), *What You Will: Gender, Contract, and Shakespearean Social Space*. Philadelphia: University of Pennsylvania Press.

Scott, W. (2013), *The Model of Poesy*, ed. G. Alexander. Cambridge: Cambridge University Press.

Sedinger, T. (1997), '"If Sight and Shape be True:" The Epistemology of Crossdressing on the London Stage', *Shakespeare Quarterly* 48 (1).

Serano, J. (2007), *Whipping Girl: A Transsexual Woman on Sexism and the Scapegoating of Femininity*. Emeryville, CA: Seal Press.

Serano, J. (2012), 'Reclaiming Femininity', in A. Enke (ed.), *Transfeminist Perspectives in and Beyond Transgender and Gender Studies*. Philadelphia, Temple University Press.

Serres, M. (1993 [1991]), *We Have Never Been Modern*, trans. C. Porter. Cambridge: Harvard University Press.

Shakespeare, W. (1600), *The Most Excellent Historie of the Merchant of Venice*. London: n.p.

Shakespeare, W. (1623), *Mr. William Shakespeares comedies, histories, & tragedies*. London. 'Concordance of Shakespeare's Complete Works', *Open Source Shakespeare*. Available online: http://www.opensourceshakespeare.org/concordance/ (accessed 20 June 2016).

Shakespeare, W. (1901), *Twelfe Night, or, What You Will*, ed. H. H. Furness. A New Variorum Shakespeare Edition. Philadelphia and London: J. B. Lippincott Company.

Shakespeare, W. (1998), *Love's Labour's Lost*, ed. H. R. Woudhuysen, *The Arden Shakespeare, Third Series*. New York: Bloomsbury.

Shakespeare, W. (2006), *Othello*, ed. E. A. J. Honigmann, 3rd edn. London: Arden.

Shakespeare, W. (2011), *The Arden Shakespeare Complete Works*, R. Proudfoot, A. Thompson and D. Scott Kastan (eds). New York and London: Bloomsbury.

Shakespeare, W. (2011), *Romeo and Juliet*, ed. B. Gibbons, in R. Proudfoot, A. Thompson and D. Scott Kastan (eds), *The Arden Shakespeare Complete Works*. London: Bloomsbury Arden Shakespeare.

Shakespeare, W. (2016), *Much Ado About Nothing*, in S. Greenblatt et al. (eds), *The Norton Shakespeare*. New York: W. W. Norton.

Shannon, L. (2000), 'Nature's Bias: Renaissance Homonormativity and Elizabethan Comic Likeness,' *Modern Philology* 98 (2).

Shannon, L. (2002), *Sovereign Amity: Figures of Friendship in Shakespearean Contexts*. Chicago: University of Chicago Press.

Shannon, L. (2013), *The Accommodated Animal: Cosmopolity in Shakespearean Locales*. Chicago: University of Chicago Press.

Shapiro, M. (1994), *Gender in Play on the Shakespearean Stage: Boy Heroines and Female Pages*. Ann Arbor: University of Michigan Press.

Shell, M. (1979), 'The Wether and the Ewe: Verbal Usury in *The Merchant of Venice*', *The Kenyon Review* 1 (4).

Shuger, D. (1999), 'The "I" of the Beholder: Renaissance Mirrors and the Reflexive Mind', in P. Fumerton and S. Hunt (eds), *Renaissance Culture and the Everyday*. Philadelphia: University of Pennsylvania Press.

Silberman, L. (1994), *The Transformations of Desire: Erotic Knowledge in Books III and IV of the Faerie Queene*. Berkeley, CA: University of California Press.

Sillars, S. (2013), 'Style, Rhetoric, and Identity in Shakespearean
    Soliloquy', in I. Callus, J. Corby and G. Lauri-Lucente (eds),
    Style in Theory: Between Literature and Philosophy. London:
    Bloomsbury.
Silverman, K. (March 2010), 'Looking With Leo', *PMLA* 125 (2).
Simmons, J. L. (1993), 'Coming Out in Shakespeare's *The Two
    Gentlemen of Verona*', *ELH* 60 (4).
Simpson-Younger, N. (2016), '"The Garments of Posthumus":
    Identifying the Non-Responsive Body in *Cymbeline*', in D. Uman
    and S. Morrison (eds), *Staging the Blazon in Early Modern
    English Theater*. New York: Routledge.
Sinfield, A. (1996), 'How to Read *The Merchant of Venice* Without
    Being Heterosexist', in T. Hawkes and J. Drakakis (eds),
    Alternative Shakespeares II. London: Routledge.
Sinfield, A. (2003), 'Cultural Materialism and Intertextuality: The
    Limits of Queer Reading in *A Midsummer Night's Dream* and
    The Two Noble Kinsmen', *Shakespeare Survey* 56.
Sinfield, A. (2006), *Shakespeare, Authority, Sexuality: Unfinished
    Business in Cultural Materialism*. London and New York:
    Routledge.
Sinfield, A. (April–December 2007) 'Coming on to Shakespeare:
    Offstage Action and Sonnet 20', *Shakespeare* 3 (1–3).
Skinner, M. B. (2005), *Sexuality in Greek and Roman Culture*.
    Malden, MA: Blackwell.
Skinner, Q. (2014), *Forensic Shakespeare*. Oxford: Oxford
    University Press.
Sloterdijk, P. (2014), *Globes: Macrospherology*, trans. W. Hoban.
    South Pasadena, CA: Semiotext(e).
Smith, B. (1999), *Acoustic Worlds of Early Modern England*.
    Chicago: University of Chicago Press.
Smith, B. (2016), 'Queer Goings-On,' *A Midsummer Night's
    Dream*. Production programme, The Globe Theatre.
Smith, B. R. (1994), *Homosexual Desire in Shakespeare's
    England: A Cultural Poetics*. Chicago: The University of
    Chicago Press.
Smith, B. R. (2000a), *Shakespeare and Masculinity*. Oxford
    Shakespeare Topics. Oxford and New York: Oxford University
    Press.
Smith, B. R. (2000b), 'I, You, He, She, and We: On the Sexual
    Politics of Shakespeare's Sonnets', in J. Schiffer (ed.),

Shakespeare's Sonnets: Critical Essays. New York and London: Garland Publishing.

Smith, B. R. (ed.) (2001), *Twelfth Night: Texts and Contexts*. Boston and New York: Bedford/St. Martin's.

Smith, B. R. (2010), 'Eyeing and Wording in *Cymbeline*,' in L. Gallagher and S. Raman (eds), *Knowing Shakespeare: Senses, Embodiment and Cognition*. New York: Palgrave Macmillan.

Smith, B. R. (2011), '"His fancy's queen": Sensing Sexual Strangeness in *Twelfth Night*', in J. Schiffer (ed.), *Twelfth Night: New Critical Essays*. London and New York: Routledge.

Solomon, A. (2002), 'Great Sparkles of Lust: Homophobia and the Antitheatrical Tradition', in A. Solomon and F. Minwalla (eds), *The Queerest Art: Essays on Lesbian and Gay Theater*. New York: New York University Press.

Spenser, E. (1590), *The Faerie Queene*. London: n.p.

Spiller, E. A. (1998), 'From Imagination to Miscegenation: Race and Romance in Shakespeare's *The Merchant of Venice*,' *Renaissance Drama* 29.

Spitzer, L. (1928), *Stilstudien*. München: Hueber.

Spitzer, L. (1948), *Linguistics and Literary History*. Princeton: Princeton University Press.

Stallybrass, P. (1992), 'Shakespeare, the Individual, and the Text', in L. Grossberg, C. Nelson and P. A. Treichler (eds), *Cultural Studies*. New York: Routledge.

Stallybrass, P. (1992), 'Transvestism and the "Body Beneath": Speculating on the Boy Actor', in S. Zimmerman (ed.), *Erotic Politics: Desire on the Renaissance Stage*. New York: Routledge.

Stallybrass, P. (1993), 'Editing as Cultural Formation: The Sexing of Shakespeare's Sonnets', *Modern Language Quarterly* 54.

Stevenson, R. (2009), '"This Senior-Junior, Giant-Dwarf Dan Cupid": Generations of Eros in Shakespeare's *Love's Labour's Lost*', *Renaissance Papers*.

Stewart, A. (1997), *Close Readers: Humanist and Sodomy in Early Modern England*. Princeton: Princeton University Press.

Stewart, A. (2014), 'A Society of Sodomites: Religion and Homosexuality in Renaissance England', in L. Gowing, M. Hunter and M. Rubin (eds), *Love, Friendship and Faith in Europe, 1300–1800*. New York: Palgrave Macmillan.

Stewart, S. (1984), *On Longing: Narratives of the Miniature, the Gigantic, the Souvenir, the Collection*. Baltimore: Johns Hopkins University Press.

Stockton, W. (2016), 'The Fierce Urgency of Now: Queer Theory, Presentism, and *Romeo and Juliet*', in V. Traub (ed.), *The Oxford Handbook of Shakespeare and Embodiment: Gender, Sexuality, and Race*. New York: Oxford University Press.

Stockton, W., M. Digangi, R. M. Karras and M. E. Sanchez (2016), 'Forum: Methodology and Queer Historiography', *Journal of Early Modern Cultural Studies (JEMCS)* 16 (2).

Story, E. (1985), *Twelfth Night*. The New Cambridge Shakespeare. Cambridge: Cambridge University Press.

Stretter, R. (2005), 'Cicero on Stage: Damon and Pithias and the Fate of Classical Friendship in English Renaissance Drama', *Texas Studies in Literature and Language* 47 (4).

Stryker, S. (2006), '(De)Subjugated Knowledges: An Introduction to Transgender Studies', in S. Stryker and S. Whittle (eds), *The Transgender Studies Reader*. New York: Routledge.

Sullivan, Jr, G. A. (2016), 'Afterword: 'A Prescript Order of Life': Memory, Sexuality, Selfhood', in J. S. Garrison and K. Pivetti (eds), *Sexuality and Memory in Early Modern England*. New York and London: Routledge.

Sullivan, M. (2016), 'Kill Daddy: Reproduction, Futurity, and the Survival of the Radical Feminist', *Women's Studies Quarterly* 44.

Taylor, J. (1635), *The World Runs on Wheels*. London: n.p. Early English Books Online. Available online: http://gateway.proquest.com.proxygw.wrlc.org/openurl?ctx_ver=Z39.88- 2003&res_id=xri:eebo&rft_id=xri:eebo:image:23550:10 (accessed 23 July 2016).

Taylor, M. (2001), *Shakespeare Criticism in the Twentieth Century*. Oxford: Oxford University Press.

Thaler, A. (1940), 'Spenser and "Much Ado About Nothing"', *Studies in Philology* 37 (2).

Targoff, R. (2012), 'Mortal Love: Shakespeare's *Romeo and Juliet* and the Practice of Joint Burial', *Representations* 120 (1).

'The Ordre for the Buriall of the Dead', in *The Boke of Common Prayer* (1552). Available online: http://justus.anglican.org/resources/bcp/1552/Burial_1552.htm (accessed 20 June 2016).

Theis, J. S. (2009), *Writing the Forest in Early Modern England: A Sylvan Pastoral Nation*. Pittsburgh: Duquesne University Press.

Tiffany, G. (Fall 1992),'Falstaff's False Staff: "Jonsonian" Asexuality in *The Merry Wives of Windsor*', *Comparative Drama* 26 (3).

Tillyard, E. M. W. (1959 [1943]), *The Elizabethan World Picture*. New York: Vintage Books.

Tillyard, E. M. W. (1991 [1944]), *Shakespeare's History Plays*. Harmondsworth: Penguin Books.

Tosh, W. (2016), *Male Friendship and Testimonies of Love in Shakespeare's England*. London: Palgrave Macmillan.

Totaro, R. (2005), *Suffering in Paradise: The Bubonic Plague in English Literature from More to Milton*. Pittsburgh, PA: Duquesne University Press.

Traub, V. (ed.) (1991), 'Desire and the Differences It Makes', in *The Matter of Difference: Materialist Criticism of Shakespeare*. New York and London: Harvester Wheatsheaf.

Traub, V. (1992), *Desire and Anxiety: Circulations of Sexuality in Shakespearean Drama*. London: Routledge.

Traub, V. (Spring 1996), 'The Perversion of "Lesbian" Desire', *History Workshop Journal* 41.

Traub, V. (2000), 'Sex Without Issue: Sodomy, Reproduction, and Signification in Shakespeare's Sonnets', in J. Schiffer (ed.), *Shakespeare's Sonnet: Critical Essays*. New York: Garland.

Traub, V. (2002), 'Setting the Stage Behind the Seen: Performing Lesbian History', in A. Solomon and F. Minwalla (eds), *The Queerest Art: Essays on Lesbian and Gay Theater*. New York: New York University Press.

Traub, V. (2002), *The Renaissance of Lesbianism in Early Modern England*. Cambridge: Cambridge University Press.

Traub, V. (2003), 'The Sonnets: Sequence, Sexuality, and Shakespeare's Two Loves', in R. Dutton and J. E. Howard (eds), *A Companion to Shakespeare's Works, Vol. 4: The Poems, Problem Comedies, and Late Plays*. Malden: Blackwell.

Traub, V. (2016), *Thinking Sex with the Early Moderns*. Philadelphia: Pennsylvania University Press.

Trevisa, J. (1495), *De Proprietatibus Rerum*, trans. B. de Glanville.

Turner, J. (2014), *Philology: The Forgotten Origins of the Modern Humanities*. Princeton and Oxford: Princeton University Press.

Varnado, C. (2013), '"Invisible Sex!" What Looks Like the Act in Early Modern Drama?', in J. M. Bromley and W. Stockton (eds), *Sex Before Sex: Figuring the Act in Early Modern England.* Minneapolis: University of Minnesota Press.

Vickers, B. (1994), 'Repetition and Emphasis in Rhetoric: Theory and Practice', in A. Fischer (ed.), *Repetition* 7 (SPELL: Swiss Papers in English Language and Literature). Tubingen: Gunter Narr Verlag.

Vickers, N. (1981), 'Diana Described: Scattered Woman and Scattered Rhyme', *Critical Inquiry* 8.

Victoria and Albert Museum (2016), 'Summary' [Girdle]. Available online: http://collections.vam.ac.uk/item/O115439/girdle-unknown/) (accessed 20 September 2016).

Vitkus, D. (2003), *Turning Turk: English Theater and the Multicultural Mediterranean, 1570–1630.* New York: Palgrave-Macmillan.

Vitkus, D. (2016), 'Circumnavigation, Shakespeare, and the Origins of Globalization', in D. Callahan and S. Gossett (eds), *Shakespeare in Our Time: A Shakespeare Association of America Collection.* London: Bloomsbury.

Wainwright, R. (2016), *Take All My Loves: 9 Shakespeare Sonnets* (CD). Deutsche Grammophon GmbH.

Wald, P. (2008), *Contagious: Cultures, Carriers, and the Outbreak Narrative.* Durham: Duke University Press.

Walen, D. A. (2015), *Constructions of Female Homoeroticism in Early Modern Drama.* New York: Palgrave-Macmillan.

Wall-Randell, S. (2009), 'Reading the Book of the Self in Shakespeare's *Cymbeline* and Wroth's *Urania*', in M. E. Lamb and V. Wayne (eds), *Staging Early Modern Romance: Prose Fiction, Dramatic Romance, and Shakespeare.* New York: Routledge.

Walsh, P. (2013), 'Reading Women: Chastity and Fictionality in *Cymbeline*', *Renaissance Papers.*

Warren, R. and S. Wells (1995), *Twelfth Night, or What You Will.* Oxford and New York: Oxford University Press.

Waswo, R. (1987), *Language and Meaning in the Renaissance.* Princeton: Princeton University Press.

Wells, S. (1980),'Editorial Treatment of the Foul-Paper Texts: *Much Ado About Nothing* as a Test Case', *Review of English Studies,* 31 (121).

Wells, S. and G. Taylor with J. Jowett and W. Montgomery (1987), *William Shakespeare: A Textual Companion*. Oxford: Clarendon Press.

Werstine, P. (2013), *Early Modern Playhouse Manuscripts and the Editing of Shakespeare*. Cambridge: Cambridge University Press.

Werth, T. (ed.) (2015), 'Shakespeare and the Human', *The Shakespearean International Yearbook* 15 (Special Issue).

Whigham, F. and W. A. Rebhorn (eds) (2007), *The Art of English Poesy by George Puttenham: A Critical Edition*. Ithaca and London: Cornell University Press.

Williams, R. (1985), *Keywords: A Vocabulary of Culture and Society*, rev. edn. New York: Oxford University Press.

Willamson, E. (2013), 'Dismembering Rhetoric and Lively Action' in *The Two Gentlemen of Verona*', in D. Uman and S. Morrison (eds), *Staging the Blazon in Early Modern English Theater*. Burlington, VT: Ashgate.

Wilson, F. P. (1999 [1927]). *The Plague in Shakespeare's London*. Oxford: Clarendon Press.

Wilson, R. (2009 [1584]) *Three Ladies of London*, in L. E. Kermode (ed.), *Three Usury Plays*. Manchester: Manchester University Press.

Wilson, T. (1572), *A Discourse Uppon Usurye*. London: n.p.

Wind, E. (1968), 'Orpheus in Praise of Blind Love', in *Pagan Mysteries in the Renaissance*. New York: W. W. Norton.

Working Group on the Anthropocene (WGA) (2016). 'The Anthropocene epoch: Scientists declare dawn of human influenced-age'. Available online: https://www.theguardian.com/environment/2016/aug/29/declare-anthropocene-epoch-experts-urge-geological-congress-human-impact-earth) (accessed 19 September 2016).

Yachnin, P. (2015), 'The Publicity of the Look', in D. Callaghan and S. Gossett (eds), *Shakespeare in our Time: A Shakespeare Association of America Collection*. London: Bloomsbury.

Žižek, S. (1992), *Looking Awry: An Introduction to Jacques Lacan through Popular Culture*. Cambridge, MA: MIT Press.

INDEX